AFTER THE WAR

After The War

A Diary

Volume III of the First World War Series

Charles à Court Repington

Simon Publications

2001

Library of Congress Card Number: 22008161

ISBN: 1-931313-73-3

Distributed by Ingram Book Company

Printed by Lightning Source Inc. La Vergne, TN

Published by Simon Publications, P.O.Box 321,
Safety Harbor, FL 34695

PREFACE

When the Peace Treaties, with one exception, were ratified and in full operation, I felt the need of a wander-year in order to acquaint myself with the new personalities and new ideas which the great war-storm had thrown up to the surface of affairs in continental Europe. It was useless to content oneself with archaic notions when all was changed, if one wished to keep abreast with the times, and there was no better way to discover what was happening than to go and see for oneself.

A mission suggested to me by Viscount Burnham enabled me to carry out my wish under favourable conditions. To him, and to many other good friends at home and abroad, my thanks are due for their confidence, their hospitality, and their assistance. Later in the year the opportunity was presented of attending the Washington Conference for the Limitation of Armaments. I offer this diary as a small contribution to the knowledge of people and events in the world of to-day in the hope that it may aid my readers to judge for themselves the proper direction of foreign policy in the future.

CONTENTS

CHAPTER I

PERSONS AND POLITICS IN ITALY

CHAPTER II

THE RETURN OF KING CONSTANTINE

CHAPTER III

ROME AND PARIS

CHAPTER IV

CONFERENCES, SANCTIONS, AND PLÉBISCITES

CONTENTS

CHAPTER V

A STATESMAN WITH A POLICY

CHAPTER VI

INFELIX AUSTRIA

CHAPTER VII

THE SORROWS OF HUNGARY

CONTENTS xi

CHAPTER X

BERLIN AND VIENNA

tion with Dr. Rosen, Foreign Minister — Return to Paris
— An exchange of ideas with Lord Hardinge — Return to
London — Off to Roumania — Munich — Some Bavarian
opinions — Vienna — A provincial procession — Austria's
mountaineers — A talk with Chancellor Schober — His first
acts — Dr. Hertz's views — Austria a colony — How Austria
obtained her best information during the war — The situation
in Austria — Only a third of expenditure met by revenue —

CHAPTER XI

NEW ROUMANIA

Country and crops — A first talk with M. Take Jonescu — Summer nights in Bucharest — Mr. Millington Drake — Mr.
Peter A. Jay and Colonel Poillon, U.S.A. — People to see —
An audience with the King of Roumania — A talk on current
affairs — The question of Transylvania — MM. Jacovaky
and Grigori Jon — Complaints of Bulgaria — Bucharest ar-
chitecture — The butterflies — Roumanian statistics — M.
Filaleki on Russia — The opposition on strike — Views of M.
Nedkov, the Bulgarian Minister — Answers to Roumanian
charges — A conversation with the Prime Minister, General
Avarescu — His account of 1916 — His views on the Straits —
A talk with M. Goga — Religions in Transylvania — Roumanian resources — Wheat, maize, and timber — Foreign capital
— Industrial concerns — Railways — Foreign trade — Banks
— Public finance — Public debt — A talk with General Niko-
leanu on the police — Mme. Lahovary on the agrarian reforms
— A talk with the Minister of Communications — A talk with
the General Staff — General Gorski and Colonel Palada —
The strength and distribution of the Soviet armies — More
complaints of Bulgaria — A conversation with the War Minister, General Rascano — Roumanian Army organisation —
M. Garoflid, Minister of Domains, on the agrarian laws —
Colonel Dundas — Consul Keyser — Mr. Guest on the oil
industry — A dinner at the Take Jonescus — The Foreign
Minister on Roumanian policy — Mr. Alexander Adams —
The Decree Laws — An investigation at the Roumanian Foreign Office — The complaints about Bulgaria — The oil industry — Statistics and observations — Trammels of the industry — The export tax — Astra-Romana and Steaua-
Romana — Mr. Charles Spencer on the future of our trade —

CHAPTER XII

BULGARIA

CONTENTS xv

CHAPTER XIII

THE WASHINGTON CONFERENCE

AFTER THE WAR

CHAPTER I

PERSONS AND POLITICS IN ITALY
JANUARY 1921

Sir George Buchanan — Colonel Détroyat — M. Maurice Pernot on Italian politics — Italy's financial position — A conversation with General Badoglio — His views on the Greeks — Talks with MM. Breski and Gayda at the *Messagero* office — A visit to M. Bergomini of the *Giornale d'Italia* — Views of Dr. Malagodi, editor of the *Tribuna* — The Hellenic problem — Italian policy — A conversation with M. Barrère on Italian and Greek affairs — A visit to Count Sforza at the Consulta — The aims of Italian policy — Emigration and commerce — A story from the Bosphorus — Italian journals — The Italian Embassy in London — Sir George Buchanan on his warning to the Tsar — Leave Rome for Athens.

Saturday, January 8, 1921. Left Victoria 8.10 A.M. A calm crossing and a fine sunny day. Met Ian Malcolm on board on his way to Egypt. We lunched at the famous Gare Maritime Restaurant so long closed to us during the war, and by dint of gossiping nearly missed the train. Drove across Paris to the Gare de Lyon in the new taxi-transport which might take on in London for station work. Dined at the Palace Hotel in the Rue de Lyon near the station and went on 9.30. No one in the sleeper whom I knew except Prince Louis.[1] Reached Modane Sunday 10.30 A.M., and Rome about 1 P.M.

Monday, January 10, 1921. Not a very comfortable journey and a poor restaurant. After an enjoyable tub and breakfast at the Grand Hotel went to the Embassy and saw Sir George Buchanan, the pink of perfection among Ambassadors. He does not think that Italy has any annexionist ideas in the Eastern Mediterranean, but he says that Italians dislike the Greeks and were pleased when Venizelos was overthrown. It was owing to Italy

[1] The Marquess of Milford Haven.

that the Allied Ministers were not withdrawn from Athens. He is more anxious about the financial situation in Italy than the political, and does not know how she will get through the next two or three years, though M. Méda, the Finance Minister, is very optimistic. He is going to see Count Sforza, the Foreign Minister, to-night to make sure whether Italy has or has not ratified the Treaty of Sèvres. I doubt whether he is kept well-informed of events by the F.O. He knew nothing of the Tripartite Treaty of Guarantees for long after it was signed, and though he believes that Giolitti met Lloyd George at Lausanne, he has no knowledge of what was settled there. He thinks that the position of an Ambassador is no longer what it was, even when he was in Russia. This is a general complaint on the part of all diplomacy, British and foreign. The Supreme Council still usurps all serious diplomatic functions, but on the other hand it hacks its way through somehow.

Went on to see Lieutenant-Colonel Détroyat, the Military Attaché at the French Embassy. He says that Italy still has three classes and some 400,000 men under arms, but that nominally there is only eight months' service. Everything seems to be provisional and temporary. He thinks that Italy has no desire to initiate any military operation and has no troops in Asia Minor. Went on to find Maurice Pernot, correspondent of the *Journal des Débats*. He is off to Paris to-morrow, but I may find him again if I return through Rome. He is very critical of Italian *désagrégation* both in agrarian and industrial troubles of recent occurrence, and declares that for a time authority lapsed in the north and did not exist in the south. He thinks that the King prevented Giolitti from acting in the northern troubles, from a generous feeling that if the dynasty had to go, it should go without bloodshed. Neither the bourgeois nor the proletariat party are organized, so they are nicely balanced. He fancies that Italy is unable to act externally and so withdraws into "her island." She has abandoned not only Albania, but even Vallona. But he thinks she is working through commercial banks and by other means to draw closer to Jugo-Slavia and Bulgaria, and hopes to dominate the Little Entente and to prevent a Habsburg restoration. He is pretty sure, as was our Ambassador, that there were secret clauses in the Rapallo Treaty directed against a Habsburg Hungary.

During my journey these last two days all the talk was about want of work, unemployment, and the hardships of the foreign exchanges. Italy's financial position is bad. The 1919–20 account showed a deficit of 13½ milliards of lire. The estimates for 1921–22 fix expenditure at 24 milliards and receipts at 14¾ milliards. In future she will need 18 milliards to meet her expenses and will have 12 milliards of revenue only. Only a reorganization of taxes can fill the void. The public debt, which was 13½ milliards, is now close on 100, of which 20 milliards are payable in gold to England and the United States. At the present rate of exchange these 20 milliards equal 82 milliards in Italian lire. Of the 85 milliards of the war debt, 35 have come since the Armistice. A large amount due to the bread subsidy, not with much effect, as the bread here is brown, sour, and beastly. Notes in circulation, 3 milliards before the war, are now 22, and were never over 9 during hostilities. The real complaint, here and in France, is that there are no clients, no buyers, and some vow that the fault was not in stabilising the exchanges at the time of the Peace Conference. No one, however, suggests how this could have been done. However much it may please English travellers and diplomats to receive 60 francs and 104 lire for their pound sterling, it is fatal to trade, and just as much to our trade as to that of France and Italy. Indeed, I begin to wonder whether the victors are not the greatest sufferers.

The Ambassador spoke most feelingly to-day about the late Tsar, but says that he, Buchanan, gave the serious warning to the Tsar which Balfour told me had been given by Milner. Hanbury-Williams had already given me the same warning. Buchanan had asked twice to be allowed to give the warning, and had been refused permission the first time. He gave it later on his personal responsibility, but says that autocracy requires a strong man like Peter the Great, and that the late Tsar, though most charming and kind, had not the character for his rôle.

Tuesday, January 11, 1921. Went off early to see General Badoglio, Chief of the General Staff. Found him in the G.S. building opposite the War Ministry. He was very agreeable and we discussed affairs since we last met just before the battle of Vittorio-Veneto. He explains the eight months' service in the Army, and the existence of a large peace strength concurrently, by saying that people have misunderstood the position. The eight months' service will only be the consequence of a long series of preparatory training of youth in drill, physical exercises, and schooling, and cannot be the prelude to this, as people imagine. He has still two classes under arms and a third now demobilising. He says that Italy has no designs in the Eastern Mediterranean and has only two small detachments, five hundred men each, on the coast of Asia Minor and five hundred at Rhodes. He says that even if Smyrna fell to Italy, he would only place a civilian consul there. He wants to revise the Treaty of Sèvres and to replace Smyrna under the Turks. He doubts that Greece can keep in the field her present twelve divisions under arms. He brought out the map that Venizelos had given him showing the present northern frontier of Greater Greece, and asked how they could defend it against Albanians, Serbs, Bulgars, and Turks with no strategic railways to permit of rapid strategic movements. Even in Asia Minor he thought that the Turks would merely draw the Greeks on, and that theirs was not a sound position. Greece was a little nation and had not the force or wealth behind her to justify the soaring policy of Venizelos. He was critical of the absence of all serious military organization in England and seemed to know our position quite well. He says that when the Supreme Council decided to occupy Batoum, Foch and he, on being consulted, advocated three divisions as a beginning. Then the Supreme ones asked who was to send them. Badoglio would not send one. Foch made the same reply, and so did the British. So the scheme fell flat. A good talk, and it is quite clear that the Italians have not the slightest intention of undertaking any adventures at present.

I went on to the *Messagero* office to talk, as advised by the Italian Embassy in London, to the Director, M. Breski, and also met his brilliant young leader-writer, M. Gayda, who did most of the talking. They told me that there were neither the men nor the means for ambitious Imperialism, but that Italy aimed at directing her future emigration to all parts of the Eastern Mediterranean which could support a largely increased white population, and that the plan was to make it a peaceful penetration with the further object of obtaining concessions and raw materials in Asia Minor by agreement with the Turks. They said that Count Sforza was well versed in Eastern affairs and knew Kemal with whom he had been in touch recently by intermediaries; but they denied the despatch of ships with arms to Kemal. The Turks understood the Italian point of view and left the Italians alone. They do not like the extension of Modern Greece and wish Smyrna to revert to Turkey. They agree that France wants to set up the Turks as a barrier against Bolshevism, but find a contradiction between this view and France's support of Venizelos's Greater Greece. They think that politically England and Italy see with the same eyes, but that economically Italy has grievances, and even politically there is a bad feeling because L. G. promised Smyrna to Italy at St. Jean de Maurrienne and then got out of the promise when Orlando was absent from Paris during the Peace Conference, on the pretext that Russia's consent had been a condition, and that Russia no longer counted.

But the real grievance is the state of the exchange and the want of raw materials. It is indispensable — though it is easier said than done — to stabilise the exchange which, they say, is ruining Italy, and more raw materials must be made available to satisfy the claims of Italian factories which have quadrupled since 1914. Agriculture wants chemical manures, and though France has plenty in North Africa she will not let Italy work part of them, though France is short of the labour to do so. A long talk round all these subjects and they promise me a memorandum upon it in a day or two. The *Messagero* is independent and under no one's orders. So they say. It is probably true, for Italian journalism stands high. I have a great respect for most of the great papers and the men in charge of them.

Went on to renew my acquaintance with M. Bergomini, editor of the *Giornale d'Italia*, who was very cordial. He says that the Italians won their share of the war, but lost the peace. The result was that those who had opposed the war came into power. Italy had won her land frontier, but not her sea frontier on the eastern shore of the Adriatic down to Sebenico, and had therefore not accomplished her strategic purpose. If all the fleets of the Allies could not defeat the Austrian Navy during the war, it was possible that Italy might be in the same position some day against another Power occupying Austria's place. I knew, he said, that the east coast of Italy was very indefensible owing to want of ports.

From all this situation and from the cost and losses of the war had arisen a serious moral depression which came to a head in the recent industrial troubles in the north and the agrarian troubles in the south and in Sicily. B. is not disposed to attach much importance to the agrarian troubles. He says that the south and Sicily are monarchical and constitutional, and that even when the people set out to occupy landed properties, they often had a priest at their head and cheered the King and Queen whose portraits they carried. But the industrial troubles were more serious, and B. admits that for a time he anticipated the worst. Things had blown over. The workmen had found that they could not work the factories and sell the products, so gradually a settlement came about, and the bourgeois classes also made better preparations to defend themselves. If, as he hoped, things were quiet till the spring when agriculture began to demand labour again, he would consider a bad corner turned. But the question of the exchange he placed first. The problem for Italy was first to live, and then to live in peace. He could not tell me of any solution that had been proposed to improve the exchange. Exchanges and the cost of living were the two greatest problems for Europe. He hoped that the Leghorn Conference of the Socialists would result in the split between the Moderates and the Extremists of a party,[1] and then the Conservatives could talk. He attributed great importance to the indictment of Bolshevism, out to-day from the pen of the Socialist leader Turati in the form of a preface to a book by the Italian Socialists who had visited Russia. He thought that it would have great influence on Italian Socialism.

Colonel Détroyat came to call in the afternoon and we had another talk on the war and the Italian position. Then I went off to see Dr. Malagodi, the editor of the *Tribuna*. He thought that Giolitti was doing well. He had bided his time at Fiume and had struck at the right moment, while Nitti had menaced and done nothing. Giolitti was everything in the Government and the rest were only his instruments. He thought that things were going well; was sure that Italy would have nothing to do with adventures of any sort, was very strong about the hardships of the exchange, and wondered why England with her two hundred and fifty million tons of coal a year could not find ten for her ally at the price that America provided it. He said that Italy only required this amount, while England wasted forty million tons on domestic uses, and Italy's ten millions would serve all her needs. The coal from England now cost one hundred lire more per ton than the American. M. thought that Italy could never

____
[1] It did.

pay her war debt to England and America. He referred to a loan from Florentine bankers which a King of England had never repaid. The prices here are awful. Things cost from three to six times the pre-war price, and exchange is declared to be at the bottom of it.

As for the German problem, here are Gayda's views. He thinks that the upheaval of Central and Eastern Europe is the dominant event, political and social, of the Continent. Europe is in search of peace, but cannot find it. There is a want of unity of ideas and attitudes. The Paris meeting on January 19 must result in precise ideas on the crisis and alleviate by discussion the asperity of their contrast. In the gigantic conflict between victors and vanquished, it is natural that the latter should draw together and follow the lead of the strongest, namely, Germany. Many people obstinately include all in the narrow confines of the text of the Treaties, with its various formulas invented by four men sitting round a table who are able to conclude in some specific case, such as the military war, but cannot confront a general phenomenon which is the world-crisis since the war. Germany has not fulfilled her disarmament engagements entered into at Spa. But Gayda does not credit a new French adventure. He thinks that Frankfort was a lesson to the French, and that English opinion has not changed. England and Italy think that the German disarmament has largely been brought about and that minor defalcations do not justify more severities. The danger is that France desires to compensate for her withdrawal from her extreme position about reparation by greater inflexibility on the question of disarmament. He accuses M. Dard at Munich of playing up to Bavarian independence and supporting the *Orgesch* to this end, and of trying to create a Danubian Monarchy and to give autonomy to the Rhine Provinces.

Clarity and prudence are needed, says Gayda, and elasticity of measure, and a compromise must be found, not forgetting that France refused to disarm at Geneva. It may mean a Government crisis in Paris, but will mean the peace of Europe. Italy's position is one of traditional moderation inspired by realistic consciousness of the complexities of the moment. He thinks that Sforza must already have pointed out that reports like General Nollet's represent real political acts which are not authorized without previous notice to friendly Governments and their consent. The present French practices may lead to the isolation of the French Government. In reparations, Italy marches with England.

It is necessary to solve the German problem, then the Russian, and finally the general problem of European economics. Each day there is more and more felt the need of reverting truly to peace which is not only a definition of a text, but a political and social form of life, to overcome all the divisions caused by the war and to revive Central Europe. These simple laws suggest the limit and the form of the reparation to be demanded from Germany. It must leave to Germany the possibility of autonomous economic existence. In the solution of the German problem we shall get the measure of the capacity of Government men to understand the problem of the world. There is a certain amount of fluff about all this, but one must grasp the mentality of Italian journalism and watch its tendencies.

Wednesday, January 12, 1921. Dr. Malagodi says to-day in the *Tribuna* that the Hellenic problem, which includes that of Turkey, depends for its solution upon events which will happen in Asia Minor. But the Allies must in any case sincerely seek a common basis for their policy in the East. England accepts King Constantine passively and the latter proposes to follow the Venizelist policy in Asia Minor, so England does not wish to revise the Sèvres Treaty. France desires to revise it, but does not desire the King. Italy favours revision, but will not look at any attack on the King, as she accepts fully the popular mandate of the Greek electorate. These three policies differ. The Allied problem is to harmonize these differences. In regard to Germany the *Tribuna* wishes to take count of the facts in Bavaria and East Prussia, not to insist too literally on the Treaty, and not to make Germany too weak internally and against Bolshevism, nor create a moral depression which may harm her growing industries and so react on the question of reparations in which all the Allies are interested. As for the latter question Italy thinks that the sword of Damocles must not be constantly suspended over Germany's head and that the gross sum due from her must be stated. Italy does not take this line from Germanophilism as some of her Allies think. She is fully in favour of the continuing solidarity of the Alliance, but has a profound conviction that it is a real interest of France to render possible the payment of reparations, and thinks that to leave the figure of Germany's debt vague is to postpone the realization of the conditions which will permit Germany to satisfy her obligations.

A correct reading of the Italian policy, I think, but all is not said, for Italy mainly looks east now, and not having had Germany as a real enemy, nor having the will or the means for future military efforts, has no intention of sharing in measures of constraint. She looks to a peaceful, diplomatic, commercial, and economic penetration of the Balkans and Asia Minor, and the diversion of her surplus population upon the eastern shores of the Mediterranean. This latter policy is big with events in future, but at present it will appear harmless. Anyhow, Italy will be a moderating influence in present troubles, and perhaps regards the general and economic situation with a broader outlook than some of the rest of us.

Note that a smart clerk at Cook's Office told me to-day that there had been gigantic speculation in Italy on foreign exchange and that the Government had been compelled to limit these dealings to half an hour in the morning and half an hour in the afternoon. He gave me 106 at the exchange to-day and thought that it might continue to fall for a couple of months and then gradually recover to 80 by the end of the year.

In the afternoon went to see the French Ambassador,

M. Barrère, at the French Embassy at the Farnese Palace. Two hours of delightful conversation with him and then a look round the big rooms, of which I admired the music room with Caracci decorations, a central room with two wonderful Boucher tapestries of very large size and exquisite quality, two other Gobelins pieces and a delightful smaller room. Found that H.E. was a great connoisseur of art and music, and we should never have talked politics had we begun by looking over the palace. I should say that the rooms may well be, as he says, unsurpassed in Rome; but his own taste in doing them up, and the paintings and tapestries from the Garde Meubles at Paris have to be taken into account.

M. Barrère's work in Italy for the past twenty-three years is certainly one of the greatest triumphs of French diplomacy. It was he who brought about an understanding between the two countries years ago, and but for him Italy might never have come into the war. We discussed past diplomacy of which our mutual experience enabled us to fit many pieces together; French politics and diplomacy; the Italian internal situation and external politics; the Vatican and its influence; Turkey and Greece; exchange, raw materials, and so forth, and in fact all the current political problems. He speaks English like a native. His father was French Professor at Woolwich and he was at school in the town. It is a loss to us that he did not follow Cambon in London.

No one knows Italy better than Barrère. I found that he thought the internal situation still much more serious than other people, except our Ambassador, had in their talks with me. He described how the red and black flags were at one time hoisted on factories within forty miles of Rome, and how Soviets had been practically instituted. He had been evidently much impressed and could not yet regard the position through rose-coloured spectacles. He says that he does not find in France or England anti-Italian journals, but does find in Italy anti-French and anti-English journals. He mentioned the *Tempo* as an example. He thought that one newspaper which he named was run and financed in a certain commercial interest, and that the *Corriere* was the only great paper and serious journal in Italy. Another paper was going down; he said that it had not now good information and articles by competent hands were rare. He agreed that the state of the exchange was a real danger and wondered that it had not been sooner taken up by the Powers, as all of our trade was being ruined by the disastrous changes from day to day. He did not seem to have heard of the rumours of coal and oil probabilities north of the Apennines.

He was interested in my views of the Eastern character of Italy and of the Eastern trend of her policy, but thought that Italy had not the men nor the means to rule the Little Entente. He had old-fashioned ideas about the Vatican, and asked what France and England would do if they had an establishment like the Vatican, with its immense moral power, cheek by jowl with the civil government. I thought that we should not mind and should just use it. I thought the Vatican Italian and that it subserved Italian policy. He admitted that it had become much more Italian than during his early days here. I thought that the Vatican would be delighted with the idea of Italian emigration to the Eastern Mediterranean, as it would increase the scope of their missions on which they set such store. He allowed that this would be so. He did not deny that the French were playing with the idea of a Danubian Monarchy, and said it was true that there was a secret and written accord in the Rapallo Treaty pledging the contracting parties to resist a Habsburg restoration in Hungary. He agreed that it was essential for England and France to keep Italy in the Alliance and that we could not afford to let her look elsewhere for friends.

He is in favour of a revision of the Turkish Treaty. I asked him if he saw any objection to the Greeks making friends with the Turks, and he said that he preferred that the Allies would do so. But it depends, supposing an arrangement, what the terms may be. He thought it probable, if we did not settle with the Turks, that the Bolshevists might be at Constantinople this year. The Turkish Nationalists did not like the Bolshies, who were arrogant and domineering, while the mentality of the two races differed, and there was their age-long hostility to reckon with, but they were comrades in misfortune, and adversity made strange bed-fellows. We agreed that the vitality of the Italian race and their flourishing natality were undoubted sources of strength and expansion, and that Italian mechanics, engineers, and craftsmen showed wonderful results. But Barrère asked whether great populations had ever meant great peoples, and said that the Fellaheen bred faster than the Italians and that it still meant nothing. It was the small nations who had been the wonder of the world.

He deplored the abasement of diplomacy, as Buchanan had done, and he seems insufficiently informed by his F.O., as our people seem to be. He told me that General Pellé was coming here in a week's time, and that P. and I would meet at Constantinople. Another good story of Clemenceau, who broke out once during the Peace Conference and said that the Italians met him with a *magnifique coup de chapeau* of the seventeenth-century type, and then held out the hat for alms at the end of the bow. Many recollections of France's errors in Egypt, of Fashoda, and of the opening of the Anglo-French military conversations. He wants French and English schools to exchange scholars for a year, for the ignorance of each other's language is a great misfortune. He finds that Englishmen can only really express themselves in their own language. Barrère is an intimate friend of Foch's and there were several photos of the Marshal in his room. Barrère is a good man and Buchanan says a good colleague, but he might become stiff and intransigent if in a high position in Paris or in London. He is very independent, says what he thinks, is frank and straightforward, but has strong views which he will not surrender easily. He says that L. G. gave Nitti his photograph and on it was the dedication "To my spiritual self"!

Thursday, January 13, 1921. Went to the Consulta at 10 A.M. to have a talk with Count Sforza, the Italian Minister for Foreign Affairs. An agreeable man with distinction and dignity. He inspires confidence and trust in his word. I told him of my mission. He spoke in English. He was practising on me, I imagine. We gradually approached the question of Italian policy. He is, of course, for the maintenance of the Entente. He does not desire the restoration of Austria in any form, believing that she would be the satellite of Germany and that Italy did not desire Germany as a neighbour. As things were, and even if the present Austria united with Germany some day, we could work the Slav and other States carved out of Austria and rule by dividing. I told him that I understood there was a secret clause in the Treaty of Rapallo directed against a Habsburg restoration in Hungary. He admitted that this was so, but said that it was not directed against Hungary. I told him how Italy seemed to me to be directing her activities eastward and to be planning an Eastern policy and directing her emigration towards the eastern shores of the Mediterranean. He admitted the Eastern trend of policy, but said that it was for commercial and industrial reasons. As for emigration, he did not think that any Italian Government could direct it away from its natural channels, and that any mass of emigrants directed to Turkey would alarm the Turks and arouse their suspicion. The emigrants would go if there were concessions and to find profitable work. I said that there was an official bureau [1] for emigration, but he said that this was for the protection of emigrants and not for their direction to appointed districts. He shares Barrère's views of the danger to Constantinople from the Russians. He would not describe the Russians as Bolshevists because all Russia was Bolshevist, and it created a false impression to describe them as anything but Russians. He was surprised that the danger to Constantinople was not appreciated in England, and wondered why it was not compre-

---

[1] There are two, one Governmental, the other Catholic.

'hended that with Turkey secured to us we should divide the two streams of Russian enterprise, one of propaganda in the West, and the other of military conquest in the East. These streams united in Turkey, and consequently it was necessary to have the Turks on our side. Why was our Government so hostile to the Turks? I put it down to the influence of the old Gladstonian policy which L. G. had inherited when younger, and said that Turkey had exhausted our patience. S. was in favour of revising the Turkish Treaty. He did not think that the Greeks could hold their present frontiers. It was one thing to eat and another to digest. Italy had not the intention of sending any troops or expeditions to Asia Minor, and even if she were given Smyrna she would not place a man there. He thought Italy's total force in the East was only three thousand men. There was only one Italian battalion at Constantinople to show the flag.

I begged permission to ask a second indiscreet question, namely, whether Italian rifles had been sent to Mustapha Kemal and whether he was in communication with Kemal. He said that Mustapha Kemal was an old friend of his. He was an honest man and a loyal soldier, and when he was once on the point of being arrested, S. had offered him the sanctuary of the Italian Embassy. Italy had never sent an official mission to Kemal, but was in touch with him by agents — like the British, added S. mischievously. As for rifles he assured me positively that not one had been sent. He told me an amusing story on this subject. A Turk had come to him to beg for rifles and had told him that one day a young and good-looking boatman on the Bosphorus had been asked by a pretty lady to row her across. He handed her in, looked at her, and remarked enigmatically, "They are sure to say so." He said nothing more and began to row. The lady's curiosity was aroused, and when halfway across asked him what his remark had meant. He replied, "You are pretty and I am young. They are sure to say that we are lovers, so why should we not be?" The Turk had applied the moral to his own request for rifles, but S. said that loyalty forbade him to accede to the request. I asked his permission to make the fact known and he gave it.

We discussed Italian journals. S. said that the French system of semi-official journalism did not exist in Italy. He saw Malagodi and named the *Tribuna* as representing best his views. The *Corriere* was a serious and important organization. Most papers were for and against the Government according to the views of the journalists engaged. The latter were very independent, lived on little, and went in neither for luxury nor parade. He thought that their moral fibre was strengthened by these customs and he had a great regard for them. I asked about a certain paper and commercial interests. He thought that such things might be, but considered X one of the most brilliant of journalists and a man incapable of writing to order. He described how Giolitti, the Prime Minister, when on a holiday, went to his little cottage near Turin where there were only two little maids, and how he spent his spare time at the village inn with the notary, the doctor, etc. This simplicity of life S. considered a great strength and I could not but agree.

We talked of Germany and I told him how glad I should be when all the Allied missions in that country were withdrawn, for their presence there might always produce an incident and was a serious danger. S. agreed and said that the Inter-Allied mission in Austria, of which an old Italian General was the head, ate up by its demands half the Austrian revenue. He had applied to the Supreme Council to close it down, but had met with a refusal at the French instance. I understood him to say that the Italians were under orders to come away.

S. admires the Greeks and thinks them a vital force, but describes them as an Eastern people. He asked me to come and see him after my return. He agreed that we three allies must keep together, but, rather by his silence than his words, left me under the impression that he was not at all enthusiastic about the French. I told him that

I knew and liked de Martino, his new Ambassador in London, but that we all regretted Imperiali who had left many friends in London. S. said that after a diplomat had been in London for eleven years things began to stagnate, and that he had to get a move on. I allowed that foreign politics were often a problem of dynamics and that a Minister long in a foreign country was apt to regard it as one of statics. I hoped that he was satisfied with the Ambassador we had sent to him and appreciated his qualities. S. was very nice about Sir George Buchanan and said that he was delighted to deal with such a loyal and straightforward man who united in himself all the best traditional qualities of the English diplomatist.

Friday, January 14, 1921. Met M. Métaxas, formerly Greek Minister in London, who hopes, I fancy, to return there, and describes M. Rangabé as Chargé d'Affaires. We had a chat about Greece, and he asked me to carry a despatch of his to Athens to-morrow which I agreed to do. Met at the house of Major General Duncan, our Military Attaché, various people including the late Greek Minister here M. Caramelos, the U.S. General Churchill and his wife on a tour of inspection of the U.S. Military Attachés abroad, and several Italian and other people. Duncan thinks that the Turks rightly determined to secure themselves by attacking Armenia and the Greeks at Smyrna. A nice young Assistant Naval Attaché present.

Sir G. Buchanan came in at five to my rooms and read my record of the talks with Barrère and Count Sforza. He also read my two articles for the *D. T.* on the situation in Italy and approved of them, telling me that his own despatches to the F.O. were on the same lines. He then recounted to me the whole story of his warning of the late Tsar. It was in the middle of January, 1917, the day that the news of Count Benckendorff's death had arrived. He described all the circumstances in which the warning was given, and the very words he had used. It was a most tragic story, and no monarch can, indeed, ever have received a more honest and terrible warning. I thought his action did him great honour and would always be a credit to the sincerity and courage of British diplomacy. I could not get the scene and the terrible and prophetic words out of my head for the rest of the day.

Saturday, January 15. Left Rome 8.30 P.M. and reached Brindisi midday Sunday, lunched on the quay and left at 6 P.M. on the Palacky, formerly Austrian-Lloyd, now Lloyd Triestino. Reached Corfu 6 A.M. Monday.

January 17. Went on at noon. Calm so far, sky cloudy. Rather chilly. Sir Edward Boyle with his wife and mother on board. We passed through the Corinth Canal early Tuesday. A great achievement and very impressive, but the banks need sloping, as they keep falling in. Our ship over four thousand tons. I believe the canal takes ships of twenty-four feet draught. Arrived at the Piræus 11 A.M. and was met by a Royal boat which took me off. A car whisked me up to Athens in no time. Am lodged at the Grand Bretagne.

CHAPTER II

THE RETURN OF KING CONSTANTINE

Athens — A talk with Lord Granville — Princess Christopher's views — A ceremony at the Piræus — Blessing the waters — Enthusiasm for the King — At Prince Nicholas's Palace — The Patriarch arrives — Greek wines — The Turkish policy — Colonel Rangabé — M. Guy Beringer on Greek discipline — Colonel Mayes on physical training in Greece — An audience with the King — His views on current events — Prince and Princess Andrew — A talk with the Greek Chief-of-Staff on the campaign in Asia Minor — M. Gounaris on current events and politics — Back to Herodotus — M. Calogheropoulos on the financial position — A conversation with the Prime Minister, M. Rhallys — Colonel Nairne — A visit to the Bay of Salamis — "*Ilthi*" — H.M. the Queen Mother — A talk with M. Stratos — Venizelist journalists at sea — Tyranny of Venizelist agents — M. Maximos on Greek finance — Admiral Kelly — Visitors — The Archimandrite of Rhodes — A luncheon with the King and Queen — The Crown Prince of Roumania — A visit to Tatoi — Colonel Pallis on the operations — Strengths and chances of Greeks and Turks — Mr. Rawlings on commerce — General Dousmanis — General Gramat on the Greek Army — Election and Plébiscite figures — — A conversation with the Italian Minister, M. Montagna — Views of M. de Billy, the French Minister — A farewell audience with the King — A final dinner with M. Gounaris at Phaleron — Corfu — The Governor's Palace and Mon Repos.

Tuesday, January 18, 1921. Delivered Métaxas's despatch and Prince Christopher's letter: then called at our Legation and had a talk with Lord Granville. I told him of my recent experiences and gave him my point of view. He told me the position here, and of the frank absurdity of the situation with all the Allied Ministers sulking in their Legations because we were cross about the defeat of Venizelos and the restoration of the King. He has not even been sent the official text of Mr. Lloyd George's speech on Greece of December 22 last, and I promised him mine and also the diary of my talks in Rome. Had a good long talk. I hope that the misconception of the state of sentiment in Greece has not done him harm, as he is too good a man to lose.

The Italians were well-informed about the elections, says Granville, and had a network of consuls who enabled the Italian Minister to warn the Consulta. Gunther, the

United States First Secretary in Rome, was also on the right side, probably informed by the Consulta, and banked on it in a long report to America. A nice Legation house with a good view of the Acropolis.

In the afternoon met Princess Christopher at Prince Nicholas's Palace and had a good talk with her on public affairs. She says that the enthusiasm on the King's return was wonderful and lasted for several days. The people were perfectly mad with joy. She thinks the King an honest man. He is a sort of god to the Greeks who regard him as their own, named him by acclaim when he was born, and believe that his and Queen Sophie's names mean the fulfilment of the ancient prophecy that the Greeks will regain Constantinople under a Constantine. She thinks the Queen broken by Prince Alexander's death, and caring little for affairs. She fears that the King's health may not long remain good owing to the strain and the effect of his recent operations. She thinks that the Crown Prince is thoroughly good. Princess Christopher herself has received tremendous ovations here. Her name taken when she became Orthodox, Anastasie, means resurrection, and to the people it is a favourable omen. Letters and telegrams pour in to her, calling her the "Star of America," and other beautiful names. She thinks the mass of the people not very highly civilised or educated, but not Bolshevist or Socialist, and easily led by a man. Many stories of excesses, murders, tortures, and imprisonments under the Venizelos régime. She declares that she has not spent one farthing on the Greek elections and authorises me to say so. She has much better use for her money, she says, than to use it for a purpose which can bring her no possible personal advantage. She says that she also would not stake her fortune against the seven million drachmas which X is said to have given to the Venizelos Election Fund, and all the public money which was spent on it. It was all wasted. The people took the money, wore Venizelos's emblem, an anchor, and solidly voted for the King. It was a sweeping victory.

Princess Christopher finds her duty here. It is severe, and if she had known what trouble she would have found she "would never have gotten into it." She must build or buy a palace now and means to spend three or four months of each winter here. The Royal Family are very nice to her. It is fortunate for her that she has married the youngest brother, and so trots about last at the functions. Albania wants her for Queen, but she has not the faintest intention of accepting. She looked at the country as she passed and did not fancy being enthroned on a trackless mountain among banditti whose only idea of a Government is what they can get out of it. She wants a quiet, peaceful life and to enjoy herself with her friends in England. Prince Christopher, who is a cheerful, friendly, and sociable man, is wholly of her view. When asked if he would like to be King, he pulled off his hat and said that a crown could never remain on his head. His head of hair is not luxuriant.

We had a talk on politics and I gave her my views, but said that I would form no final opinion till I had had a good look round here.

Wednesday, January 19, 1921. Sir Edward Boyle, his wife and mother and I went off in a car with Count Mercati, the King's Maréchal de la Cour, to the Piræus to see the ceremony of blessing the waters. It is a ceremony as old as Christianity, but no one can trace its precise origin. A lovely drive along the coast from Phaleron. At the Piræus a dais was raised over the water and the ships and houses round were black with spectators. All the Guilds were represented by their standards, all with the cross of St. George at the top. A great gathering of civil and military dignitaries. We were given a good place. After a service in the church, the King and Princes with the Crown Prince of Roumania walked in procession to the dais on which our party were also given places. Soon there came all the priesthood, ending up with the Patriarch of Athens, a venerable, white-bearded figure in red and gold vestments, and with a gold and red orthodox head-dress like an inverted flower pot. There were five or six more, equally magnificently attired. The Patriarch suffered much under Venizelos and was imprisoned in a dirty cell among rats. The people received him with shouts of "He is worthy!" The King had a fine reception. There was a service on the dais, with chanting and the burning of incense. Then a cross was thrown into the waters after being blessed and sprinkled with holy water. The Patriarch had blessed the King and Princes and saluted them: they were all bare-headed. It was fortunately a lovely sunny morning. As the final act was performed, the whole crowd broke out into frantic cheering, sirens sounded, the bells rang, and there was a great scene. The King's reception was very enthusiastic. The crowd pressed on to him. A woman threw herself before him in front of me and kissed his hand, and then fell flat upon the ground before him. There is no getting away from the fact that the King is the popular figure in Greece, and that the people are devoted to him.

Met Granville and Admiral Howard Kelly, formerly of the Gloucester, and went on later to Princess Nicholas's Palace to lunch with her and her Prince, three nice daughters, pretty and with delightful manners, and a Lady-in-Waiting, with Prince and Princess Christopher. Princess Nicholas is the daughter of the Grand Duke Vladimir. A striking figure, handsome, deeply draped in black owing to her mother's death, and dignified. We had scarcely begun lunch before the Patriarch was announced. He had come to bless the household. We trooped out and the Patriarch blessed them all and they kissed a cross. He extended the cross to me and I bowed. At lunch some Greek wines which are good if one knows which to get and where to get them: Mavrodaphne, like Tokay, rather sweet and very strong. Achaia or Domestica is a good light wine which King Edward liked. After lunch a long political talk about events.

I found Prince Nicholas cool-headed, well-informed, and perspicacious. He has also a good acquaintance with the old architecture of Athens and has a cultivated mind. I told him my views; that Greece could no doubt beat the Turks, but could set no limit to her conquests, and could not afford the cost of keeping the fourteen divisions mobilised. As France and Italy wished to square the Turks and revise the Treaty of Sèvres, I saw no way out to accommodate all interests but for the Greeks themselves to arrange with the Turks, but whether it was best for the Greeks to ask the Allies to join with them in doing so, or to act themselves, I could not yet decide. Prince Nicholas said truly that Greece believed she was carrying out the Allied mandate in her action at Smyrna, but that she would make friends with the Turks to-morrow if England gave a hint that she would support Greece in doing so. They asked me to talk to the King as I had to them, and I said that I certainly would. They asked how England viewed affairs and I referred them to Mr. Lloyd George's speech and said that we supported the Greeks if the King could make good, but that some people thought his task very difficult. They all admitted the serious character of the financial problem. There were some contemptuous remarks about Germany at lunch, which rather surprised me.

At the ceremony this morning I saw M. Rhallys, the old Prime Minister whose character Princess Christopher had sketched to me the day before. Rather a strong old face with a beaky nose. He watched the attitude of the crowds with close attention, blinking like an old owl. I was introduced to M. Gounaris, the War Minister, who seemed very glad to see me, and I found a note from him on my return, bidding me welcome in the kindest terms, and saying that Colonel Rangabé, brother of the Rangabé in London, has been appointed to show me round. The latter came to call and we had a short talk. He places three Greek Army Corps each of three divisions in Asia Minor, one in Thrace of three divisions, one division at Salonika as reserve, and one other — total fourteen of 120,000 aggregate ration strength in Asia Minor and 40,000 in Thrace. In all about

185,000 under arms. He thinks Kemal has three Army Corps, all weak, but admits that in the last operation they were found better organised than before, and that the strain of the Greek lines of communication had become considerable.

Returned cards on a lot of official people who had called. In the evening the Granvilles and Sir Edward Boyle and his ladies dined with me. Talked alone to Granville afterwards and told him what Prince Nicholas had said about an agreement with the Turks, and that I was to see the King in the morning. What did he wish me to say? He first thought of wiring Prince Nicholas's remark, and then decided to await my talk with the King. He advised me to let the King talk. Granville wanted to know who the next Prime Minister would be, when the Government would be formed, and how long the Greeks could go on in Asia Minor. He said it was quite true, as Prince Nicholas had declared to me, that the Greeks were fighting the Turks at our instance, and that Prince Nicholas was right in saying that the Greeks believed that they were following out our policy. But all this is surely a little out of harmony with the instructions to our Ministers at Athens to avoid the King, and also with the withdrawal of our financial support.

Mr. Guy Beringer, Reuter's agent here, came to call. He had been in the Smyrna area in August last and declared that the Greek discipline was rigid, and that the Turks told him that if there were a plébiscite, they would vote for the Greeks as the Kemalist bandits murdered the Armenians and robbed the Turks.

Thursday, January 20, 1921. Colonel Mayes of the Canadian Army called. He is in charge of physical training in Greece; our other missions here are for Navy and the Police. He describes forty per cent of the Greek people as illiterate, or "blind" as they call it, but says that there are some of the most brilliant intellects in Europe here, and that children of eleven to fourteen know more about politics than men of twenty-three at home. He considers that eighty per cent of the country are Monarchist, but this does not mean that eighty per cent are anti-Venizelist. The culminating error of the latter was that he asked the people to choose between him and the King. Mayes is convinced that no other régime but the present one can work. The physical instruction of the people has been neglected. He describes the Greeks as unaccustomed to give or return blows in personal contact and for this reason does not think them as hardy as our men. He would not be sure of them against a well-organised army of Turks if there were one. He came back to lunch with me and we had a good talk on the subject. His duties take him all over the country, so his opinion is of value.

At 11.30 A.M. I went to the Crown Prince's Palace for an audience with the King and stayed talking with him till lunch time. I found him very much incensed against Granville for his attitude, and the King even attributed to him the refusal by Admiral Kelly of the Grand Cross of the Redeemer. I defended Granville and said that a British Minister had no authority to allow or refuse permission to a British subject to accept a decoration, since this was the privilege of our King. King Constantine does not realise that it is not Granville but our Government that dictates policy, and said he did not see how he could work with Granville, who was, he said, accredited to him and not to the Government. He said that the Allied Ministers would have to present new credentials, but did not think that Ministers already here need ask for an agrément. I found the King more set on operations against the Turks than on making peace with them. He said that he had 120,000 men in Asia Minor and that Kemal had 30,000 Regulars, while some 20,000 irregulars might join them for short operations. I asked how long the Greeks could go on financially and he said "a month to six weeks." He was not quite sure of the figures of the cost. I asked when the new Government would be formed and he said that he would keep strictly to his constitutional rôle and would allow the Parliament to decide this matter. He did not think that

Rhallys would stay long. He thought that Gounaris was likely to have a sufficient majority to control the Chambers. We discussed French and Italian policy in the East. He told me that he had heard from Prince George that Briand was very well-disposed towards Greece, but a Reuter message from London of January 19 creates an unfavourable impression here, as it makes the support of England to Greece in Asia Minor depend on the success of Greece in maintaining her position, and this she cannot do for long unless financially supported. He said that a German archæologist (by name Dechtold, I think) had seen the Kaiser lately and that the latter had found great fault with the King's attitude. So, said the King, I am a pro-German for England, and the Kaiser does not approve of me!

I told the King that before I came here I hoped for an amnesty, and even for a reconciliation between His Majesty and Venizelos, but now thought the latter idea hopeless on account of the intense bitterness I had found between the two sides. I told him that so far as I understood our policy we wished to support the Greeks if he could make good, but that many doubted whether he would be able to do so. It would not be very wonderful, he interrupted, when we have an army fighting the Turks at the instance of the Allies, and the latter not only do not lift a finger to help me, but hamper me in every possible way.

We talked of persons and events. All seems quiet now in Greece and the new territories. He said how hard he found it not to reward all who had suffered for their loyalty to him. Some people had to be displaced to make room for his adherents, but those who had been dispossessed by Venizelos were far more numerous. He had to receive to-day a party of maimed people from some island. They had been assailed by Venizelos's troops and many of both sexes, and all ages, had been killed and wounded. It was incredible what sufferings Venizelos's agents had caused the people. I hear the same story on all sides here. He said that he had given orders that I was to be shown everything and particularly recommended to me M. Maximos, the Director of the National Bank, for financial and commercial matters

Had tea with Princess Christopher and met the Prince and Prince and Princess Andrew. She is Prince Louis of Battenberg's daughter and very good-looking and agreeable. We had an amusing talk of people and events. In the evening dined with the Granvilles at the Legation. A party of eight, including M. de Billy, the French Minister, M. Teniers, a witty French member of the International Financial Commission, Admiral and Mrs. Kelly, very pleasant people, and a number of Greeks, some of whom came in after dinner when we played the "pirate" Bridge usually played in Athens. In the second game if one gets doubled and loses, one is minus 400 above the line. Too restless a game for the English.

Friday, January 21, 1921. Went off at 11 A.M. to talk to the Chief-of-Staff, General Vlachopoulos, who goes away in a few days to command an Army Corps in Asia Minor. A capable man, but not much personality. He showed me all the dispositions of the Greek and Turkish forces in this theatre. The Greeks are holding a front of some seven hundred kilometres, but their main forces are near Broussa in the north and Uschak in the south. At each point an Army Corps and one in Reserve. One division at Ismid under Harington. About 130,000 mouths to feed. In a short time an operation will be carried out to drive the Turks from the two railway junctions which they occupy at present. He thinks that the Kemalist Army is a bluff and that they are not worth much: their divisions often worth only a regiment and a half. Many parties of irregulars marked. The Turkish positions seem to be all known. What is behind Kemal's force does not appear to be known. Most of the Greek line is a mere chain of strong points. There is nothing much against them on the southern front on the Meander opposite the Italian sphere under the Treaty. In the last fight the Turkish A.C., which had drawn too near the Greeks of Broussa was driven back seventy kilometres and dispersed. The Greeks then retired as directed by their original operation orders. He thinks the French and Italian views about the Turks are a mere pretext and disbelieves in a Kemal-Bolshevist combination. The losses are light: seventeen officers and one hundred and fifty men killed and wounded in the last affair. The Greeks are now considerably beyond the frontier assigned by the Treaty. General Vlachopoulos will be succeeded by General Gouvelis next week.

Saw M. Gounaris, the War Minister, later. A pleasant, capable man with a good presence. We spoke of political affairs. He thinks that Rhallys will be left in control as Prime Minister for the time. Gounaris authoritative and speaks well. Like everyone else here he fails to understand the French. He thought that they had lost their political sense. It is incredible what lies are published about Greece in the Western papers of Europe.[1] A typical example is the report that Venizelos was beaten because the Greeks were tired of being in the field. Actually there are five classes under arms, each of 30,000 men, but the 1920 and 1921 classes would be with the colours in any case, as there is two years' service here, so there are only three classes more in the field than in peace-time. Gounaris spoke all over the country before the Elections and said that the question of demobilisation never came up at all and that he never referred to it. All the people accepted the campaign as a national policy and no one dreamed of opposing it.

Gounaris would mobilise five more classes to-morrow if they were needed, and even a general mobilisation would be accepted. Now that "The Son of the Eagle" had returned, the people were ready for anything and all their patriotic songs were of battle, victory, and glory. I said that we seemed to be throwing back twenty-three centuries to the time of Herodotus, and I asked whether the main theme of the father of history, namely, the hostility of

---

[1] See the explanation by M. Venizelos and Prince George, entry for *February* 11.

Europe to Asia, was not reproducing itself after all this lapse of time, with the Greeks in the van once more. Gounaris agreed and said that Asia had not the power of revival possessed by the West and would always be beaten. I had sent on to him, through Princess Christopher, from London a string of questions about Greek affairs, financial and commercial, and he gave me a useful paper in good English with full replies. He felt assured that Briand would help Greece. If the Treaty were not revised, Greece would stand firmly by England. It was inconceivable to him that England should join with Turkey to coerce the Greeks, and falsify English principles. France and Italy wished to exploit the Turks because they could not exploit the Greeks.

I saw M. Calogheropoulos, the Minister of Finance, in the afternoon after lunching at the Russian Restaurant with Colonel Rangabé, his wife, and the Chief of the General Staff. The Minister gave me his views of the financial position. He says that they can go on for three or four months. They are spending over three million drachmas a day in Asia Minor or ninety-eight millions a month. If we can lend them three million sterling a month they can go on fighting later, or, if peace comes, they can hold their ground with one million sterling a month for a short time till their new territories are opened up and exploited. He saw his way to make good the present deficit to some extent by changing the incidence of taxation, and in suggesting some new taxes. He thought that the Greeks were prepared to go on till they had nothing but their shirts to fight in. Dined with M. Vlasto and Prince and Princess Christopher in M. Métaxas's house.

Saturday, January 22, 1921. Went to see the Prime Minister, M. Rhallys, at 1 P.M. A strong old face: he is very deaf and does not always catch what is said, while he does not speak at all clearly. He began by compliments neatly turned and called me "Your Excellency" which he said I deserved for political and intellectual reasons. The King had told him of His Majesty's talk with me. M. Rhallys was very cordial, but the real purpose of his talk was to get me to inquire unofficially whether our Government would consent to the King visiting his Army in Asia Minor, not as King but as Commander. The Army wanted the King, who was all a soldier, but he would not go if the British Government did not approve. It was thought that the King would finish off Kemal in two months. M. Rhallys did not like to inquire officially, as he evidently did not want a direct refusal. The King would go as Commander rather than King, and the Army desired his presence amongst them. I understood him to say that he wished me to obtain this information for him, but M. Rhallys speaks indistinctly and sometimes does not hear one's observations. So to make sure, I went in to tea with Princess Christopher where I met the Crown Prince of Roumania and pretty Princess Hélène. He looked better without his military war hat and seemed much in love with the attractive and charming Princess. Much talk of the coming wedding. The Orthodox marriage service seems to be pretty terrible. They are to stand on a raised dais, and the service appears to be more than commonly crude and blush-raising. Princess Christopher told me afterwards that she believed that this was so, but that, as she did not know a word of Greek, it did not matter to her when she was married. Princess Christopher says that the ceremonials here are very well done and that the Master of the Horse department is very efficient. A merry party.

When they had gone, Princess Christopher sent for Prince Nicholas, as I wished to make sure that I had correctly interpreted M. Rhallys's indistinct commission. Prince Nicholas went off to the King and came back in half an hour to say that the King, in pursuance of his constitutional rôle, could only say that, if I had understood that the Prime Minister had requested me to make the inquiry suggested, he could only advise that I should make it. It appears that the Government have hitherto prevented the King from going. M. Rhallys had reminded me that the Smyrna territory under the Treaty was not yet officially Greek, and that they did not want to act contrary to Great Britain's views. M. Rhallys placed the Greek combatants available at 85,000 men. I told him that, as the Treaty of Sèvres was not yet ratified, I did not see why the King should not join the Army, but M. Rhallys thought it was a question of tact and not of right. He did not want the King to go there if his presence would prove an inconvenience to the British Government. He said that the King desired to show the British Government his intention to co-operate cordially with them. In the afternoon went to the Acropolis with the Boyles. Fine sunny weather, but a brisk wind. Very interesting. There is no other capital in Europe so dominated physically by the past as Athens.

Colonel Nairne, our Military Attaché, dined with me and we discussed the military situation. All had gone well in the last fight, but there is a suspicion among the foreign colony that the men were better than the officers. Nairne complained of the recent appointments here of the Commandant de Place who held the same post in the December 1916 affray, and of another officer, sentenced to twenty years' imprisonment for betrayal and surrender.[1]

Nairne says that Jugo-Slavia is reorganising her army on the basis of thirty divisions, and could smash Greece. He is Military Attaché there too. He has heard from Harington that the latter awaits his news from Greece. Nairne has been awaiting Harington's from Constantinople, so Nairne is going to see Harington. I gather that Harington's reports on the Greeks are favourable.

Sunday, January 23, 1921. Went off with the Boyles, Colonel Rangabé, and M. Rediadis, deputy for the Cyclades, to Xerxes's throne over the Bay of Salamis, where Rediadis most kindly and fully explained to us the battle of which he is a competent historian. I had little recollection that there were 200,000 men in the Persian fleet and 60,000 in the Greek, or that 40,000 men were killed in that

---

[1] I referred this to the Greeks and warned them that such acts made a bad impression.

September day of the year 489 B.C., which was, perhaps, the most decisive battle in history for the greatness of its political results. A peasant came out of a cottage and brought us a tray with wine. He gave as the toast "Ilthi," meaning "He has come." The Greek peasant does not accept tips or bribes. A mechanic came out to help to repair our car when it broke down. He worked like a horse for half an hour and would accept no tip. Is it pride of race or what? It is something to find one unsophisticated people left in Europe.

Nairne came after lunch and we walked together and talked Greek affairs. A good soldier and most trustworthy. Had tea with Admiral and Mrs. Kelly. I thought the Admiral a sound, sensible man of much strength of character, indeed, rather a formidable personality, as I fancy the Italians found in the Adriatic. He thinks that Greece must now begin to build up from the foundations, and that it is useless to project a naval port to cost eight millions when there is scarcely a penny for the Navy. Like most others, he believes the King to be the only salvation for Greece. He is sure that the French and Italians want to exploit the Turks and Asia Minor, and are hostile to the Greeks because they cannot be exploited. Finance seems to be at the bottom of most affairs here. MacAlpin's, Jackson's, and another firm, Wells, I think, are competing for the Piræus plans.

In the evening I dined with the Prince and Princess Andrew to meet the Queen Mother, a very kindly and most dignified old lady. Princess A. told her that I had criticised, in my War Diary, the Royal practice of keeping people standing up, so the Queen Mother sat down and made me sit too. Princess Christopher says that the insides of Royal persons must be constructed on different principles from ours. Two very pretty and delightful daughters. Athens is a perfect treasure-house of beautiful, charming, and accomplished Princesses, all brought up in a thoroughly English way. A pleasant dinner and then a large number of people turned up for a reception, including

Prince and Princess Nicholas, Prince and Princess Christopher and others. I was the only Englishman there. I made the acquaintance of M. Stratos, the leader of the Conservative Party, so called, but really of his own party, for Greek politics are personal. We had a good talk on Greek politics. The anti-Venizelist Union will act together in their choice of a President for the Chambers to-morrow. Gounaris has 100 to 150 followers in the House, Venizelists perhaps 100, and Stratos 50, while Rhallys, Calogheropoulos and others have their small groups. There is a band of some fifty independent and young members who have not yet taken sides. Princess Andrew a charming hostess. Stayed late and had supper there.

After lunch to-day there came in Dr. Sfikas of the *Embros* journal, who told me that his paper, though termed independent, was, in fact, strongly Venizelist. But neither the Venizelist papers nor the Venizelist deputies had any guidance or any *mot d'ordre* from anyone, and they asked me to suggest a line of conduct for them. I said that the wish of England was to see all Greece pulling together, and that she was too small to allow herself the luxury of political divisions, exile, imprisonments, etc. But I refused to express any opinion upon what the Venizelists should do. This was their affair. I also said that I could not give him my impression on the general situation, as I had not yet completed my study of it.

French influence here has been practically destroyed by France's own faults during the war and after it. Opinion is quite unanimous on this point, and on the fact that English influence is supreme. France seems to have lost her political instinct as Gounaris declared, and maybe that the loss of her Russian Ally has destroyed the basis of her Eastern policy.

I am impressed by meeting shoals of people who have been imprisoned, exiled, or ostracised by the Venizelists. It is really a tragedy in real life, and carries one back to the Middle Ages. I had no idea before I came here how utterly Venizelos was discredited in Greece, *solely* on account of his internal policy. It may be mainly the fault of his agents and subordinates, but the fact remains that he is loathed. Hardly a person I meet but has suffered by Venizelos's reign of terror. He kept up the censorship to the last, so England is still most ill-informed. Stratos said to-day that Venizelos's tyranny was terrible, but that it was really weakness and not strength. The eternal answer to tyranny had been given at the Elections. But the country is to a man in favour of the foreign policy of Venizelos, and later on, when the misdeeds of his Cretans are forgotten, Greece will erect a great statue to him and admit that he deserved well of his country.

The high esteem of England held in Greece, and the low esteem of France, are partly due to the reports from Macedonia of the behaviour of the two armies. The reports about the British are most gratifying. The nicest things are said of them. It is declared that the French employed bad troops, and the latter are accused of all sorts of acts of indiscipline and crimes.

Lent Gounaris's paper to Charles Bentinck, who is getting out some financial report for the Foreign Office.

Monday, January 24, 1921. Saw M. Maximos, Governor of the National Bank, at 10.30 A.M. A short, dark man with a clever face. It appears that he wrote, or caused to be written, the report on finance, etc., which Gounaris gave me, so now I understand why it is so good. The main new thing which he told me was that Venizelos, when last in London, had received a promise [1] from Lloyd George to give Greece a loan of $3\frac{1}{2}$ million sterling a month to help them to carry on in Asia Minor. Maximos was in favour of Gounaris going to London when the matter was *en train* again. I asked for the date of the promise, as the exchange might since have operated to our advantage, or that of Greece, but he could not give it. Maximos talked of ample security for the loan, and when I approached the

---

[1] I asked later for proofs, but was told that Venizelos left no records, and the only reference to the promise is an entry in the proceedings of the National Bank at the time, when Venizelos made a statement on the subject to the former Director. For M. Venizelos's explanation see entry for *February* 11.

question of interest he talked of 5 to $5\frac{1}{2}$ per cent, and then went as far as 6 per cent. We talked over the whole position of Greece financially. Greece did not understand cheques which were never used here, so there was a large issue of notes, and a holder of notes could redeem them at any time by a bank cheque on London, Paris, or Washington, at which capitals were kept the Greek cover.

Venizelos's financial policy had been unfortunate. He had used the cover in America for recent transactions, and the King had only found the depreciated supply of France to play with. It was also the fact that Greece found great difficulty in extracting her own money from abroad, as treasuries and not banks now held it, and all sorts of difficulties and delays were now encountered. An English Under-Secretary of State had even given an answer in the House of Commons some time ago implying that these were British monies, and Maximos could only suppose that he had been misinformed. Maximos had gone to Paris to see Venizelos last July and had told the latter that he had to consider the chance of defeat at the elections. He had advised him to bring the King back, and to go for a united Greek policy. He had told Venizelos that he was wrongly informed about the state of opinion in Greece, and that his financial policy was unsound. He had tried to convince him for an hour and a half, but Venizelos was immoveable and in the clouds. It was only a week or so before the elections that Venizelos had realised the true position and then it was too late.

Maximos said that surely the duty of a British Minister at Athens was to maintain neutrality between parties and to hear both sides. He thought that Granville had regarded every question from the Venizelist point of view. I defended Granville and said that Maximos's ideas were criticisms after the event, and that it was not proved to me that Maximos and I would not have made the same mistake in Granville's place. We must remember the whole story of Granville's association with Venizelos, the policy of our Government, and the state of war. Maximos allowed it, but said that we still had the right of private criticism. I said that I wished that a word might be passed round that these attacks on Granville might cease. I heard them everywhere, and they did not please me. They might result in ill-feeling against Greece, and they served no Greek end. They might even have the opposite result of what was intended by them.

Maximos said that the depreciation of the currency and fall of exchange were due to natural causes and could not be helped. He saw no royal road to improvement except action on a steady and gradual incline to recover parity. Greece had great resources, but needed time to exploit them. Macedonia and Thrace would greatly aid with wheat in time, but there would still be a minor deficit for Asia Minor to fill. Exploitation of the good Greek lignite would help in coal, but large works were needed for proper exploitation.

Maximos said that when Greeks spoke of the Allies, they now meant England who had the mastery of the world. France's influence was dead. Italy not of much account. Greece wished to act with England, but without financial help in Asia Minor could not long continue to carry out the Allied policy. He agreed that Greece required fifty years to solidify her gains by the war, and I warned him of ambitious projects against Constantinople which would ruin everything. I told him that we must retain a card of re-entry to the Black Sea in order to act against the Bolshevists in case of need, and the international control was the only solution that I could see for the present.

Saw Granville, who has been laid up in bed for two days, and told him of Rhallys's question and asked him how to reply. Granville said that when the press had talked some time ago of the King's intention to go to the Army, he had asked the Foreign Office to advise him on the point, and they had told him that the question was one for the Greek Government. After some consideration he thought that I might tell Rhallys this, while adding that he could not commit the Government to a definite undertaking. He, Granville, was all in favour of the King going out to the Army, but advised me to add, as my own opinion, that the King should not perform acts of Sovereignty, especially in Smyrna, but merely act as Commander-in-Chief, and go more or less straight to the Army Headquarters. I said that this concorded with the opinion of Rhallys that the King should go out in a military capacity.

Prince and Princess Christopher called and took me to the Conrad Caftanzoglubs' house to lunch. These Athens feeding functions are interminably long. The Princesses and their pretty little daughters are the pick of the feminine basket here. Their homes all seem English, and all the families talk nothing but English.

Tried to see M. Rhallys, but he was at the Chambers. Left a message that I had a reply for him. Asked the Christophers to tell Prince Nicholas that it was all right, but gave them no details. Just while I was dressing for dinner, M. Rhallys asked me to come round, so I went to him at 8.30 P.M. and gave him the reply. The Ministers of War, Marine, Finance, and another were present. It was a sort of private meeting of the Chief Ministers into which I found myself flung as a thick curtain was drawn aside by the old Prime Minister. Then it appeared that M. Rhallys also wanted to know whether Granville had received a reply to a request by Rhallys a good time ago about a journey of Rhallys to London. Granville had never had a reply, as I knew, but Rhallys wants the question repeated, and wishes to go to London in two or three weeks. He had asked me to inquire so as to avoid another official snub.

Dined with the Kellys and Lady Granville. Much amusing talk about the recent crisis. It seems that waiters and cooks are or were Venizelists and all maidservants Monarchists. School children of three or four are divided into the same parties, and have battles. Greece lives on politics.

Tuesday, January 25, 1921. I notice that I have omitted to state that I was informed that Venizelos had warned the late King Alexander that the elections might go against him, and had suggested that in this case Venizelos might practically rule in the Smyrna district, and had asked King Alexander to consent. The latter had informed Prince George of the conversation in Paris.

In the morning interviewed an intolerable number of people who come to see me every day and ask for advice and for my views on all sorts of subjects. The last visitor was the Archimandrite of Rhodes who came in full canonicals, and made a long complaint of the Italian administration of the island where there are 40,000 Greeks, including 8000 Jews.[1] The Italians have 1000 troops and gendarmes. He had brought a written protest and signed it in my presence, and that of Colonel Rangabé. He was in very deadly earnest. His main complaints are the Italian failure to give the local Government promised, interference with trade, and the refusal to allow the return of Rhodians who had left the island during the last eight years, or the departure of Rhodians from Rhodes. I don't suppose that we can do much, as Greeks have given away Greeks, but Lord Burnham will have to decide.

Went to lunch with the King at 1 P.M. Queen Sophie, the Crown Prince of Roumania and his fiancée, and one other daughter. The little youngest girl of eight came in later and sat with us. She is a pet. Sat afterwards in one of the sitting-rooms. The Queen showed me the garden in which she takes great pride. We all talked, and then I talked to the King alone. I am sorry to hear from the King that the Comitajis have appeared again on the Bulgarian frontier. He says that the Bulgarians have not given up all their arms, and have 7000 officers in excess of the stipulated number under the Treaty. He wishes to appoint Count Mercati as Greek Minister in London, a good choice, as he is a very agreeable and gentlemanly fellow.

I found Queen Sophie quite good-looking and very agreeable, but she looks terribly sad, and I am told she

---

[1] Count Sforza told me later that the population was equally divided between Greeks, Turks, and Jews.

spends long hours at her son Alexander's grave at Tatoi. We did not touch on any political subject in conversation together.

I told the King about the talk with M. Rhallys. He asked what the latter had said. I told him that he had said nothing for or against the King going to the Army when I gave him my reply to his question. The King said that he never could understand what M. Rhallys said — neither can Granville nor I. He took the advice about Asia Minor in very good part and said that he would follow it. This advice was that the King should not have a Royal progress at Smyrna, but should go out at the last moment to G.H.Q. and act as Commander-in-Chief only and not as King. He objected that G.H.Q. was at Smyrna. I replied that he could make his advanced headquarters somewhere else, and that political and military considerations recommended this course. He would not wish to give the Turks warning of an impending attack.

The Crown Prince of Roumania very agreeable. A very homely family circle. All these Greek royal palaces remind me of English country houses, and the presiding spirit is British so far as it is not Greek.

Went off with the Prince and Princess Christopher in the afternoon by open car to Tatoi, the King's country house. That of Queen Olga is near by. A stately little Byzantine chapel on a hill in the woods, with the graves of King George and Prince Alexander outside. Lonely and solemn. A vast area of the woods round, and the King's house, were burnt in a fire attributed to the French during the occupation. The village folk gave the Prince and Princess a very hearty welcome everywhere. Saw various people in the evening after tea at Prince Nicholas's Palace. Tried to concoct a formula with a Venizelist editor later for a demand from our Government for the protection of the Venizelists. They want us to do something for those who aided us during the war, but I think they have no grounds for their fears of reprisals. There is not one of the Venizelists even in prison.

Dined late at the hotel.

Wednesday, January 26, 1921. After visiting our Legation went to see Colonel Pallis, Chief of the Staff of the Greek Army in Asia Minor, who is in Athens for a few days. A good staff officer and a man of capacity who expounded to me for two hours over the maps and with great lucidity the whole situation of the Greek forces in Asia Minor. They are mainly in two groups. First Corps about Uschak and Third Corps at Broussa with a curtain of troops between holding the interval, and the Second Corps in reserve forming also the curtain. The Third Corps has one division under Harington holding the zone east of the Bosphorus.

The season is cold and will continue so till March when rains are expected most of the month, and by April it will be suitable weather for campaigning. There is plenty of wood on the ground and the troops are housed in huts. Food and moral favourable. The troops have warm clothing. There are about 110,000 altogether, and Colonel Pallis places the combatants at 60,000 with 400 guns. The Turks are along the railway and the main points are at Afiun-Karahissar and Eskishehr. Colonel Pallis rates the Turkish Regulars at 30,000 men and 100 guns, but believes the figures to be nearer 20,000 men and 50 guns. They have scanty ammunition and only three aeroplanes. They are much dependent for transport on their railways. He considers their defeat to be an easy task and is sure of the fact. He thinks that if all goes well for the Turks in Armenia, they may have 10,000 more to bring up, but cannot do it within two months. The Bolshies, even if they joined the Turks, could not arrive before next summer. He thinks it useless to regard the Turks as a barrier to Bolshevism, as the Turks have no men nor organisation. Their losses in the recent wars have been immense. The Greek position is offensive and aids future strategy which will aim at great results. It is only justified because either block of Greek troops can hold their own against the Turks. Colonel Pallis says that if the Turks had the forces sometimes attributed to them they would have attacked long ago. It would be possible, if necessary, for the Greeks to attack before April. In the last raid the water in the water-bottles of the Greeks froze. There are some 10,000 men in a Greek division. No Turkish division is over 3000 strong.

It is possible for the Greeks to place 300,000 men in the field by a general mobilisation, but there are enough now for the present purpose. The occupied territory behind the armies is divided into regimental zones, one regiment per zone, and three in all. Other regiments will be needed to hold the country as the Greeks go on. The Turks are happy under the Greeks and many come in from the country outside the Greek lines for protection. The 25,000 armed bands of Kemal — the figures that I am given on this point vary a good deal — are a sort of mounted infantry. There are three large bands and many others. They follow some resolute leader and ill-treat the people, who are quiet folk and sick of war. Colonel Pallis thinks the bands useless for fighting, but they shoot the Regulars when they retire and act as battle police. Kemal's regulars are about 10,000 old soldiers and the rest men forcibly recruited. As Kemal requisitions young men, and the money and food of the rest, his rule is unpopular. In the last operation, 10,000 of the civil population followed the Greeks back to their lines. Eskishehr is a large town of 50,000 inhabitants, and it was not in the interests of the Greeks to occupy it in the recent attack, as the population would have been massacred or thrown on Greek hands. No Bolshies or Boches have yet appeared. Colonel Pallis thinks that French and Italian traders supply Kemal. An Italian ship was stopped by a British destroyer off Adalia and found to contain clothing. French machine guns — brand-new with the polish fresh, and with ammunition — have been recently taken and are on their way to Smyrna. Kemal has Fiat cars which come from Italy. Colonel Pallis thinks that certain foreigners act as *agents provocateurs* to stir up the Turks to make complaints, and that they also inform Kemal of the Greek position. There were no complaints before these foreigners came.

In the afternoon went to see Mr. Rawlings, commercial attaché. The Board of Trade, Foreign Office, and Overseas Trade Department seem all to have some share in the new commercial arrangement. Rawlings describes himself on his card as First Secretary of Legation, and this gives him a better position with the officials here than if he were a representative of some other department. The consuls are also now better paid. They report politically to the British Minister, but commercially to Rawlings. They should keep a Minister informed of what is going on, but all depends on how they are treated and whether their advice is listened to. I have never known this to be properly done except under Sir William White at Constantinople in old days. The Germans used to understand the system best and to send for consuls and talk to them at length. Rawlings thinks that economics lead politics now, but that politics may make or mar trade. They mar it in Greece. We were in a privileged position until we closed the door financially to Greece who had drawn on $3\frac{1}{2}$ millions of the account opened for them and then found it closed, and the King not recognised. It would all have come back to us in the form of contracts, concessions, and trade profits. Now trade is dead, and the warehouses are encumbered with goods in bond which the purchasers will not take out if the exchange has fallen since they purchased, and they cannot be made to pay because of the moratorium which is constantly being prolonged. Even if they could be made to pay, it would be useless to ruin customers. Rawlings thinks that we are playing into the hands of Germany. The fluctuation of the exchange is fatal. In whatever direction we change our course we find snags, for if our exchange went down we could not afford to buy abroad and as we are a great importing nation this would not suit us. Rawlings thinks that our recent political action against Greece has been most foolish so far as trade is concerned and has reported this opinion officially.

The French have comparatively little trade and so the course into which they dragged us harms them much less. M. Teniers, the French member of the I.F.C., told me to-day that the Supreme Council had put off the Eastern question matters to February 21 when it will consider it in London. He also said that the real Greek deficit was not 500 millions, but 1500. To show advances as assets was fallacious. It was all *un truc*. But the real figures appear clearly in my Maximos memorandum.

Dined with the Boyles and the Serbian Minister here M — something — itch. He held forth much on Balkan politics and finds the Croats very contumacious. He admits the clause in the Rapallo Treaty against the Habsburgs.

Thursday, January 27, 1921. Paid a lot of calls on French and Italian Ministers, on General Gramat, Chief of the French Mission, etc., and lunched with Mr. Charles Bentinck and his sister and Mr. and Mrs. King, both of our Legation.

In the afternoon went, at his request, to see General Dousmanis who surrendered Roupel during the war, and was condemned to hard labour for life. He tried to convince me that he was not a pro-German, and thought that the northern frontier of New Greece was very insecure and had been settled by Venizelos in a hurry without any regard to natural frontiers.

Tea with Princess Christopher and a long talk. She told me of her duties as a Royal Princess and they seemed to me to constitute a dog's life. She says that "any bob-tailed Greek" can write to ask for her photo, and she has to send it. A long talk over the situation.

In the evening was to have dined with Nairne, but he had a high temperature, so Colonel Schallenberger, the U.S. Military Attaché, whom I had met on Pershing's Staff, and his pretty wife dined with me, and we had a good chat. He lives usually at Belgrade, and shares most of my ideas about Greece. So does his Minister, I gather. He says that the Jugo-Slavs have sixteen divisions formed, and that the United States thinks it shameful to withdraw its promise of financial aid just because the Greeks wanted the King back.

Official confirmation came to-day that the consideration of the Eastern question is postponed until February 21, when it is to take place in London. Greece is to be asked to attend, and the Turks, including Kemal or his representatives. The Greeks far from pleased, but I tell them all that it is a perfectly reasonable course.

Friday, January 28, 1921. Had a walk round "Shoe Lane" with the Boyles and visited a very exquisite old Byzantine church. Went on to see General Gramat, head of the French Military Mission. A short burly officer, competent and without fire. He told me that there were nine Greek divisions in Asia Minor and five in Epirus, in all 183,000 men, of whom 30,000 in Thrace and 100,000 in Asia Minor, the latter with 65,000 to 70,000 combatants. They have in Asia 36 long French guns of 120 mm. and 36 English 6-inch howitzers. The transport is defective, and the roads so bad that the motor lorries can only carry one-fourth of full loads. They have secured only 600 camels. He thought the Greek Army pretty good and well-found, but they ought to have three months' reserve of wheat in Greece and there is no reserve. He thought that the information about Kemal's Army lacked precision. The dépôts are empty in Greece and the last division sent out was to make good strengths. There are six classes now under arms, three of serving soldiers, and three of reservists, but the Class 1913 counts as two owing to some administrative change. They can call out fourteen or sixteen classes in all, and had 300,000 men under arms and fifteen divisions in 1918, but there would be deficiencies in guns and material if the attempt were repeated now. The Greek field guns are 65 mm. mountain and 75 mm. field. They have very few aeroplanes, possibly not ten, and though the aviators are good they break many machines. Greece needs spare parts for lorries and planes, and a skilled repairing staff of mechanics is greatly needed. In the highlands of Asia Minor, where the Greeks now are, the average level above the sea is 3000 feet and the climate is severe. He puts the French force at Constantinople at one strong division and the English at as least as much. With the fleet to help, Constantinople is safe. The average Greek contingent is 22,000, excluding the new territory. There are many deserters and absentees who do not return from leave, about 16,000 altogether, but he did not mention desertion at the front.

Lunched with M. and Mme. Giro, M. Rangabé *père*, and Colonel Rangabé and his wife. A comfortable and large house. M. Giro has been many years in India in the Ralli firm. Mme. Giro said that while her maid was brushing her hair to-day she inquired anxiously about the London Conference, and asked what it meant. All the servants and children discuss politics endlessly. Someone of the party had been away in the hills recently, and at night the people were discussing politics — French, English, and Italian — practically all night. These were common people.

Colonel Rangabé brought me a paper that I had asked him to procure at the Ministry of the Interior, namely, a return of the elections and the Plébiscite with the official figures. This shows that about 732,000 voted at the last elections and over a million at the Plébiscite. In the latter voting, only 10,000 votes were given against the King. In Crete, where 17,000 voted, the Venizelists were all returned, seven in number, but in the Plébiscite in Crete 12,000 voted for the King. There were some 56 Venizelists returned in Thrace under martial law rule, but, as the Royalists had not been allowed to nominate their candidates, the elections might be invalidated. Some thirty out of the fifty-six Venizelists said that they had only posed as Venizelist to get their names put forward, and now expressed their wish to join the Government parties. The Tribunals had still to decide the legality or otherwise of numerous elections. Nominally about 110 Venizelists were returned, but the figures look like coming down a good deal.

Went to have a talk with M. Montagna, the Italian Minister, who told me how it came about that he, alone, of the Allied Ministers, was properly informed about the recent elections. He had found his two colleagues hand in glove, and in close touch with Venizelos. While friendly, they did not show much disposition to consult him and he was somewhat *tenu à l'écart*. He was "thrown on his own modest resources" and so mobilised all his means, namely, the rather large staff of the Legation, all the consuls, and the Italian missions for fisheries, gendarmerie, archæology, etc., etc. He had not a penny to spend on all this. He applied the whip to the consuls, and in fact obtained a fine intelligence service, and soon became aware that the people meant to end the Venizelist tyranny, which by its oppression and cruelty had utterly disgusted the people. He said that the treatment of the people by the Cretan bravos was terrible, and that one could not so much as bow to a Royalist friend without being thrown into prison. They spied even upon him and upon everybody. He could not consider that Venizelos had no responsibility for these acts of his Government, though this is what was being said now.

M. Montagna's opinion of the military position accords generally with mine. Italy, said Montagna, desired pacification and then exploitation. Would the continued presence of the Greeks in Smyrna, he asked, permit of exploitation? Smyrna was the chief port of Asia Minor. If they give you facilities for your trade, will you be satisfied? I asked. He said that he thought so. And you will, of course, give reciprocal facilities in the Italian Zone? This he did not seem to hanker after, but in the end, after a long talk, I did not find that his views differed seriously from mine.

He thought the Greek people good and solid. He asked why we monarchical countries did not support the monarchical principle instead of throwing every difficulty in the King's way, and treating him like dirt. Whatever a King might be elsewhere, in Greece he was everything, while we were injuring our trade and nationals by our foolish behaviour. He thought that the folly of the present placing of the King in Coventry and cutting off financial supplies, injured British trade and interests more than any other. Italy had no great commercial interests in Greece. France's influence was dead. Here was a country which was a fortress of monarchy in a liquid world, but if we rendered the King's task impossible Bolshevism might creep in here too, and Italy did not wish that.

We discussed the prospects of the London Conference and the names of the Greeks who might be sent. I thought Gounaris, Pallis, and Maximos would be the strongest team of the men I had met. Rhallys, we agreed, would be no good. Montagna thought that his health would not stand it, and I felt sure that Lloyd George would never have patience with an old man who could neither hear nor be understood. Tea with M. and Mme. Montagna and their staff.

Saw Granville later, and told him about my talk with Pallis and about the election figures. Granville thinks well of Stratos, and does not ignore the chance of a combination to upset Gounaris. Montagna, on the other hand, told me that he expected the Venizelists to disappear in a month. They were being drawn to the other parties. The Greek Venizelist papers these two days have been preaching unity. The sinking Venizelist ship is being deserted by the rats. I doubt whether there will be enough places to fit them into!

X suggests that I should hint to the Ministers that Gounaris is not well seen in London, but I said that it would be against my judgement, as I thought he was the best man to go to help Lloyd George.

Saturday, January 29, 1921. A long talk with Princess Christopher in the afternoon, and with Count Mercati. Went to see Nairne, who is still laid up. Nothing yet decided about the Greek representation at the London meeting on February 21. Spent the morning at the Museum with the Boyles and Mr. Wace who is one of the experts and interested us enormously. Should like to spend many days there. Colonel Rangabé lunched with me. Dined with the Boyles who had the Granvilles, Rawlingses, the Serbian Minister, M. Mélas, the Venizelist deputy for Janina, and one other man. The Janina deputy talked Venizelism to me most of dinner without throwing any fresh light on the position. The Serbian Minister does not believe in any serious trouble ahead in his part of the world, but says that they will want ten years to settle their own internal affairs which are difficult owing to the intransigence of the Croat peasant party who want autonomy. But he says that the cleavage in Jugo-Slavia is, with this exception, not that of nationalities fortunately, but of political colour, i.e., radicals, democrats, socialists, communists, etc. He says that the study of a State in a condition of gradual formation is a most interesting one. A bluff, hearty, boisterous, clever old bandit with a strong face. So different from Greeks like M. Mélas, impeccable in dress and diplomatic in conversation.

Sunday, January 30, 1921. Saw M. Robert de Billy, the French Minister, at the French Legation at 11 A.M. A pleasant, well-informed, and cultivated man, Granville's most intimate colleague. He has the usual tendency of intellectuals to scepticism and sarcasm. We discussed art first and then came to politics. He thought that Venizelos's fall was due to his own failings. He had great ability, but was always in the clouds, had a board-school child's notions of finance, and let others carry on the internal policy while he was interesting himself in the big questions of foreign policy. Venizelos well knew that he would some day have to carry out a huge programme of internal reform after he had got his New Greece. The country was in a bad state administratively, and an immense work awaited the new Government. Venizelos had carried on by his subordinates a system of tyranny which had proved his ruin. It could be excused during the war, but not after it. He admitted that the Greeks could smash the Turks, but did not see what the limit of their action could be. He did not much believe in the barrier of Turks against

Bolshevism. He did not think Rhallys would be a success at the coming Conference, but heard that he wished Politis to join him. As Politis was Venizelos's right-hand man this would displease the Monarchists, but certainly if Politis came he had the faculty of presenting a case well, with all the facts marshalled. Perhaps old Rhallys wished to implicate Politis in a failure. I do not think that de Billy much approves of certain action taken here. He knows too much of Greece, and says that the big people think that by saying a thing is to be, it will be, whereas it will not so be in Greece. The psychology of the Greeks was very special. They ruled their Government and were not ruled by it, as France and England were. The Greeks still regarded the world as made up of Greeks and Barbarians and thought it a condescension when they said that Greece was with this Power or that. They were astounded when they found that this Power was not with them. The Greeks were very subtle and trained to politics from infancy. They ate, drank, thought, and dreamed politics. When Rhallys came to apologise to Madame Politis for having her windows broken, the lady said to her boy of six how nice it was for a Prime Minister to have taken such a step. "Pish! It was only a phrase," scoffed the infant. We thought that Kemal would not come to London, but might send a man who would probably not dare to return to Angora if he failed, as he would probably get his throat cut. So he would probably remain in London.

De Billy seemed to have no idea of the death of French prestige here, but I did not allude to it. It is certainly not his doing. He was all for the renewal of relations with the King, as the other Allied Ministers are. He was not in the least contemptuous of the Greeks and showed sympathy with them. He ought to go to the Conference.

Went to say good-bye to the King. I thanked him for all the facilities that had been given me. We discussed the Greek delegation to London and agreed that Rhallys was too old and would provoke impatience. I thought Gounaris, Maximos, and Pallis the best team to help

Lloyd George. The King agreed, but said that Rhallys might have to go. He would arrange with Gounaris that the latter should take the lead. I told him of the ill-feeling against Gounaris in certain Allied countries, but said that I thought Gounaris would live down this feeling if he went, and that one could not exclude the real Prime Minister and leader of the strongest party in the Chambers. It seemed to me idiotic from all points of view. The King now thought that they could carry on until March financially. He shares the views of Pallis about Asia Minor. He ended by saying that even if the Greeks were ordered out of Asia Minor, they might refuse to give way to anything but force.

Lunched with M. Montagna and his wife, the Italian Military Attaché, called San Martino, and one or two more. Montagna said before lunch, when we were alone, that some British reports which he had seen showed an extraordinary variation between the different estimates of Kemal's force. One report gave his figures to be 180,000 and another report under 20,000. I told him of our experiences in Afghanistan, and thought that large numbers might turn up for a battle, but would go home after a few days. Neither Montagna nor de Billy has really explained to me what their countries want. "Pacification and exploitation" are the watchwords of both, but as these mean pacification by giving the Turks Smyrna as a *pourboire*, and the exploitation of the Turks afterwards, it does not mend matters, nor much advance them.

Said good-bye to Princesses Andrew and Christopher. Saw Granville at four o'clock.

Mercati came and told me, to my surprise, that I had suggested that the Queen should see Admiral Kelly and that she had said that she wished to do so to talk about Prince Paul who was a Naval cadet. I told Mercati that I had not suggested this to Queen Sophie, but had merely said that the Queen would like him if she saw him. Reported this to Granville and the Admiral in order to avoid any misunderstanding.

M. Gounaris called for me at 8.30, and motored me down to dine at Phaleron, where we hoped to be quiet. But we found a dance going on, and all the youths and maidens trooped in to talk to Gounaris as the custom is. The girls are particularly fond of him, it seems, because he has promised female suffrage. We got rid of them all at last and had a good talk. Gounaris went at some length with Venizelos's persecutions, which were really intolerable. It was a species of terror. No one could call his soul his own, and everyone was always liable to find himself arrested during the night. The people did not rise because Venizelos had force on his side, but they bided their time for the vote. The outside world knew nothing of what had been going on. The Press was fed by Venizelos, and the few voices of the exiles were regarded as tendencious. Anyone would have made the same mistake as our diplomacy and Press made, for the Venizelists took charge of all foreigners and fed them upon lies. The Greek people had been very moderate in victory. No spirit of personal vengeance inspired them, and they only wished to forget the past. We had a long talk about the whole political and military situation, but I got back too late and start too early to-morrow to jot it all down.

Monday, January 31, 1921. Motored to the Piræus with Rangabé and embarked on the *Bucovina,* a little Lloyd-Triestine boat of some three thousand tons. A slow boat, very full: three in a cabin. Prince Andrew came on board on his way to Corfu. Played Bridge most of the night to avoid going to my cabin. My stable companions were asleep when I went down. Opened the porthole and so slept well. When I woke up, I saw two faces in the other bunks the living images of Potash and Perlmutter — shining, oily, and genial, but hating the open porthole like the devil.

Tuesday, February 1, 1921. A very lovely journey yesterday and to-day through the islands and the Corinth Canal. Reached Corfu about two o'clock. What wonderful lights and soft colour effects! Prince Andrew invited me ashore to see his house and the last British Governor's old palace. A launch came for him. We tossed up and down in going ashore. A crowd of people received the Prince very well. We motored together to Mon Repos, a charming old Georgian house about two miles away, with fine views over the bay. He took me over the house. A lot of harm done during his enforced absence since 1916 — much wet come in and roof wants repairing, but it is a most charming place and only wants a little money to be spent on house and garden to be an ideal winter resort. The house in very good style, and might have been taken bodily out of some English county about 1780. Prince Andrew then drove me to the Governor's palace which has been left exactly as it was when the last English Governor left it, in 1863 I think. We did things well in the eighteenth and early nineteenth centuries. Possibly there was less supervision from home. All in the best Georgian style, and all the furniture, decorations, portraits, etc., left exactly as they were under the English rule. The result is a perfectly ideal old Georgian model with nothing out of taste. The Hall of St. George in the centre of the first floor very fine. The entrance hall most dignified. A throne room with a throne chair at one end, with the English Crown still on the chair — three circular steps up to it. Full-length portraits all round, including one of George IV, and allegorical pictures of St. George. In the Council Room are portraits of distinguished Corfu statesmen. What a heavenly country house this would make in England! The name of the man who designed and decorated this place should be preserved. He was an artist. In one of the bedrooms used by the late King of Greece is a wardrobe with a looking-glass on which there are the signatures of distinguished visitors. The German Kaiser's signature is among them, written with a diamond ring, I suppose.

The launch took me back. It was rough, and we had been tossed about like a cork on landing. The gratitude of the stout Greek officer sent to escort me was comic when I took leave of him at the landing-stage, and did not ask him to accompany me on the journey to the ship again. An acrobatic feat to jump on the companion ladder as the launch danced up and down. Transferred to Prince Andrew's cabin and was alone there.

CHAPTER III

ROME AND PARIS

Consul-General Eyres — The British Embassy — The *Fascisti* and the
hotel strike — An official dinner — Some Roman beauties — Another talk
with M. Barrère — Princess Jane di San Faustino — Princess Radziwill —
Another conversation with Count Sforza — His success at Paris — His
views on Greeks and Turks — The London Conference — The Italians and
the Czechs in agreement — Sir George Buchanan on Russia — M. Beneš
makes a favourable impression at Rome — Good influence of Count Sforza
— Miss Buchanan's "City of Trouble" — Leave for Paris — Thoughts on
Italy — A conversation with Marshal Pétain — A talk over Asia Minor —
Strong position of the French Army in Europe — A conversation with M.
Venizelos — His strenuous work for Greece in London — He will never
work with the King — Herodotus and the Greeks — Visit to Prince and
Princess George of Greece at St. Cloud — Hopes in the French — Views on
events — Visit to M. Philippe Berthelot — Reparations and Greece — A
fair deal between France and England — Bismarck on the value of a man —
A talk with M. Briand — He wishes to withdraw the French troops from
Cilicia —The lies about Greece — M. Briand has reached the limit of con-
cessions to Germany — The French Chambers a difficult team to handle —
Bonaparte and Briand — Lady Millicent Hawes — Return to London.

Wednesday, February 2, 1921. Reached Brindisi 7 A.M. — a
long wait till 6.30 P.M. when I took train for Rome. Mr.
Eyres, late Consul-General at Constantinople, and Captain Mars, King's Messenger, lunched with me. Eyres's
knowledge of the Eastern Mediterranean most valuable.
He is a perfect mine of information.

Thursday, February 3, 1921. Arrived at Rome at 10 A.M.
and found that Sir George Buchanan and Lady Georgina
were expecting me to stay at the Embassy. All the hotel
servants are on strike and the *Fascisti* are assisting in the
waiting and house-maiding, so the haven by the Porta
Pia was a godsend, especially with such a charming host
and hostess. I found myself in a lovely room overlooking
the garden with bathroom and sitting-room attached.
After lunch took a drive with Lady Georgina and Sir
George, and we visited various places of interest and several curio shops. They both have fine taste in old and
beautiful things. Sir George rather fussed by Italian

press attacks on us, and German propaganda strongly
suspected. The *Popolo Romano* the chief offender.

In the evening a big dinner of twenty-six, including
Count Sforza and his Countess and a lot of pretty women
and their husbands, including the magnificent Duchess of
Sermoneta, the Torlonias, the Odescalchis — she was
Dora Rudini, Labby's daughter, and retains her looks —
Princess Radziwill, very brilliant, and various others.
Took in Princess Radziwill and found her as good company as ever and in great looks. Had a good talk with
Count Sforza after dinner and found in him the same
spirit of conciliation and broad statesmanship which have
won him such renown of late. He was wearing the Annun-
ciata, the great Order of the old House of Savoy, which
gives him precedence over all but Royal Princes and
makes him the cousin of the King. We agreed to meet
again before I left. Then talked to M. Caramelos, late
Greek Minister here, who had come without his beautiful
wife, to our regret. He is in bad odour in Athens for having advised the King to resign in favour of the Crown
Prince.

Friday, February 4, 1921. Have begun my articles on
Greece and they keep me busy. Another tour by car in the
afternoon with Her Excellency and Edward Cunard who
is here on a visit. Later went to see M. Barrère, the French
Ambassador, and told him the results of my trip to Greece
which were not calculated to cause him much joy. We had
a long talk about it all. I told him frankly what I thought,
but he could not give me the French policy for Greece and
I am in some doubt whether he or anyone even in Paris
has one.

It struck me, on second thoughts, that the eighteenth-
century tapestries and other joys are out of keeping with
the fifteenth-century Farnese Palace, which demands
sterner furniture and decorations. The Farnese is most
magnificent, but our Embassy is a better house for the
purposes of diplomacy and garden parties, and much
more habitable. I am told that we might have bought the

Barberini Palace at the time for the same sum. It would have been fine for official receptions and a most profitable investment as it contains about five sets of apartments, each good enough for a Legation at least. Still, taking one thing with another, I like our Embassy best of all.

Saturday, February 5, 1921. Worked, and then went to Princess Jane di San Faustino's for lunch. We were alone and had a great talk over the affairs of Greece and Italy. She is in the Barberini Palace, and has some large and beautiful rooms with suitable furniture. A large fountain in her dining-room lit up by light from below. She told me of the troubles in the Fiat Works which her son-in-law and his father control, and of all the difficulties of Italy, house-keeping, etc. Later it was scandals, the crew of Taormina, etc. A very pleasant, clever, and well-informed woman who is one of the stars of Rome. A most amusing talk over the Roman personalities of the day, and their loves and troubles. She says that Italians think of nothing but love.

Went to the Russian ballet in the evening.

Sunday, February 6, 1921. Worked, and then lunched with Princess Radziwill and a pleasant party of Prince Ruspoli and some nice Americans. She told us of her party last night with M. Scaletti, who had given out that he meant to invite the twelve prettiest women in Rome and the twelve smartest young men. They included the Sermoneta Duchess, of course, the Radziwill and Odescal-chi beauties, Mrs. Grant, Eddy Wortley's lovely girl, the Medici beauty, and several more. Maurice Pernot came to see me and I presented him to the Buchanans. Pernot always delights me. He is so broad, and so cultivated.

Monday, February 7, 1921. Went to the Consulta and had an hour's talk with Count Sforza, the Foreign Minis-ter, with a view to discovering what Italy really wanted to change in the Treaty of Sèvres, and what line Sforza meant to take in London. I congratulated him on his action at Paris the other day in bringing M. Briand and Lloyd George together. He said that the first day was very stormy and that there was some difficulty in arranging matters. I asked how it was that Briand did not know of the arrangement made at Boulogne. Why had not Berthelot informed Briand? Sforza said laughingly that there were some diplomatic mysteries into which one did best not to look too closely. Then we agreed that for a man of the world to be Foreign Minister was an advantage to a country, and he told me how he had realised what modern democracy had lost by not comprehending this.

Turning to the Greeks, and after a long discussion, in which I told him my views, he said that life must be made more endurable for Turkey, and he evidently wished that Thrace should be restored to Turkey, leaving to Greece a "privileged economic situation" there. He also still wants to treat with the Turks and use them against the Bolshevists, and he explained his view of the future danger presented by Russia, and his regret that Lloyd George paid so little attention to it. Sforza thought that Greece aimed at Constantinople, as of course she does. He told me that Kemal's representative was coming to the London Conference via Adalia. I told him my views. He seemed particularly impressed by my argument that the Treaties were the public law of Europe, and that if we began tinkering and altering them, we should have no peace. He agreed that Kemal was no good, but did not think that the Greeks could stand the strain for long. I told him that the Greek Army controlled the situation in Asia Minor and that a Turkish stick to beat Bolshevism would prove a broken reed, but that we must keep our international garrison at Constantinople because no better solution presented itself. Personally, I was for the Treaty and all the Treaty. Those who wanted it changed should say precisely how they wanted it changed, not vaguely, but in set terms.

Sforza is undoubtedly all for peace and reconciliation, but with economic benefits for Italy to follow. He is not prepared to send an army to Turkey or anywhere else. He has seen M. Benès, the Foreign Minister of the Czecho-Slovaks (de Salis distinguishes the two new States as the Checks and the Jugs), and both Sforza and Sir George

Buchanan agree in stating that Italy and the Czechs are agreed on political, economic, and commercial policy. So Sforza says that there is no need for a Treaty, and Italy will not at present join the Little Entente. But undoubtedly Sforza will press for the revision of the Sèvres Treaty. Three Allies and three policies! Therefore nothing doing, and a general muddle!

I saw M. Métaxas later in the day and he is ciphering to Athens my news about Sforza's and Lloyd George's approval of the recognition of the King, and about Sforza's view, also expressed to me, that no Greek should be placed on the Index at the Conference on account of his supposed unpopularity with the Allies. Sforza preferred, he told me, to meet such men, and especially leaders like Gounaris, face to face, and to find out if and where we differed from them. He was not for harassing the Greeks by excluding their leading men. Métaxas told me that Rhallys had been replaced by Calogheropoulos as Premier, which pleased me. He also said that the Greek papers were all full of my doings in Greece, and recorded my every movement. Lucky that there was no Maid of Athens on my list! Byron was in luck. He lived before journalism. How amusing it is, by the way, that the only Greek line in Byron is ungrammatical! The result of a Harrow education, no doubt. I was also much amused in Greece to hear that at the last Olympic Games we sent our choicest Greek scholars, and that they made flowery speeches in their best Greek and no one understood a single word of them!

The Kennards and Mr. McClure dined at the Embassy, and Mr. Philip. McClure and I discussed the *Times* who have discharged him, though he has an almost unsurpassed knowledge of Italy.

Tuesday, February 8, 1921. A talk with the Ambassador in the morning. He told me that Benès thinks that the Bolshevists will break up in the spring, or at all events this year, and that their rule will be succeeded by five years of anarchy. He expects the Social Revolutionaries to upset them, but Sir George does not believe in them and says

that some of them are as bad as the Bolshies. A talk of
Siberia declaring autonomy. Sforza told me yesterday
that Benès feared an attack by the Bolshies on Poland
formerly, but now does not credit it. But he and Sforza
think an attack on Roumania possible.

It occurs to me that Sforza cannot carry far his views
about taking Thrace from Greece, since Bulgaria renounced in favour of Greece all her rights in Thrace under
Article 42 of the Treaty of Neuilly, which has been ratified
and is in operation. We are surely not going to upset a
second Treaty!

Note that Benès has created a very favourable impression here and is much liked both by Sforza and Sir George.
I think that Sforza is a man who realises that his task is
the restoration of the peace and the unity of Europe. His
optimism in foreign policy is less a mask than the real
nature of the man. His main practical aim is to pacify
Europe while securing economic profit for Italy. He will
always oppose a Greek occupation of Constantinople, and
considers Russia a real menace, or pretends to do so. His
head is cool and he regards politics without passion. He
may not be a Bismarck, but a Bismarck would be highly
inconvenient just now. I think that Sforza adds something to the moral forces of our post-war world. But I dis-
agree with his Greek policy all the same. I told him of the
petition from Rhodes, but on Sir George Buchanan's advice did not show him the text, as the language was rather
strong. McClure, and M. Gallenga, a Deputy, lunched at
the Embassy to-day — Gallenga told numerous stories.
One of Clemenceau after Deschanel's accident: "I was not
made President because I was too old. But I got as far as
the third cataract, and Deschanel could not get as far as
Montélimar."

Finished reading Miss M. Buchanan's book on Russia
called "The City of Trouble." A charming and pathetic
little volume, well written and deeply interesting. A very
nice girl with a real good heart. Walked round the garden
with His Excellency in the morning. Admired the ilexes

and the Aurelian wall from the top of which there is still a fine glimpse of the distant mountains, though part is now shut out by new buildings.

Left 3.30 P.M. for Paris, carrying a Foreign Office Bag with me. M. Métaxas came to bid me good-bye at the station and gave me his latest news. Said good-bye to the Buchanans with real regret. Most kind and hospitable people who make all who visit them feel happy and at home. I delight to see an Embassy kept up in the style and dignity of the old days, as this is. Sir George exactly the man for Italy.

I see that I have not referred to the *Fascisti*. These are a strike-breaking anti-Bolshevist organization composed mostly of the young men of the better classes who turn out like special constables to keep order, and to keep things going in factories, hotels, etc., when workmen strike. They have arms — so have the workmen. Giolitti's aim is to disarm both. The *Fascisti* are popular with the proper-tied classes. So are Nitti's *Guardia Regia* of old N.C.O.'s and soldiers, a body which must be very numerous now.

Rome to-day and a month ago has been full of these men and of soldiers who are seen in courtyards everywhere as if trouble were expected. But I see no reason to change my view that Italy is over the worst of her internal troubles, even if the people are not yet all setting resolutely to work except in the south, and even if there are still too many loafers about the streets. Emigration has again become a safety valve, and the figures are growing yearly, though as yet only a third of the immense pre-war figures. The trans-oceanic emigration is still to the United States, Argentina, and Brazil in the main, while France takes most emigrants in Europe and Germany not one thousand a year yet. I am told that in normal past times the amount of money sent home by Italian emigrants amounted to a million dollars a day, and that the majority come home after eight to twelve years abroad when they become part of the small-propertied bourgeois class, which must be essentially anti-Bolshevist.

A difficulty is that the people of Italy have given up eating maize which Italy produces, and have taken to wheat of which Italy can produce very little. Wheat and coal are Italy's main needs, but iron and steel and all kinds of raw materials not produced in Italy are greatly needed, and are difficult to buy from countries with higher rates of exchange. What has happened to macaroni I don't know. It can scarcely be bought.

Arrived Paris 10.30 P.M. — two hours behind time. Took the F.O. Bag to the Embassy and found a room at the Ritz.

PARIS BEFORE THE LONDON CONFERENCES

Thursday, February 10, 1921. Walked to the Embassy and found that Lord Hardinge was in London for his son's marriage. Sir Milne Cheetham, Minister and acting temporarily for Hardinge, saw off Lord Curzon to London on the return of the latter from the Riviera and then came to lunch. He told me how affairs were going on here and I told him of affairs in Greece and Rome for him to pass on to Hardinge. Cheetham no more able to define French wishes in the East than I am, but he has only been here a month, and I must try to see the French F.O. people. We had a good talk. Hardinge took no part in the Conference at Paris. Lloyd George stayed at the Crillon, and Curzon at the Ritz.

The arrangements made by the Allies for the disarmament of Germany and reparations are provoking intense fury in Germany, and we shall see how things go in the London Conference of February 28 after the Eastern Conference.

Saw M. Métaxas, Chargé d'Affaires of Greece here. The press gives the names of the Greek delegation under Calogheropoulos which comes here next Monday. No mention of Gounaris nor of Pallis yet, but Sterghiadis, the competent Governor of Smyrna, said to be coming, and Maximos. Métaxas confirms my news that Venizelos is working hard here and in London for the Treaty, but also against the King. Métaxas finds that the French Foreign Office is not glad to see him, and fob him off as best they can. He tells me that he published in certain French papers the gist of the private wire I sent through the Greek Foreign Office to Lord Burnham. Métaxas said that part of it appeared in the *Daily Telegraph*.

Went to see Marshal Pétain at five o'clock at the Boulevard des Invalides. Found him looking well and stouter than during the war. He was in civilian kit. We had a good talk about the war in Asia Minor over the map. I noticed that the figure of Kemal's forces was placed at 63,000? and the Turkish "Army of the East" on the side of Armenia at 36,000? (Both figures had a query after them.) I told him the Greek estimate, and their assurance of success. I also told him that if the Greeks were ordered out of Asia Minor the Constantinople position would be uncovered, and the French in Cilicia liable to be overwhelmed. He agreed, and after a long talk we thought that the only solution was for Greece and the rest of us to hold our present positions, and that if any change were to be made, it should be made by kicking the Turks out of Constantinople. He said that he had four French divisions in Cilicia; they were bad troops, mostly black, and were hard-pressed by the bands attacking them. But as he was speaking an officer came in to report the capture of Aintab, and Pétain was pleased and said that it was an important place with 70,000 inhabitants.

Pétain was quite unaware of the reasons for the fall of Venizelos, and was much interested in my explanations of them. He thought the whole problem of Constantinople, the Powers, the Greeks, and the Turks extremely involved, and that no solution presented itself. He did not want Russians or Greeks at Constantinople. An international garrison, and elsewhere for all the Allies to hold what they had, seemed best. That is precisely what I think.

He said that the French Army was all right, that the mobilisation was all worked out, and that they could place sixty divisions in the field immediately. He thought the

Chambers aggressive, and that the country would follow them to a man if it were a question of making the Boche pay.

Pétain thought that we should occupy and exploit the Rhineland first, and if taking it over and taxing it were of no avail, we should send the whole German population over the Rhine and replace it by the French *mutilés de guerre*. This plan was similar to the German plans for Northern France which the French had discovered, but had not yet published. They would do so when the time came, to show that they were taking a leaf out of a German book.

Friday, February 11, 1921. Lunched with M. Métaxas and his wife and a party of Greeks. Not much fresh news.

M. Venizelos came at five o'clock to my rooms and talked till 6.15. I began by telling him that I did not wish to talk to him under false pretences: that I did not agree with his internal policy and proposed to say what I thought about it, but that I wished to help to save his Treaty with which I was heartily in accord in common with the whole of Greece. He told me that before I judged his internal policy, I should hear his side, which I offered to do when he pleased, but we agreed that the Treaty was the main thing for the moment, and he declares that he has been working strenuously for it here and in London, and is well content with his talks in London with politicians, and newspaper people, including Burnham, who had, he says, a good article last Tuesday, and undertakes to support his point of view. *Times, Daily News, Westminster Gazette, Chronicle,* and *Manchester Guardian,* all coming into line.

As to the King, Venizelos thinks that Serbia will never forgive him for betraying her, and he fears that Serbia and Bulgaria may some day unite to crush Greece. But he regards the King as an episode, and expects him to die before Germany and her recent satellites recover. He will never work with the King, and was perfectly decided that it was wholly impossible.

I asked about the promise said to have been given by

Lloyd George to lend Greece $3\frac{1}{2}$ millions a month while the operations continued. Venizelos said that there was no formal promise, but that on one occasion he had put forward a Greek occupation of Constantinople, which he did not press, and a Greek enclave on the Black Sea about Trebizond where there was a large Greek population, and a loan of $3\frac{1}{2}$ millions a month. He said that Lloyd George described this latter as perfectly reasonable, but beyond that he did not go. As to the Treaty, we were perfectly in accord on all points, and I see no reason to alter the five articles which I have now completed on the future of Greece. Nearly all my arguments he repeated word for word. He traced the lying reports in the French press to the agents of a certain bank who were working in the interests of the Turks. There are a lot of Frenchmen on the Board. He thought that people were greatly impressed because he, Venizelos, though fallen, was supporting the Greek cause. He thought with me that the Conference might fail, since we could not compromise if the French and Italians maintained their positions. We should then all go on as we were, and the Treaty would remain, even if unratified.

He said the Versailles men had placed the force to hold the Greek Zone in Asia Minor at three divisions when peace was made, and thought that Greece could find these from her normal peace effectives and volunteers. She would help in the gendarmerie to be created under the Treaty, and he was for evicting the Turk from Constantinople.

I asked about a limit to the Greek offensive. He thought that the Baghdad railway line should be the limit, with Angora.

He said that the Greek birth-rate meant a population of thirty millions by the end of the century, and declared that with the present population she could find a million soldiers. I told him my view, i.e., that we were going back to Herodotus, and showed him the map in Bury of the Greek settlement in Asia Minor about 500 B.C. He was interested and said that the same thing had gone on later, and that the coast always became Greekicised, no matter what was done.

He was looking very fit — rather stouter than when we last met, while he seemed to have a fuller beard. I scarcely recognised him when he came, but he has not lost his old volubility and fire, and poured out a lava of words.

Went off to St. Cloud to dine with Prince and Princess George at their villa, 7 Rue Mont Valérien, across the Pont de Suresnes, up the Boulevard de Versailles to the Café de Vol d'Or, and then to the left. It takes a bit of finding in the dark.

The Prince is more like the late King than the other brothers. The Princess is quite a character, literary in her tastes, has written a book of which she gave me a copy with a nice inscription — "Souvenir d'une fidèle lectrice," and is rather more than nice-looking and very intelligent. Prince Waldemar of Denmark also there and a daughter of the House, besides another lady whose name I did not catch. I found Prince George on the high horse about Venizelos, and much *monté* against poor Granville whom I had to defend once more, and against the English for not supporting the Greeks with gifts of money. His hatred of Venizelos dates from Cretan days when he said that Venizelos betrayed him. He and the Princess very hopeful about Briand. They felt assured that he would support Greece. Prince George had also heard that a certain bank had paid for the recent lies about Greece, and said that a paper which has been unusually bitter had received 2,500,-000 francs! He also named the sum, fantastic it sounded, which had been paid out of the Greek revenues to suborn a certain press before the late elections. He confirmed the story of Venizelos, Prince Alexander, and Smyrna. An amusing talk after dinner. The Princess subtle, elusive, and the best of company. Briand telephoned to me to-day, by the way, that he would be out of Paris till Monday, so I think I will not wait for him, especially as I shall see Berthelot in the morning.

The house full of pictures collected by Prince George, while his collection of Napoleonic snuff-boxes looks particularly interesting and valuable. A pleasant evening with amusing conversation. Prince George has been offered the throne of Hungary, but says the pheasant shooting is the only attraction that he would find there!

Driving back to Paris found our bridge closed by gates and had to motor miles down-stream to another bridge to get across. Just like the French Jacks-in-Office! Why close the gates at all?

Saturday, February 12, 1921. To the Quai d'Orsay at 11 A.M. I had a talk with Philippe Berthelot, who was very cordial, and we ran through the Greek question. After a little beating about the bush he told me exactly what I wanted to know, namely, that France was chiefly interested in the German reparation question and we in the Greco-Turkish one. We had given Briand a definite undertaking to support him in the reparation question, and France was, therefore, prepared to adopt our views about Greece. Berthelot even hoped that Lloyd George would decide to *tenir le bâton du chef d'orchestre* on the 21st. I said that it was curious that I had just written in the same sense to Lord Burnham, and as this was Berthelot's view I would not detain him longer, for it was exactly what I felt myself about it all. I need not bother about Italy, he said, for when France and England were agreed, the Italians always kept silence. He rather sneered at my praise of Sforza, and thought him a ladies' man and a *diplomat de salon*. He paid a high tribute to Benès whom he thought far superior. He told me that Bismarck had once observed that to weigh the value of a man one should subtract his vanity, and then see what is left afterwards. But Sforza has no vanity! How has he got across Berthelot? I did not like to ask about Briand's ignorance in Paris the other day of the Boulogne arrangement. Berthelot was sure that the Boches would give way about reparations if the Allies remained firm and united, but they would only give way at the very end when they were convinced that we were all in earnest, and not before.

Berthelot then rang to see if Briand had gone out, and finding that he had not, I went down and was shown in without delay. After some mutual compliments, Briand, who was looking very well, asked for my news from Greece and I told him my conclusions. He seemed to agree entirely with Pétain's and my point of view about the danger of making the Greeks quit, and said that the real wish of France was to be able to take away her troops from Cilicia where they number 60,000 and are costing a great deal of money. I spoke about the lies published in the French press about the Greeks and asked why he did not stop them as he must know their *provenance* as well as I did. He said that he had stopped a great many. He was all for the recognition of the King and for ending the comedy of the sulking Allied Ministers, as Berthelot was, but could not say if it could be done before the Greek-Roumanian marriages.

I told him of the loss of French prestige in Greece and thought that it could be restored if France acted reasonably. All that he said about Greece, her future, and the Conference, led me to think that he did not mean to take a line strongly opposed to ours, but he certainly spoke openly for the revision when the last Conference took place in Paris, and I do not quite see how he can change his note now.

He said that he had gone to the utmost limit of concession about reparations from Germany, and could not proceed an inch further without being abandoned by the Chambers. The Chambers were full of young men from the war, and were a difficult team to handle. If the Boches would not agree to our terms, all France would march and sanctions would be imposed. I said that France had the only great Army in Europe now, and that I was very glad not to find Bonaparte sitting in Briand's chair, for the conquest of Europe would seem easy to him. Briand said that such ideas were far from him, and I replied that I was sure of it. I then rose and took leave, and he asked me to see him in London when he came over.

Went to lunch early with Lady Millicent Hawes, formerly the Duchess of Sutherland, and her new husband Colonel Hawes, a very pleasant and nice-looking fellow. They both seem very happy and have a very nice flat overlooking a garden. He is employed at Furness's shipping business. They have taken a farm in the country, thirty miles east of Paris, and are doing it up. We had a good talk of events and people.

Finished my series of Greek articles and sent them off. Dined with Captain and Mrs. Lock; he is the *Daily Telegraph* man in Paris and is doing well.

Sunday, February 13, 1921. Left by Boulogne 9.45 A.M. and crossed in the *London,* a good boat with all arrangements very perfect. I have never known our seas so calm in winter before as this year.

Reached London 6.30 P.M.

CHAPTER IV

CONFERENCES, SANCTIONS, AND PLÉBISCITES

The London Conference of February 21 — The Eastern Question and Reparations — Leave for Paris — The French position — Düsseldorf occupied — Marshal Pétain's views — M. Herbette's opinions — The Abbé Siéyès on Germans and victory — General Buat and Lord Hardinge prefer a blockade to sanctions — M. Barthou on events — A conversation with M. André Lefèvre — The Ruhr plus blockade — Economic sanctions — A lunch with Marshal Pétain — Some shooting stories — I go to Cologne — General Masterman on aircraft control in Germany — General Nollet on the military position in Germany — War material not delivered up — Mr. Julian Piggott on the economic sanctions — A visit to Düsseldorf, Ruhrort, and Duisburg — General Gaucher — Berlin — Views of our Embassy — Breslau — "The Victors" — Journey to Oppeln, Upper Silesia — General Le Rond — M. F. Bourdillon — Views of various Allied authorities — Motor tours round the Plébiscite area — Major Robin Gray — Colonel Wauchope's brigade — The industrial triangle — Voting day, March 20 — M. Korfanty — Germans win at Oppeln — Enthusiasm — Rough returns of the voting — Facts and figures about the mining area — Major R. W. Clarke, R.E. — Motor to Breslau — Prince and Princess Blücher — Their views on Germany — Major Piper on his control work — The English and the French mentality — I am robbed at Breslau — Journey to Prague — The Germans to-day.

London, Friday, March 4, 1921. We have had a fortnight of Conferences here, the first over the Treaty of Sèvres with Greeks and Turks to the forefront, and the second over reparations with the Germans. In the first Conference the French did not support us, as I had been led to believe they would, and Italy maintained her opposition to the Greek claims. L. G. took no strong line, and eventually, at Turkish initiative, it was resolved to ask Greeks and Turks whether they would consent to the despatch of a Commission to Smyrna and Thrace to make fresh investigations. The National Assembly at Athens promptly and unanimously refused. The Turks gave a conditional assent. An excellent chance of settling the question has thus apparently lapsed, but the decision of the Allies is not yet announced.

Meanwhile there had begun on February 28 the investigation of the Reparations question. The Germans, led by Dr. von Simons, their Foreign Minister, put forward preposterous proposals amounting only to a fraction of our demands from them, and L. G. at once spoke to them severely about it. On Thursday, March 3, he made a detailed indictment of the German attitude and gave them till Monday, March 7, to accept the Paris decisions of January 29, or to produce equivalent proposals, failing which certain acts of constraint would be at once applied.

Saturday, March 5, 1921. In view of these events I crossed the Channel to-day and came to Paris to be handy in case of trouble, and to escape any possible delays owing to curtailment of cross-Channel services if the Germans remain recalcitrant on Monday.

I am very disappointed that we have not supported the Greeks and have observed such a coldly neutral attitude. I have seen much of their delegation in London. They are much disillusioned, though we must await the decision before anathematising L. G. and Curzon. It may be that Briand's political position rendered it inadvisable to conclude the Eastern Question until the settlement had been made with the Germans. At all events L. G. has kept his word to the French even if they have not acted as Briand and Berthelot promised me they would.

Sunday, March 6, 1921. A quiet day. Hardinge away at Biarritz till Wednesday. Cheetham laid up. Loch lunched with me and we had a good talk. Our view is that there will be a fresh attempt to-morrow to come to terms in London. We both dread the consequences of the famous "sanctions," not immediately, but in their ultimate results, and we do not see how the measures proposed, i.e., occupation of Duisburg, Ruhrort, and Düsseldorf, will bring the Boches to heel. Walked and left cards on Marshal Pétain and his wife at 6, Square Latour-Maubourg. They were just going out for a drive, but the glimpse I had of her showed an agreeable and distinguished figure. Spent the day in studying all available French and German papers. The Boches seem to me as utterly unrepentant as they ever were, unready to acknowledge their responsibility for the war, neither willing to express regret nor to atone for all the miseries which they have brought upon the world, and as destitute of tact and feeling as of old. They are to some extent disarmed for the time, having given up or destroyed 35,000 guns and some $3\frac{1}{2}$ million rifles and so on, but under various disguises they keep up about a quarter of a million *Reichswehr* and *Schützpolizei* (late *Sicherheitspolizei*), while there must be at least three to four million rifles unaccounted for and 10,000 machine guns. As there are still some six million trained men in Germany, a guerilla war is not an impossible contingency, and the German hatred of the French is intense.

As for the French, they are as determined to exact full reparation for all their fearful sufferings as the Germans are to evade it. We have 100,000 French and British troops in the Rhineland, and there are the Belgians and Americans besides. We can spare but few more, as all our troops are either in Ireland or in occupation of conquered territories or plébiscite areas. We have no reserves to speak of and not 100,000 Territorials. In fact our military situation is much more abject than in 1914 except that we have a mass of war material rotting and rusting in store, and could, if the people were willing, call on our five million of trained men after furbishing up the Registration Act and reinstituting the Service Acts. But it would take a cataclysm to induce the politicians to consider such a thing, and the general public at home want no more fighting. The French seem ready for anything, but we know little of the real feeling of the mass of the French people, and I see already appeals to the communists and the proletariat of Europe to prevent the sanctions. The French think that they can carry out the first moves without mobilising. No doubt they can, but what with incidents, troubles, strikes, and so forth the future is obscure, and I should prefer to shut down the German frontiers to all trade and trust to blockade rather than to military measures which may lead the French to Berlin, if not to Moscow. But this may not be the French view. I feel sure that Foch's desire for the military frontier of the Rhine remains unchanged. The French are not convinced that Germany is adequately crushed and prevented from reviving. There is no real peace, only an enforced truce, and while we have broken up our old friend Austria we have made Germany more united than ever. So one must regard the general prospect as grave, and while admitting constraint to be indispensable one need not approve of the pending methods of applying it. A blockade is our most effective instrument, and it is better to take this course than to start out unconsciously on the road to Berlin.

Dined at the Ritz Restaurant with Jemmy Durham, Lady Agnes, and Mr. Hankey. The old pre-war throng again and a dance afterwards. Lady A. and I watched the dancing for some time. The ladies had few clothes and none on their backs. We thought the whole proceedings undignified, indecent, and vulgar. We felt sick of this sort of thing which belongs to a dead past. Maurice Rothschild and Lady X skipping about like two-year-olds. The band was quite good and the new world seemed to be amusing itself in much the same way as a hundred years ago after the other great war in France. We felt very old-fashioned and out of date. The modern post-war public dance is the most blatantly vulgar and insolently indecent performance imaginable. The most suggestive stage dancing is prim in comparison. One can bear almost anything except lack of taste. The war seems to have killed off everyone except the vulgarians.

Monday, March 7, 1921. We hear this morning that there was much hurrying and scurrying, lobbying and negotiating, till 2 A.M. this morning in London and that L. G. has produced a new proposal which is duly reported in the papers and frightens the French to death. Another division said to be going to the Rhine under Cavan in case of the sanctions. The French correspondents in London are evidently fearful that Briand may be forced to make some fresh concessions by L. G. and Sforza. In the afternoon late came the news that the Conference had broken down, and that there was an open rupture. The Boches had refused the L. G. compromise and had put the fat in the fire. I received a wire from Burnham asking me to go with the French and to send an appreciation. There has been a meeting of the Conseil Supérieur de la Guerre to-day under M. Millerand, the President of the Republic.

Tuesday, March 8, 1921. Went to see Pétain this morning. The Allies have not been long in applying the military sanctions. Düsseldorf was occupied peacefully this morning at 6 A.M. and the other two towns later. Pétain sarcastic about the whole proceeding. He expected nothing from the occupation. He thought that we had all been wasting our time in interminable discussions and that the desire to please the English had always held the French back. We should be made fools of, as usual. If the Boches said "yes" we should go back, and when we were gone the Boches would say "no." Pétain would prefer to occupy the territory necessary to bring the Boches to reason, would administer it and take its revenues, and would tell the Boches that he would stay there till all the debt was paid. He did not care whether it was five years, or thirty years, or fifty years. The Boches would have to pay before he left. I said that we had always spoken to one another very frankly during the war, and that I asked him now whether the French only wanted to make the Boches pay, or whether they had other and unavowed wishes. He assured me that they had no other *visées*, and that he knew the English distrusted them, but that they should have confidence in France. Drew blank at the French War Office. Barthou away and the whole place seemed quite deserted, so different from the war-time and the days of Clemenceau when the anterooms were always thronged. There was not one soul in them. Had a talk with M. Ladmirault, the chief of Barthou's civil cabinet, a very nice fellow. Pétain advises me not to go to the Rhine now as there is nothing to see, but to await events. M. Herbette, who writes the leaders on foreign policy in *Le Temps*, came and had a good talk. We think that the occupation will do no good, but that the customs duties may if generally applied, and we preferred that they should be applied all round Germany, and not upon one fraction of one frontier. Like Pétain he favoured remaining till the Boches paid.

I told him of my projected trip to Vienna, etc. I got out the map of post-war Europe and told him that I could find no policy in London on all this question. I wanted him to give me the French policy, or at least his own. He thought, like Pétain, that we had made a bad peace, and regretted the break-up of Austria as I did. Czecho-Slovakia now stretched across to Europe and was like a cartridge of dynamite, hating everybody round them, but appearing to him more Slav and pro-Russian than anything else. Austria was bound to go to Germany some day, and Germany would then extend over Hungary next. He thought the new Serb State had more possibilities than any other carved out of the old Austria. We agreed to differ about the Greeks. He thought that we were laying up great trouble for ourselves in future with Russia, owing to our backing of the Greeks and because of the little Baltic States which we had created. A revived Russia would sweep all this away. He was critical and suspicious of L. G. and was sarcastic about the manœuvring in London last Sunday. Briand would certainly have been upset had the Boches accepted L. G.'s compromise, but fortunately they refused the terms. They were our wisest councillors, said M. Herbette.

Went to see "Le Chasseur de chez Maxim" in the evening. Very funny, but long, and the theatre very hot. Audience as scrubby as in London nowadays. Risky French plays are really rather harmless to English people, as so few know the *argot* of the fast sets or can follow the play upon words and all the *nuances* of the best French acting. These plays are written for Parisians and only Parisians can understand all the allusions.

After reading masses of French papers, I find opinion wholly favours the present military sanctions, but not one

gives any reason for belief that they will make the Boches
pay.

Wednesday, March 9, 1921. All quiet on the Rhine. M.
Dato, the Prime Minister of Spain, murdered. Distressed
to hear of the serious illness of Princess Christopher.
Wrote an article for the *D. T.* on the comparative merits of
military and economic pressure on Germany, concluding in
favour of the latter and of blockade to finish matters speed-
ily. Lunched with the Countess Cahen d'Anvers, Lady
Townshend and her daughter, and her nephew, Count de
Fretteville. A house full of beautiful furniture, boiserie,
tapestries, china, and the Townshend pictures from the
sale of 1904. Count C. d'A. still ill and in bed. Lady T. in
her old form, very bright and intelligent. The nephew was
in the French Artillery, and then in the French Flying
Corps, 1915 to 1918, and ended in command of a flight.
He was never wounded even, which was almost a record
for the long period that he was flying. He says that the
French F.C. lost eighty-five per cent of their officers, of
whom twenty per cent while training at the schools owing
to bad instructors. He worked for a fortnight last year at
Krupps' as a common workman, and is sure that Krupps
produce guns which escape our Commissions of Control
and that they have been arming the Reds against Wrangel.
My view is that the Boches have certainly over four million rifles still at their disposal and perhaps 10,000 machine
guns. They may have many guns. These things may help
to account for their provocative attitude now and for the
refusal to meet us over reparations. Saw Lord Hardinge
for a few minutes. He is just back from Biarritz. We
spoke of d'Abernon's attitude in London. It has provoked
great criticism among the French correspondents. I said
that diplomats usually supported the country to which
they were accredited. H. agreed, but said that while he always supported France about French interests, he always
placed England first when our interests and those of the
French were in conflict. It takes a strong, resolute character to take this line.

Burnham wires confirming his previous suggestion that I should go to the Rhine, and asks me to go on to Upper Silesia. The Plébiscite takes place on the 20th. Commandant Weil came to see me to-night, and we had a long talk over the French translation of my War Diary which he is superintending for Payot's firm. Here are two very apposite quotations from letters from Siéyès to Talleyrand which Weil gave me:

"Dès que vous entreprenez de prouver que vous avez raison un allemand croit que vous reculez." (Berlin, March 12, 1799.)

"Quand une cause a été jugée par la victoire c'est la remettre en question que d'imprimer des phrases."

Sent off a strong article to the *D. T.* in favour of pressure by blockade.

Thursday, March 10, 1921. Busy paying visits in the morning. Lunched at the Embassy with Hardinge, his daughter, and one of the Hamilton girls. We had a long talk over the position. He believes that the Council of Ambassadors will be asked to direct the Rhine customs war, but will have nothing to do with the military sanctions. He does not care even to contemplate the occupation of Germany, as he considers that the administration of the country, railways, etc., would be a tremendous task in view of Boche ill-will and ill-temper. He is all for a blockade. Little has been said about this yet in any part of the press, French or English. He hears that our Government is very discontented with the present sanctions. He does not think the Greeks strong enough to hold their position in Asia Minor, and does not consider the Greeks in that country to be real Greeks. The Oriental question is being fixed up to-day in London. H. thinks that the Council of Ambassadors gets through three times the amount of work in a given time, now that Derby and the American Ambassador — neither of whom could speak French — are out of it. There is no translation now, all the work is done in French. H. has given up the old room of the Ambassadors looking over the courtyard, and now works in a charming room looking south. Much more cheerful. The Board of Works critical for fear the carpet may become worn!

I saw General Buat, the Chief of Staff, a very capable and shrewd man, as he proved himself to be during the war. I was agreeably surprised to find him wholly in favour of blockade as a means of constraint. He and I discussed a guerilla war in Germany. He does not think that the South African analogy applies because of its larger spaces and because in Germany we could levy money on towns, and squeeze the country more easily, but he does not want to undertake an occupation of Germany. He considers the *Reichswehr* an army of cadres and that all the plans are made for an eventual expansion. Our present advantage is largely due to the Boche want of artillery, but when the Commissions of Control are withdrawn there will be no obstacle to the restoration of the old war material, or better. All the studies of a new army and new appliances are in full swing in Germany, and B. regards the Boche offer of payment on the Paris scale for five years as an indication of the period which will be needed for Germany to recover.

Saw M. Louis Barthou, the War Minister, at six. De Castelnau was there and I had a little talk with him first. Barthou says that Louis Barthou agrees with Colonel Repington about blockade, but that M. Barthou, the War Minister, has to await the decision of the President of the Council. He was very agreeable and we had a talk about my coming journey. He asked me to see him again as I returned through Paris. He has been fourteen times Minister, but never at the War Office before. I told him that he was about the twentieth French War Minister that I had visited. He agreed that the British system of Parliamentary Government was far better than the French; with the latter system there was no chance of carrying out a long-considered policy. He told me that his last news from Silesia was that the Poles were likely to win in the mining areas, which was the really important matter for us.

Buat told me that I would probably have great difficulty in reaching the Plébiscite area, as the Commissions of Control were placing every obstacle in the way of arrivals and the Boches would not want me to go there either. A cheerful prospect!

Lady Townshend dined with me, and we went off to the Capucines Theatre, so much appreciated by King Edward, to see a most amusing piece, in which many French politicians figured, especially Loucheur and Mandel, under their own names, and made up to resemble them. We do not accord this liberty to our playwrights. A real good show, the place crowded and very hot.

Friday, March 11, 1921. A lovely day. Met Ian Malcolm just back from Egypt, and we compared notes. He thinks that as independence comes nearer the Egyptians realise that they are not ready for it, or at least not ready for it all at once. Went to the Chamber of Deputies, and had a long talk with M. André Lefèvre, late War Minister in the Governments of Millerand and Leygues. A striking character of whom we shall hear more if he lives. About the strongest man in Parliament here, not Jingo, but with a fixed idea that any measures are preferable to the resumption of the war with Germany, which event he considers certain within five years unless we adopt drastic courses. He confirms Buat's estimate of the Boche preparations and puts their rifles down at four millions and their Maxims at many thousands. He also tells me that many essential parts of submarines are under construction, and I asked him to publish the information at once if it was authentic. He said that he would. He also believes that orders for arms are being executed in Sweden and elsewhere and that they are for the Germans eventually. His view is that directly the Commissions of Control are withdrawn, Germany will recommence to arm, and that it will not take her long to become the old Germany. If the United States and England had kept to the Treaty of Guarantees he would have been quite satisfied, because the Boches would not venture again to confront such a combination, but the United States had taken the line of pretending that European affairs did not interest her, and England had scrapped her armies. He would prefer to retain the Commissions of Control permanently. If France had an assurance that Germany was disarmed, he would make no point of the maintenance of our present occupation, but as things stood he found it indispensable.

He scoffed at the absurdity of our present methods of constraint. He was sure that they would fail. If they did he was for a combination of blockade with the extension of the occupation to the whole of the Ruhr Valley. How many people will you control? I asked. About six millions he thought. I said that there was all the Rhineland population besides, and that if we took this action we must have the whole machinery ready for feeding these people and for supplying raw material for industry. He admitted that this was so. I preferred a blockade on our present line to avoid this responsibility for the Ruhr, but he said that if the Poles won in the mining area of Silesia, and we controlled the Ruhr, German industry was disarmed for want of coal. He preferred the combination of my method with his. As for the occupation of Germany, he thought with me that this was an immense affair and he did not favour it. He thought that the Boches could wage a great guerilla war, and was not at all inclined to doubt it, or to underestimate it. He reminded me that he had not voted for the Versailles Treaty. He had refused amidst the silent resentment of the Chambers, with a few others. He thought that the marriage of England and France should be regarded as permanent and that neither could do without the other. He was not convinced that Germany was not backing the new revolution in Russia and was not in doubt of a German-Russian combination if this came off. We discussed the whole situation in its various aspects, talking in a Committee Room where we were alone. I was struck by the attention and respect paid to him by other deputies as we strolled back through the lobbies and the Salle des Pas Perdus. He asked me what our F.O. policy was in the

East of Europe and I said that I could not discover that they had one. Then you are living from hand to mouth? he asked. I said yes. He asked me to explain the English hatred of Poland, Roumania, etc. I replied that no such feeling existed. He also could not comprehend why England did not understand how grave the situation was in Europe and that we were practically recommencing war. I asked him to remember that we were an island and had only joined in the war for a special purpose. The war over, we reverted to our oceanic interests. America was in the same position and her greater detachment was due to her greater distance and insularity. It was an affair of geography and interests, and was not due to any double dose of original sin.

Saturday, March 12, 1921. Lefèvre is as good as his word, and prints in the *Journal* of this morning the details of Boche preparations for building submarines. L. is a competent technical authority. Spent part of last night in studying L. G.'s speech on Thursday in the H. of C. A most ineffective opposition which took quite the wrong line of criticism. My view is that when we take fifty per cent of the cost of German manufactured goods, the Boche contractors will cancel all their contracts unless the German Government undertakes to indemnify them, and I do not think they will. As for the Rhine customs I do not see why the Boches should walk into our Rhine trap when all the other holes remain open. My article sent to the *D. T.* does not appear, but a *Times* man at Cologne warns the public of the futility of the operation. The huggermugger scheme of London will come to nought. I see that L. G. counts in Poland and Czecho-Slovakia in his total of a sixty million a year German exports expected. But it remains to be seen whether the Poles and Czechs will join in our customs reprisal scheme, and, anyhow, how can we wait a year, and what is the use of such small sums to us when we want milliards of gold marks? The sole test of the efficacy of the present sanctions is whether they will make the Boche pay. L. G. says the Boche must make fresh proposals. Dr. Simons says that they have none to make. He is much attacked by the Right in the Reichstag for offering too much!

It seems to me that the origin of all our present troubles is the detached attitude of America. She has protested her signature to the Versailles Treaty, has not ratified the Anglo-American Guarantee to France, and has rendered the League of Nations ridiculous by not joining it. She pretends that Europe does not interest her. We shall see whether she does not find that it interests her very nearly. I think that Hardinge will revert to sane policy if he be given time and is not rushed. Hardinge told me the other day that Auckland Geddes lives a dog's life at Washington. He and his family are preceded, followed, and surrounded everywhere by detectives, even his children at their playground. Our politicians have only had one vitally serious domestic problem to settle in my lifetime, namely Ireland, and they have completely failed in it for fifty years. Our Army has had about fifty problems during the same period and has solved them all. Of all the lower animals of creation the politician is the most ineffective.

Lunched with Marshal and Mme. Pétain, General Buat and his wife, Comte Clary and another man at Mme. Pétain's house. We had a good talk over the situation and I did not find any reason to change my views. Buat is already looking into the question of feeding the Boches in the Ruhr. I asked how many souls there were in the Ruhr and Rhineland together. He thought fifteen millions. I told him that he might have to supply the raw materials for the industries as well as food. He thought it clever of the Germans to send the raw materials from Prussia to the Rhineland to be made up, and then to be sent back for finishing. This tied the Rhineland to Prussia economically. I thought that we were in for great trouble owing to want of forethought. They are facilitating my mission to Silesia and Buat is writing to-night to General Le Rond, the Frenchman at Oppeln, to get me through. Pétain expects fighting if the Poles win on the vote. We all agree upon the folly of allowing the émigrés in Germany to come into the area and vote on the same day as the rest. They put it down to L. G., but I believe it was Berthelot who brought the question up in London, when it had been practically settled that the voting should be a fortnight later for the émigrés.

Clary is a great shot. We talked shooting. Pétain was shooting at some big shoot the other day. He said that C. never aimed; he just put up his gun and the bird fell, he thought from fear. He tried to do the same, but a game-keeper reproved him, saying that C. was an artist and it was no good trying to imitate him: "Visez seulement M. le Maréchal." So the Marshal viséd and then got on all right. C. said that Clemenceau's father was buried at his own wish in a perpendicular position, as though standing up. C. told us of Jules Ferry's shooting exploits. He fired at anything anywhere, and generally hit somebody. One day Waldeck Rousseau was the next gun. Ferry fired, and W. R. fell into a ditch, nothing being visible but his boots. People ran up. "Qu'as tu donc?"... "Mais je n'ai rien"... "alors pourquoi"...? "Oui! mais ce malheureux à un second coup à tirer!"

It seems that Pétain's report on the war is finished. He said that I might consult it when I wished, but that he had to submit it to Foch before publication. P. and B. thought that historical documents on operations were often mis-leading. People looked to some short order and found in it the genesis of some great operation, whereas usually it was merely the launching of some great plan that had been worked out by others weeks before. We talked of past War Ministers. Pétain had a great regard for Painlevé, but he worked till three in the morning. Barthou till 1 A.M. Millerand was a man of settled habits and hours. One al-ways knew when and where to find him. They both thought that men who could not organise their work did no good. They thought Lefèvre most attractive, and honest, but an artist, and rather dangerous. He was a fine speaker with much fire and was highly esteemed in Parliament. They asked if I held to Burnham's plan, and I said yes. I thought that the politicians would take some time to work out their customs plan; it would then take a week or two for the French to discover that nothing would come of it, and by that time I hoped to be at Vienna to await the Marshal's wire to see the next move.

Pétain said that he had known his wife since she was five, that was so and so years ago. "Merci, mon ami," replied Mme. Pétain with some vexation. He calls her "Mon Maître." They teased me about Greece, and both seemed to know everything that I had done and said and written, no doubt from the diplomatic reports. "Mais l'Angleterre a lâché la Grèce?" "Il parait." "Qu'en pensez-vous?" "Nous avons perdu la manche, je n'ai plus rien à dire!" They found this *très beau* and the real sporting spirit. Buat and I, driving off together, extolled the Marshal's exploits in the war. We both think that he has no equal.

Cologne, Sunday, March 13, 1921. Left Paris 8.10 A.M.; arrived Cologne 7.47 P.M. Captain Macduff, R.T.O., met me. Room taken for me at the Town Major's Mess at the Kölner Hof. Clean and comfortable with a perfect bathroom. Met in the train on my journey General Masterman of the R.A.F. in charge of aircraft control on the Inter-Allied Military Commission in Berlin, and the French General Nollet, President of the Commission. They were all returning to Berlin, Masterman with his wife and Captain Plugge of his staff. Masterman says that they have seized or destroyed 14,000 German aeroplanes and 28,000 engines, but that the German commercial metal aeroplanes are coming on fast and may have great value in a war. They are slower, but much safer than our planes at the end of the war, being built for safety and to travel at economical speed. With 160 h.p. they can do all our English planes of 300 h.p. can do and at half the cost. The Germans were ordered to stop building them because they had not carried out their engagements under the Treaty, but they took no notice. M. says that about December last the tone of the Germans changed. He could not give the reason, but supposed that they thought themselves strong enough to resist.

General Nollet put down the change of tone to between September and November last, but he could not assign any special date or cause to the change. He agreed that the number of rifles undelivered was still in the region of four millions, and that there were still heaps of machine guns. These things were easy to hide. When he asked the Germans for their statistics of production, they pretended that all the papers had been destroyed during the Revolution. None of the seven or eight big Berthas had been found yet. They are said to have been destroyed by the Boches, but Nollet did not affirm that it was so. He regarded our present sanctions as merely a warning and believed that a blockade would have to be imposed. He and another of his officers thought that it was by far the most effective measure, in fact the only one.

Nollet considered that the Silesian plébiscite was of immense importance, and did not appear confident about the result. One of his staff remarked that all the plébiscites yet held had gone in favour of the country with the best exchange, and in this case German marks were of more value than Polish. But against this would be the reparation to pay if the regions remained German.

I told General Nollet that I had been impressed while in Paris by the serious character of the German situation. Was it true that unless the control was permanently maintained the Germans could recover their old position in five years? He said it was. He thought that materially they could recover their power in two years, but that to work up the whole military machine again might take five years. On the other hand, he said that a permanent control was morally impracticable as it was not in the Treaty. It might be imposed as a sanction. He did not credit young Count de F.'s story [1] about the guns at Essen. Nollet had staff officers permanently attached there, and he

<hr>

[1] See entry for March 9.

thought they knew everything. It was not in the German interest to make the guns. Their interest was to get us out of Germany. We had enough trouble in Germany without adding more. But he confirmed Lefèvre's story [1] about the submarines and said that the facts were known to our Naval Commission.

We agreed in regarding the whole position as grave. The Anglo-American guarantee of France would have covered everything, as Germany would never have faced it again, but now America was out, and the English had no army, nor even the machinery for making one. So naturally the Germans were planning a revenge and we should do the same in their place. In the same way he did not lose his temper over German evasions of disarmament, as he thought it natural. But the Germans certainly had not carried out their engagements, quite apart from reparations. He has 450 officers under him including 120 French. A good, cool, capable officer.

Monday, March 14, 1921. Saw Lieutenant-General Sir Thomas Morland, Commanding our Rhine Army, and a number of other officers in the course of the morning. Learnt that four out of our eight battalions here have gone to Silesia under Wauchope, the battalions sent averaging only 400 men each. Mr. Julian Piggott, the representative of the Rhineland High Commission, lunched with me. I had seen him yesterday, and had found that we were fully in accord. But he threw much new light on the most difficult situation. He is not in principle opposed to the L. G.'s fifty per cent scheme, *provided* that it is imposed in agreement with Germany, and he tells me that Simons thought the scheme a good one when he talked with a member of the German F.O. on returning from London. But the scheme is useless *without* an agreement, for unless the German Government recoup the German traders their loss of fifty per cent, they will either increase their prices correspondingly, making us pay reparations, or obviously will not trade with us, and there is no sign of an intention

---

[1] See entry for March 11.

on the part of the German Government to put down the money. As for the Rhine customs barrier, this is to be established on the actual line of the Rhine. A part of the German personnel now working on the western frontier of the Rhineland are to be transferred to the eastern frontier and are to work under Allied supervision. The Tariff is not yet laid down. If it is low, it will not repay the cost of administration, which will be important, and if it is high, it will deflect trade from the Rhineland. The Tariff is now being considered by the Inter-Allied High Commission at Coblenz. Only this morning a big textile firm in our area notified Piggott's Labour branch that they expected to have to dismiss 25,000 workmen when the customs barrier was imposed. Goods are already being rushed out, and inward contracts being broken. Financial and commercial chaos is fairly well assured, and the main object of making the Germans pay reparations is no nearer. The Rhineland is bound to suffer from the present plan and to have to deal with serious unemployment which may need an increase of our garrison.

To take over the money from the German customs officials is one thing. To set up a customs barrier of our own is another. From the Dutch to the Swiss frontier along the Rhine must be some three hundred and fifty miles and it will be a big affair to organise this if we are unable to enlist Germans for the job. The R.H.C. has not been consulted by the Supreme Council. Some eighty per cent of the raw materials used in the Rhineland industries come from Germany which also takes a large part of the finished goods. We shall presumably tax the flow each way, and what seems certain is an increase of prices, deflection of trade, and unemployment. We are dealing with a trade which cannot, however taxed, bring in a tithe of the amount needed monthly for reparations, and the one thing certain is that the payments from Germany are brought no nearer.

Piggott and I agree in disliking anything in the nature of an extended occupation, whether of the Ruhr Valley, or of

Germany as a whole. He will not admit blockade because of the world's obloquy which will follow. But he suggests the prolongation of the Rhineland occupation until all claims are met, and thinks that this may satisfy Foch who will then keep his garrisons on the Rhine. Piggott wants us to reopen negotiations with the Germans.

It seemed to us both that we were in presence of a very skilful German plan of campaign, as dangerous as in 1914, and that we were replying by an opportunist and light-headed policy which was bound to fail. All remedies seemed to us nearly as bad as the disease, and the worst feature of all was that no one in London appeared to comprehend the situation.

Dined with General Morland at the G.O.C.'s house where I formerly stayed with Sir W. Robertson. A party of eight men including Sir George Ashton, Colonel Fuller of the General Staff here, and Colonel Longstreet, U.S.A. A pleasant talk and we played Bridge till late.

Tuesday, March 15, 1921. Started soon after 10 A.M. and motored with Colonel Fuller and Hutton-Watson west of the Rhine to Düsseldorf, where we saw General Gaucher commanding the French and Colonel Brown commanding the 14th Hussars and our troops here, which include four Tanks. We visited the billets and stables of the 14th. They all lunched with me and then we motored on to Ruhrort and Duisburg, returning to Cologne about 6 P.M. Düsseldorf a fine town with pleasant boulevards, avenues, and gardens. General Gaucher, whom we visited at his H.Q., says that there are 475,000 inhabitants and that 125,000 workmen are employed here. A tall, genial, capable, resolute man. He has found the 1500 *Schützpolizei*, or green police — mostly old N.C.O.'s — contumacious, and has got rid of half already. He says that the Belgians have claimed the command at Duisburg and Ruhrort as they have the bulk of the troops there. Is the famous unity of command gone so soon? I asked. It is always difficult to get, replied Gaucher.

Ruhrort is a revelation. It is the port of the Westphalian

coalfield, and on the Rhine and its affluents and in basins and canalised branches there are thirty-two kilometres of quays, alongside of which and in the stream are hundreds of coal barges and steamers. The trade must be immense, as from one-half to two-thirds of the German coal comes this way, and so to its purchasers all over Europe. The whole country here seems like the busiest part of Lancashire, the towns and factories extending endlessly. Everything is peaceful. The Allied troops all walk about without arms and the Germans take little notice of them. But our small numbers are almost lost in these huge overgrown manufacturing centres, and how on earth we are to set up a customs barrier here, or to supply the people if a tariff arrests trade, no one can suggest. Finished an article on my brief visit here. I think that we have got into a fine muddle, and it will be curious to see how we get out of it. I am told that the coal output of Germany is 120,000,000 tons in Westphalia, 30,000,000 in Upper Silesia, and a few millions more from other smaller fields. Thus the importance of the Ruhr port and of Silesia is palpable.

Berlin, Wednesday, March 16, 1921. Started early for Berlin. After traversing the ravaged area of France last Sunday, I was hating the Boche so badly that I would not speak a word to any fellow-travellers. Arrived 9.30 P.M. My telegram of yesterday morning had not yet reached the Adlon Hotel, so I was sent on to a vile place called Iderna in Charlottenburg. No bath! Too late to change quarters. In the train to-day I thought the fields looked fairly well, but rather dried up. Considerable development of trade traffic. Permanent way good. Material so-so, and carriages very dirty. In the restaurant car chiefly pig to eat. No butter or sugar. Bread black.

Thursday, March 17, 1921. Took my things to the Aldon early. Met Lord Kilmarnock at the Embassy and we had a talk. Have to get a French visa for the Silesian visit. Later lunched with the Kilmarnocks at 6 Parizer Platz, very well placed. Addison and Fane of the Embassy — Fane a stepson of Cis Fane's — and Major Beasley of the

Control Commission from Dresden. Kilmarnock told me that he had seen Dr. Simons last night and that the latter had told him that the rumors of a German concentration on the Polish frontier were untrue; that Germany would rather receive an affront than give one; but that if the Poles took part in any sanctions they would be resisted. K. also said that the Control Commission had denied to him the truth of the rumors about the concentration. The rumour had come in the form of a Polish communiqué which Reuter had sent on. So I sent a wire to the *D. T.* about it.

Much talk of the Conference, the Reparations, and the Sanctions. I fancy the general opinion of the Embassy is that the Boche cannot pay the Paris claims, but that no one is honest enough to state the fact to the public. They think that the economic sanctions will do us at least as much harm as the Boche. A nice girl of the Kilmarnocks and her governess also at lunch. My first visit to Berlin since the war. A great come-down since old days. I missed the soldiers and the officers in the Tiergarten. The *Sicherheitspolizei*, now *Schützpolizei*, are quite obviously regular troops. Beasley told us much about the work of the Control Commission. They give Germany a year to rearm if the control is removed. If the Boches had been wise they would have met us in every way in order to get us out of the country. But they never are wise.

Left 3.30 for Breslau. The train crowded with men and women on the way to vote in Upper Silesia. Talked with a former Judge from the Tarnowitz area who was also on his way to vote and was in my compartment. They all seem very cocksure of winning. Some 200,000 to 250,000 people who were born in Silesia are coming in from outside to vote. The organisation appears to be good. The Polish mark is only worth seven pfennigs, and stands in relation to the German mark as the latter does in relation to the pound sterling. They say that there is a Polish law which compels all debts to be paid in Polish marks, and that the difference in the exchange will heavily influence the vote.

All the stations decorated, and crowds to see the outvoters. I asked whom they were waiting to see and they said, "The victors." This referred to the men who had fought in the war and had not been back in Upper Silesia since. They call them "victors" because the idea still is that the army won the war and the Revolution lost the peace. Went to the Monopole at Breslau. Full up. Got a good room at the Goldene Gans, but found that the bath here was *alles kaput*. What chance of a bath at Oppeln I wonder? During the talk in the train to-day the Judge said that there would be another Conference, probably after Easter and in Italy. I said that the atmosphere was different in Italy. He smiled and agreed. It may be the best way out of all this muddle, but maybe Briand will not think so. As wonderful a March as a February. Quite hot and brilliant sunshine still. Kilmarnock's girl fined yesterday for having a Japanese spaniel unmuzzled. She referred the policeman to the English Botschaft. He said he didn't worry about the Botschafts and made her pay.

Oppeln, Friday, March 18, 1921. Started 7.47 A.M. for Oppeln. A great crowd which swarmed in and I could not find a seat. So enlisted the station-master and he put me in with the Dienstabteil, some five or six train guards and attendants, some old soldiers. *Rauchen* was *strengverboten,* so I gave them some cigarettes and we were soon all happy. We talked soldiering. One chap had been in the 6th Uh-lans, had fought at Ypres, Arras, and in Russia, had been four times wounded, had had malaria and typhus, had been made prisoner in Russia and had been knouted by his Russian guards when he did not work hard enough, though he remarked that the German prisoners in England were playing football. He had been nearly frozen to death in Siberia and so on. I was not surprised to hear that he was fed up with war. They thought Hindenburg the best German general, and made grimaces when I asked about Ludendorff. They thought the Grand Duke Nicholas the best Russian leader and said that the English and French had good generals too. At Breslau, and all along the line, bands, crowds, decorations, and cheering at the stations, but on reaching the plébiscite area all this ceased, as the Commission has forbidden all music, flags, and demonstrations. They have also wisely stopped all spirits for three days before the plébiscite. The drunken Pole is a real terror. The Germans very submissive. They were delighted to hear of British troops on the Polish front. All the German organisation for the plébiscite working well, and as the trainloads of the outvoters pass down the confidence increases. From a railway point of view it is a practice mobilisation.

But on reaching Oppeln found the Poles equally confident and also their French friends. Saw General Le Rond and Colonel Percival for a few moments. Went to the office, and Mr. F. Bourdillon, the English civil member of the Commission, most kindly offered to put me up in a tiny room in a flat which he only takes over to-day, but lucky to get any room with all this mob here. Robin Gray turned up from Warsaw, and we lunched together. Lumby from Warsaw, and Macartney, the *Times* man from Berlin, here: there are eighty-five foreign correspondents already arrived! Had a good talk with several well-informed people. Wrote and sent off a wire to the *D. T.* on the situation and about the prospects of Sunday's vote. It seems likely, according to the views of the experts, that the eastern quarter of Upper Silesia will vote Polish including the industrial triangle which has its apex at Gleiwitz and its base south of Tarnowitz to south of Myslowitz. But all west of the Oder, and a good part east of the river, besides the Kreuzberg area, expected to vote German, with most of the large towns throughout. The Germans have the pull of all the administration being in their hands, and the fall of the Polish mark to the value of some seven pfennigs also helps them. The Commissions seem to have taken a very firm hold and combine firmness with impartiality.

In the evening at 9.30 P.M. called on General Le Rond by appointment at the Präsidenz, a large building where are the offices, council chamber, etc. The General is well protected. He has double sentries on all sides of the house, and the only entrance at night is through the French guard-room in the court behind. A shortish man, rather lean, with a nervous keen face, much intelligence and more vanity. He was in command of French artillery most of the war and now has an Army Corps. He says that he was on Foch's staff during the Peace Conference and has been in Silesia fourteen months. He gave me an interesting account of his administration. He said that his triumvirate of himself, Percival, and the Italian General de Marinis ruled despotically without a Parliament, but through the German administration which they controlled. He had gradually cut off many of the links and wires which united Upper Silesia with Breslau and Berlin. He had a regular government in several departments, including that of Finance, and after meeting all expenses he had a surplus of 300,000,000 (marks, I suppose), which were in banks here and would be handed over to any government which came about from the plébiscite. He did not tell me of his government debts. He had endeavoured to disarm the people, and had collected between 30,000 and 40,000 rifles, but arms came in from both sides, Poles and Germans, and he did not pretend that the district was not still full of arms. He thought that all men had rifles and many had two. There were at least eight million rifles at the time of the Armistice, and even if 3,500,000 had been collected by the Control Commission, 4,500,000 remained. I asked the General about the green police seen about. Why had he kept them while Gaucher had suppressed them? They were not, he said, the *Sicherheit* lot. They were a special plébiscite body carefully selected [1] from Germans and Poles in equal proportions, and every patrol, etc., was similarly constituted. They acted as checks on each other and it was the same for the officers. They wore blue bands on their caps and tunics to differentiate them from the *Sicherheit* lot.

He thought that he had proved the possibility of an

---

[1] When the Poles rose in May, most of the Polish police joined them.

allied government of at least a considerable province. He said, however, in answer to a question of mine, that though the Poles had responded to every request of his, even to a stricter watch along their own frontier, he had reason to complain of the Germans, but did not give me any proofs except about arms concerning which, it seems to me, both sides are equally to blame, and probably each has acted from motives of fear of the other side. He said that after the vote on Sunday it would take three weeks to check and confirm the figures. Then the Commission would have to consider the results and advise their Governments. Then the matter would go to the Supreme Council, and it might not be till the first fortnight in June that the fate of the country, or the terms of a partition, would be settled.

I told him how good the German *Heimat-treu* or German outvoters organisation appeared to me to be. He claimed more or less the credit of it, as he had arranged for the trains and the control of arrivals at the plébiscite frontiers. But I think the matter is in all serious respects of German planning, and the reception arrangements here are excellent. The trains are all met: there are wooden houses outside the stations where the arrivals are told where to go and how to get there, and are given a free meal and everything they want including writing paper. The return journey is arranged in the same way. We concluded our talk by discussing the general situation and his own career. He is evidently very proud of his work, and did not mention in his laudation of it the names of any of his fellow-commissioners or assistants.

Saturday, March 19, 1921. Went off in a car with Major Robin Gray of the Grenadiers from Oppeln to Lublinitz, two hours fast travelling, where we found Colonel Wauchope's flag in the act of being hoisted outside the Schloss of some Count a little to the north of the town. We walked a bit with him and his B.M. and then lunched. A very comfortable Schloss, bed and bath rooms very perfect. All the third floor given up to him and some six officers and a French liaison officer. A good talk over the position. The

British troops extend along the Polish frontier from Rosenberg to Beuthen, a "front" of about one hundred miles held by 1600 men! I have seen the British Army in many countries and many strange circumstances, but never expected to find it on the frontier of Poland looking out over the mournful Sarmatian plains.

Our H.Q. are at Lublinitz with the 1st Black Watch and two companies 1st Middlesex besides details. H.Q. 1st Middlesex two companies, Rosenberg: 2d Royal West Kent at Kreuzberg: H.Q. 1st Sussex, Tarnowitz, and one company at Beuthen in the mining area which begins at Tarnowitz reckoning from the north. Wauchope is a good man and a good soldier, with all the charming and chivalrous courtesy of his uncle Andy Wauchope who fell at Magersfontein. Morland and the Rhine Army staff have fitted out Wauchope's force right well. They have all they need including wireless with each battalion, trench mortars, motor cyclists, good horse transport, and lorries to allow rapid movements of detachments. They have thirty days' supplies besides a train of food sent weekly from the Rhine. A French 75 mm. battery attached to them. There are eight control posts of six to twenty men on the actual Polish frontier, but if the Poles wish to cross, or to send arms across, they can, as the posts are much too far apart to stop such traffic, and this is inevitable from the weak numbers. They are merely on the frontier to control the main roads and to protect the inhabitants. The Germans are delighted to have them there. Bright sun, and keen wind. It was snowing when our men came here, but now the drifts only remain on the north side of the fences and woods, and in the ditches.

The road from Oppeln runs through seemingly endless fir woods which are beautifully kept and regularly cut and replanted. The trees are planted a few feet apart and shed their lower branches as the straight stems grow up leaving no knots in the wood. Gray described to me how well the German women looked after the forestry nursery gardens during the war while he was a prisoner in Germany. The rural district is not unpleasant and farm houses not unpicturesque, but the flatness of the whole country is depressing. It is said that the Alpine chasseurs who are here were sent because the district was "Haute" Silésie, and the French thought it must be mountainous! So also it is said that Colonel Hawker of the Coldstreams and two other good pundits on Eastern languages were sent here because Silesia was confused with Cilicia!

The mining area begins at Tarnowitz and continues right down to south of Myslowitz running up westwards to Gleiwitz. It is typical Black Country with almost limitless coal of some seams thirty-six feet thick extending, it is supposed, right down to Pless, but all the southern area is unexploited so far. There are iron, zinc, lead mines, etc., and what with the power stations, railways, pumping arrangements, and interdependence of one part of the industry on another, it will be a most formidable task to partition the mining area between two States. Germany has done a big thing in organising and directing the work here, and I can find no one who believes that the Poles can manage it. We went through the mining area to Beuthen and Königshütte, and turned back through Zabze, Gleiwitz, and Gross Strehlitz to Oppeln, I suppose about two hundred and fifty miles, arriving 8.30 P.M. frozen cold and stiff [1] from the keen air and fast pace. Bourdillon had the Percivals, Miss Chapman, and Colonel Tetbury dining. Sat down as I was, very unkempt, and took an appreciable time to thaw. A pleasant dinner, and much talk of the events round us. All reported perfectly quiet on all sides.

Sunday, March 20, 1921. Voting day in the plébiscite area. As trouble was most expected in the mining area and on the Polish frontier, I went off there early with Colonel Hawker of the Coldstreams, Captain Turner of the Indian Cavalry, and Major McVey, a professor. The car went ill, and we were much delayed, but reached our destination Kattowitz and lunched with a clever barrister in uniform,

---

[1] Less than three months later poor Robin Gray was dead. A fine soldier and a good comrade.

Major Stevenson, and Craig of the Food Commission. One of Hoover's Americans came and talked mining to us at lunch. We went on to Myslowitz and got out to walk to the frontier and had a good view of Poland beyond the little river boundary. I was amused by the British corporal off duty who said that he was going to walk down "to have a chat with them Poles." It must have been a treat. All seemed quiet. There were no guards on the railway and footbridge here. Hawker had suggested them to Le Rond's military department on the advice of the railway people, but the M.D. had turned the proposal down alleging want of troops. Accounts of the Polish forces across the frontier vary. There is certainly a cordon, and Hawker says 40,000 men in arms all told.

I forgot to note that Gray and I yesterday at Beuthen went to see Korfanty, the former Polish Deputy in the Reichstag, now an honorary member of the Warsaw Parliament. He is the soul of the Polish cause here. One of the active spirits thrown up by these tempestuous times. A man under fifty, formerly a miner, strong and stoutly built, medium height with a good head and much intelligence. He has a savage-looking wolf-dog who barks when anyone says "*Heimat-treu*" and often bites too. He bit Wauchope one day! Korfanty lives in an hotel strongly guarded by his supporters. The stairs have steel bars to check a rush, and the windows have thick wire over them to keep out bombs. He told us that he expected to win up to the Oder, but that several big towns would have large German majorities. He had come into possession of, i.e., had bought from German agents that morning, all the German plan of provoking the Poles in case the Election went in Polish favour. I asked him what he meant to do in case of a disturbance. He said that he would give the Allies forty-eight hours in which to suppress it and would then call out his people. I passed this on to Percival last night.

We visited a few other places and returned to Oppeln by about 9.30 P.M. after another long day. Dined at Forms Hotel. At about 11.15 P.M. the figures were out for Oppeln

town — not the Kreis — giving a German majority of
some ninety per cent on the whole vote. Crowds assembled,
flowing in from all parts, and marched up and down the
main street in front of the Präsidenz in more or less military array, singing *Heil dir in Siegerskranz*, and other
patriotic songs. They were perfectly orderly, but as Le
Rond is at the Präsidenz, and two French guards were
within a stone's throw, it must have been trying for the
French, and I wondered what was taking place in the mining area. Got back about midnight. Bourdillon got home
a little later.

I should have noted that during the day we went to see
some polling-booths and found them well organised. There
is a President, a *Stellvertreter*, a clerk, and a representative
of the Germans and of the Poles. As each voter comes in,
he or she has to show a photograph and give evidence of
identity. The names are checked in the communal lists.
Each voter is then given two cards, and, after selecting the
one, destroys the other in a secret cabin where a candle
burns. There is thus no evidence how the votes go, or who
votes one way or the other. The card selected is placed in
an envelope and dropped into the voting-box or urn. All
necessary precautions seem to be taken. There was no
crowd at any polling-station. The crowds reserved themselves for our Tanks and for the post-offices where the
plébiscite endorsed stamps bearing to-day's date have a
great vogue.

Monday, March 21, 1921. Spent the day in Oppeln seeing people and hearing news. As the day wore on and the
returns came in, it became clear that the forecast which I
had sent to the *D. T.* on Friday was coming very nearly
true. The Poles have a very small majority east of the line
Upper Oder-Kosel-Rosenberg, and the Germans to the
west of this line, but the towns throughout the plébiscite
area have voted German. Therefore the problem for the
European Governments remains the same, and the only
change is that it has become better known. Figures are still
incomplete, but broadly there seem to have been 670,000

German votes against 480,000 Polish over the whole area. As there were 188,000 of the *Heimat-treu* outvoters, they practically decided the Election in the German favour over the area as a whole. The heaviest voting figures were in the mining area, where there voted 260,000 for Germany and 210,000 for Poland, the town vote going for the former and the land vote for the Poles. Such result was unexpected, but the Germans have lost Gross Strehlitz which is a great blow to them. I saw General Le Rond in the late afternoon. I do not think that either he or the Poles are very contented with the results. However, he says that an Allied Government has been found practicable, and the plébiscite has been held without disturbance, so there is now nothing left but to reach a decision. He did not think this easy and asked for my views. I said that the mass of German and Polish voters were on the west and east of the Oder-Kosel-Rosenberg line respectively, and that this seemed to me a good line if partition was decided, but that for the mining area alone I thought partition was economically inadvisable, as the whole was so interdependent in relation to railways, water, power, light, and sand supply. The Commissioner favours the Kosel-Rosenberg line, but the Poles have apparently not all voted Polish, or were less numerous than was thought. The good German propaganda may have turned many voters. I suggested an Inter-Allied régime for a period of years over the mining area, and the General seems to favour it.

To-day I went into the situation and statistics of the mining area with Major R. W. Clarke, R.E., the extremely capable head of the mining department of the Commission which at present controls and practically commands the whole output and marketing of the coal. Clarke has a profound and probably unique knowledge of Central European mining. This Upper Silesian coalfield is carboniferous and belongs to old measures. It has been most closely surveyed and the reserve supplies estimated. They amount to 113,000,000,000 tons largely in the still unexploited area running south to Pless, and the coal is called "long-flame," or what we should call steam and house coal, suitable for industries and for any steam boilers. The defect of the basin is that there is little coking coal for the blast furnaces and for steel-making, so the coke has to be brought from outside to a large extent. There is a big coal measure fault on the line Rybnik-Gleiwitz where the strata are two thousand metres lower to west than to east and so at an unworkable depth.

In the main field the coal measures are quite accessible and the deepest mine is only seven hundred and eighty metres. The average depth of the best seams is three hundred metres, and the thickness is usually eight to ten metres, and runs up to the extremely unusual thickness of thirteen metres. The area is almost all mined by private owners who form their own companies. Their profits were formerly immense, but now, although coal fetches two hundred marks a ton at the pithead, not ten per cent of the mines pay dividends. This is due to the six hundred per cent increase of miners' wages and to high cost of materials. The former profits have enabled the best machinery to be installed, and all the arrangements for the railways, water, power, light, and so on have been systematically and expensively organised for the area as a whole, or what Clarke calls the industrial triangle.

The Silesian coalfield is not very conveniently situated for markets, and the loss of the Russian market seriously affects its prosperity. The coal sales are arranged by the Commission. About 36 per cent of the coal goes to Germany, 8.8 per cent to Poland, 6.3 per cent to Austria, 2.4 per cent to Italy, and 2.5 per cent to Czecho-Slovakia. The remainder is absorbed by the local Silesian industries. Reckoned in another manner, about 15 per cent of the coal goes in reparations to the Allies, 40 per cent to Germany for public uses, and the remainder is available for general trading. The collieries work two or three shifts a day and six days a week. The miner or hewer is actually at work for only five and one-half hours a shift. He gains three hundred marks a week and about one thousand a month.

The mark on the exchange compared with our money is as 1 to 12, but in practical life its value is as 1 to 3 in Germany. The output has fallen from 1.3 tons per man per day in 1914 to .55 ditto now. I am told that fifty per cent more men since wages went up produced twenty-five per cent less coal than before. Clarke thinks them bad hewers and says that discipline ceased with the Revolution, and the men were also underfed up to a year ago. Not all that he can do to coax the miners to work more by dint of pay and rations can get more than one per cent more coal out of the mines. The hewers are mainly Poles, but all the skilled direction is German and so is the skilled labour in the mines and in iron and the steel industries. Were the Germans to lose this area it would take five years to train eight thousand certificated officials alone. In the Saar the German skilled staff left and there resulted a drop of forty per cent in the output. The Germans who left were absorbed by the other industries of Germany.

The other industries in the triangle are zinc, lead mines, and iron and steel industries. All the "*hüttes*" vote German because they are such industries and the greater part of the work is skilled, and so German. The Poles have heaps of coal in their Dombrova field which has a proved area of seventeen hundred square kilometres, but is not properly exploited. The Poles have no real need of the Silesian coal, and what they take they are not now paying for nor do they return the coal wagons.

The triangle may be to a large extent worked out for coal in sixty to one hundred years. The great reserve is in the south running down to Pless where the coal is proved, but not yet worked. One solution is to give all this unworked area to Poland with a few neighbouring mines now working and to leave the triangle to Germany. Clarke entirely opposed to partition. As I told him and Le Rond, it seemed to me the problem of Solomon and the baby.

One of the interesting features of these large Silesian mines is the use of sand and water to fill in the mined pillars as these are hewed out. The sand and water are led in by pipes, and in two days congeal into a solid mass and work can continue alongside of it. It would be a tremendous and most unsatisfactory affair to run a political dividing line through the mining area owing to the interdependence of the whole in utility services. The two great power stations are near Hindenburg and at Charzow.

Private citizens are allowed to work the Crown lands if they prove a workable field, and the concession is given to the first person who produces the necessary samples of the coal gotten by testing. Clarke thinks that there will be a great world surplus of coal soon, and that this complicates the whole situation.

The two books from which details are usually drawn — to suit every thesis — are the *Handbuch des Oberschlesischen Industriebezirks*, published by the Oberschlesischen Berg and Huttenmannischen Verein at Kattowitz in 1913, and the *Jahrbuch für den Obergamtsbezirk Breslau*, also published at Kattowitz in 1913. But these are really only useful for comparison. For the present purpose they are out of date. Dined with the Percivals, Colonel Hawker. Major Gray, and Tidbury. A great talk, and we played Bridge. I like Percival, who is a good man working under inconceivable difficulties.

Tuesday, March 22, 1921. Went to Tidbury's office where the coloured map of the results is nearly finished by Bourdillon. It is a mosaic of red for Germany and blue for Poland. Bourdillon checked up the results east of my Oder line. They give 386,070 Polish votes to 371,000 German, so it is a very near thing. Said good-bye to the very good lot of fellows at work on a thankless task, especially to my most kind host Bourdillon, who is a charming character. Motored to Breslau. Stopped three times on the way by the French and two German control posts, who examined my passport. Uninteresting Middle Silesian country, very flat and dull, but appearing prosperous. The towns neat, the churches attractive with quaint towers. At the Monopole. Saw and talked to Major Piper and his pretty wife after dinner. He is on the control of German effectives, and says that not only is the police an army, but is a very efficient one consisting of the pick of the old N.C.O.'s. The pay offices for pensioners are practically the old dépôts and expansion is arranged. The General Staff, abolished by Treaty, goes on just the same except that the officers are nominally retired and wear mufti. It is impracticable to stop it.

Wednesday, March 23, 1921. Went to a bank to get some Czech money on a letter of credit. They did not seem to understand it and kept me hanging about for nearly an hour. The Directors came down to examine me as if I were a new beast at the Zoo. Lunched with the Pipers, and afterwards, on hearing that I was here, there drove over to see us Prince and Princess Blücher from their place some fifteen miles out from here. The Princess and I had a talk about our respective books both published by Constable. We were not jealous of each other, as each book has run into ten impressions. She tells me that her original book was nearly twice as long as the book she published, but she had to cut out all the accounts of and reflections upon many persons, so the real book will not see the light in our day, I suppose. We talked of exchanging our original MS. or of joining the books to make one. She sees few English here now except Princess Münster and Princess Daisy of Pless, who is going to get a divorce and does not see why it should prevent her living at Pless's house! It seems that Princess B. has found out that her denial of the Lusitania Medal having been struck in Germany is incorrect. One Karl Görz of Dresden struck the medal and is proud of the fact, only complaining that the English had it copied! She says that it is quite hopeless to make the Germans understand that they began the war. They are firmly convinced to the contrary. It is not their fault. They honestly believe themselves to be right. It is the result of persistent propaganda. Only a few of the higher administrators admit the truth.

She went away to Princess M. about four and the Prince stayed and talked with me for an hour. He said that our idea that Germany is not highly taxed must be based on inaccurate information. He has paid his capital levy of forty-five per cent without waiting the forty years allowed, and he is also paying fifty per cent income tax. He says that all pay heavy taxes, but where the money goes to nobody knows except the governing people who get hold of it. He says that his wages bill for 1500 acres is now 14,000 marks a month instead of 4000. His foremen get thirty marks a day: his labourers one hundred and fifty a week with free board and lodging. He thinks that grass alone will pay before long and that a land strike is not improbable. He says that the effect of the collapse after the war had been appalling. Many of the old aristocracy cared for nothing but the army and could do nothing but soldiering. Now this was gone and they knew nothing else. Many had died of broken hearts or had shot themselves: others had become doddering. Many of the old civilian officials were starving. He himself was employing an Austrian Rittmeister in his stable. He found that everyone's nerves were still on edge in all classes and that no one could follow up an argument or even begin a job properly. It had all been too much for everybody.

The Princess told me that the ex-Crown Princess of Germany lived near here. She is very popular and a very clever woman. She does not get on with the ex-C. P., but gives up her time to the care of his son with a view to his ultimate succession. They all feel that Germany is unfinished without an Emperor, and believe that when affairs are cleared up it will be either the C. P.'s son or Rupprecht of Bavaria who will be elected. Rupprecht could come back now as King of Bavaria, but says that he does not wish to break up Germany. When the democrats have finished the reparations the Empire will come back. It is not likely that the Kaiser himself will be restored. All the same they think him more sinned against than sinning, and excuse his flight to Holland by showing that his abdication had been announced at Berlin to quiet the people before he had decided upon it. The Prince told me much about the present position of the best families in Bohemia and Austria.

Major Piper has told me a great deal more to-day about his control job. He thinks that, though we know more than the Germans think, we still, on the whole, only know what the Germans tell us. The dépôts or bezirks commands, camouflaged as pension offices, may very likely have all the old lists of men, and a mere law would enable them to recall these men. There were lately found the full lists of the Posen district which had been sent elsewhere for safety when the Poles took over, and probably the Germans contemplate using the lists some day. He also wonders whether all the armament that cannot be found may not be kept in rolling stock and be sent away when a control inspection threatens to discover it. The train full of war material that came into Upper Silesia by mistake the other day and was there discovered came from Neisse, and undoubtedly some German officials were cognisant of it. Piper says that the Socialists are keeping a sharp eye on the *Orgesch* [1] and the potential *Putsch* [2] leaders, some of whom he pointed out to me, and will not allow them to renew their exploits without resistance, but still their unofficial organisations continue more or less with Government connivance and it is all very unsatisfactory. So I think, but when we withdraw our control there will be nothing to arrest German arming, and so we must either continue the control indefinitely or admit that Germany will arm and become strong again, and adopt the necessary precaution against that event.

I am impressed by finding everywhere throughout Germany such a marked difference of mentality and of attitude between our officers and civilians and the corresponding French officials. While the latter are hard, domineering, and unforgiving, we are impartial, patient, and not unsympathetic. The difference is marked everywhere

[1] Organisation Escherich. So called from the name of its founder.
[2] The Kapp Putsch was first given this name, and after Kapp had failed many who favoured it still kept on at work on the same lines.

that I have been. We are not pro-Boche, though some French now speak of us as "les Boches Anglais." It is merely a racial and temperamental difference and reminds us in a somewhat uncomfortable way that we are racially and temperamentally more akin to the Teuton than the Latin. The Italians, it is true, generally share our moderate views, but for political reasons mainly, I think. Neither of us has had a huge area of territory ravaged as the Boches ravaged Northern France. That may account for much, but it does not account for all. After all, the difference has not been unmarked on the Supreme Council.

Dresden, Thursday, March 24, 1921. A most exasperating experience. Left early for Prague via Dresden. A surging mob of people in the train as I got in. People shoved against me fore and aft as I got into the narrow passage. As I thought they were fussing for seats, I did not fret, but found on gaining a seat that the rascals had relieved me of my letter-case with about £42 in German and French money and with my ticket and baggage registration. Reported to the police, but hopeless to do anything. Fortunately I had put some Czecho-Slovak notes into my hat-box and so was able to pay my way, but lost my train at Dresden by having to explain all the circumstances before I could get out my registered luggage. Great civility on the part of the Dresden railway authorities. Went to the Bellevue for the night. The Dresden people told me that it was a very expert band of international thieves. I was not the only sufferer in the train. The news comes of a considerable communistic activity over Central Germany. Before one trouble ends another begins.

Prague, Good Friday, March 25, 1921. Train Dresden to Prague 11.55 to 4.30 Travelling by train on the Riviera is like travelling along a flute and looking out at the keys. Travelling from Dresden to the frontier is like a moving-picture show. The Elbe Valley here is fine, backed by high, precipitous sandstone cliffs topped with fir woods. Many barges working towed by tugs. A hectic time at

Tetschen,[1] the frontier station, since one had to get every package passed by German and Czech and there was a rare crowd. Found fair rooms reserved for me at the Hôtel de Saxe. Unpacked all my things for the first time since Paris.

I am glad to be out of Germany, especially that flat, dull, dusty, ugly part of Germany where I have been. Dresden is a beautiful town, but anyone may have my share of Berlin and Silesia. I never knew a people so changed as the Germans since the war. I think that they are still dazed by their fall. They not only fell, they crashed. They cannot get over it, understand it, or account for it. They are fearfully humiliated and very sad and sorry for themselves. They indubitably regard our view, that they began the war, as a fiction, and consider that the chief duty of German statesmanship must be to expose that fiction.[2] They put down the original cause of the war to the encircling policy of England and avow that Russia mobilised first. So they regard the Versailles Treaty as shameless brutality, and their clever if coarse caricaturists represent poor Michel — the German peasant — as a sort of saint, a harmless unarmed creature exposed daily to fresh bullying by the Allied Powers. I doubt whether the men who fought in the war, and the older men who did not, will ever get over their experience of these years. Youth is more elastic, and it may be the German youth who may restore Germany to a high position. At present one hates talking to a German and a German hates talking to us. If the soldier servants of Wauchope's staff get on like a house on fire with the Count's serving *mädschens* at his Schloss, it just ends there as a rule. We are civil when forced to talk. We do not seek to talk, but the contrary. What we have to remember, too, if we wish to get paid, is that Germany is not a rich country except in

---

[1] Not to be confused with Teschen.

[2] Karl Kautsky did the reverse when he published *Die Deutschen Dokuments zum Kriegs-Ausbrach*, containing the German diplomatic despatches with the Kaiser's marginal notes on the originals — a very damaging publication for the German case.

Westphalia and Upper Silesia. She is a poor country which has become rich by the industry and science of her people. If that industry be checked, we shall not be paid. We are not dealing with a Darius and his heaps of gold, but with a formerly industrious people who are only returning to work with nonchalance, doubting whether it is worth while with the figure of the reparations claims in their minds. I do not believe that they are dreaming of war, but some of them at one end are certainly longing for a restoration, and at the other end for a commune. In appearance, habits, taste, and so forth the average German remains the utterly uncongenial being that he always was to us, and this is all the more marked now that the aristocracy and gentry have retired to their properties to wait for better times.

CHAPTER V

A STATESMAN WITH A POLICY

Prague — Palaces — Slovakia seeks autonomy — Two Englishmen on the
Czechs — A conversation with Dr. Benès — He explains his policy — En-
tentism and free trade — The German danger — Sir George Clerk —
Czechs, Austrians, and Italians — Population, area, and industries of Czecho-
Slovakia — The political position — Dr. Krammarsch — The British Legation — King Karl enters Hungary — The Czech Constitution — Agrarian
reform — Abolition of nobility, orders, and titles — Commandeering of
private houses — The Czecho-Slovak Army — Resources of the State —
The German fringe — What the Czechs want from us — General Husak,
the War Minister — The King Karl adventure — The Czechs ready to
move — Beauty of Prague — Conversation with the Prime Minister,
M. Cerny — Another conversation with Dr. Benès — He thinks Germany
can pay — His system of alliances — No formula for his confederation of
Central Europe — A ten years' programme — Leave Prague for Vienna.

Prague, March 26, 1921. Prague, Prag, Praha — I think I
prefer the last. Spent the day in finishing my articles on
Upper Silesia and in visiting the town. Saw Lady Clerk
and Mr. Aveling at the attractive Legation house, rented
for twelve years from Count Oswald Thun-Salm-Hohen-
stein. Sir George and everybody else away till Tuesday.
A fine town. The home of the rococo and the baroque.
A new republic in an old capital, and much out of place
there. The palaces of the Schwarzenbergs, Thuns, Clan
Gallases, Kinskys, Czernins, etc., all either not inhabited,
or commandeered by the State, or the owners living in a
corner like Count Waldstein. All titles and orders abolished. The droshky man tells you how long you may stay
when you call. Mine gave me ten minutes at our Legation
and then sent in for me. I fancy that his feeling was that
he had had the graciousness to hire *me*. For full-blooded
tyranny commend me to a new republic. Republics aside,
what a beautiful old town! Either Prague or Cracow is the
capital of Central Europe, and I don't know which. The
Palace and the Cathedral of St. Vitus on the hill across
the river are superb and the lines noble. President
Masaryk living in a wing of the Palace is still very ill and I

shall not be able to see him. Various Government offices in the rest of the huge building. Only the Archbishop's Palace remains tenanted by the original incumbent. The Vatican must be laughing at the disappearance of all the earthly potentates while the Cardinal Archbishop keeps his Palace. But is even he quite safe? I hear that people already talk here of a Czech Church with all the services in Czech. The Czechs look to me a much more alert race than the Germans and with a better moral. They look gay and happy and confident, which is more than any Boche does now. Their women-folk are better-looking too.

Went to the Foreign Ministry and saw M. Jean Bröz. He has arranged for me to see M. Benès on Tuesday, and Benès is to arrange my visits to the Ministries of War, Finance, Commerce, and Interior. Made a prolonged visit to Wallenstein's Palace and am glad to have the picture in my mind of the home where that great general lived. I think the picture of Christ's head by Guido Reni must be an original; it is in the family pew of the chapel in the Palace. I liked Wallenstein's grotto bathroom where all the stones flung water at him. It is approached by a secret staircase from his rooms. I expect that anyone who fought campaigns in Central Europe must have discovered the want of baths. Why did Wallenstein's name become corrupted from Waldstein? Was it only to suit Schiller's verse? It is vexatious that the names of an Irish and Scottish officer who took part in the murder of the hero on the instigation of the Emperor should have been preserved and should be told to all visitors.

Easter Sunday, March 27, 1921. A pity to have arrived in this holiday season. Most people away and nobody working, not even the washerwomen. Sent off three articles to the *D. T.* on Silesia. Read the local German paper, the *Prague Tagblatt.* Amused to see that a Professor of the Pressburg University writes an article demanding the full-blooded State autonomy of Slovakia which numbers some three millions out of the fourteen millions of this country. He says that it is the new political gospel that each people should make its history with its own strength, its own will, and under its own responsibility. What a sweet revenge for Austria to find that

> Big fleas have little fleas upon their backs to bite 'em.
> Little fleas have lesser fleas, and so ad infinitum.

The Professor says that the Czechs and the Slovaks have a totally different character, spirit, and temperament. The Germans in Bohemia may say the same thing. We appear to be on the threshold of another period of tribal rule. How acute was Pershing's officer at the end of the war who told me that he was reading "The History of the Future," and then produced, not Old Moore, but "The History of the Middle Ages"! There is another article on the Franco-Czech alliance which Benès is supposed to have signed in Paris. It is regarded in Berlin and Vienna as another part of the web of alliances which France, Italy, the Czechs, and the Serbs are spinning. It is supposed to destroy the Danubian Monarchy idea, and to mean that the new allies will consider a Habsburg restoration as a *casus belli.* France is said to have withdrawn from the scheme of a Danubian Monarchy. The new alliance, combined with the Little Entente, is creating a circle of allied states round Germany. But I suppose that Benès will tell me that it is all merely an accident insurance policy. We are still elementary people in Central Europe. News of the assembly of the League of Nations at Geneva does not seem to have reached us.

Met at Zavrels, a nice little restaurant which Mr. Aveling recommended to me, Mr. Smith, whose Nobel firm have a concession for making all the explosives in the country, and Mr. Wilson, his Scottish technical man. Very nice fellows. We walked across the river and up many steep streets and stairs to the Castle and back by the Belvidere, a purely Italian building. We found a great football match of Danes *versus* Czechs going on and went in to look. The result was a tie. There must have been 14,000 people there. It is extraordinary how football has caught on everywhere in Europe lately. My two acquaintances told me much of the people here. They did not see why the new State should not get on, as it was in the happy position of being self-contained in all raw materials, [1] both food and minerals, and had besides much to export, notably sugar. It had coal, iron, industries of all kinds, and very fairly good railway facilities, while the barges went down to the Elbe and thence to the sea at Hamburg. They find bribery much too common and put it down to the ridiculously low salaries. They do not rate the Czech soldier high. They say that German and Czech mix as little as possible and cordially detest each other. They say that the present Government is one of permanent officials, no party having a clear majority. Also that the Czech Catholics are aiming at a Church of their own with the Czech lingo instead of Latin. It is quite on the cards that the people may want a king some day. They find that liberty only means that they are still conscripted and made to pay heavier in taxes than under the Austro-Hungarian Empire. They are a sober, steady, hard-working people, and not at all warlike. They are still mortally afraid of Hungary. Wages here are much as in Silesia, one hundred and fifty crowns a week for an agricultural labourer.

The Czechs are very musical as Kubelik's compatriots should be. The Germans say that in every Czech cradle is placed a violin string and a ten heller piece. If the baby selects the string, he becomes a musician, if the heller piece, he becomes a thief. It is sure to be one or the other according to the German. To the German the Czech in the past was a hewer of wood and a drawer of water. Now he is master. For how long? The Germans say that he has never been able to govern and never will be. But some Germans cannot really believe it, as they had a journalistic competition the other day to decide whether Germans should learn Czech or not. By a sixty per cent majority the vote was that they should learn it. Some of our

[1] Not quite correct — some thirty per cent of the wheat comes from outside.

people who wish to get on here will have to learn it too. I
have not heard of one Englishman or foreigner who can
speak it. I am told that there are not a dozen English in
the country. There was one Dutchman who could speak it.
He was the Dutch Minister here. They would not allot
him a residence, so he left a vice-consul at Brünn and
went away. Then he came back and was so insistent with
Dr. Beneš that the latter gave orders for the wing of some
palace to be evacuated and given to him. The Dutchman
went to the department concerned and the head of it sent
for the official who was occupying the wing. He told him
in French that he had to clear out, and then added in
Czech, which he supposed the Dutchman would not
know, "This is all humbug, I am not going to allow you to
be turned out. We will gain time and wear out the Dutchman." The Dutchman then blandly observed that he
knew Czech and understood what had passed. Far from
being overcome, the head of the department told him that
his action was *très inconvenante* and that it showed a grave
want of tact in a Minister who knew Czech not to make
the fact known!

Tuesday, March 29, 1921. Went to the Foreign Ministry
to see Dr. Beneš.[1] An agreeable man with a clever face.
Impeccably honest, wholly without vanity, clear and most
frank. Such was my first impression of the man. I told
him that I considered him the defence minister of Czecho-
Slovakia and not General Husak. When he asked why, I
pulled out my map of modern Europe and asked how a
country like his, one thousand kilometres long and not
two hundred broad, surrounded by five potentially hostile
States, was going to be defended by anything but a Foreign
Minister. He agreed, and said that this had been his view
from the first.

He then gave me a clear and interesting sketch of his
policy. When the Armistice came about he said that
Czecho-Slovakia was surrounded by enemies or dubious

---

[1] Five months later Dr. Beneš became Prime Minister of a Parliamentary
Government, retaining his portfolio of Foreign Affairs.

friends, so he felt that, unless he moved and worked on a settled plan, all the Treaties might come to nothing and the legend — as he called it — of the Balkanisation of Central and Eastern Europe might come true. He had left German-Austria and Hungary to the last. He had made a definite plan and had steadily followed out a fixed policy. He had first made a binding political and military alliance with Jugo-Slavia and then a less comprehensive arrangement with Roumania. With Poland, which he evidently regarded as a dangerous and fickle neighbour, he was now quite friendly, and he had made good terms with Italy, terms about to be strengthened as he hoped by the meeting at Porto Rosa. He would not attend that meeting, as he wanted it to be confined to economics. If the politicos went they would quarrel about the causes of the war or something else, so he preferred to stand out. He was quite satisfied with his Paris talks and I think has secured himself on that side against Polish risks. He has arranged commercial treaties with France, Italy, England, Germany, and Austria, while by the recent meeting at Bruck he has initiated an understanding with Hungary, and has, as it were, reintroduced this State into the European field of politics.

He had refused to march against Russia in the earlier days because after the war nobody wanted to march and adventures were not to his liking. His method of combating Bolshevism was by economics and social reforms, but for these the State must be safe first, and he thought that he had made it safe in two years by his treaties and agreements including the Little Entente which he had joined.

Is it really as good as the old confederation under Austria? I asked, and how do you propose to break down all these interminable and harassing barriers of frontiers and customs wherever one goes? He thought that an economic confederation would take the place of the old political link. He had begun by strict customs barriers in and out because all had to be organised and consolidated. But very soon he meant to turn this system upside down by opening up trade in every way and by only making a few exceptions to the general rule. It is easier for you than others, I said, because you are nearly self-contained. Yes, he said, and our position now is superior to that of any other country in this part of Europe. Oil? I asked. Yes, it had just been opened up in Slovakia. It was still all a question of tariffs and especially communications. He found all ready to deal, and was very satisfied with the results of all his missions. He doubted that we could do anything with Russia for twenty years.

In view of the possible recurrence of the German danger, with which might come danger from Austria and Hungary, he felt that Czecho-Slovakia's interests were bound up with those of the Western Powers — England, France, Italy –– and he had proceeded on those lines. I said that instead of being the cartridge of dynamite that someone had called Czecho-Slovakia, it seemed to me a centre for radiating the warmth of peace, but I supposed that he had many difficulties internally, and mentioned the Germans, Magyars, the Slovaks, and the religious question. Yes, he said, we have 2,800,000 Germans, but on account of the natural frontiers of Bohemia and on economic grounds they could not be given to a defeated Germany. They were somewhat troublesome. The Magyars were 600,000. Are they not rather a weakness to you? Yes, they were, and he thought in time there might be room for a rearrangement here. As for the Slovaks, they were uneducated and strong Roman Catholics. The Church meant much to them, but much less to the rather free-thinking Czechs, who preferred to have a National Church. He had seen Cardinal Gasparri, and had told him that they could settle it between them, for he thought that it would be unwise to start a Kultur-Kampf at this stage, and said that he did not intend to tackle the question yet awhile. Slovakia's real needs are met by a comprehensive educational policy. He thought that the greatest danger to Czecho-Slovakia was its protuberance into Germany, and the encircling position of Germany and Austria round its western frontiers combined with the presence of Germans within. He said that German-Austria had tyrannised over the Czechs, who had no share in the old Government. The Church had made itself the instrument of this tyranny, and neither could be forgiven by the Czechs.

Lady Clerk and Mr. Aveling lunched with me, and afterwards I went up to the Legation and saw Sir George, who was just back. We had a good talk. I found him on the whole disposed to believe that Czecho-Slovakia would survive. There were great difficulties, but the people were confronting them bravely. Benès was politically the child of Masaryk; but he was not yet a great political figure in the country. He was a tremendous worker and his value was fully appreciated. He had certainly raised the prestige and influence of Czecho-Slovakia greatly, and Sir George could not but admit that both at Prague and even at Vienna matters had improved during the past year. We discussed the sanctions. Sir George had been instructed to ask Czecho-Slovakia to impose the fifty per cent plan. It was not certain whether it would go down here, for it would seriously affect trade and Germany might make reprisals.

Studied the press again. The Bruck talk has resulted in an agreement to group all the questions pending from the Treaties into categories, namely into four commissions for political, financial, economic, and transport questions in order to regulate the accord between the two States in accordance with the Peace Treaties. This practically admits that the Peace Treaties will be applied and that the hostile and distrustful attitude of the two States may change into a better feeling. An atmosphere of peace and confidence may return if both sides comprehend the international position of Central Europe, and if the Hungarian Premier, Count Teleki, and M. Gratz, the Foreign Minister, terminate the attitude of open opposition which has hitherto been maintained towards the execution of the Peace Treaties.

The Czech-Italian economic accord also helps matters on. It is for five years and contains general rules for the normal economic relations of the two countries. Tariffs have not yet been inserted in a convention, since in both countries tariffs are under revision. The question of a differential tariff for Trieste, Czecho-Slovakia could not agree to, but the principle has been adopted for merchandise reaching Trieste under the Czecho-Slovak flag which will help to create the future Czecho-Slovak merchant fleet. Czecho-Slovakia also gains advantages in the use of docks and the installations at Trieste. All these matters will help on affairs at the Conference at Porto Rosa between the States successors to the Austrian dominions.

As for Austria, Czecho-Slovakia is rather contemptuous of the Austrian lamentations and inspired articles and asks why Austria does not help herself. She thinks that Austria is really beginning to look up, and that her good means of communication, favourable situation, and the development of her industry and resources make it foolish to despair. Czecho-Slovakia does not add, as she might, that Prague has no decent hotels, no pleasures, no meeting-places for business men, and that Vienna has all these advantages and is attracting both capital and industry.

Czecho-Slovakia is the only State in Europe whose exports to the United States exceed its imports. The Czecho-Slovakian census of February last not yet out. It is based on nationalities and not on mere language as formerly, so it will make the real situation much more clear. The last Census of 1910 gave 13,811,755 inhabitants. The territory of the Republic has 142,745 square kilometres. Coal is most important for the Czecho-Slovak industries. In 1920, 395 independent industries exploited mines of which 150 lignite and the rest coal. There were 126,000 miners of whom 75,000 employed in coal mines. The output increased twelve per cent over 1919. The miners worked 5.24 days a week, but the output per man decreased. A new and special institution deals with all the questions connected with the working and the use of coal. This is called the Uhelna Rada or Coal Council, and M. Kovalik, the Minister of Public Works, addressed its first meeting on March 8. In 1920 Czecho-Slovakia produced thirty million tons, namely eleven million coal and nineteen of lignite. Czecho-Slovakia has an industrial crisis, and second-grade coal is not so much demanded. Most of the industrial enterprises formerly used the good steam coal of Silesia. Without it the cost of production is greater Czecho-Slovakia took 6,460,000 tons from Upper Silesia in 1913, and one million tons from Westphalia. Now she only receives 6,200,000 tons yearly under the Treaty recently made with Germany. After deducting five million tons for exports and the same for use of the mines, the twenty million remaining of Czecho-Slovak production is not enough for industries and domestic use. Therefore production must be increased and Upper Silesia more drawn upon. Czecho-Slovakia is in no hurry for nationalisation. It is considered not a political question, but one of economics which can only be settled by an accord between all the interested parties.

The present Cabinet in Czecho-Slovakia is a provisional Government and not an ordinary parliamentary Government created by a majority. There is no regular party majority on which a Government can count. This is mainly due to the crisis in Czecho-Slovak socialism which is broken up into eight groups. It is therefore not a normal position, but the Government have got through much useful work, and revenue nearly balances with expenditure, which is quite the exception in Central Europe. M. Englis, the late Finance Minister, also did a good thing when he suspended the issue of paper notes without cover. Czecho-Slovakia has shown herself determined to pursue a policy of peace and conciliation with her neighbours. The Social Democrats have always supported the Government on essential questions, and the attempt of the Communists to destroy the authority of the State ended in a fiasco. The Germans of the Czecho-Slovak Republic have not yet evolved the definite character of their relations with the Czechs. Some German agrarians have given hopeful promises of collaboration, but the German Nationalists have shown systematic opposition and no practical result has come from the conferences between the Czecho-Slovak and German Social-Democratic parties. In Czech politics the "Council of Five" (or the representatives of the Social Democrats of the Right, the National Socialists, the Agrarians, the National Democrats, and the Catholics) exercises a great influence in Parliament. Thanks to it the Government has been saved on many occasions. The research of a stable party majority is highly desirable. Note that the return of the clearing houses of Vienna, Pesth, and Prague in 1913 gave figures to show that the amount of business done at Vienna was seven times, and at Pesth three and one-half times, the amount done at Prague. In 1919, however, the amount done at Vienna and Pesth combined was only one-third that of Prague, the figures being 12,137,419,300 Czecho-Slovak crowns for Vienna and Pesth, and 41,535,733,000 Czecho-Slovak crowns for Prague.

Wednesday, March 30, 1921. The Clerks having most hospitably invited me to the Legation, I moved there this morning and found it a delightful haven. Many floors with fine rooms and terraces, and on about the fourth floor, where I seem to be, comes the garden and behind it the wall and ramparts of the Royal Palace. A perfect and quite unique place, most suitable for fêtes and entertainments. The Krammarsches lunched. He was the first Prime Minister of the Republic, a strong man with a powerful physique and decided views. She is Russian and must have been handsome. He told us of his twenty-six months' imprisonment in a small damp cell, and of his condemnation to death, and reflections whether he would choose hanging or shooting. It seems better to be shot in these regions because hanging is only a crude form of strangulation. He is very pro-Reactionary Russia and does not like Benès's policy which is apparently to let anyone come here who likes and to trade with them like the England of L. G. to-day. Lockhart, the Commercial Secretary at the Legation, with his great knowledge of Russia, does not think it will make any difference whether we trade with them or not. He thinks it would have been best to have done nothing at all when Russia went out of the war. Krammarsch cannot understand how the England of Gladstone can trade with men whose hands are stained with blood and whose pockets are filled with stolen money. He was most amused at the Italian idea that they won the war. He thought that the Czechs and others who wished to break with Austria had won the war. It was their work in the interior and the *mot d'ordre* passed to the front that started the *dégringolade*. There was suddenly no front. The Italian talk of prisoners and guns captured was all eye-wash. He said it was a wonderful time in Bohemia. One has yet to find the country that does not think it won the war.

This morning there had come the news of the ex-Kaiser Karl's visit in a motor car to Budapest on Easter Sunday. He went with some reactionary friends to the house of a reactionary Bishop on the Austrian frontier, and thence motored to Budapest. A very silly move and the reason is not yet fully explained. Krammarsch calls him "un fou." He seems to have had a chilly reception by the Hungarian Premier and to have returned. As Italy, the Czechs, and the Serbs are all in league against a Habsburg restoration, the *Putsch* was silly. Krammarsch thinks that Germany will become a Great Power again soon and the arbiter of Europe. He thinks we are giving Russia into Germany's hands. Sir G. took me to Ressource, the "Jockey Club" of the Ur-Adler or primeval nobility. We played Bridge with Prince Mansfeld and his brother, then adjourned to the Legation to dine, and went on playing till 1.30 A.M. The Ressource has been largely commandeered and the members restricted to two rooms, much as if the Marlborough had to give up its first floor to Mr. Smillie. The primeval nobility express primeval sentiments on the subject.

Thursday, March 31, 1921. Occupied in talks with Sir George and Mr. Lockhart, the commercial attaché, about the politics, finance, commerce, and interior policy of this country. Needless to say that they are both exceedingly well-informed. I also ran through the Legislative Summary of the Parliament, or rather the Assembly, since the Revolution, i.e., from October 20, 1918, to May 26, 1920. Very instructive to see how a Socialistic Republic regulates its affairs. The Constitutional Law of February 29, 1920, seems to me a good law, carefully elaborated, with many reasonable safeguards and enough authority left to the President to secure the safety of the State. There are two Houses, most power residing in the lower. I have not found a new Republic yet which ventures on Single Chamber rule.

The Assembly in its salad days practically declared all land to belong to the State, and as early as November 9, 1918, passed a law on the seizure of large properties. Other laws on agrarian reforms followed. The Czechs were in a hurry to repair what they considered wrong done to them during the past centuries regarding the possession of land, and protest that they did so without too radical changes and without too cruel injustice to existing rights. It is questionable whether this reservation is justified. The agrarian laws include measures for the protection of small farmers, but the law of November 9 is most drastic, and so is the law of April 16, 1919, modified by that of July 11, 1919. By this legislation the State assumes the rights over all domains in excess of one hundred and fifty hectares of cultivable land and two hundred and fifty of land in general. On seizure the State acquires the right of possession, and the alleged spirit of the law is that the land must be given first of all to those able to farm it. A further law of February 12, 1920, deals with the exploitation of land seized. The compensation is fixed at pre-war prices, but, as at present rate of exchange the value of the crown had depreciated ten times, the compensation is largely fictitious. How vitally this restriction of landholding to one hundred and fifty hectares affects Bohemia may be judged by the fact that the largest landed proprietor, Prince Schwartzenberg, owns 700,000 acres and employs 30,000 people. There are many other great landowners, and so what is involved is an agricultural revolution, for which the only excuse to be made is that it possibly prevented a Jacquerie. What with levies, taxes, and seizures it is reckoned that Schwartzenberg will have to pay thirty million more crowns than the value of his property! But it must be added that confiscation has not been largely carried out yet, and most of the old nobles continue to reside on their estates. Only in a few cases have farms been seized and industries depending on them have had to close down. To change great estates into small farms means, of course, any amount of new farm buildings to be constructed, and the petty marketing of the small farmer means a wholly different set of agricultural economics from that of the great estates.

Another blow at the old German-Bohemians is the law of December 10, 1918, which abolishes the nobility, and all orders and titles granted as honorific distinctions except for science and letters. Our O.B.E.'s will now know what a socialistic government will do with them when it comes.

Further laws of 1919 have the effect of enabling the Government to seize private town houses to provide lodgings for those who need them and to secure Government offices for all the new Ministries and the Administration, the numbers of which here are said to be equal to those which formerly ran the whole Austrian Empire. This power has been very extensively used in Prague, where an immense number of great palaces exist, seldom tenanted by their owners during the Empire, as Francis Joseph and the Court scarcely ever came to Bohemia. The Palaces have mostly been taken over, and the owners allowed a few rooms in a wing. But the same thing has happened to the houses of the bourgeois classes who are similarly served. I really wonder whether Article 112 of the Constitution, which guarantees inviolability of domicile, is not the finest piece of sarcasm ever embodied in legislation.

Another point which interests me is the divorce law, as one sees how the Socialist looks at it. In the Law of May

22, 1919, there are nine causes for divorce. The last two are "grave incompatibility of character in the couple" and "invincible aversion." In the latter case an application can be made a year after the petitioner has lived separately.

The Army is eventually to be organised on the Militia basis. Military service is obligatory and equal for all: there are no exemptions. Men serve from the age of twenty-one to fifty, and professional soldiers are liable to the age of sixty even if retired. A man can join at the date which suits him between January 1 in the year when he becomes twenty and the 30th of December in the year in which his twenty-second year ends. Regular service lasts fourteen months, but men called up in 1920, 1921, and 1922 serve for a supplementary period of ten months, and those of 1923–25 for four months more. There is a first reserve up to the age of forty and a second over forty. Reserve service may mean four training periods each of fourteen weeks. The peace effective for the four years after 1920 is fixed by law at 150,000 men. Voluntary engagements are permitted. I believe that one hundred and sixty-six battalions are maintained in peace, but are very weak.

For 1920 the whole State expenditure was estimated at 10,416 million crowns and receipts at 7750 millions. The Government was authorised to procure the sum necessary to meet all deficits up to 2666 million crowns.

Now if we turn to the commercial and industrial side of the life here, it is certain that this little State is the most *viable* of all in this part of the world in its industrial present and future. It comprises about three-quarters of the riches of the former Austria, and though it is short by about thirty per cent of the annual foodstuffs required, it has almost everything else needed for itself and much over for exportation. It is a good going business concern, but as it lives by its industries it competes with us, and owing to the high rate of exchange it cannot buy our goods, while the control of the Government over imports and the cheap production here make our merchants wary. There is scarcely any trade between Czecho-Slovakia and the countries at the top of the tree in the exchange scale. We might find a large field for banking here, but nothing is done, and the Germans are nearly sure to seize this outlet before long. There is no doubt that the western end of the country and all the fringe of land running along the Czecho-Slovak side of the Erz Gebirge are the richest parts of the country and contain the greater part of the most promising industries. This part is German, and the attitude of Czechs to Germans, and of the latter to the Czechs, is not friendly. But the German industrialists recognise that they profit from being Czechish subjects, since they can promise themselves protection against other German competition. All the same, it is not to be denied that Czecho-Slovakia without this German fringe would not have the good prospects it has now and might not be able to go on. Yet this eventuality does not suggest to the Czechs, who are suffering from swelled heads just now, that they should make advances towards the Germans of Bohemia. The Czechs rather play the Germans the game that the Germans formerly played them, and it is dear price to be paid some day for the sake of paltry revenge. The aristocratic Germans sulk in their homes and wring their hands. They hate the Czechs whom they have always considered an inferior race. They never even learned the Czech language, and now they refuse diplomatic appointments which Benès offers them and take little part in public life. There are in fact faults on both sides. Perhaps common interests will hold the two together for a time, but I do not see a recovered Germany failing to attract their Bohemian brother Germans now that the old German-Austria is in such low water, and the old Empire is no more. One sees that the Peace Conference could not give beaten Germany a strip of Austria, but still the mountains on the west are not the dividing line between the races by any means. A broad belt as deep in as Pilsen is German. Were a plébiscite taken here, a large German majority would be assured.

Dined at the Legation with Lady Clerk. Sir George out

at a students' dinner. A pleasant talk afterwards of pictures, painters, books and writers.

Friday, April 1, 1921. This morning went to the Ministry of Commerce and then to the branch for foreign trade to discuss various matters with Dr. Fafe and Dr. Peroutka. I find that in 1919 Czecho-Slovakia sent 238 million crowns worth of merchandise to England and bought 328 millions from us. Czecho-Slovakia also sent 800 millions worth to Germany in 1919 and took 780 millions worth from Germany. I discussed the sanctions question. In so far as the fifty per cent plan serves as a protectionist tariff against competition in Germany, it will please the German Bohemians who compete against her, but there is a risk that a policy of this kind may interrupt Czecho-Slovak trade by the Elbe to Hamburg and elsewhere. Czecho-Slovakia might become almost an island in a hostile Central Europe and the Czechs are not in a hurry to run risks. Looked into what the Czechs can send us that we want — or don't want. It includes sugar, malt, hops, mineral waters, beer, fruit, timber, spirit, gloves, caoline, pulp, paper of all kinds, glass, china, clothing and underclothing, collars, cuffs, neckties, wooden toys, wood mouldings and frames, and bent wood furniture. Czecho-Slovakia wants from us tea, coffee, spices, copra, soya beans, oleaginous seeds, hides and skins, mother-of-pearl, india-rubber, resin, copal, vegetable wax, ferro-manganese, pyrites, tin and nickel, cotton, wool, jute, fine cotton yarn over No. 70, combed woollen yarns, fine cloth, iron and steel, textile machines, machine tools, soap, chemicals, soda, and mineral oils. A good long list for our traders. I find that the Czecho-Slovak iron ore is not good enough for the best steel and that Austria has always taken better iron from Sweden and Lorraine. About sixty to seventy-five per cent of the former Austrian industries are now concentrated in Czecho-Slovakia.

There lunched at the Legation to-day young Masaryk, son of the President, General Husak, Minister of War, General Mittelhauser, Pellé's successor in Czecho-Slovakia, and his A.D.C. Picot. Madame Husak, a pretty and agreeable woman, also there. Lady Clerk, who is a very pretty woman with a fine figure, makes a perfect hostess. Husak told me that up to yesterday he had regarded the ex-Kaiser's escapade as an operetta, but the news to-day was more serious. Karl's statement that he would never leave Hungary alive might be bombast, but the declaration had been launched and it might be that Colonel Lehar, whom Husak described as the best officer in Hungary, was pushing him on. The ex-officers in Hungary numbered 30,000 and there were battalions composed entirely of officers. The men called up for training were also all told off to certain duties on mobilisation, and he thought that 70,000 could rapidly be assembled and that Hungary would not lack for men and arms. Czecho-Slovakia kept quite calm because within a week some twelve divisions could be collected with a formidable artillery, and the Jugo-Slavs would move too. We should know in a few days. It was a bad sign that Julius Andrassy appeared to be in the movement, as he was clever and experienced. The telephone wires to Pesth had been cut, but news came by car from Pesth to the Czecho-Slovak frontier in two hours. Austria might be in the movement. Clerk doubts this, but he says that the Hungarians would not like the summons of Benès and might fight. Husak says that Horthy is jealous of Karl, but that Teleki's attitude is less certain. Mittelhauser generally shares Husak's views and regards the position as rather serious. Husak thinks that the state of readiness of the Czecho-Slovak Army is not known in Hungary, and he says that his men are war-experienced and the young officers trained in France are good. Husak asked me to visit Skoda where I should see the German plans for its ten-year programme.

In the afternoon called on M. Courget, the French Minister, who was very agreeable and we talked Czechish problems for an hour. Later Sir G. talked on the telephone to Vienna which told him that all was quiet and that Hohler at Pesth reported that everyone there was against Karl who is still apparently at Steinamanger on the Austro-

Hungarian frontier. I decided that if anything happened it would be best for me to accompany the Czechs, and that if it all fizzled out it was not worth while to go to Steinamanger. I hope that Burnham will agree. Dined with the Italian Minister, Sir G. and Lady Clerk, Miss Boyle, a capable lady on the Legation staff, Aveling, Lockhart, and Chichester, and Michiels, the Dutch Minister, son of my old friend Baron Michiels at The Hague. A pleasant talk and we played Bridge.

Saturday, April 2, 1921. This wonderful Italian weather continues. My window at the Legation gives a view over the garden and up the walls and slopes of the Castle. The silence is profound. The early morning sun colours all the walls with a soft pink shade. There is a simplicity about this front of the Palace that is wanting in Prague, the baroque generally. Certainly one cannot deny the beauty of Prague. The view from the eastern end of Karl IV Bridge looking west has perhaps no equal in any other capital. The baroque style may seem extravagant, eastern, laboured, and heavy, but when a whole town seems sixteenth and seventeenth century, as if it had become architecturally passionate and disorderly all at once, one forgives a good deal. It is strongly infected with Easternism. It is too unquiet for English taste. One likes it against one's will. But one likes it because it is not mean, nor even prettily rococo, but in the grand manner and virile in its way. Compared with an old English town Prague reminds me of a Middle Ages dining-hall covered with barons of beef, boar's heads, and roast swans. The appetites may have been coarse, but they were those of strong men. I expect it is a town to remember, and one would remember it better were the hotels here anything better than dirty, ill-served pot-houses.

This Legation is a joy. There seems to be no end to the floors, rooms, strange winding staircases, concealed and otherwise, and terraces and gardens where one least expects them. Of course there is a ghost, Matthias of the Clan Thun, who steals up the spiral staircase, rattles at your door, shrieks with laughter, rings bells, and altogether behaves himself as a good ghost should.

Went to see the P.M. Monsieur Cerny before lunch and had to take the Czech Secretary at the Legation, M. Bubola, with me. He translates very well. Cerny of the Benès type, shortish, serious, trusted, and courteous. I fancy that he thought it was a press interview which would echo through Europe the next minute, as he returned prim official answers and looked horribly alarmed. I ought to have told him that he could speak plainly. A go-between is not of much use in a talk after all. A conversation through a third party is ridiculous. We discussed Czecho-Slovak legislation, especially the agrarian policy and the sequestration of houses, and he gave me to understand that this legislation dated from the early revolutionary days and would be much amended and not carried out in practice. He told me that the sanctions against Germany, which Czecho-Slovakia is said to have adopted, could only be carried out within the limits assigned by Czecho-Slovakia's special position regarding Germany. He knew that the Deutsch-Bohmer nobles had many relations with England and did not think their fears of complication justified. He would be very glad for the German nobles to come into the Government if they became one of the regular parliamentary parties. Not much of interest, but he said that his one aim was peace.

Counts Ledebur and Kinsky lunched with Sir George and me. We had a good talk about political matters. Ledebur speaks boldly in the Senate. He is one of the few who has taken up the cudgels in the interests of the great nobles. He speaks in German, but the speaker has to speak in Czech always. He tells me that they — Germans — are four millions in Bohemia, but we must wait for the census returns. His view is that Austria and Czecho-Slovakia must eventually come within the German constitution, and the other parts of old Austria in an Eastern confederation. Sir George and Aveling went off to shoot with Prince Colloredo. I was asked, but am still full of my

Silesian chill. Chichester took us to the Russian ballet. Poor. We came back and played Bridge. A young Murray, son of the Oxford Regius Professor of Greek, struck me as a boy with a future. He is here with the Students' Conference. Pretty good for a youth of that age to stand up and speak boldly in an International Assembly and in French as well as English.

Sunday, April 3, 1921. Went to say good-bye to Dr. Benès at the Foreign Office. They do not revel much in week-ends here and the hours on Sunday are from eight to eight with two hours for meals.

I began by telling Dr. Benès that the P.M. seemed rather alarmed at my conversation with him yesterday, and I begged B. to tell him that I did not publish my talks in the press without sending copies to Ministers concerned, so he need not be anxious. All that I wanted was to know the views of Ministers for my personal guidance. Then I told B. that in our last talk we had restricted ourselves mainly to Czecho-Slovak policy, and that I wished before I left to know his views of various aspects of foreign policy in a larger sense. For instance there was this question of the sanctions, concerning which I told him my views, namely, that they were dangerous and ineffective and that I preferred the blockade to end the thing quickly. I was interested to find that B. was entirely of the same opinion. He said that Germany could pay, but did not want to pay. She had concocted a Bankruptcy Budget to mislead us and appeal to our pity. But she had offered B. two thousand milliards of marks as a loan when his application to France for one hundred million francs had failed, and she had also made a similar offer to Roumania which might or might not be accepted. The Czecho-Slovak Finance Minister had wanted to accept, but B. would not let him, as such dependence on Germany would be bad for Czecho-Slovakia and besides disloyal to the Allies. But the offers showed that Germany's plea of poverty was all gammon.

B., in Germany's place, would have signed and would

have done his best to pay for one, two, or three years. He would also have asked for an Allied Financial Control Commission to prove Germany's good-will and to satisfy the Allies if, in fact, Germany could not pay. All the questions pending between the Allies and Germany were largely psychologic. He believed that the blockade was the best means of closing the accounts and he was ready to share in it. Countries like Holland, Switzerland, and Austria could be roped in by being compelled to declare the origin of all goods sent abroad. B. thought that in a month or two this course would produce a surrender. He did not deny the influence of an occupation, as it might prove to the Germans that they had been beaten, but he preferred the blockade, because it was not easy to say when the occupation would cease. Czecho-Slovakia was prepared to join in any virile measures, but the present sanctions promise to injure us without effecting any useful purpose. Entirely my view.

I then asked B. to allow me to submit another point to him. I said that England had been very friendly with Austria in the past and that even up to 1878 we had found ourselves often acting with her. Austria's illiberal policy had alienated England afterwards, and finally had come the smash, but all through the nineteenth century our men of affairs like Palmerston had regarded Austria as the pivot of the balance of power. What I wanted to know was whether B.'s policy, which he had before explained to me, gave the hope that it might restore the lost pivot on which peace had long turned.

B. thought it would. The system of understanding and alliances had for its eventual aim the creation of the United States of Central Europe within which should come Czecho-Slovakia, Jugo-Slavia, Roumania, Poland, Bulgaria, Austria, and Hungary. It was not a case of a fresh Empire. It was a political and economic federation, based on democratic principles, each State preserving its full sovereign rights, and the various States arranging matters with each other by mutual agreement. The formula for the Confederation had not yet emerged, but the aim was clear; and he considered, as he had told me before, that he could count on ten to fifteen years of tranquillity for carrying out these great designs.

I said that these things seemed to me of extraordinary interest and asked whether B. had spoken of them to any Western statesman. He said that he had not. All his available time had been given up to the settlement of practical matters as the different points came up, and each visit of his to the great capitals had been fully occupied, while at home every sort of *mesquinerie* had to be dealt with. But he hoped to go to London soon, and I suggested that he should explain his ideas to L. G. over a map, as I thought that he would rise to such a big idea. It was B.'s intention, I learned, to do so. We talked for about an hour and a half. He was sometimes interrupted by telephone messages or by despatches brought to him. After each interruption he continued the conversation precisely where he had left it without any break of continuity at all. An orderly memory.

In the late afternoon called upon M. Krammarsch at his house which occupies a wonderful site in the most prominent position at Prague, where an old bastion of the City walls was, and indeed still is. He showed me round the place outside first and took me to the end of the garden where there is an unsurpassed view up and down the river in the valley below, seven bridges being visible. The house is well built in a reserved baroque style, chiming in well with the general architecture. Very nice inside too, and the whole well defended by iron grilles, gates, and so on. I could hardly get in or out. Quite the home of the successful and retired revolutionary! I found him still immersed in his Russian book and Russian ideas. I threw out the Benès scheme as a fly, very briefly and without mentioning its origin. K. was sceptical about it, and said that it would only be the old Austria over again, but this is not B.'s idea at all. I did not stop to argue about it. He gave me many interesting details about the past. Mme. K. gave us tea. In the evening dined alone with Lady Clerk as H.E. is still not back from his shoot. A pleasant evening and a good talk.

Monday, April 4, 1921. Said good-bye to my very kind host and hostess and the Legation staff and caught the 4 P.M. train for Vienna. A gorgeous day and Prague looked its best in brilliant sunshine. I am glad to think that Sir George is where he is. It seems to me the crucial point in Central Europe so far as I have seen yet, and I think Sir G. one of our best diplomats.

CHAPTER VI

INFELIX AUSTRIA

Vienna, Tuesday, April 5, 1921. Macartney came to see
me in the morning. He has been down to Steinamanger,
but could not see Karl. Lunched with Sir T. Cunninghame, our Military Attaché. He has Franz Ferdinand's
old house with the old furniture and fixtures as they were.
A delicious drawing of Franz Joseph in the white uniform
at the age of eighteen or twenty, and many more treasures of real historic interest. Cunninghame thinks the
Austrian Army not worth discussing. It has three thousand of the old officers, but is run by soldiers' councils,
and is only a toy. He says that it is useless for all practical purposes, except to stand between the people and the
police, and that Austria would have been just as well off
without an army. C. does not think much of Hungary's
troops either, and says that they have only forty guns.
He admits the great progress made by Czecho-Slovakia
lately. He asked if they would have moved if Karl had
taken up the reins. I said yes, with twelve divisions in a

week. Had I seen Skoda? I said no, but General Husak
had asked me to go there to see the ten-year programme
which the Germans had planned for it. From what C.
tells me, it is a pity that I did not go. The French are
trying to civilianise it to prevent it from competing with
Creusot. Perhaps this is what Husak wanted me to realise.
I do not blame the French after what we suffered from the
Krupp dominance in Europe. C. says that Husak and Mittelhauser are sure to quarrel soon.

Went to see the Vienna Emergency Relief Fund people.
They are still feeding 60,000 children under six in their
homes. They have spent half a million. The Americans
are feeding 300,000 over six in special buildings. We are
closing down in May. It has been a creditable work and
Cunninghame has been managing it. The Americans and
the Quakers are still carrying on. Walked through the
Hofburg. Impressive but deserted. The double Eagle
remains on the Palace here. At Prague it is being removed.
Walked round the main streets. I met Count Albert
Mensdorff and asked him to lunch to-morrow. He was
looking very much older, but seven years have no doubt
altered us all, and such years! Macartney dined with me
and we talked Europe. All accounts here accord that
Vienna is looking up. The wages have so increased that the
people can buy enough food. Sour brown bread to-day, no
butter nor milk. Hot baths only three days a week.
Vienna shops show all their old attractions and the people
in this part of the town — the Innere Stadt — look bright
and well off. C. says that it is the same thing in the
suburbs. He says that he does not know one factory here
that was not kept going throughout the war. A Vienna
Jew called Baron Heitzes, who is now a Pole, paid twenty-
three million kronen and two millions tax for a writing-
table of Napoleon's at a sale here the other day. C. and I
had a good talk of Greek and Czech politics to-day. I
don't gather that I shall find much to interest me at
Vienna, but Hungary, C. says, is an extraordinarily
charming and attractive lunatic asylum. Wrote two arti-

cles for the *D. T.* on the Czechs and had a nice letter from Burnham.

Wednesday, April 6, 1921. Worked in the morning and took a stroll over the town. Count Mensdorff came to lunch and we had a long talk over the future of Austria, the origin of the war, the treatment and behaviour of the Bohemian nobility, Mensdorff's enemies, Kaiser Karl's frolic, and much else. I was very interested to discover that M.'s desire for Austria is an economic union with the small States round her, and not the *Anschluss* with Germany, which he strongly opposes. This is practically the policy of Benès. M. says that the old Austria came about, not from love marriages of the "tu felix Austria nube" type, but from business alliances to join neighbouring provinces which could not get on without each other. So it was now. These States all wanted each other, and all the same had raised all their idiotic boundaries and customs walls against each other. If the opinion is general, the task of Benès in Austria should be easy.

M. admitted that the condition of Vienna was improving. Men were working. It was only the poorly paid officers, officials and professors, clerks, and paid employés who were really badly off still. He was severe upon the Treaties, especially in the Tyrol, and said that the people ceded to Serbia and Roumania were badly treated and beaten. Everything, of course, had gone that he had cared for. He wishes that he had died before 1914. He would not talk much about the origin of the war, but declared that Tschirschky was a very bad influence at Vienna at the critical moment. He, M., was always sure that England would come in if Belgium were violated. This act he considered a vital error. He talked of X. X, he said, hated the Comtessen of Vienna who would not accept him in society. He hated the Catholics, the Hungarians, the Court, the Army, and the Jews. There was nothing else much left in Austria for him to hate or like. M. thought that Israel had won the war. They had made it, thrived on it, and profited by it. It was their supreme revenge on Christianity. He thought that the good management of their estates by the Bohemian nobles had saved Austria by providing food during the war. He did not think that confiscation would be carried very far, but said that as long as the sword of Damocles was suspended over them it was fatal for the estates. He is going to ask me to talk with some of the older Austrian statesmen still living. As for the accusations against him, he was away in Silesia with the hospitals when a Society of which he was President published an attack on England's treatment of the Austrian prisoners and put his name to the statement without his knowledge. He had protested when he heard of it and had withdrawn from the Society. He had done his best to refute the charge by letters to friends and the press in England, but only the *D. T.* had the fairness to print his letter. Recently the charge had come up again when he had been sent to Geneva, and he had written again to the *Neue Freie Presse.* As for Kaiser Karl, M. said that no one in Vienna or in Hungary knew of his intention, nor could now account for the indiscretion. He had heard, as I had, of other Pretenders, but said that Monarchists must necessarily be Legitimists, or must give away the most sacred principle of Monarchy. The German Kaiser was in a different position as he had renounced the throne. Mensdorff told me that he had frequently met Conrad von Hötzendorff during the war, and that the latter had told him that I was the only man in the enemy's press who understood the real situation. Dined with Sir T. Cunninghame and his cousin and had a pleasant talk about Austria and other affairs. I am thinking that there is little of interest here. But after all I have hardly begun to look yet.

Friday, April 8, 1921. Had a heavy day's work yesterday indoors, writing letters and finishing articles. Today began to see some authorities and first Baron Pitner, of the Wiener Bank Verein, to whom Mensdorff took me. A clear head and a broad mind. We talked of Austria's State finance, the means for putting it to rights, the feelings of Austria and Hungary, the animosity of Austria against the Czechs, etc., the antipathy of the country to Communism, the sentiments respecting the Habsburgs, the *Anschluss* and the causes that might bring it about — until at last we ran into the luncheon hour just as we were getting on to the special problem of Vienna, so I asked him to dine to-morrow to talk more.

Pitner is well-informed and in close touch with the Government, as befits a wise banker. He is a Monarchist. But he says that Karl is an unbalanced person who never does the right thing. As Kaiser he was as often changing his opinions as he was his counsellors. He was personally pleasant. The Army came home raging against him and against the Kaiserin, who was absurdly reported to have sold plans to the enemy! There was no feeling for him in Austria, and in Hungary only among the Christian Social-ists and the Centre Party. If there had been any strong feeling the people would have risen the other day when they found him at Budapest. P. admitted the justice of Mensdorff's plea about legitimacy in Monarchism, but said that it did not prevent a large number of the Jockey Club members being in favour of the Archduke Joseph who had been very Hungarian in his sympathies. Many people longed for a King back, but not for Karl. When the question arose, it would go to the League of Nations as a formal application from the people. It would not come from a *coup d'état*.

In the same way, though P. is against the *Anschluss* or union with Germany, he thinks it may come if all else fails. In this case some outlying province like Tyrol or Salzburg might apply to the League to join Germany, and then the others would follow if they saw no other way. The Austrians wished to remain Austrians, but they could not stand having to reply in soft words to Serb or Czech impertinences: they could not stand being bullied by those whom they had accounted an inferior race, and if it be-came a question of being trampled on they would rather share the process with sixty million other Germans than suffer it alone.

The real point was that Austria was not *viable*. It was true that she was better off now that reparations had been almost rescinded, and that people were beginning to work, but the exchange was going to nothing and unless she was put on her legs financially there would be a crash. There were three ways to do it: (1) by a loan from the Allies which was scarcely practicable in view of the Allies' own needs; (2) by an operation by a group of foreign bankers who might take the tobacco monopoly as a security now that this was out of pawn; and (3) by facilities given to Austria to raise a loan abroad. What was uncertain was the amount and the period of time for which the loan was needed, but he thought that sixty million sterling would put Austria on her legs again. They could not go round with a drum and beat up foreign bankers, and no bankers had come to them. I said that I thought there was a big future for a foreign bank in Central Europe, and that people did not yet seem to understand that there were assets to be offered as securities and a very fruitful field to cover. As things were, said P., it was Hugo Stinnes who had bought from Italian proprietors the Styrian iron mines near Leoben which were the biggest industry in Austria. The Italians had bought them cheap when Austria wanted money badly, and the latter had thrown away a great asset.

P. did not worry about the chance of Bolshevism in Austria. It might come to Vienna, but in this case the country districts would starve out Vienna. They hated Bolshevism, but did not want their Kaiser back. P. was in a conservative part of the country for Easter, and did not hear a word said for Karl when he made his *Putsch*. I threw out the Beneš scheme tentatively to see what P. would say about it. He thought it impossible, but as we discussed the needs, the ways, and the means, his opposition to it grew less. His argument that each little country hated the other so that it would not make a move did not convince me, and at last he admitted that the thing might come in fifty years.

He said that it was not realised in Europe that all the States of Austria had their Provincial Assemblies under the Empire and were therefore prepared for provincial rule. This had really come now, and the Provinces looked to their chief towns, and not to Vienna. Hungary had really always been independent while pretending not to be. She had behaved abominably to Austria during the war, having closed her frontiers and starved her. P. admitted that the old Empire was *viable* because it contained almost everything that its people wanted. Then open your frontiers in Central Europe and you will get back the old conditions, I said.

In the afternoon went to call on Dr. Schüller at the Austrian F.O. in the Ballhaus Platz. Walked through the Hofburg which seemed full of ghosts. Such magnificence and now no magnificos. Had what Colonel House would call a good gloom over the Ball Platz. The same old building with the grilles on the lower windows and the sedate air of the perfect lady! What schemes, what intrigues, what follies were born within those walls. Shade of Metternich, what has it all come to but the ruin of an Empire! Vanity of vanities!

Schüller was very friendly and helpful. We met at Franckenstein's table one day in London and he was prepared for my arrival. He will arrange for me to see the President and Dr. Mayr and the other people who can tell me what I want to know. He himself will also prepare some short papers on certain subjects not easily handled in conversation. I was interested to hear that the President's pay only amounted to eighty pounds a year in English money. S. said that Austria had 230,000 officials on her hands, but the figure was really deceptive, for about half of them ran the State monopolies and were really workmen and managers of business concerns. Out of the 125,000 remaining, only 35,000 would be classed by us as civil servants. Their wages were very low. He himself could not afford a new suit of clothes. Fortunately most of the present rulers were men in very modest circumstances before, so they felt it less, but out of twenty men in his branch at the F.O. four had left in the last two months because they did not get a living wage and had found something better.

We talked of Karl. S. says that Erdödy was his adviser. He was both wrong-headed and malicious. Karl had been told by everyone who came to Switzerland that Hungary was longing for him, and the Kaiserin no doubt thought Easter Sunday a lucky day. He had had reported to him some civil remarks by French officers to somebody and Karl had magnified this into French acquiescence with his action. One could not really get over the fact that Karl was a very stupid fellow. It was a pity that Dr. Gratz, the Hungarian Foreign Minister, had resigned, as he was a good man. S. much in favour of a big foreign bank in Central Europe. But it must be so arranged that there is no head office at Vienna and succursales in other little States or they would all rebel. They must all be on an equal footing. I said that I was struck by the great opening for business and the assets available. S. said that few people in Europe realised this. There was a vast volume of business of all sorts. Is it ignorance, or the supposed political instability of this part of the world, that chokes people off? I find Prague and Vienna more stable than revolutionary England just now. The accounts of the strike which began at home on the suitable date of April 1 are really heart-breaking, and I do not know how far it may not extend. It is the usual story of a revolutionary minority trying to secure by direct action that overturning of authority that cannot be obtained by a popular mandate. The very worst form of tyranny.

What a pleasant town Vienna is! With a saving clause for Dresden, it is the only really civilised city that I have seen since I left Paris. Fine buildings, broad streets, shops full of every kind of goods, nice civil people, pretty ladies and pretty frocks, a real upper middle class, and not at all a few of the old régime lot with all the old Austrian attractiveness and charm. Can any country afford to dispense with its governing class, and the traditions, taste, and tact of centuries of accumulated experience? I doubt it. There are too many things in life which books and board-schools can never teach.

Saturday, April 9, 1921. To most of us Austria is still Austria. How few of us realise that an Empire of 240,000 square miles has been reduced to 32,000 and a population of fifty-three million to six million! It had a seaboard and it is now land-locked, an army where now it has a Socialist guard. It had a currency of twenty-four crowns to the pound sterling and it is now twenty-five hundred to the pound. But this little rag remnant has still much of the culture and most of the pride of the old Empire.

The last election gave some eighty-four members of the Christian-Socialist Party divided into three groups of the Vienna intelligentsia, the peasants, and the intelligentsia of the provincial towns: the Social Democrats returned sixty-eight members, the Pan-German, twenty-six. The figure of the latter disproves the claim that the *Anschluss* was desired by the mass of the people at the time of the election. Dr. Heinisch is President, a colourless man they say and not a success. The Government is a more or less informal combination of the Christian Socialists and the Pan-Germans. Dr. Mayr, the P.M., is a peasant and school-master from Innsbrück. A Jewish name, but not a Jew. In these Tyrol districts the chief man on a farm was called Major from the Roman Majordomos. There are no Jews in the Centre or Christian-Socialist Party, though I fancy Dr. Grünberger, the Food Minister, must have a touch of Jew. The chief men of the Christian-Socialist Party are, except Mayr, not in the Government. Dr. Seidel, who is a priest, is practically chief of the party. Mataja is another influential member of it. Seidel and the Speaker practically issue orders to the Government. The Pan-Germans prefer the Christian Socialists to the Social Democrats, but no party has a clear majority. Being totally unable to rest their authority on ultimate appeal to force, the Government have a limited scope. There are two Houses,

No more than at Prague does Single-Chamber government smile upon practical republicans.

The idea has been given to me that the almost self-contained old Empire deliberately contrived to make each Province produce something different with a view to trouble when a break-up came. This is too far-fetched. Each Province produced its natural resources, and because they were part of a single Empire all could interchange them freely. Now one shuts out what another wants to give, and is itself shut out from giving what it has to give. Surely it only needs time for the policy of Benès to appeal to all.

I don't think that people in Austria are thinking in political terms. The *res angusta domi* makes everyone think of him or herself in economic terms. I am told that Austrians frequently say, well, anyhow we are by ourselves now, and need no more worry ourselves about what the Czechs, or Croats, or Magyars want. I am also told that the Entente Ministers here have been constantly feeding the Austrians with hope of material support which never materialises, and that Governments here have made their book on it.

Went to see M. Alexandropoulos, the Greek Minister, at 14 Allergasse, to see if he had any news of the Greek campaign. He has no more than has been in the press except reports of Turkish massacres and outrages which he read to me. I fancy that the Greeks have had a set-back. One can't wonder if they have. After the Conference where they were let down by England, and sold by the French and Italians, they should have retired on Smyrna, and waited. That was the correct policy and strategy. Now the King goes out next Wednesday.[1] Métaxas [2] is with him and three more classes have been called out. I have an idea that Harington will be feeling pretty uncomfortable now. All this thing hung together, and when the French made terms with Kemal the situation wholly changed, and the

---

[1] He did not go till June.
[2] General Métaxas refused to rejoin the King.

Greeks should have recognised it. A. says that no bulletins about Princess C. have been published for four days and we hope it means that she is better.

Sunday, April 10, 1921. The Supreme Council having transferred their responsibility for reorganising the finances of Austria to the League of Nations, the Financial Committee of the League will soon arrive here. Much private discussion of a possible basis. Will all the creditor Allied States forgo their claims on Austria's assets for a term of years, as Austen Chamberlain wisely proposed on March 17? This is not yet certain, except for the Great Powers, but it seems a vital preliminary move. There will then be some securities for loans, and the Greek pattern of International Financial Control seems to me a good model to copy.

A lovely warm, spring day, the first without the bitter wind for weeks past. Walked round the town. Whatever faults the Habsburgs may have had, they certainly made old Vienna into a very dignified capital of a great Empire from an architectural point of view. The spaciousness of it all, the broad boulevards, the uniformity of the architecture, in spite of the presence of many different styles, the magnificence of the public buildings, the worthy statues, the churches, opera, and theatres, the many great palaces of the old nobles, and the pervading sense of elegance and finish make a most impressive whole which no other capital on the Continent but Paris can rival. It is truly an Imperial City. The parks and boulevards were full of the middle class and common people to-day. The talk I heard chiefly of food, dress, and the krone. The Viennese are not "political animals" like the Greeks. I don't think that the majority bother their heads about it. Can this great city die, or be replaced by any other as the natural trysting place of Eastern Europe for pleasure or business? I doubt it. The equipment, enchantment, and apparel of a great capital are not so easily duplicated. Neither the music nor the finesse of Vienna can be transplanted, nor its peculiar business aptitudes and adaptability, nor yet its less reputable enchantments. Hither must always drift Czechs, Magyars, Serbs, Croats, Slovenes, Roumans, Ruthenes, Slovaks, Bulgars, and Turks. So I think. It is the Paris of Eastern Europe, irrepressible and irreplaceable. Some strong young people may one day march and sack it out of spite, for Austria to-day is like a crab that has shed its shell, but more likely it will enfold the victor and assimilate him. The culture and civilisation of Europe are hence disseminated *in partibus*, and perhaps as a passive resister to barbarism Vienna may shine more than as conqueror in the Habsburg panoply. It may be that Maria Theresa with the statesmen and generals, Eugen and the Archduke Charles, the poets and the musicians, must still look down regretfully from their plinths upon a terribly changed world. Vienna stands. Her soul has fled with the comtessen. The sword and the sceptre are broken. Vienna, if it is to reign still, must reign by the mind.

Monday, April 11, 1921. Am impressed by studying the Austrian papers. They seem detached and indifferent about foreign affairs, but are full of accounts of all sorts of new or extended industries springing up, and I counted twenty-three pages of commercial advertisements in Sunday's *Neue Freie Presse.* I read or hear of every kind of old industry being extended and of some new one opened. New machinery is being employed, and on the farms prize stock are being bought and farm buildings improved by the rich peasants who throve on the war. From Upper and Lower Austria, Styria, and the Tyrol, it is all the same story of new developments, and what is really going on is an endeavour to make the new Austria less dependent on her neighbours and less forced to buy abroad in markets made fearfully dear by the exchange. I do not wonder that Benès contemplates a hasty change in his protectionist policy. He will lose his Austrian customers if he does not hurry up!

Had long talk to-day with Police President Schober,[1] a very wise old Austrian, and with Hofrat Dr. Friedrich

---

[1] He afterwards became Chancellor.

Hertz in the Bunderskanzleramt. The latter is largely charged with economic duties. I found them both strangely in line with the Benès policy for Central Europe. Schober is a charming character and a regular Austrian of the old type, and Hertz a convinced Republican of a moderate type, but they were quite in accord on the general economic aim of Free Trade and open frontiers. The real difficulty is the obstruction of the Austrian Provinces separately. They have tried not to let anything in the way of food go to Vienna, and in fact are little stuck-up feudatories who almost levy taxes on their own account and generally make themselves an infernal nuisance. How, Dr. Benès, will you unite seven little States in an economic unity, if in each of these seven little States there are a packet of little statelets trying to run an economic policy of their own?

I find a general accord that Austria wants about sixty millions sterling to put her State finance on its legs again, but I have not yet found the bases of the calculation. I find that Vienna's improvement in food conditions is in some small part due to the fact that there are 80,000 allotment holders in the environs. This practically means that the eight-hour day is extended to twelve and so balances the loss. Quite a good remedy when it can be used. For the industrial State the allotment is the best agrarian reform. A man will work while there is any light to cultivate his own patch. There are also 100,000 men who want to convert the Tiergarten into allotments and work on them. I am becoming convinced that there is nothing for it but free trade within the old Austrian boundaries. Selfishness and obstinacy may prolong the settlement, but it must come, and each State will have to wallop its own provincial nigger who won't play the game. There are so few great properties here that the Czech agrarian legislation is not copied, but the commandeering of houses is. It is carried to such lengths, and fixity of tenure is so secure, that, as rents may not be raised, the prospective house builder is frozen out, while house properties for want of adequate rents slowly deteriorate generally. People think that the Socialists have quite come down off their perches. They find their theories impracticable. They know it, and can't afford to admit it. They are very mild now. As for the Communists, they only polled one-half per cent at the late election, and have not one member in Parliament. I find that two-thirds of the Austrian deficit is due to food subsidies, chiefly bread. A loaf of 1260 grammes is now sold for nine kronen, but costs sixty kronen to the State. Even a Rothschild is paid therefore fifty-one kronen by the State for every loaf he eats. It would be better to stop the subsidies even if salaries and wages were raised proportionately. The price of nine kronen is merely that of baking and distributing the bread.

Tuesday, April 12, 1921. Went to the F.O. in the morning. Schüller gave me a typed statement by the office on Austrian foreign policy. It had been seen, very slightly altered, and approved by Dr. Mayr, the Chancellor and Foreign Minister. It came to this, that Austria's foreign policy was mainly economic and that food and work for their people were the aim. It said that no people had been hit so hard as Austria by the Peace. Scarcity of coal is strongly commented upon and the absolute need of foreign credits, the critical situation arising from the need of them being pointed out. It says that an economic union of the Succession States cannot be thought of, but that Austria is ready for normal commercial intercourse, as before the war. Sent it off without comment to the *D. T.*

I saw the President of the Federation, Dr. Heinisch, to-day at the Ball Platz. A tall, dignified man of some sixty-five years with a good presence. Also with a beard. We talked in Metternich's old working room. I told him why I had come and we had nearly an hour's talk on politics and finance, food supplies, farming, and kindred subjects. He was very pleasant and shrewd, especially on agricultural subjects and finance on which he is an acknowledged authority. Writing at the close of a day when I have had talks with many people, I cannot recall that he told me anything particularly striking except that the Swiss cattle did best in Austria; that he produced good flour, but that his baker turned it into sour bread by a bad mixture of barley and maize; that he had no oven to do his own baking; that whereas Vienna used to get 600,000 litres of milk a day she now only gets 70,000. We have to remember that half of the Austrian soil is given up to Alpine farming, and only twenty-three per cent bears wheat, while the remainder is forest or unproductive. He did not throw much fresh light on the questions of Central European politics or of finance, but hoped that the League might act quickly about finance. He struck me as a good, steady, and rather slow man of calm mind and moderate views who would neither commit follies nor set the Danube on fire.

Afterwards I saw the Chancellor, as he is called, alias the Prime and Foreign Minister, Dr. Mayr, who was suffering from neuralgia. A good, clear-headed man who took care that I should realise the position of the Government in the *Anschluss* question. There is to be a plébiscite in the Tyrol on the 28th on the question of uniting with Germany and perhaps in Styria and some other provinces in May. The Government do not want the plébiscite, but the Pan-Germans do, and as the Government owes its life to the support of the Pan-Germans, it cannot stop an *Anschluss* plébiscite, as this is the main plank of the Pan-German Party. A German majority of anything from sixty to ninety per cent is expected. But Mayr said that it would only be platonic and would mean nothing. The attitude of the Government was regulated by the Treaty of St. Germain, and Mayr said that he had quite agreed with Curzon when the latter had told him in London that the question of Austria joining Germany was not one for Austria to decide. I discussed the Benès plan with Mayr and found him entirely in favour of free trade between the Succession States, but he, like all others, flouted the idea of any political union, and all similarly agree that there is no pro-Habsburg sympathy in Austria just now. Even in Hungary yesterday a vote was passed approving of the Hungarian Government's action in their treatment of Karl, without one dissentient voice, which is almost amazing in such a fanatically monarchical country. Mayr had given such a clear account of Austrian taxation when he was in London that it was not necessary for me to reopen this question.

We talked for an hour round all the Austrian questions, and then I had a look at Metternich's portrait, apparently by Lawrence, who painted him several times. A fine figure and a good pendant to his colleague Castlereagh, I should imagine. Also went to look at the room where the Congress of Vienna sat. It is in the F.O., and has been left quite unchanged with the old chairs covered in yellow silk. The room and trappings white and gold. Some large lustres and mirrors. The long table would take about thirty-six people. Not a very big room, but a pleasant one. All the old Habsburg furniture and pictures remain in the F.O. It is like the home of a county magnate who has nothing left but *meubles*.

Dr. Schüller very helpful again to-day. I went with him into the main figures of debt and food. With a revenue of twenty-eight milliards Austrian crowns there is an expenditure of sixty-eight milliards, or a deficit of forty milliards. There is an uncovered note issue of forty milliards. The large deficit in proportion to revenue is due to the depreciation of the exchange. The total amount of cereals required annually to feed the people is about 900,000 tons. Of this amount the farmers contribute 100,000 tons nominally, or one-quarter their crop at a price of twenty kronen for a hundred kilograms, which is half its value. The peasants use perhaps 300,000 to feed themselves and their men, and have about 100,000 tons to sell freely. The balance of 500,000 tons comes from the United States, the Argentine, and Jugo-Slavia. The population of Vienna by the census of 1920 was 1,841,326, of whom 851,302 were men. Of these 975,904 were engaged in industry, trade, traffic, agriculture, liberal professions, and public and domestic service.

Motored out to Schönbrunn. I suppose the only Palace extant with 1441 rooms and 139 kitchens. Quite hideous, huge, gaunt, and bare, painted a horrible yellow colour and with no view. A formal French palace garden, with radiating broad walks, clipped tree hedges, sculptures, fountains, etc. Very little turf. The walks now all a dreary grey gravel. The only decent thing in the garden is the Neptune fountain. A most depressing country house, quite apart from the bill from 139 kitchens. Who would be a Kaiser and live in such sterile, uncomfortable, and pretentious grandeur? Not surprised that the poor little Duc de Reichstadt died there. The only wonder is that he lived there.

Looked in at some churches. St. Stephen's a great Gothic masterpiece, and the Votive Church a most attractive modern Gothic jewel, but too dark inside. Went to have a dish of tea with Baron Pitner and there met Herr Metaya, one of the leading agents of the Christian-Socialist Party. A long talk over Austrian affairs. The Baroness came in later. A pretty and pleasant woman. P. says that the old régime still talk as if one could order a regiment out of barracks, and maintain order, but the 25,000 or so of the *Volkswehr* were strongly infected with Socialism and had no offensive value, as most of the officers and N.C.O.'s would go one way and most of the men the other. They had put in a man to try and reform this body, but he had not succeeded. The Government could not really count on force as every Government should be able to do. The best force they had was the six thousand Vienna police, but it was not strong enough to suppress large movements. In the Provinces the gendarmes were pretty good. In the Provinces the old double government of the Central Government and of the Province still *de facto* continued, though the Landeshauptmann and the Statthalter had been united in one person. Metaya made a point of the immense numbers of persons who had been thrown out of their work by the recent upheaval. All agree that Vienna must remain the chief business centre of Eastern Europe.

It has all the plant and the knowledge, besides still great resources, and I think that the banks are doing a great business. The mere game of money-changing for the needs of foreigners here is a profitable business, aided, of course, by the separate currency of each State.

Austria became an economic entity in 1775 long before the Zollverein in Germany. It was within the Empire that Austria built up her industry, and this business prevented her distance from the sea proving a serious hindrance. It is the obstacles to such internal trade that are really impeding Austria now, combined, of course, with the dispersal of her old resources among the Succession States. She is cut off from the sea, has only one-half per cent of her old coal assets, and is hedged in by tariff barriers. The debasement of the currency make it almost impracticable to buy in England except at prohibitive prices. There has resulted some political as well as economic prostration and the Provinces of new Austria herself, always enjoying a large share of local Government, have become even more independent of Vienna, a movement fortified by the natural antagonism of the country and the towns which has been one of the prominent features of modern political developments. The international popularity of Vienna, far from helping her at first in her material difficulties, rather had the contrary effect, since it exasperated the Succession States who were so jealous of Vienna. Vienna is perhaps safe because the Succession States could not bear to see one of their number aggrandise herself by taking this great centre of attraction.

I was told to-day, either by the President or by the Chancellor, that England, France, Italy, and almost certainly America would waive their rights to reparation and that Czecho-Slovakia and Roumania would probably concur. This will remove one great obstacle in the way of foreign investment here, for there will be assets as security for loans.

I thought it strange to-day while examining the portraits at the Ball Platz to observe that nearly all the Austrian Foreign Ministers since Metternich, except Haymerlé and Aehrenthal, had been Hungarians, Poles, Slavs, and anybody but Germans. Berchtold and Forgach were both Hungarian, though the former has property in Moravia. From the accounts I get of him here, he must have been a frivolous boulevardier without any sense of responsibility. He never seemed, after he fell, to have displayed the slightest realisation of the odious part that he played in July, 1914, and though he had intelligence he had no character and was a mere tool for more active intriguers. He is said now to live the same life of frivolity in Switzerland. It must also be said that the Habsburgs kept foreign politics and the Army out of the hands of parliaments and the public altogether, and that the Austrian people had little share in the responsibility for the war. Tisza, as we know now, was strongly against war at first.

Wednesday, April 13, 1921. I think that the Anglo-American Relief Mission of the Society of Friends have done a great work here. One of their wisest acts has been to buy, and to help Vienna to buy, Swiss and Dutch cows. The President told me that the staff are most capable and well-informed. When the Vienna *mölkerei* increases its single boiler and its one hundred and sixty-eight employés to the pre-war eight hundred employés and eight boilers stoked day and night, and gets back its other admirable arrangements, one of the most baleful hardships of the present time will be removed. I wonder how the Reparation Commission dare ask Austria to deliver all those eight thousand cows to the Succession States and Italy!

I fear it must be said that owing to want of many articles of food and high prices of other articles, the people of Vienna are still badly off. The pawnshops do a thriving trade. Perhaps exploitation of the gold in the High Tauern of the Austrian Eastern Alps, which might yield three thousand kilos of pure gold a year, will be one of the attractive investments of the future.

In the afternoon Mensdorff called for me and took me to the official residence of the former P.M. Baron Beck whose wife gave us tea. There was a little circle of the *ancien régime* including Baron Plener, frequently Minister, Count Colloredo, the President of Police Schober, an Austrian Ambassador formerly at Washington, Spitzmüller, the Governor of the Austro-Hungarian Bank, etc. We had a good talk of affairs and they were all very interesting. On the whole it is thought that the ruin of Austria is in full swing, since there is no authority except Schober's, no one to say no to anybody, and blocks of people had only to demand more pay or wages and there was no one to resist them. So the thaw of orderly administration had set in. Baron Beck said that in the old days, when one rang up the Statthalter of a Province from the Chancellor's office, an order was given and was executed. Now they might ring up from Herrengasse 7, but the Provinces did as they liked. Even the new Vienna Province at No. 10 in the same street. They thought that the workmen were now swimming in money, but the upper classes had mostly left Vienna, as they could not afford to live there, while the middle classes were badly off too.

Mensdorff says that there are never more than two or three people whom he knows at the opera or theatre, and the old names on the boxes and at the race meetings have disappeared. Vienna is given up to profiteers and foreigners. The old glory has departed. There is neither fashion, taste, nor elegance. It is the end of a period. A famous demi-mondaine here had apologised to one of the old lot for taking up with the new side, but said that she could not afford the luxury of her old friends, as she could not reduce her standard of living! Much sarcasm about the Treaty of St. Germain, and it was supposed that the people there had been deceived by the names of the Austro-Hungarian Bank and had supposed that it was a Government establishment, whereas it was only a private bank with certain privileges just like the Bank of England, and utterly unbearable burdens had been thrown upon it. It was in liquidation. Sir W. Goode's proposal had been turned down. If the League of Nations proposed an internal loan it would

not succeed. Everybody very despondent about the future,
but I expected nothing else among the old Imperial set.

So there it is. Europe's failure.

Thursday, April 14, 1921. Had intended to go to Budapest by the Danube to-day, but stayed to see Sir W. Goode,
who is at the Bristol, suffering like others from 'flu and
throat brought on us all by the extraordinary season, dust,
and chilly winds. He impressed me favourably in spite of
the criticisms I had heard of him in London. He told me
that L. G., his own P.M., had turned him down in Paris.
Curzon had made a good speech leading up to Goode's conclusions and suggestions, when L. G. had butted in and had
made the famous *gaffe* about not caring whether Austria
went to Germany or not. The French papers had got hold
of it at once, and as usual had spread it abroad to diminish
our prestige in Europe. Goode thought that when L. G.
was immersed in home affairs, he had no patience with
foreign problems and would not listen to anything. I have
no doubt myself that the general conclusions of the Reparations Commission dealing with Austria were the correct
ones. Sforza asked whether L. G. wanted Germany on the
Italian frontier, and Crowe said that the only thing left for
Austria was a first-class funeral.

Goode showed me the last figures of Austrian expenditure on the bread subsidies. They are *monthly* 2,762,000-
000 kronen for food generally including 2,300,000,000
kronen for cereals. This is really what is sinking Austria. It is still true that Austria cannot exist without
external assistance, but that if she were tided over the
next five years and internal reconstruction effected she
might become self-supporting. A foreign loan of sixty
millions sterling, the control of Austrian public finance,
the foundation of a privileged bank of issue, and the fund-
ing of the services of the Austrian foreign debt are among
Goode's proposals on the financial side, but it has all been
turned down, and the League financial people seem to be
coming here with a brand-new plan which Goode fancies
no practical banker will look at. He says that Barclays'

believe in the financial rehabilitation of Austria, but with
L. G. omnipotent nothing can be done. Caught the 2 P.M.
train to Pesth. Where we struck the Danube it was some
two hundred to four hundred yards wide, not blue, but
steely grey. Reached Budapest latish. Major Lyons met
me kindly. My room in the Hungaria faces the river. A
beautiful sight when the moon rose and all the lights
twinkled on the heights beyond the river. Dined at the
hotel and made the Maître d'Hôtel give me the local
gossip and tell me who was here.

CHAPTER VII

THE SORROWS OF HUNGARY

Budapest — The British High Commission — Lord Bertie's correspondence — Major-General Gorton — A new Hungarian Government — Hungary's losses — A waiting policy — The Archduke Joseph — "The Royal Hungarian Government" — Accusations against Roumania — Situation of the Danube Navigation Company — The Mannheim-Regensburg Canal — The Danube Commission — Agricultural statistics — Two good diplomatic stories — Count Bethlen announces his policy in Parliament — Count Julius Andrassy — M. Czabo — Prince Windischgrätz — M. de Barczy — The scene in Parliament — Hungary and the Roumanians — A conversation with Count Banffy, Foreign Minister — His definition of the Government — The crown of St. Stephen — A Protectorate — Cromwell and Horthy — Tales of the refugees — A conversation with Count Albert Apponyi — The outlook of people changed — Apponyi at the Peace Conference — Confidence in English justice — M. Hegedüs, Finance Minister, expounds to me his great programme — Colonel Alfred Stead — A tour round Lake Balaton — The country and the crops — Vienna — A party at Sir William Goode's hotel — Foreigners and night life at Vienna — Police President Schober's opinion — Mr. Walker D. Hines — Return to Paris.

Budapest, Friday, April 15, 1921. The Danube is a nobler river than the Moldau, but Budapest has a strong resemblance to Prague, with its heights and palaces on one bank and the lower part of the town on the other. Went up to our Legation. Hohler has been and still is seriously ill with 'flu and bronchitis. Saw Athelstan-Johnson, the First Secretary, and looked over the Legation — I beg its pardon, the Headquarters of the British High Commission [1] — which has a beautiful view over the river from the heights close to the old cathedral. Very comparable with Sir G. Clerk's view from his terrace over Prague, but the Legation here is much smaller. A charming place of an old-world type with arched and vaulted roofs and an inner court. Left a card and note on Count Albert Apponyi who is away. Lunched with A.-J. in his house and we discussed European politics. He thinks that the old nobles party here is losing ground, and that the various countries round hate each other too much to combine. He would approve of the final

---

[1] The Treaty of Trianon had not yet been ratified.

break-up of Austria, part going to Czechs and Serbs and part to Germany and Hungary. I said that I did not see the continued existence of Czecho-Slovakia on these terms and that Italy would not like Germany on her borders.

He told me that Lord Bertie's correspondence was lodged at Welbeck in two strong boxes and that it would not be published for fifty years. I asked if it included the private letters written to the F.O. and were they not very Rabelaisian? Yes, he said they were. Bertie had copies of them all, for he was a bureaucrat and had kept everything. I grumbled because we should never see these gems. A.-J. said that they were a most faithful and accurate representation of Bertie's time in Paris during the war.

Went on to see Brigadier-General Gorton, my old friend of past Intelligence days, now at the head of our Military Mission here. The French press seems to be quite off the rails in belittling the Little Entente and in boosting a Karl Kingdom here and in Austria. I am amazed that they seem quite off the Czechs. The Frenchmen ought to travel a bit and they would see how the land lay. I saw Mr. Barber of our Commercial Branch, Mr. Humphreys being away, and am to come in and gain a little trade wisdom from him to-morrow. Went to the opera with the Gortons at 6 P.M. A good house and a competent orchestra. "The Evening Star," by Meyerbeer. I have never heard it before. Very well done. Went on afterwards to dine at about 9.15 with the Gortons and General Bellini, the Italian Military Commissioner, and his wife. I asked the Italian General whether Italy's natural frontier on the Alps appeared to him worth the passing over of the Tyrol to Germany, as seemed to me likely to happen eventually. He thought it was worth even having Germany on the border for Italy to gain the natural frontier. Doubt whether Sforza will agree with this opinion. Am afraid that our own people at home are too much immersed in their Martha-like worries to understand where all this affair is leading. The abandonment of Austria is the beginning of a great future disturbance which will entail the ruin of the Benès scheme and of

Czecho-Slovakia, and the eventual spread of German dominion over not only Austria, but Hungary, which is too hard beset by Roumanians and Jugo-Slavs not to seek refuge in a German, or in fact in any combination which is against the Roumanians.

Saturday, April 16, 1921. A Hungarian Cabinet crisis which followed the Karl *Putsch* has resulted in the retirement of Dr. Gratz from the F.O. here and his replacement by Count Banffy. Count Stefan Bethlen, aged about forty-eight, becomes Ministerpräsident, or P.M. I am told that one effect of recent losses of territory by Hungary has been to leave about fifty per cent of the present population Protestant with some affinity to the Wee Frees. This accounts for the visit of the American and English Unitarians to Transylvania last autumn. The Magyars had shrieked about their treatment by the Roumanians. The parsons after a three months' tour gave the Roumanians a rare dressing-down, and said that it was like placing Mexicans over two million Americans. Had an innings with Mr. Barber about trade and commerce. He gave me some interesting and relevant facts. I never realised before that Hungary was now only one-third her former size and population; had lost all her mines, iron ore, forests, half of her coal, headwaters, etc., and was reduced to the status of a large farm. Albert Apponyi recommends a waiting policy, sure that the peace is untenable, but also that no basis exists yet for modification. In fact — *pensons-y toujours!* Quite sound. Colonel Alfred Stead is specialising here in films, oil, river transport, banks, and other speculations. I have a suspicion that the clauses about Danube navigation are the most sensible things in the Peace Treaties. They are the only things not demonstratively cursed by everybody. I must look into them. I am told that the Hungarians secretly do a night's drill a week. They can place 70,000 men in the field, but of course one cannot neglect their old war-trained veterans whom Gorton puts at 800,000 men. Pesth very full of officers in uniform. Not quite the old aristocratic-looking lot. Expect they are all pretty hard hit. Ministers here get the equivalent of thirty-six pounds a year.

Motored with Gorton up to the golf course on the Downs behind Buda. Fine air and views and a perfect mass of wild flowers of all sorts. The Gortons dined with me. He told me that the Archduke Joseph stayed on here all through the Bela Kun Bolshevist régime and called himself Joseph Anschut from the name of his country house. Joseph a regular Magyar and speaks the lingo. He is forty-eight. He means to call himself Lorraine instead of Habsburg as he is entitled to do by his descent from Maria Theresa. It would evade the proscription of the Habsburg, but Gorton tells him that the Allies might see through the plan. He is a tiptop shot and a fine sportsman. The Hungarian Habsburgs seem to have been little in touch with F. J.'s crowd. When F. J. came here he stayed with the Andrassys, etc. When Karl came here to be crowned he scarcely left his railway train. G. says that the reverence of the people is not for an individual, but for the sacred crown of St. Stephen. Last night at the opera the Archduchess occupied the Royal Box. Met the American Military Attaché Enslen and his wife. Nice people. One thing I must say for F. J. He was the greatest builder of towns in modern history. History will admit it if we do not.

Sunday, April 17, 1921. Wrote on Austria; then lunched with Mr. Davidson, of the *Chronicle*, and Mr. Dicker, of the *Chicago Daily News*. They have been about in this part of the world all the winter and were interesting. We are all agreed that the opening-up of all frontiers of the old Dual Monarchy is the only economic salvation for Austria and the Succession States. We walked down to St. Margaret's Island and had tea there. Athelstan-Johnson dined with me in the evening and we had a good chat and wrangle over Central European affairs. A capable man with strong and decided views.

Ex-Kaiser Karl is still King of Hungary and has never abdicated in this capacity. The Government is still the "Royal Hungarian Government" and uses the Royal

Crown on its official paper which I have examined in order to make sure. The Governor Admiral Horthy is a kind of Protector. In fact he is Regent. All who swore allegiance to Karl and the sacred crown of St. Stephen still adhere to him. If they did not — and some were away — they consider themselves free agents. The mass of the people are Monarchists, but do not want the King back just yet. Quite a number would like to elect a King. Joseph is much liked, but they say that there are other reasons why not many like to plunge in that direction. Albrecht is talked of as a substitute. He is very rich, whereas poor Karl is said to be very broke. Still I would back Karl from belief in the "*moriamur pro rege nostro*" 1741 sentiment of a loyal peasant people, and because one cannot get over the fact that he has been crowned. Why are my friends in Vienna, Mensdorff apart, backing Joseph? Why does not Austria like or wish for Karl? Is it from jealousy of Hungary? Perhaps it is all of scant practical import because all feel that the matter is not urgent. There is a King to be had if the people want one, but Karl is not a great figure, and he has done little to make Austria stand up for him, while in Hungary many think that there is a period like our Commonwealth to be got over before a Restoration. There is so much else to be done first! All the same the Hungarians seem to be so deeply incensed against Roumania, which now bullies two million Magyars in Transylvania, that they will join any combination against her which promises success, and they might want a King then.

I don't much care for all the reports here against Roumania. She is said to be rotten, everybody bribed, no governing personnel fit to run her new territory, railways hopeless for military and commercial uses, etc., and altogether a very sorry story of graft, incompetence, and peculation. Not good when Germany must have such a grudge against her and the Hungarians are always ready for any mischief on her borders.

It is also very enlightening to study here the new map of Hungary and to size up her losses under the Trianon

Treaty. Especially to note that all the headwaters of her rivers are cut off from her to the north and east and the foresters in the north unable now to float down their logs to Budapest. One peasant of Tlemcen was asked how he got on under the Czechs. He said that when the Vag ran to Prague upstream instead of to Budapest, it might be all right. Population, mines, forests, salt, iron, the grain of the Banat, and much more all taken away. A peace of justice? How can the Magyars think it?

Monday, April 18, 1921. The *Corriere* correspondent here came to talk. Lunched with Captain Thomas Domaille in charge here of the Danube Navigation Company, run by Furness's house in London, chiefly by Sir F. Lewis, and by Cox's Bank through Eric Hambro. The Fleet consists of the D.D.O.G. (Austrian) and M.F.T.R. (Hungarian) fleets on the river, of which fifty per cent were annexed by Roumania and Serbia, who say that Paris can decide what they like about the ships, but they are not going to give them back. The fifty per cent remaining, now the Company's, include fifty-six steamers, sixty-eight tugs, seven hundred barges, and eleven motor barges with a total personnel of some six thousand people. D. is keen about taking over and improving the Mannheim-Regensburg Canal. This is little used now, and only three feet deep, but a million would make it fit to take the D.N. Company's barges, and they could then ascend the Rhine and pass by the Canal to the Danube and deliver a ton of steel at Budapest at twenty-seven shillings a ton. The other way costs forty-five shillings a ton up from Galatz alone. It is energetic of England to have got hold of the Company, but I doubt that it more than barely pays its way yet. The Regensburg scheme offers great possibilities. A great fault in the International control of the Danube is that one set of men look after the actual navigation, and another after dams and agriculture. It is a fault because everything done to the banks, etc., affects navigation, rate of current, fall of water, and so on. The Danube is a five-knot stream; the Rhine, they affirm, only one to one and one-half knots.[1] So it is much easier to ascend or tug up the Rhine than the Danube. I doubt whether the Danube Commission in Paris is much good. The riparian States play tricks as they please.

Spent the afternoon in studying agricultural facts and statistics. Much hampered by want of figures since the Peace; all statistics are for the old Hungary. The Alföld, the great Hungarian basin or lowlands, has lost all its timber by the recent partition; i.e., about six and a half million hectares out of seven and a half; much of its live-stock and its fodder, twenty-four per cent of its horned cattle, thirty per cent of its sheep, and forty per cent of its horses, half of its coal supplies, and 128,000,000 out of 144,000,000 of tons of its iron ore. All its salt supplies are gone, all its gold, silver, lead, copper, zinc, quicksilver, antimony, cobalt, nickel, and aluminium mines, and its natural gas. The splitting-up of a hydrographically united economic whole is especially fatal to Hungary. The problem of water power will now be difficult of solution, and irrigation most precarious. The sources of energy and the reservoirs should be, and now are not, in the same hands as the territory to be watered. The new arrangement is like handing over the Assuan Dam to the dervishes. The Vag (Waag), Tisza, and Maros can only carry their timber to the timberless Lowlands, and are not allowed to do so now. The tobacco factories and sugar refineries in the mountains will also languish, as their raw materials come from the Lowlands. The appeal of the Hungarian Geographical Society to the world is, to my mind, one of the strongest arguments against the recent so-called settlement. But what settlement, here or elsewhere, was ever made but by force?

The chief agricultural products of Hungary are wheat, rye, oats, and spring barley. Potatoes are widely grown, and clover and lucerne among the fodder plants. Wheat is the chief product of the Alföld. Maize is a big crop. So

---

[1] Quite incorrect. The Rhine stream between Mainz and Coblenz is at least eight knots an hour.

is sugar beet. That remarkable publication, the *Magyar-orszag Gazdasagi Terkepekben*, or *Economics of Hungary* (1920), shows in a series of maps in the most striking manner the loss to Hungary by the settlement in every class of crop and industry. It is painful reading. I wonder if the victors at Paris will allocate those forty million saplings to the afforestation of the barren tracts that the Hungarians used to do. What will happen to the Forestry High School at Selmeczbanya? I wonder how the extensive irrigation system will get on when it has been broken into by the new boundaries. But the more one looks round one in this part of the world, the more one wonders and at last one ceases to wonder, for one's capacity for wonder becomes exhausted. Don't know whether the world has been made safe for democracy, but am sure that democracy has shown itself unsafe for the Austro-Hungarian world.

I have seen figures which show that large estates under the intensive farming system, compared with the small estates, often produce double the crops. Deep steam ploughing in the autumn, frequent hoeing, good manuring, a proper rotation of crops, adequate capital (sometimes), and efficient management are the main causes. Many of these large estates will soon [pass into the hands of the small farmers under the Agricultural Reform Act, so it is unsafe to speculate on the results.

Nemesis is evidently reaching the selfish Succession States too. I hear on all sides that they are losing by their protectionist tariffs.

Two good stories at dinner to-night. One, the receipt of a letter by the Hungarian Government from the League of Nations requesting them to establish a sanitary cordon on the Polish frontier to prevent the spread of typhus. The fact that there is no such frontier is not yet known at Geneva. The other, an F.O. letter refusing to send petrol to Budapest, but saying that a lorry would be sent out via Trieste and that it could travel backwards and forwards from Budapest to Bucharest for supplies which, they believed, were available there. A rough calculation showed that the journey to Bucharest and back was one thousand miles or nearly as far as from Budapest to London. I wished that Henry Labouchere had been alive and in diplomacy here to answer that letter. He would have made the F.O. squirm.

Tuesday, April 19, 1921. Went off to the Parliament to hear Count Stefan Bethlen announce the new Government's policy. A huge and uncommonly late Gothic pile, the central part with a dome too narrow at the base. Fine and most well-arranged inside. Had a front seat in the diplomatic box. Three tiers of public galleries, quite full, except behind the Presidential Chair where there is only one [tier all round the house. I should say some two thousand of the public could find places. The horseshoe system of talking-shop with tribune and president's desk. The Ministers sat in the front row of the horseshoe facing the tribune. Good light and air. Bethlen was speaking when I arrived and he spoke for about an hour. His wife, an attractive lady, in a gallery on my left. B. rather like Lord Lansdowne twenty years ago. He spoke clearly, his notes in his left hand, and using the other for gestures, mainly up and down as if he were hammering in nails. A strong Calvinist, without the agile flexibility of Teleki, and wanting in the sense of humour. Captain Rapaics, the High Commission liaison officer, translated for me when there were important points in the speech. The chief things seemed to be that the whole Parliament was in unison, that it would take three years to carry out the legislation already proposed, that the question of a King was not yet safe to discuss, and so forth, ending up with a quotation from Lord Salisbury about strong and weak nations.

I saw the P.M. in his private room after his speech, and afterwards saw Count Andrassy, Count Albert Apponyi, Mr. Czabo, the head of the Small Holders' Party, Prince Windischgrätz, Count Pallavicini, Mr. de Barczy, and several others, and had good talks with them all. I liked the look of the members. They resemble what our House of Commons used to be twenty-five years ago. I asked them how it was they managed to get such a nice lot of members out of universal suffrage, and they said that formerly Budapest had sent its carpet-baggers round to be elected, but that Bela Kun's Bolshevist rule had so disgusted the people that they had all elected their own natural chiefs locally. I liked Bethlen. He is going to give me a paper for publication with his views. We had a brief talk of affairs. Czabo farms thirty-five acres. He does not talk any language but Hungarian, though I believe he reads French. We had a little talk through de Barczy, who has the curious post of sort of permanent secretary to Prime Ministers, and is a sort of Chief Whip as well. A young man, alert, and capable. Czabo is a good peasant type, squarely built, medium height. Wearing high boots to the knee, crinkly at the top. He controls the largest party in the house, namely, the Small Holders' Party, which has some eighty-six members. We had some talk of the agricultural and irrigational consequences of the Peace Treaty. He is Minister of Agriculture. He is popular, though Pallavicini grumbles that he is a trifle Bolshie.

Count Julius Andrassy is getting on in years now, but these Magyars wear well, and both he and Count Albert Apponyi, who is seventy-five, are very spare, hale, and hearty. Andrassy is an interesting figure. He told me how he had always loved and admired England, and how deeply disappointed he and others had been that England had deserted her old principles and had put her name to such an act of injustice as the Trianon Treaty. Hungary had never hated England all through the war; since the Peace her sentiments had changed, but it was not the England that Hungary used to know that had made the Peace. Windischgrätz told me that it was his grandfather who had made the famous remark that "no one counts below the rank of a baron." It seems to be the other way about now.

Bethlen was well received by all the House. They seem a very united Parliament. I am found fault with when I call them conservative. I can believe that they often get too excited and interruptious. The House was built for a larger body than the present members. They used to be 413 and now are little over 200. The number of empty benches is a perpetual reminder of Hungary's loss. The House of Magnates still exists to the north of the Parliament House, but is not in being. Feeling is more or less liberal when not quite democratic, I am told, and the continuance of a House of Lords is regarded as an anachronism. But a Second House or Senate is to be created, probably on a basis of county representation. Many are for proportional representation in order to secure the middle classes adequate voice in affairs. The Houses suspended the sitting for about a quarter of an hour when Bethlen sat down, and then I had a talk with him on the general results of the Treaty, but he was soon called back to the House. I did not see Kovacs who is said to be the brain of the Farmers' Party. All these figures might easily be duplicated by members of our House of Commons. They all talk English except the peasants. The Magyars have marched with the times, but it is odd to find a Windischgrätz an advanced radical! Generally speaking, the oldest noble families are losing ground somewhat, and it is the Bethlens and the Telekis who are coming to the front. A critical, interested, and very attentive House. Ditto the public in the galleries. Lunched with the Gortons; the Greek Minister and his English wife; the Roumanian Military Attaché and First Secretary; Mr. Athelstan-Johnson; Mr. Robinson, the English Consul here; the American Military Attaché and his wife, and a Spanish diplomatist. A nice garden on a terrace at the back of the house looking over the river.

I was amused to hear that the Roumanian Minister had not got a house yet, and that the Military Attaché had only a room some 2x2 metres for a bedroom and office. They had purchased a house, but the tenant refused to turn out, and it is most difficult to put one out under the present laws. The Magyars detest the Roumanians on account of their looting during the occupation following the Bela Kun régime. They rejoiced at their arrival, but the Roumanians really came in order to treat Hungary as they had been treated by Germany. They are accused of having stolen everything moveable — plate, pictures, carpets, linen, furniture, even down to the cloth off billiard tables. They took the best thoroughbreds and let them die in the train for want of food. They took twelve hundred locomotives and left the Hungarians only four hundred. In my hotel Bela Kun had done five million crowns' worth of damage. The Roumanians did seven millions worth. They took literally everything, and the rooms are still without telephones as a result of their brigandage. This, of course, is all the Hungarian account of what happened. The other side of the story must be heard in Roumania.

The Roumanian Military Attaché, by name Margaretezen, or some such, tells me that he is followed by three agents and cannot go anywhere without his movements being reported. He gives the Magyars a bigger force than most people, and two hundred and fifty guns. He thinks that the country is stiff with rifles, and declares that German equipments keep on flowing in. He does not believe that when the Reparations people come here they will discover much, for the watch-posts stop travellers everywhere and communicate with their friends when anything has to be concealed. The American thinks that this is all exaggerated, but admits 600,000 men capable of being mobilised if arms, guns, and equipment are here for them. I saw Hohler after lunch. A pretty sick man still and was only in an armchair for an hour or two before returning to bed. He is fully of opinion that great injustice has been done to the Magyars under the Treaty, and we had a good talk over it all. He gave me a note to the Finance Minister Hegedüs. A capable representative, and I wish I could have found him fit and well.

Went on later to the F.O. and saw Count Banffy, the new Foreign Minister, who was very courteous and interesting. I told him that I found a difficulty in describing what the Government here was, for there was nothing quite like it anywhere else. Whitaker's description of it as

a Republic seemed incorrect when they called themselves
a Royal Hungarian Government, but I was not sure
whether to describe it as a Monarchy in suspense, or what.
Banffy said that the meaning of the Crown of St. Stephen
to the Magyars could not be understood except by Magyars. Every single Magyar was a member of this Crown,
and regarded it as the sanction of his personal rights and
liberty. The Golden Bull was only a few years after Runny-
mede, and the development of Hungarian life and political
thought, except for the one hundred and fifty years of
Turkish domination, had followed English lines. English
constitutional history was well known here and our political precedents were frequently quoted in Parliament when
they had none of their own.

It was true that Karolyi had declared a Republic in 1918,
but in March, 1919, the Bolshevist reign of Bela Kun had
begun, and to this succeeded a Governor, now Admiral
Horthy, who was much what Cromwell was in England in
his day. The feeling of the whole country was undoubtedly
monarchical, but it was realised that considerations relating to foreign policy made it highly inconvenient to raise
the question now. Why had not Karl understood this? I
asked. He said that the facts were not yet all fully known,
but that the whole history of this affair would eventually
be set down. No one knew of his coming. Perhaps he had
expected support in various matters. In any case B. said
that every Hungarian had done his duty and that the
Government had given Europe proofs of its good-will and
of its desire not to disturb the Peace.

He said that if Benès opened his campaign for freeing
the customs within the old Empire, Hungary would be
with him, but that Hungary's great difficulty was the millions of Magyars annexed to the neighbouring countries,
and the incessant complaints of ill-usage which they
brought back with them. Scarcely a day passed without
the return of refugees with these stories, and the result was
that opinion in Hungary was so incensed that it would be
difficult to make Parliament accept any economic agree-

ment that did not take into full account the interests of these unfortunate Magyar minorities. Who looked after them now? I asked, and why was it left to Scottish and American Unitarians to represent the hardships of these people? The Allies had forced the Treaty on Hungary, and it seemed to me their duty to control the execution of it. Yes, said B., but after the ratification he presumed it would be the League of Nations. This question of the four million Hungarians in the neighbouring States evidently gave him great concern and will affect his foreign policy very much. I told him that I thought Benès was ready for accommodation. Without it I doubt that Banffy can go far. The Magyars are a chivalrous, warm-hearted people who will always support their unfortunate fellow-countrymen.

We had a talk about the other effects of the Treaty and B. confirmed all my opinions of it. I also gather that. Sir George Clerk's intervention here was most happy when all was in disarray. Clerk told them they were not divided on any essential matters and that they should have a coalition Government and get on at once. They seem to have followed the advice exactly, and it all worked out, though not fully till the Socialists were put out and the present lot came in.

I talked for an hour with Banffy on these and other matters, and went on to see Count Albert Apponyi with whom I stayed till nearly eight discussing the general situation. He tells me that he is an independent and has not joined any party. He is Karlist. He watches events. He says that the main result of the war has been to change completely the mentality and outlook of all people. The masses, who fought the war, and expended so much blood, courage, and fortitude, now look for compensation to a larger share in the Government, and Apponyi is prepared to support them. They have lost faith in the old leading circles who brought about all their sorrows. He was biting about the ignorance of the Peacemakers of all the conditions of Eastern Europe. They had to be shown the positions of the largest towns. He, with Teleki, Bethlen, Hegedüs, etc., were in Paris. He had found that they were given no opportunity of explaining their views, so had written to the Big Four, and finally was allowed to explain the situation on the express understanding that there should be no discussion. He spoke in French and then in English. L. G. seemed struck by his remark that particular blocks of Magyars had been violently and unnecessarily detached from Hungary, although they were physically in contact with her. L. G. had passed a note to Clemenceau and afterwards had asked for further explanation and A. had brought out his ethnographical map. He had heard from an English friend that L. G. had trounced his staff for the treatment of the Hungarians, but unfortunately nothing had been changed. The injustice remained. A. thought that the Treaty could not stand, but they had no intention of doing anything to upset Europe. It is pathetic how all these Magyars confide in the legendary justice of England and in her power to put matters right. I tell them all that the mass of our people were too much preoccupied with affairs more vital to them to worry about little Hungary, and that I felt sure that few outside the official classes knew of the measure meted out to her and what it all implied.

Wednesday, April 20, 1921. Hegedüs, the Minister of Finance, is the financial magician of Hungary and will either be described hereafter as a genius or a lunatic, I don't know which. I went to see him this morning on H.E.'s introduction. I found a deputation with him demanding higher salaries. He told them that he had doubled their purchasing power by raising the crown from 2200 to 1000 for the pound sterling and that this was his system and he would do no more. A man of devouring energy, rapid thought, and torrential speech. He has, in fact, raised the crown as he says, and hopes to raise it to 500. This is our English comparison; actually these foreigners' standard of value is usually the Swiss franc, and the crown is compared with the number of centimes that it is worth in the Swiss money, but it is all one. He has stopped the printing of paper notes, and contemplates the destruction of masses of them still in circulation. He is dead against foreign loans. He is the apostle of self-help. How does he work?

He regards every taxpayer as a congenital liar and so shuns valuations and income-tax returns. He thinks direct taxes useless because so much is paid in kind for work done, and the values cannot then be appraised. He does not like inquisitions and knows that Hungary is not accustomed to them. He goes to work a different way. He increases the indirect taxes, and incidentally mentioned a new tax on cigarettes which would bring in several millions. He taxes the war profiteer by taxing him double amounts on all increases since 1914. He takes for the Government a first mortgage of twenty per cent on all houses. Here the value has to be stated, but if the value of a house is understated he may buy it, and sell it again. He calls upon all companies of whatever kind to increase their share capital by fifteen per cent. He takes these new shares and sells them back to the companies if they want them, and if not, then in the open market, or keeps them and his mortgages as securities to use for any purpose. This avoids all question of prying into capital and profits. He takes twenty per cent of all moneys on deposit in the banks. He proposes to take two, three, or four years' annual rent from all estates except the large ones as a capital levy on them, and if he cannot discover the amount of the rent he judges by the nearest farm from which figures are available. From large estates he takes twenty per cent of the land and sells it to peasants and small farmers, thus making an agrarian law of his own; and from all these sources he reduces his deficit, which he found when he came in, of twelve milliards by seven milliards, and proposes to cover the remaining five milliards deficit by an internal loan. He has a foreign debt which he places at 130 milliards, and thinks that as he is the debtor of France and England these countries will give him time, say ten years, as France has already undertaken to do, to pay the debt. Before that time he hopes to have re-established Hungary's financial stability and to have brought back the crown nearly to the pre-war parity. The payment of this foreign debt will not then cost the country what it would cost to pay it now.

He thought the Treaty, when he first read it, not bad, but good, because it was so bad that it could not endure. Had it been better it would have been worse. He has passed twelve out of some twenty-one Bills which complete his programme, and if he gets through his capital levy and agrarian schemes he thinks that the whole programme will be completed. It is coming up to-day. Much depends on what he is asked to do about reparations. He hopes that his efforts to restore Hungary's credit without appeals for help may be taken into consideration, and that a fair amount of Hungary's debt may be allocated to the Succession States which have annexed her territories and populations. He is against what he calls the morphinisation of a country by foreign loans. He tries to copy English finance, and by copying England and America in stopping the printing of notes he hopes to advance in time to their standards in exchange. He is most ardently in favour of free trade in the Succession States, and says that England ought to help as she can sell nothing to them at the present rates of exchange. He is furious with Roumania for allowing no letters to go from Hungary to Magyars now in Transylvania, and says that his relatives and friends are constantly returning, as they find themselves unable to endure Roumanian rule from its cruelties, exactions, and corruption. He says that the Hungarians are the only race in Europe who are neither Slavs, Germans, nor Latins, and would hope that we should extend our protection to them. He amused me by saying that the first thing he looked at in the morning was not the state of the exchange, but the meteorological reports. The recent slight rain, he said, meant milliards to him. We had forty-two days of drought before it came.

Whatever the result of all these schemes may be, it must certainly be admitted that Hungary is facing her difficulties bravely and helping herself. It is only to be hoped that the reparation people when they come here will not be such a great expense to this little country as they have been elsewhere, or try to exact payments from a people who are trying to avoid appeals to Europe. The best reparation is to allow Hungary to recover economically and then trade.

Alfred Stead came in late and told me much about his efforts to galvanise British trade into life again. He too is doing something and is one of the few Englishmen really working here. He gave me his views about the future of the Danube. Dined with the Greek Minister and his wife.

An interesting visit and am sorry that it is so short, as there is much more that I should like to have seen and done here. The real obstacle to progress in this part of the world is the racial rivalry of all these people, who are all embittered by the war, while the vanquished are still more embittered by the Peace and by the loss of so many of their people by the transfers of territory. All the same I find that Austria and Hungary are ready in principle for free trade and I think it was a pity that free trade within the old Empire was not enforced at the Peace. I expect that I shall find more objections to sensible economics in Roumania, Jugo-Slavia, and perhaps Bulgaria than I find in Prague, Vienna, and Budapest. I think that we should reconsider our attitude to Hungary. It seems to me that Hungary, Jugo-Slavia, and the Czechs are the strong people in these parts, and I doubt from all accounts whether Roumania will prove any serious barrier against Bolshevism if a barrier be needed.[1] Hungary, I think, will, and all except Jugo-Slavia are horribly afraid of her. Her martial reputation has survived defeat. Altogether Central Europe is full of fascinating problems, but one must keep a more or less open mind till one has visited Bucharest, Sofia, and Belgrade. Then one can conclude.

Thursday, April 21, 1921. As there was no direct train

---

[1] I altered my opinion after visiting Roumania.

to Vienna to-day, I made a virtue of necessity, started at dawn, and made a long détour through Hungary round Lake Balaton and so to Vienna by 7 P.M. Very glad to have seen this country and to have gained this bird's-eye view of Hungary's wealth. The crops looking better after the few days of light rain. A general air of content. The black soil looks amazingly rich. Flocks of sheep, large droves of pigs, plenty of horses and cattle, extensive vineyards, much beekeeping, and any amount of farmyard fowls. The houses well-built and looked comfortable. Usually single-storied, brick and tile. Balaton of great length and fair breadth. Hardly any coal on the railway: the stations had piles of wood. Went to the Imperial again, and managed to get dressed in time to dine with Sir William Goode at the Bristol, where I found a party of a dozen men, largely Americans, including General Churchill, U.S.A., Walker D. Hines, just back from looking into the division of enemy Danubian shipping, the American Chargé d'Affaires, and a few Austrians, like Police President Schober and the clever doctor who has done so much for the Vienna children.

I was glad to see Schober again and told him that there were a few things I wanted still to know from him, especially the value of his police and the gendarmerie, and the composition of the crowds which painted Vienna red every night. Were they foreign or Viennese? He thought that his police were very trustworthy, and that he had full control. The gendarmerie in the Provinces were some nine thousand and were also good. The so-called Army was no good at all. Why not abolish it and increase the police forces? Schober said that it was a Socialist toy. They came to him privately and admitted that it was useless, but publicly they had to support it. Schober wished that Austria might be allowed to have Militia service with compulsion. So, no doubt, would Germany. I then asked him about the night life of Vienna, and told him how it had disgusted many people in view of Vienna's food condition. I had heard various explanations given, what was the right one? He said that Vienna, like all great capitals, catered for public wants. Vienna had always laid herself out to entertain her visitors and did so still. He had made a number of perquisitions, i.e., raids, on the various night haunts and had found that ninety per cent of the people attending there were foreigners, and that the remaining ten per cent were the new rich, largely Jew, and not four per cent real Viennese.

Mr. Hines a thoroughly capable American with a judicial turn of mind. He thinks that the riparian States will accept his decision about the ships. The real trouble is the frontier question. The Danube is only in principle free. Also the trade is mainly up from Galatz and not down. But he thinks that there will be a big surplus of wheat soon, and that if coal were sent out at that moment the emptied barges could take coal up the river. He and the American Chargé d'Affaires were most bitter about France who, they say, will soon be cordially detested everywhere. The French Government, or at least their Minister here, had committed a folly in protesting here against the *Anschluss* Vote in the Tyrol, and had declared that the Reparations Commission would resume its work and credits be withheld, but as everybody here knows that Goode is winding up and going away next week, and that there are no credits, this leaves the Austrian Government cold. The result of this folly, to which we weakly adhered, has been to give an immense fillip to the Pan-German Party, and there had been a big meeting at Vienna and the French had been hissed. I think the English too, and there is going to be another meeting. This is all exactly contrary to the suggestions which I sent to Lord Burnham, for I told him that the movement were better not taken tragically and were best ignored, as it was platonic and the Government here were quite sound. But now public feeling has been aroused. It is difficult to cope with such light-headed policy.

There was a British officer present who was shortly going to Budapest on the military control to look into

Hungarian armaments, to see the Trianon Treaty ratified. He asked for my views. I told him that if there were arms and so on they would have been concealed long ago, and he would find nothing: also that I did not think it was any disadvantage to us if Hungary were strong. In any case she is entitled to the Armistice scale until the lapse of a certain period after the Ratification. Goode said that the Americans here all knew my views and had read my last book. He had intended to dine with me alone, but the Americans had insisted upon coming to meet me. Several of them offered to help me in every possible way. I told Hines that the Americans would have to come into European politics again, for we could not do the Atlas business much longer. We were too small a country and our internal difficulties were too great. If the Americans did not come in things might begin to crumble. Under the rule of demagogues and agitators who put the nose of our F.O. out of joint, we could not control affairs abroad, and they must see how their own trade was being paralysed. They were much interested in the financial policy of Hegedüs. But I can never recall his name. I can't get nearer to it than Habakkuk.

Vienna, Friday, April 22, 1921. With great difficulty got a ticket to Paris and a sleeper. Wrote a first article on Hungary. Wet and cold.

Saturday, April 23, 1921. In the train for two days and a night bound for Paris. Met an intelligent Director of an Anglo-Austrian Bank. We agreed that Central Europe had not thrown up any man of distinction except in Czecho-Slovakia, and that the inability of the Austrian Government to impose its will on the Provinces was a very serious matter. Met also an educated better-class Pole, one of the many foreigners I have met lately who are travelling for American firms, not to do business, but to watch and report events so that the United States may be ready for any business going. The state of the exchange practically prohibits business. Many of the traders have suffered heavily because they have not protected themselves properly in their contracts against the practice of Eastern Europe to refuse to pay until the exchange improves. The United States are flooding Eastern Europe with their travellers and expert observers, and they choose foreigners of some position probably on account of the general American ignorance of foreign tongues, and because they find it necessary to deal with leading people who will not talk to the ordinary trade traveller. My belief is that we shall need to make a great effort to prevent Germany, with her depreciated exchange, from dominating all these markets after reparations are finally regulated.

CHAPTER VIII

PARIS AND THE SANCTIONS

The conversations at Lympne —Upper Silesia, the sanctions, and the Ruhr
— Views of Lord Hardinge and Mr. Arnold Robertson — Sir Milne Cheetham on French vigour — Colonel Baldwin on Danube affairs — Mr. Robertson on Rhine customs and the proposed occupation of the Ruhr — His alternative proposal — Marshal Pétain in readiness — He invites me to accompany him — His views on subject races — The census of Paris — Germany's liabilities fixed at 132 milliards of gold marks — Sir Basil Zaharoff
— Boucher pictures — The business honesty of different nationalities — A
story of the Chinese — Zaharoff's gold plate — Comfort and civilisation —
The Dutch Loan Exhibition — A conversation with M. Clemenceau — An
unchanged host and house — He will write nothing about the past — He is
opposed to the occupation of the Ruhr — France financially exhausted —
Views on Marshals Foch and Pétain — Clemenceau's love of Burma —
Clemenceau's life — His wound — His reply to the Sister of Charity — A
good story of Clemenceau — Prince Ghika and Count Zamoyski — Preparations for a move into Germany — The situation — A motor trip to Princess Murat's house — The 1919 Class called out, but the Essen *coup* put off
— Painful moments at the London Conference — A brief visit to England.

Paris, Sunday, April 24, 1921. Arrived from Vienna about
noon. David Loch dined with me and we exchanged news.
A huge and over-dressed (i.e., under-dressed) crowd at the
Ritz: about seventy per cent American and ten per cent
French; saw a number of friends from England. A perfect
Babel of noise: most strange dresses and precious little of
them, but rivulets of jewels and a blaze of lights. Not a
good place to choose for a quiet talk. Had forgotten that
it was a Ritz Sunday. What an odd thing humanity is.

Monday, April 25, 1921. Finished my Hungarian articles
and sent them off with my diary to Burnham. The French
correspondents give such excellent accounts of what happened at Lympne that one might almost have been there.
Berthelot must have posted them up. Conversations not
decisions. The latter are reserved for an Inter-Allied
Supreme Council in London next Saturday. Germany
twisting and turning to evade the French spear. She has
failed to induce America to arbitrate, but is to send her
proposals to Washington and Harding is to send them on

to us if they seem to meet the case. The French fixed upon the occupation of the Ruhr. A big job. Our press warmly supporting them. Lunched with Lord Hardinge and Evelyn Lady Alington at the Embassy. He is, of course, not informed yet of anything that passed at Lympne and so dares not see Briand and admit his ignorance. A fig for diplomacy!

H. agrees with me that our treatment of Greece is the greatest disgrace of our diplomatic history. He also agrees that Hungary and Greece are States worthy of our support. We discussed Upper Silesia, the sanctions, and the Ruhr. Robertson, of the Rhineland High Commission, tells him that the British can hold the Ruhr with four battalions, but it will need 250,000 French to hold it. The French propose to send six divisions and to call out the 1919 class. But I think that the Germans will meet us and that matters will be squared. H. told us that he and Grey had bought up the Constantinople quays in 1906, squaring the French by half the loot, and at the expenditure of £260,000, which the Bank of England had advanced, had made £80,000 profit. When the war broke out, Parliament knew nothing of the transaction. The profits had been spent on secret service during the war, but now they would be accruing again. I said that it was Dizzy's Suez Canal *coup* on a small scale. H. had made the Ambassadors here transfer their Rhine responsibility to the R.H.C. because they were the proper technical authority. A very sound move. The four battalions of ours sent to Silesia were now even in England and the French were demanding them for the Rhine. H. says that all the spare troops from Palestine are also back in England and that Harington's position in the Straits is an anxious one because the Greek division at Ismid is leaving to join its Army and the French have refused to allow their troops to pass to the Asiatic shore of the Straits. This is the French idea of giving Harington the command! We had a good talk about French politics. Lady A. not changed in nature since she was a girl. We talked of the old days at Amington. She remembered every

corner and every picture there. Much talk of my trip and
of events in Central Europe. A meeting of the Conseil
Supérieur to-day under Millerand, and then he held a Conseil des Ministres after Briand's return.

Tuesday, April 26, 1921. Saw Sir Milne Cheetham in
the morning and Mr. Challis later; also Spring-Rice, First
Secretary. Cheetham thought the French extraordinarily
vigorous people, for they were pushing their interests
everywhere and seemingly cared nothing for the general
enmity that they were arousing. We thought that a
settlement might take place with Germany, but we are
still without the German note to the United States and
Harding's view of it. Met Lady Juliet Trevor who is
staying with Princess Murat, and was looking wonderfully
well. Also pretty Mrs. Felix Doubleday. Tried to find Mr.
Arnold Robertson who is at Princess Hotel, Rue de Press-
bourg, and Colonel Baldwin of the Danube Commission
at the Vieullemont Hotel, 17 Rue Boissy d'Anglas. Both
out. Went on to the Boulevard des Invalides and saw
Millescamps, A.D.C. to Marshal Pétain, who tells me that
the Marshal is *débordé* just now, so I suppose that they are
really fussing to get ready for the Ruhr.

Colonel Baldwin came in to see me later. He is not only
on the Inter-Allied Conference here, but on the International Commissions on the Lower Danube, Elbe, Rhine,
etc. He tells me that the Mannheim-Regensburg Canal
would have to be rebuilt to serve larger barges, and cannot
be deepened owing to technical difficulties. If it is made,
the Germans are bound by the Treaty to apply the international rules for navigable rivers to it. The rule is that
navigable rivers traversing the territories of more than one
State are free and must be regarded as the sea and not be
subject to dues and rates or obstacles to trade. He finds
the greatest difficulties to arise from the small minds of
Roumania and Serbia, who try to make out that they can
do what they please with a river of which they have the
two banks in certain places. If they do not ratify the Convention, they cannot be made to do so! Therefore the Con-

vention must be arrived at by agreement. He says that the Roumanians hate the old Commission, dating from 1856, which rules from Braila to the Black Sea, but we hold to it because six thousand ton ships go up to Braila and we have forty per cent of this trade. He would like the future H.Q. of the Commission for the Danube from Ulm to Braila to be at Budapest, but Czechs, Serbs, and Roumanians resist this and each wants it in his own territory, i.e., at Bratislava (Pressburg), Belgrade, or Braila.[1] So he hopes to get it at Vienna, in spite of jealousies, and thinks that if he can get it there for five years it will remain there. He thinks that the question of the Iron Gates is most important. He is interested in the French Strasbourg-Basel Canal which will allow two thousand ton barges to go from London to Basel under their own steam, but as the Canal is to have eight locks and will take from twenty-five to fifty years to build, the plan is not of any use to trade in the near future. This section of the Rhine, already bad, would cease to be navigable, as the French would divert the water into the Canal in order to secure power. B. says that the London Chamber of Commerce oppose the scheme and that so do the Swiss who are doing much propaganda in London through a man called Palliser. I still think that an improved Mannheim-Regensburg Canal, giving us a clear international water highway from the Port of London to the Black Sea, would be of great service to us and to all the riverside States, not only in itself, but as a protection against high railway rates. I wish it had been in the Treaty as an obligation upon Germany. He tells me that his French colleague is a very good fellow and works with him cordially. So would the Germans, Austrians, and Hungarians, who will eventually join, but at present have only a right to attend and express their views, and not to vote. The Conference will simply tell them what to do. B. thinks that however difficult the French may be, our best policy is to maintain the Alliance. He thinks that Austria must go to Germany. I told him all the grave objections to it. The

---

[1] The place chosen was Bratislava, for a term of five years.

Tyrol plébiscite has gone warmly for the *Anschluss* by over-powering majorities, some ninety per cent. The Italians not at all pleased.

Wednesday, April 27, 1921. Mr. Arnold Robertson, the British Commissioner on the Rhineland High Commission, lunched with me. His colleagues are still M. Tirard, the President, who is clever, and the Belgian M. Rolin Jaeque-myns, who is a sound capable lawyer. Tirard is always in close touch with his Government. Robertson was never consulted about the customs line, and has not been consulted upon the pending Ruhr operation. He has a staff of one hundred and fifty-seven people. He wants back the missing four battalions very badly. The customs line is estab-lished. It holds up all the main trade and he is not worrying about small smuggling. He has taken the Germans' customs laws and has applied them to the extent of twenty-five per cent: he will raise it to fifty per cent and then to the full figure later, but it was thought best not to hit the Rhineland too hard at first. He says that all the German customs, all round all their frontiers, only brought in twenty millions sterling last year, and he does not expect more than one and a half millions from the Rhineland. His own staff are very good and all speak German as well as English.

He tells me that the fifty per cent scheme of L. G.'s has merely had the effect of arresting German trade, so that will bring in nothing and only destroy our German trade, in and out. He disapproves of the proposed occupation of the Ruhr by the French and says that he expects trouble, though it is impossible to say how far it will go. He doubts that the French can manage the mines and thinks that they will make as big a mess of it as of the Saar where the output has fallen by sixty per cent. He expects the miners to strike and says that the French will need 200,000 men. He personally would simply hold, administer, and exploit the line we have now and make the German coal barges at Ruhrort pay dues. He would take over the whole Rhine-land and says that it would only mean another fifty men on his own staff. He would, as a sanction, withdraw all undertaking to give up the Rhineland and the other points. He is convinced that the war will recommence and that we should therefore place ourselves in the most favourable position. The constant infraction of their undertakings by the Germans gives us every right to secure ourselves. He believes that the Germans can pay and should be made to pay. There were three thousand high-powered German motor cars at a Rhine race-meeting the other day. A rich German told him that the capital levy did not hurt anybody much, as it was based on the capital of 1917 in gold and was now payable by the same amount of paper! Also one of his friends who made his return in 1919 was not assessed yet. Robertson thinks a guerilla war possible, but regards passive resistance and strikes as the worst danger. If the Germans do these things the French may treat the Ruhr as the Germans treated the French and Belgian factories and mines, and wreck them. I said that it all seemed to me very grave and as serious as August, 1914.

He does not know whether he will have anything to do with the Ruhr affair. If he has, he will need one hundred and twenty more people to keep him informed about everything. He is not very keen about it, as he will have little power and will have to cover everything done by the French. If Robertson's scheme fails, he would apply the blockade and thinks America might come into it. We do not think that the French will accept the new German offer through America. R. is against the Germans taking over the Allied debts to America. It will put the latter on the German side afterwards.

I saw Marshal Pétain at four. He was looking well and told me that I looked younger every time I came to see him. We talked of my tour first. He summed up General Le Rond's qualities with precision. He said that he presumed Degoutte would put through the occupation of the Ruhr. It would be simple as a military act, but what would follow no man could say. He thought that there should be a Governor to combine civil and military powers. He did not expect much trouble from the miners if they were fed, but the direction might have to be taken over by French engineers. All was ready. Only one Class would be called out. He did not think it worth while for me to go to the spot for this business. But if opposition arose, it might become necessary to occupy Berlin. Then there would be a partial mobilisation, and if thirty divisions were sent to Berlin it would be the French Army and he would go in command of it. The French mobilisation was very supple. It was divided into échelons, a first, second, and third, to meet such a case as this, and there would have to be plenty of troops on the L. of C. I said that he could count on our moral support, at least, if he marched. We agreed that the psychological effect of occupying Berlin would be great. I told him that Benès would help, but preferred blockade to occupation. I hoped that the Silesian mines might be looked after, as half of Central Europe depended on them. Would the French classes come out willingly in case of a partial mobilisation? He thought they would if the reasons and scope of the operation were clearly explained to them. He invited me to accompany him in the march on Berlin and I accepted. He thought that we had had enough of discussions and that it was time to stop talking and to act. He chaffed me about the Greeks, and said that we had deserted them. I said yes, and did not defend our action, but declared that the French and Italians had betrayed them and us by making peace [1] separately with the Turks contrary to our common stipulation.

Pétain said that he had received bad news of our position in India. I said that it had never been good, and that as we were trying to govern three hundred millions of natives by two hundred thousand whites the thing was bound to break down sooner or later. Pétain said that if one left subject races in their native ignorance one was abused for it, and if one raised them up the first thing they did was to revolt. It was just the same in West Africa, but the only way was to take timely action and to trust to the feelings

[1] The French tried, but failed. They did better later.

of gratitude which would follow. Later went on to see Sir
Basil Zaharoff at 53 Avenue Marceau. Still very crippled
from his motor accident. He is seventy. M. Bignon, the
big Deputy, was there for a bit too. Sir B. declares that he
is a Frenchman and is strongly for a resolute policy in
Germany. He thought that Burnham had "la religion de
la presse" and was very public-spirited. He was quite
satisfied with L. G.'s statements in the H. of C. about the
Ruhr and said that we should all have to adhere to this
point of view whatever we thought of it.

Thursday, April 28, 1921. The census of March 6, 1921,
gives Paris a total population of 2,863,433, and the whole
Department of the Seine 4,343,346. The latter figure shows
nearly a quarter of a million increase since 1911. The Paris
figure a small increase of 16,000.

The French Government have informed Washington
that the German proposals have produced an impression,
"nettement et unanimement défavorable." (Later this
was clumsily denied.) The Commission of Reparations has
unanimously fixed the total of German liabilities at 132
milliards of gold marks. This figure includes restitutions
already made or to be made, but not the Belgian debts to
the Allies, which is 250 millions sterling. Lunched alone
with Sir Basil Zaharoff. We were quite agreed on public
affairs concerning which there is little more to be said until
we know the result of the Conference in London next week-
end. So we talked of more amusing matters. He has many
of his favourite Boucher pictures including an exquisite set
of four small ones and two portraits in character of Boucher's Irish mistress, Miss Murphy, who lived with Boucher
in his best days and figures on so many of his tapestries.
Boucher is, *qua* artist, less meretricious and finnikin than
most of the French eighteenth-century school, I think.
That led us to talk of love and fidelity.

We talked of the business honesty of various people. Z.
had been much struck by reading in a book of American
statistics that there were fewer bills protested in Spain than
in any other country. His experience confirmed this idea.

Have you not found the Chinese very honest. I asked? Z. smiled and told me a story. He had almost completed a large contract with the Chinese when the chief Chinese man began to make endless objections about the quality of the materials. So Z. went to see him and told him that the Japanese had been perfectly content and would take the contract if the Chin did not. The Chin remained entirely imperturbable. Z., exasperated, at last said, "How much do you want to make you report that the material is perfectly satisfactory?" "Two hundred and fifty thousand francs," said the Chin blandly. Z. went off and got it. The Chin counted the notes with the utmost deliberation, and took out two or three which were a little torn and asked to have them replaced. Z. began to take hold of them to take them away to change. "No, don't do that," said the Chin, "you can bring fresh ones here." So Z. did, and then the Chin handed over the contract signed, evidently thinking that he had been a scrupulously honest business man.

Z. has some wonderful gold plate. He told me that he picked up ten pieces at a sale some fourteen years ago, and Boucheron had every year made him a few more to match. So now he had a complete dinner service of pure gold (not silver gilt) for thirty-six people, and the only one in the world, he said. The pieces are fearfully heavy. We talked of Clemenceau. He had met him in the Bois this week, full of life. He would not write anything, not even of his recent voyage in the East.

Z. is not exactly broken down from his accident in which his head went through the top of his car, but he has attacks of giddiness in which he forgets everything. Between the attacks his brain is as good as ever. He is retired from business and says that his young men think him out of date. But I fancy he still runs things at Vickers. We talked of comforts and civilisation. I said that I thought that they did not exist in Europe outside England and Paris. Z. said that they never had. They were spurious elsewhere or individual to certain men who were cosmopolitans. We reminded each other that hotels of the present class had only existed for a very little time, and had come from America. It was not till the Ritz hotels started that hotels became really good. Ten years ago a bedroom with a bathroom was a rarity. Now people would not go to an hotel where they could not get it. Z. quoted an advertisement of a country house in England in the *Times* where he saw that there were fourteen bedrooms and only one bathroom. He thought that the English food was the best in the world, but not the cooking. When there was a good restaurant abroad, it was always French. If there was a German manager over French chefs, there was always something wrong with the place and the meals. We talked of the changed situation in Europe, and how people were going on believing wrongly that nothing was changed. All business habits had to change, we thought, and Z. agreed with my plan of barter on a large scale through Government clearing houses and said that Goodenough of Barclays' believed in it. It was the only reply to depreciated exchanges.

Z. fancies himself as a cook and is often in his kitchen. His food is first-rate. He has a special little dish made of transversely sliced bananas. They are cooked inside a *bain marie* and kept constantly soaked by melted sugar poured over them. I hate bananas, but he made me try them. They were quite excellent. Huge strawberries, and grapes with the stalks in water which keeps them from getting dry and shrivelled. This was his discovery and other people had begun to copy it. His cigars are sent every month from Cuba. He opened a box dated April 4. They were quite soft, and he says that fresh cigars, or green cigars as he calls them, are to old cigars like grapes to raisins. But every cigar is thrown away on a cigarette smoker, so I would not try one.

Went to see the Dutch Loan Exhibition at the Jeu de Paume Court. A bad picture gallery, light all wrong. But a fine exhibition. I have never seen so many Rembrandts together before. They were from The Hague and Amsterdam, with fine specimens from private collectors, notably Sir G. Holford, M. Schneider, etc. The Jan Steens delicious. A few good Franz Halses including the big family picture which turned up one year in an Old Masters' Exhibition at Burlington House, and now belongs, I see, to Otto Kahn. A very characteristic Hals. Lord Crawford also sent several good ones, and his Hals "Le Bouffon" is delightful. And to think that thirty years ago old Martin Colnaghi used to buy Hals portraits at the price of scrap iron and store them because no one would have them. What sheep we all are! But everything good in art is like water. It is bound to find its right level at last.

Friday, April 29, 1921. Went off to see M. Clemenceau at his old address 8 Rue Franklin at 9 A.M. The same old commonplace bourgeois den, with the dark enclosed court all surrounded by other houses, and in the dining-room, where I waited for a few minutes, the same dirty old woodwork on the walls, crying for coats of paint, and the ordinary, almost lodging-house furniture, and the red carpet worn threadbare and in patches at the entrance. What a home for the man who won the greatest war in history! Clemenceau came out of his room to find me. He was in the same old clothes and with a black half-turban cap on his head, and an almost imperceptible bit more stiff in his gait. But directly we sat down opposite one another at the well-known writing table, I saw that there was all the old fire, the alert brain, the rapid thought, the clear word, the penetrating sarcasm, in fact the old master who won the war and the tiger who destroyed so many Ministries. I could not see a vestige of a failure of his intellectual powers, and the eyes danced and glared and flashed, and the fun came rolling out with the same old humour, witticism, and profound knowledge of character and human nature.

I told him that I had come to consult him on two matters. First a point of history, second the present position. I said, you are among the very few who know what really happened in 1918 and at the peace. Every lie is current. You only sit still and say nothing. You are growing old.

When you are dead, they will tell more lies, many more, for they are still afraid of you. You cannot roar at them from beyond the tomb. Are you leaving any records of this tremendous time? Even if you are contemptuous of your contemporaries, will you not admit that we won victory at frightful cost, and that France at least deserves that you should show where the faults were made as a warning to her for the future?

No, said C., he had said nothing, had written nothing, and was not going to. He took no interest in controversies about the past which was over. He had lived through the greatest period and had done his best. It was enough to contemplate in silence the grandeur of it all. He took pleasure in his disdain of all discussion over the past. He had been too deeply concerned in these events, and the events had been too tremendous, for him not to feel it unworthy of him to waste his remaining years in sterile discussions. He did not care what people thought or said. It was all one to him. He had succeeded, and all those who had failed owed him a grudge for succeeding. Yes, he could destroy many reputations by a word. But that was no service to France. If he said what he thought of X, he would make bad blood between England and France and that was of no service to either. Let them talk. He knew that he was credited with a bad character because he spoke the truth, but that was the way of the world, and he did not care. He admitted the high cost of the mistakes of the war, but was not going to change his point of view. He thought it would be mean, petty, and dishonouring to such a great epoch if he began to say or to write that on such and such a date someone or other said, or wrote, or did something or other. It was not for him to defend himself. He regarded such littleness with scorn and preferred silence, and his contemplation of great grandeurs.

Then we turned to the present. Clemenceau is opposed to the projected occupation of the Ruhr. It was not certain that it would bring the Boche to heel, and there one would pile in tens of thousands of men and there might be shooting which would be bad, and then strikes, and masses of workmen would have to be fed and perhaps have raw materials found for them. It was not the right way to proceed with the Boche. If the latter had not kept his word, he should be made to do so by a march on Berlin after a serious mobilisation which would give ample means of suppressing risings in rear of the armies. I said yes, it is really more a psychological than a political question. C. agreed, but said that while, during the war, he could mobilise every sort of financial resource, and print masses of paper money, France was now financially exhausted, and he did not see how her finances could bear the new strain which might be long and profitless if restricted to the Ruhr. He preferred more drastic measures to get the business finished quickly.

I happened to mention Foch. A slightly sarcastic smile passed over C.'s face. He told me that he appreciated the services which Foch had rendered, but said that on several occasions he had had to speak severely to Foch who owed him a grudge for it and had shown it. I do not think that he approved of Foch for allowing the Ruhr operation. I told him that I expected the march on Berlin to follow and that I hoped to go with Pétain who had invited me. C. was pleased. He approves of Pétain, of his silence and reserve. He has a very high opinion of him. He thinks that the whole course of the negotiations since the Peace has been deplorable and that we have gone on from one mistake to another. He foresaw the certainty of this, and rather than remain a spectator of these events he went off to the East and was delighted to meet in India so many of his old friends of the old front in France. C. loves Burma as much as I do. The gaiety of the people, unknown in India, where C. never saw a native woman smile, the colours and the lights and the rivers, but he wished that the Burmese ladies would not smoke those large cigars, as it was out of the picture. C. was not in Parliament now. He would not accept a seat. But he was always occupied and talked of philosophy. He had begun work at 4 A.M. this morning.

His wound? It did not trouble him at all. The bullet was still there, and he pointed to the spot a little to the right of his breast-bone below the throat where it lay transversely. It was quite happy there and had found a resting-place. His Sister of Charity had described it as a miracle of Heaven that this was so. C. had replied that if Heaven had intended to perform a miracle, it would have been better to have prevented his aggressor from shooting at him at all! The doctor's card came in and I rose to leave. C. begged me to write to him whenever I was in doubt and wanted advice. He pressed me to give him a promise that I would, so I agreed and he asked me to tell him everything that I was thinking. Did not the others consult him? Yes, some of them, but when he said disagreeable things to them, they did not come again. "But when I say, as I say to you, Colonel Repington, I am your friend, then it was different, and we could write our minds to each other." What a pity that Rembrandt could not paint Clemenceau! He was so like a Rembrandt to-day. Futurity will never understand from any photos and portraits the force and fire and vital energy of the man.

Spring-Rice lunched with me. He told me a story of Clemenceau. A tree in the garden of a home of the Jesuit Fathers next door to him had grown so large that it overshadowed C.'s study. So he wrote to ask that it might be slightly trimmed. The Father wrote back to say that it would not only be trimmed, but entirely removed. C.'s letter of thanks began:

"Mon père,—Je crois avoir le droit de vous adresser de cette manière puisque c'est vous qui m'avez donné le jour . . ." Very neat.

S. and I had a long talk over the desperately involved situation here now unless the Germans gave way at the last moment. He thought that the French would be much put about if the Ruhr brought them in no money. His reports agreed with my view that the Boche is still much below par owing to constant ill-feeding for so long, but certainly they have invested largely abroad since the censorship was abolished, and he says that they are now buying up the press of Central Europe including the Hungarian. Also judging from the wealth of the Hungarian peasants, who possess literally chests full of paper money, I expect that the German farmers are as well provided.

Went to see the Roumanians and Poles to-day to prepare for my next tour. I saw Prince Ghika and Count Zamoyski. The former is advising Bucharest and will tell me to whom to apply. He spoke at some length of the ruin wrought in Roumania by the war, of the sufferings and want of the people, of the difficulty of restoring the administration of the railways, and of the hostile action of the Hungarians who seemed to regard the Roumanians as inferior and almost black men. He was glad that the ending of the Karl episode had removed the necessity for Roumanian military action, but said that the Western Hungary question was still open and that its determination might arouse serious difficulties.

Count Zamoyski expatiated on the troubles of Poland, on how it had been the scene of constant wars, retreats, occupations, and disturbances, and how fearfully difficult the whole situation was. He thought that the Polish mark was at a false standard. He told me that little was feared from Bolshevism this year, for Lenin was in a process of evolution towards a new and democratic form of Bolshevism based on the peasants and the security of property! Lenin was now against expropriation and altogether his views were greatly changing. But Trotsky did not follow him and led a middle party, while at the other extreme were the Terrorists. All the intellectuals and men of position had been murdered or exiled, and Z. thought that the Russians never understood organization and had no genius for it, least of all the present people in control. Perhaps in a couple of generations leaders might appear from the new strata, but meanwhile we were in for fifty years of chaos. A nice prospect!

Spent the evening looking into the German trouble. If

the Germans make no fresh proposals, or those which they make are unacceptable, it is probable that about half the 1919 Class in France will be called out in a few days. Men of this class in the devastated districts, abroad, or in certain categories of scholastic training will be exempt. The preparation of the movement and its execution will probably take a fortnight. The French intend to seize the whole Ruhr Valley, starting from the junction of the Wapper and the Rhine, passing through Solingen, Elberfeld, Barmen, Hagen, Unna, and then along the left bank of the Lippe back to the Rhine. They proposed to place a tax of twenty gold marks per ton on all Westphalian coal entering Germany, and expect to get from it one hundred and fifty to one hundred and sixty million gold marks a month, or two milliards of marks a year. They say that this will help us, as German coal costs under one pound a ton, and our coal double, so we shall recover our markets when the coal strike ends, but so far as the one hundred and fifty millions a month are concerned, the calculation is all based upon the Germans in the Ruhr continuing to work, which seems to me quite conjectural. There is also a prospect, as the French admit, that there may be troubles in the Ruhr, and that Germany may prevent food from going in, in which case the three or four million workmen of the Ruhr will have to be fed from elsewhere.

In general the position of France at this moment is that Germany has shown flagrant bad faith by refusing to meet her obligations over reparations, by refusing to disarm her secret forces, and by neglecting to prosecute her war criminals. She demands the moral support of England in the measures of coercion which she is now compelled to begin, measures which will apply to the centre of the Imperialist and reactionary agitation. L. G. has publicly declared the German proposals to be "thoroughly unsatisfactory" and has agreed in principle to the Ruhr occupation. The Belgian Press seems solid with France.

Dr. Simons speaks again in the Reichstag and says that Germany has only one thousand guns left. D'Abernon has left Berlin for London, but apparently only with explanations of the German offer, and no new offer.

It is certainly necessary to bring the Germans to book. But are we doing it in the best way? I should prefer a blockade on our present line, which would cost little and probably take effect sooner. It is not certain that the seizure of the Ruhr will bring the Germans to heel and then we shall come to the march on Berlin plus the Ruhr. I see no end to the evil consequences of this action, whereas the silent pressure of the blockade avoids them all. We must all back the French heartily because we are in for it, but we have no troops to spare, and no chance of getting any with Ireland and all our other troubles. Our military decrepitude will cause many other things to be done that we do not like. It is all a very bad business.

Saturday, April 30, 1921. Went to see M. Barthou, the War Minister, in the morning. He was very agreeable, and advised me not to go to London next week, as they meant to begin to act in the middle of the week, I should judge by Wednesday early. So I reluctantly gave up my plans and wired to England. He asked me to see him Monday at noon by which time he will have fixed up my plans for me with General Buat. He seemed in good spirits and to believe that all would go well. Afterwards called on Lieutenant-General Joostens to see about a Belgian permit. He was very official at first, but soon expanded and ended by saying that I was to regard his house as mine. He gave me a card which will serve in the Ruhr. Ordered some 1/200,000 maps. Lunched with the Countess Cahen d'Anvers, Lady Townshend, her daughter and nephew. Confidence in England seems only relative. We seem to be urging another ultimatum on the French. The latter are opposed to it and think it needless, as they regard the Treaty as the gospel. But I think it would throw on Simons and the Reichstag the responsibility of saying yes or no and would engage their responsibility directly. Whereas if we say nothing, they will do nothing, and this is the line of least resistance for their weak Government.

Philippe Millet foreshadows a financial control on the lines suggested by Benès. The Conference will probably begin this afternoon in London. Lovely weather, warm, soft air, and very pleasant. Went to see "Le Roi" at the Variétés at night and enjoyed this amusing piece and some perfect acting.

Sunday, May 1, 1921. A lovely day. Paris looking its best. Wrote a telegram to the *D. T.* on the situation. Lady Juliet lunched with me, and then we motored out to the country cottage of Princess Eugène Murat near Jouy-en-Josas, southeast of Versailles. Found there also Mme. M. and Princess Michel and Mr. Dodge. A charming place with some ten acres of orchard and gardens, thorough country and very peaceful. The idea of taking away the upper storey to make an airy living-room at one end of three cottages built together seemed a very good one. A perfect place for resting and writing. We passed Longchamps on the way and were glad we had not attended the races. There were thousands of smart cars there. Much talk of many things and people. It turned wet as we motored back to Paris. Road bad except through the Bois which was looking perfection. Dined at the grill to avoid the Sunday mob; Lady Harcourt dining there too. She has been ill. We had a little talk. All the news is of a very sad London.

Monday, May 2, 1921. The Conference in London was not in agreement yesterday. The main difference appears to be about the question of an ultimatum. We want Germany to be notified how she is to pay the 132 milliards fixed by the Reparations Committee as the total of her debt, and to suspend the occupation of the Ruhr till the reply comes a week hence. We also appear to object to taxing the Ruhr products. The French want to act at once. So do the Belgians. The Italians and Japanese support us. Much talk. I went to see Barthou's Chef de Cabinet this morning at midday. The telephone had been working badly and Briand's message this morning was not clear, but he was to telephone again at 2 P.M. and I am to call later at the French W.O. to learn what is decided. Made up my stationery kit for a fresh voyage in case of accidents. Saw Jemmy Watson looking wonderfully young and very smart.

Called again on M. Ladmirault and found that Briand's instructions are not coming till between six and eight to-night. It is believed to-night that the ultimatum party have won, but that Briand will be allowed to collect all the troops ready for an advance by the 8th or 10th, by which time the German reply to the ultimatum must be in. "Another delay," says every Frenchman, with a groan and a snarl. But it is the proper way to do things. The only trouble is that Briand will be expected by his own people to occupy the Ruhr in any case as hostage, whereas we seem to think that this will not be necessary if the Germans agree to our terms. Some uncertainty remains on the point. Our action in London has not been presented in a favourable light by some of the French journalists. The French are simply *aching* to get hold of the Ruhr, and I don't think that they can keep off it.

Tuesday, May 3, 1921. Saw M. Ladmirault and then General Hergault, the respective heads of M. Barthou's Civil and Military Cabinets. The intended Essen *coup* planned for Wednesday is off, and I am not sorry. They are making arrangements for me to join General Dé-goutte's staff on Monday next and will send me my instructions here by Sunday.

The impressions derived from the accounts of the London Conference are still not good. My impression is that the French mean to carry out the occupation of the Ruhr whether we like it or not, and that only an American voice can stop them. The 1919 Class was mobilised late last night after a telephone talk between Barthou and Briand. The French cannot withdraw all the young men from their occupations only to send them back again if the Boches accept the ultimatum. So they say. We have evidently come near to a rupture in London. Sauerwein says that "there have been the most painful moments that can be imagined." I wonder if they understand in London that Briand, or anyone else, will be upset at the *rentrée* of the Chamber on the 19th if, by that date, no action is taken. The French are perfectly sick about the procession of Conferences which have taken place, and have ended in smoke. I told Hergault that "par acquit de conscience" I wished to tell him the serious objections to the Ruhr occupation which I entertained, the cost, the risks, the danger of a strike both of staffs and workmen, and the fearful economic crisis that might follow if Upper Silesia also struck, as seems is happening, owing to the statement that the Poles are not to have the industrial triangle. I said that if we needed eight thousand certificated men to replace the German directing staff in Silesia, how many should we need in Westphalia, with its four times greater industry? I thought the blockade a far better, cheaper, and more effective weapon. But there it is, the French are set upon it.

It seems that the Ruhr will be encircled by two divisions on the north and two on the south, with a cavalry corps about Griffon to the east of the industrial area under General Férand. Each part will make detachments to protect the technical staff and the new customs staff. The 5th Cavalry Division was intended to make the raid on Essen. I suppose it will now await events at Düsseldorff. It is under General Simon and arrives to-day. They say that there are only one hundred and fifty French engineers to replace any German engineers who resign. A drop in the ocean. Hergault told me that the workmen were well-disposed and I told him that I had heard other opinions. The movement is to begin at "H. o'clock" — an hour to be named from Paris.

There seems to be some 10,000 German police, green or blue, and gendarmerie in the Ruhr, and 15,000 Reichswehr chiefly the 6th Division 11,000 men, and the 3d Division of Cavalry 4000 men near the neutral region. It is supposed that three other Reichswehr divisions (2d, 3d, and 14th) could come up in six days. But the danger is not here. It is in a general strike as a protest, in which case all public utility services may be suspended and the district return to anarchy. It is another industrial triangle with one hundred kilometres of front, Wesel-Hamm, Hamm-Solingen. The real German Commander is Herr Hugo Stinnes.

Wednesday, May 4, 1921. Nothing to be done at Paris till next week, so crossed to London to see Burnham. Found at Dover that the Allies were pretty well agreed, but it is clear, from Austen Chamberlain's statement in the House of Commons yesterday, that he thinks that the Ruhr will not be occupied if the Germans surrender. I am not confident that this will be true for the French. They all lead me to suppose that they will occupy it as a "gage" *in any event,* and it is necessary to ascertain whether there is any want of clear understanding on this point. There are many interpellations awaiting Briand on the 19th, and he will be under much pressure to act. Things bad in Upper Silesia. The Poles have begun a movement, half strike, half insurrection.

Met Lady Kilmarnock at Dover straight from Berlin. D'Abernon seems to remain optimistic. However, in eight days the situation must be cleared up one way or another.

CHAPTER IX

WITH THE FRENCH ON THE RHINE

The Allied ultimatum of May 5th — I return to Paris — The revolt of the Poles in Upper Silesia — Arrive at Mayence — The Saar — General Michel — French plan of concentration — The 1919 Class — The New German Government — General Degoutte — A long conversation — Wealth of the Ruhr — Berlin and the Rhineland — "Black" troops — The railways in German hands — The Kaiserin's funeral — Mr. Lloyd George on Upper Silesia — The hidden formations of the German Army — German informers — Wiesbaden — Fury aroused in France by Mr. Lloyd George's speech — Wiesbaden races — Another talk with General Degoutte — His hatred of war — General officers in France — Our incomprehensible Prime Minister — Dangers from future Napoleons of commerce — General Claudon on the Rhinelanders — A good repartee — Commandant Philippi on our new customs duties — A lucky bargee — The Mayence Cathedral — The Gutenberg Statue — Our new *douane* at work — A visit to Coblentz — Mr. Arnold Robertson — A conversation with his staff — Captain Troughton — Captain Georgi — Their views on the customs and the Ruhr — Ruhr statistics — Our battalions ordered to Silesia — Lunch with M. Tirard — A talk with M. Rolin Jaequemyns — General Allen's opinions — Return to Mayence — M. Briand's great speech — A German bank director on the economical situation — Levies, taxes, and wages — A review — Visit to Frankfort — The Stadel Gallery — The Lenbachs — Consul-General Gosling — Goethe's house — A talk with the editor of the *Frankfurter Zeitung* — A final conversation with General Degoutte — Conclusions from three weeks on the Rhine.

Paris, Sunday, May 8, 1921. Returned to Paris from London to-day.

The Allied ultimatum to Germany was handed to the German Ambassador on May 5 at 11 A.M. in Downing Street. The time limit expires May 12. The Germans are invited to carry out the directions of the Reparations Commission, as well as the disarmament and the trial of the war criminals, and to notify their resolve to do so, failing which the Ruhr Valley will be occupied, and such other naval and military measures will be taken as may be required.

There is a slight balance of belief in the probability of a German surrender, but no certainty, and Berlin is in confusion from the resignation of the Government. Meanwhile the Poles rose in Upper Silesia on May 2, and practically control the country east of what is called the Korfanty line. The French troops are not attempting to suppress the rising. The Italians have had some losses in trying to do so. We have no troops there now. It is an attempt by the Poles to forestall in their favour the decision of the Supreme Council on the plébiscite, and it is said to be due to Polish knowledge that the English and Italian Members of the Commission had not given the industrial triangle to the Poles. Who told the Poles? They seem to have learnt the story just before Le Rond set out for Paris.

It is at least a curious coincidence that the Poles rose on the same day that the French intended to seize Essen. The Germans ask the Powers to suppress the revolt and clearly leave it to be seen that they are prepared to do so if we do not act. A nice state of affairs! The Poles are a lawless people, and the French, instead of acting judicially, are supporting them for political reasons.

In the evening German opinion appeared to be hardening against acceptance. One of the obstacles is the inability of the Government to make Bavaria disband her *Einwohnerwehre* who now number 320,000 men, and have, by the explicit admission of Dr. von Kahr, 240,000 rifles, besides guns and machine guns. Theoretically this is a private organisation, but it is paid by the Reich and Bavaria, and its H.Q. are in the Ring Hotel at Munich. The men are carefully selected and are trained and do musketry. The whole thing is dead against the spirit and letter of the Treaty (Art. 160).

Monday, May 9, 1921. Called at the French W.O. in the morning. I am to go to Mayence and report to the Commandant Camus of the Q.G. at the Palais de Justice. Took tickets. Left at night 9.15 P.M.

Mayence, Tuesday, May 10, 1921. Arrived Mayence 1 P.M. The usual plentiful crop of customs houses. A French douane at Forbach, a second Saar Government douane at Nambonn, and a third German investigation at Turkimuhle. The Saar seemed very busy and prosperous, but a German fellow-traveller employed there told me that they were overstocked and were only working four days a week. Owing to shorter hours and five years of underfeeding the output of the basin was only about two-thirds that of 1913. There had been trouble at first between French and Germans, but all was peace now.

Went to the Hollander Hotel on the Rhine. General Degoutte, the Commander of the Inter-Allied Army of the Rhine, is away for the day at Düsseldorf. Saw his Chief of Staff, General Michel, at 4 P.M. and had a talk. The concentration goes on. He showed me the plan of it day by day. It will not be completed till the morning of the 15th, but there will be enough troops by the night of the 12th to carry out the Ruhr *coup*. There are six French and Belgian divisions of Infantry, three French Cavalry divisions, and a small British detachment of three squadrons and some Tanks. The operation orders are provisional, and will not be carried out until the word comes from Paris. I said, "Then you, at least, are en règle, mon général." We thought that if the Boches did not give way, Briand would fall if no action were taken before the 19th. M. has no idea what the Germans will decide, but he thought that they would postpone a reply to the last moment. He told me that the 1919 Class had come up well and showed a good spirit. There were no shirkers, but they were much incensed against the Boches, and showed their feeling towards the tame Rhinelanders. M. thought that the total available Allied force was 80,000 men, but said that I could say 100,000, and he imagined that Paris had still not settled what to do about the civil side of the Government. He thought that the state of siege would be proclaimed at first and that the soldiers would rule. Also that the workmen would be quiet, and probably the mining staff too, as he did not think that they would sacrifice their business for mere political objects. Michel a good clear-headed man, very French, tall, and uses glasses.

I thought that all the German part of this valley and the hilly region between it and the Saar looked wonderfully rich and well-cultivated. The crops, vines, and fruit trees were most promising. There are some *tirailleurs Algériens* here; very smart chaps: they are on duty at Headquarters, and I should be sorry for a Boche who tried to force the *consigne*. There is also a regiment of Morocco *tirailleurs* hereabouts, reckoned of the first quality. Degoutte formerly commanded the famous Morocco Division. These are very serious troops. Black troops there are none here now. One must not call the North African troops black, because they are not, or at least very few of them. The Rhine here is fearfully low, the lowest known for one hundred and sixty years, they say. The boats can hardly use it and only at one-fifth to one-third of their usual loads. The Alps without snow in the winter and the present drought are cause and effect. If Nature makes up for it by a wet summer, where will be our harvest?[1]

Degoutte's A.D.C., Lieutenant Chapel, of the Cuirassiers, dined with me and we had a great talk about events and politics. He says that Degoutte works from 9.15 to 12.30 and from 2 to 7 and never stops working.

Wednesday, May 11, 1921. This morning came the news that a new German Government of the Socialists, Democrats, and Centre had been formed and that the Reich had accepted the Allied ultimatum last night by 221 votes to 175. Later there came the official confirmation to H.Q. here, but from the Belgians and not from Paris. The text showed that the acceptance was complete and without reservation. I went to see General Degoutte at the Palace of Justice at eleven, talked with him alone for an hour, and then walked round with him to the Grand Ducal Palace where we lunched together alone, in overheated rooms, and stayed talking there till 4 P.M. We covered much ground in these five hours, and discussed the Ruhr operation, the conduct of the Germans, the profits of the Ruhr stroke, future dealings with Germany, the chance of an-

---

[1] Nature did not. The summer was abnormally hot and fine, producing a great wheat crop, except in parts of Russia, where the crops were burnt up and a terrible famine was caused.

other war, the state of Central Europe, and the case of Austria, besides many other points of politics, economics, and commerce. The very deuce of a pow-wow.

In general, I am not sure that General Degoutte is very sorry that the operation in the Ruhr is apparently off. He did not anticipate many difficulties if he still had to march, but there is an element of uncertainty, though he will not quite acknowledge it. He declares that one-fifth of the whole wealth of Germany is contained in Westphalia and that in French occupation it would be a paying concern. He tells me that he is exactly informed of the state of German opinion in both Ruhr and Rhineland, and that all the opinions of the Socialistic and Bolshevist parties are known to him. Like General Michel, he is sure that the directing staff will remain and that they will be punished by the German Government if they leave and return to unoccupied Germany because the products of the Ruhr are quite indispensable to German industry. He is sure that the workmen will remain if they are fed, and declares that he will improve their position, and that the savage repression of their rising by the *Reichswehr* put them against all the Right parties in the Reichstag. He looks to the imposition of a *dime* on all Ruhr products; thinks that it may amount to two hundred milliards of francs a year; that France can recoup herself out of this indemnity without paralysing German trade, and that the rise of German prices will help both us and France. He admits that it is impracticable to replace the German staffs of industries if they leave, but he does not believe they will. He is not surprised at the German surrender, and eight days ago had reported to his Government that this would happen.

He could not admit that the operation would still take place unless some new fact came out, for France always kept her engagements, and it was clear to him that a German surrender implied the abandonment of the plan. But Paris and public opinion might be very disappointed. They would not get their *gage*, nor their money immediately, and of course it would be said that there was just one more German promise and that it would be broken like all others.

He had received no fresh instructions from Paris. The concentration would go on, and he was off to Düsseldorf for forty-eight hours to-morrow to inspect newly-arriving troops. He meant to congratulate them on having caused the German surrender.

General Degoutte reminded me that we had met at General Gouraud's Headquarters in 1916 — I remember the occasion well. He said that when he arrived here, in succession to Mangin, he had done his best to ingratiate himself with the Rhinelanders and had promised to do all that could be done for them to make them happy. But before long — and apparently about the same time that General Nollet's Commission of Control began to encounter obstruction at Berlin — Degoutte found that Berlin was putting spokes in his wheel and issuing secret orders to the Germans to have no dealings with the French officers or French members of the Rhineland High Commission. Berlin sent Prussian officers to take control of every sort of service and to instruct youth *sub rosa* in patriotic duties. These men ran everything because the Rhinelanders were so submissive, and there came about a great change in the behaviour of the population towards the French. Even his Generals had been hustled, French flags [1] had been torn down, and there had been other incidents. This accounts for the strict *consigne* to the Algerian and Moroccan Troops who guard the Headquarters and the Grand Ducal Palace. D. told me that he could not afford that the *grand chef* should be *bousculé*, so he always took his car to his house, not two hundred yards distant, except on this occasion when he walked round with me, and when he wanted exercise he motored out some miles and then got out to walk. I noticed that he even unlocked with his own key the various doors in his Palace. But all the same he had told someone that he would only care to

---

[1] The British practice of hauling down the flag at sundown is not generally followed by foreigners.

be Kaiser of the Germans, if he were Kaiser at all, as they were so perfectly obedient to any *mot d'ordre*. .

D. is an omnivorous reader and an indefatigable worker. He seems very well-informed of everything that is going on. He believes that the Germans intend to wage a war of revenge at the first favourable moment and does not see how it is to be prevented. He watches them as a cat watches a mouse. We thought that if the Control Commission remained for some years and the French held the Ruhr, the Germans could not do much, and D. only asked for five or six years' grace until France had restored her finances and general position. He approved of the Reparations Commission in its new Control shape at Berlin, but did not know whether it would be effective. .

D. said that he had not intended[1] to take any so-called "black troops" into the Ruhr. They were not really black, being Berbers from North Africa, and in the two large native guards which he inspected as we walked to his house there were only two or three real blacks. All the others were fairish men, fine-looking chaps, the Algerian and Tunisian men with the red chechia or fez, and the Moroccans with the khaki chechia. They had been much abused by the Germans who hated them, and there had been a row the other day in which a German had been killed. The man who had killed him was before a *conseil de guerre* and would probably be condemned to death, but D. said that he might find a difficulty in approving such a sentence, since all the native troops knew how constantly they were insulted by the Germans. Troops are generally on the move in Mayence with tambours and clairons — making a racket. The native troops make a good impression when under arms. They are smart and steady. Our conversation was so long and ranged over so much ground that I cannot jot it all down. Degoutte is short in stature and short-sighted. He has pleasant manners, is very steady, and has much breadth of mind and coolness in judgement. He does

---

[1] He told me later that this had been imposed upon him, but did not say by whom.

not spare himself and keeps a very sharp eye on the Germans and all their works. He was particularly cordial and thanked me for all that I had done for France since 1906. I think that he would have kept me talking till night had I not at last risen to go out of sheer fatigue of talking.

Walked about the town in the late afternoon and wired a message again to the *D. T.* The name of Conrad Tack on a bootseller's shop would have appealed to Dickens, I thought. Decided to await events here for a short time. One could not find a better centre in present events.

Thursday, May 12, 1921. Went round to see General Michel. There is no news except that Marshal Foch has sent instructions suspending all movements until further orders. This does not affect the concentration which proceeds according to plan. I asked about the German management of railways from the French frontier. Was this wise, and could not the German personnel *saboter* the lines on a word from Berlin? Michel thought they could, but all the lines used for the concentration were being guarded by the Allies, including Americans and British, and all the main bridges were held. So the Boches could not do much, and minor damage could be quickly repaired.

The arrival of French *cheminots* in case of need had been foreseen. The telegraphs were also in German hands, but the French had their ciphers, and all the main groups of forces, besides Paris, of course, were in wireless touch. Michel thought that the 1919 Class would probably remain till the end of June, and be replaced by the young Class in July. The latter had come in on April 15 and had not done much training owing to the 'flu, but would be fit enough for police duties, he thought.

The satisfaction which I feel on account of the very correct attitude of the French soldiers here is considerably mitigated on reading the French Press of the 12th on its arrival here this afternoon. It seems almost to gloat over the difficulties which Germany will find in meeting our demands for reparation and disarmament, and, after giving long lists of both, lays stress on a promise said to have been given by L. G. to Briand at the London Conference to the effect that the Ruhr sanction would be applied on the report of the Reparations Commission or of the Military Control Commission affirming any want of obedience on the part of Germany.

It will be only too easy to *constater* this fact with a little ill-will, and I see that there has been a conference at the Élysées on disarmament at which Millerand, Briand, the chief Ministers, Foch, and Weygand were present. The object appears to have been to discuss the measures to be applied to carry out the disarmament indicated by the Allies in their letter of January 29, 1921. There will not be much difficulty in convicting Germany of *manquements* if it is still desired to occupy the Ruhr. Here also is Provost de Launay in the *Éclair* talking very large of immense armies which Germany can mobilise in a few days. He talks of seven divisions of cavalry and twenty-one of infantry supported by innumerable formations of *Einwohnerwehre*— all leading up to the conclusion that the Ruhr must be occupied at once.

I must ask Degoutte on his return who has been posting up P. de L. during his tour in this part of the world. D. certainly told me that the Germans had done marvels, and that he was much struck by the organisation which was better than anything he could have devised, but de Launay's story is a bit thick, and I personally cannot conceive how the Germans can dream of war after all their sufferings which every soul here remembers so well. Even now the people here have black bread, no butter, and there is no milk except for the children, while the taxes on the working people seem to me far higher than ours. The real trouble is the abandonment of the Anglo-American guarantee of France against another German attack. The French now know that they must protect themselves and are nervous about the future. The camouflage of secret German armaments adds to the anxiety. The French have a sense of being tricked and are ready to believe anything.

Did X's commission and bought a good Zeiss No. 8 race-glass with good leather case and strap for £4.15.0! Took the opportunity of having my eyes examined by the best German oculist here. He charged me 2s.6d.! Also he found my eyes quite sound and fitted me out with a pair of glasses for reading the infinitesimal print of Bellows and Dr. Feller. I suppose that in London I should have had to pay seventeen guineas for the opinion and the Zeiss glasses instead of £4.17.6. I was rather amused in one shop to see that the hilts of officers' swords are now made into stands for electric lights; not quite swords into ploughshares, but very near it. The windows are filled with photos of the Kaiserin's funeral. It seems to have been a tremendous Imperialist demonstration in which crowds of old officers, officials, students, etc., took part, the whole thing on an imposing scale and all the best-known old leaders present. I don't wonder that it made the French thoughtful. The Mainz public crowd round these photos, very silent and respectful. There was no doubt where their sympathies lay. There is about as much real Republicanism in Germany as there is in Pall Mall.

Friday, May 13, 1921. Wrote and sent off a longish article to the *D. T.* on the French attitude towards all this German trouble. Had a talk with General Michel in the afternoon and am to begin my investigation of the secret German organisations to-morrow. There is no news and all is quiet, except in Upper Silesia on which subject our press seems to be speaking stiffly of French partiality, and I do not wonder. Took a stroll round the town. All the old names, the Kaiser Strasse and the rest, remain as of old. Rather a pleasant town, with old and modern buildings in turn and with fairly good shops. Am amused to find the stupendous difficulties in the way of sending the glasses to X. The formalities and papers to be signed are interminable. In fact every conceivable difficulty is thrown in the way of sending anything out and of getting anything in. I am following it up as a practical experiment.

Talked to various people. The six German regiments in garrison here in 1914 are said to have lost 30,000 men killed in the war. I doubt whether there is a first favourite for the future throne. But they all admit that they want a Constitutional Monarch, and some one to represent Germany worthily. Ebert, they say, was a distiller, then kept a pub., became an editor, and is now President. How could he talk to Queen Mary? they ask. Why should he? I mentally reply. Degoutte and I had a long talk of Russia the other day. I said that I preferred the Bolshies to a reactionary Government which would surely join Germany. It was better to have the Soviets and fifty years of chaos than a Russian reaction leaning on Germany. Degoutte wanted a sealed-pattern Republic, and I thought we could not get it in Russia.

Saturday, May 14, 1921. All quiet on the Rhine, but in upper Silesia things still bad. L. G. makes a statement in the H. of C. of a firm and notable character, so far as we can judge by the summary, against the Polish action, and says that we shall not accept the *fait accompli*. It was quite time to speak out. Wrote an article on Travel in Europe, and after a talk with General Michel on Upper Silesian matters went to his Second Bureau to talk with Commandant de Charry and Captain Florange on the hidden formations of the German Army. At my request they gave me a map showing the distribution of the *Reichswehr*. It is pretty strictly on the lines of Versailles, but it is also considered more than probable that the organisation pursues the old aim of restoring the twenty-one Army Corps of 1914. Each regiment of infantry is known, or believed, to possess three complete sets of arms, clothing, and equipment, and the seven divisions could become twenty-one on expansion, while the cavalry could become seven divisions.

It is necessary that the redundant arms and equipments should be given up. There are also more engineers than are allowed and the bridge-trains are enough for an Army Corps. The dépôts might similarly expand. The twenty-one divisions, if formed, might number 300,000 men, and it is probable that they would be completed as fast as the

Reichswehr was made up when it went to put down the Ruhr Revolt. This the French think to be only a covering force. The National Army is expected to group itself behind on the *Schupo* or *Schützpolizei* nucleus, which is the old dog in a new doublet, namely the old *Sicherheitspolizei* abolished by order of the Allies, but in fact handed over to the Ministry of the Interior and only renamed. It has 80,000 men in Prussia, and in all 150,000 men. It is considered to be the *cadre* of the future national army. How they will be formed is not precisely known, but the *livrets* or small books of 7,000,000 men are in existence and touch is kept with men through the pensions officer. There is also a system of passing men through the *Schupo* for nominally experimental training stages, which looks ominously like the old Prussian camouflage after 1806. Given the many rifles and machine guns known to exist, and the probability that many guns are also concealed, a good-sized body of troops could be formed, probably 1,500,000 it is thought, and the idea is that the triplicated *Reichswehr* would delay an enemy until this force was assembled in the interior. Such an idea had been formulated by a German General and is becoming a sort of doctrine.

Behind all this is the *Orgesch* (organisation Escherich), the *Einwohnerwehren*, and other nondescript bodies whose disbandment the Allies are expected to demand. If they go, Florange expects the old *Kriegerverein* in a new form to take their place. This old institution has been suddenly galvanised into life again in the last three weeks and is in course of formation on a regimental, battalion, and company basis, but nominally, of course, only as an old comrades' association. It takes in all the men who fought in the war, or may do so. It is an organisation which was not explicitly forbidden at Versailles, but was forbidden to occupy itself with military matters. Even if it is suppressed, something will revive in the guise of sporting, athletic, or gymnastic clubs. Even football is now regarded not as a sport for sport, but as a sport for war training. One must apparently regard every German football team as an eventual platoon!

We had a talk over it all. Florange is well-posted and has everything at his fingers' ends. I said, "Do you really believe that a people who have suffered so much want war again?" Florange said, No, the people did not, but the old Imperialist and reactionary parties wanted to re-establish a strong Germany and it was difficult to prevent them from doing so. This disastrous docility of the German people, and the hankering of all but the Socialists for Monarchism, made many things possible. There was all this huge mass of officers out of work who longed for the re-establishment of their prerogatives, and these people naturally wished to act soon, as they could not afford to wait. If we could put off the possibility of a war for fifteen or twenty years, until this class and the trained soldiers were *hors de cause*, and the old military spirit had given way to the civil spirit, we might get over the danger of a fresh German aggression. It was also necessary to bring many fortresses and coast defences into line with the Treaty. Könisberg, for example, is only allowed (I do not know when this rule was made) to have twenty-two heavy guns and actually has seven hundred or eight hundred. The Bavarian *Einwohnerwehren* have 240,000 rifles on their President's own admission, and all this was quite outside the Treaty rights, so there was a good deal to be done. Nollet and his people had done marvels. The Germans were champion informers (*dénonciateurs*) and frequently gave away for money the hiding-places of arms. Even if Nollet and his people came away, Florange assumed that we should leave in Germany a good service of information. I asked about the cavalry squadrons being called by the names of the old regiments. Did this mean that each squadron would be the nucleus of this old regiment when it was resuscitated? Had they its uniform? No, said Florange, they all had the same uniforms, but there was a badge of the old regiment on the right arm to recall the traditions of the old regiment, and one could deduce from that what conclusion one liked.

Whit Sunday, May 15, 1921. Wrote on the German

Army for the *D. T.* till late last night. Motored to Wiesbaden. The consul undiscoverable.[1] A fine town with solid
buildings and pleasant, broad, shaded streets, with avenues
of limes and chestnuts. Lunched at the Kurhaus. Many
people, but no English. Pretty gardens with lake and
shaded walks. An agreeable spot. Cooking awful. Company common. The only pretty women were French.
Came back through Bibrich. The French are in all the
German barracks which have been rechristened "Quartier
Joffre," "Gouraud," and other French Generals' names.
The Rhine continues to fall and huge sandbanks appear in
the stream. The defect of Mainz is the want of hills near
the river, such as those which give such distinction to
Prague, Budapest, and Coblenz. It is flat and dull, but
beyond Wiesbaden one gets to the lower Taunus and there
are some wooded hills which look agreeable. The Kurhaus
seems to have every attraction in the form of music, gam-
bling, reading-rooms, gardens, and so on.

L. G.'s speech against the Polish *Putsch* in Upper Silesia
makes the French wild. It is perfectly justified, so far as
Korfanty's banditti are concerned, but I think, on reading
the text, had better not have been delivered, as it is in-
directly a severe criticism of the French, does no good, and
only embitters the controversy, already acute enough.
Briand replies in an address to French journalists, and says
that France accepts no orders from her Allies. L. G.'s suggestion that the Germans might be allowed to retake Upper
Silesia is a serious matter. I fancy the Germans will not
use the *Reichswehr* in Silesia for fear that the Polish Army
may cross the frontier. They seem to be collecting bands
to oppose bands. If they attack the Poles, L. G.'s speech
will be considered responsible, and the Germans are pretty
sure to come in conflict with the French, who will immediately occupy the Ruhr. All very unpleasant. Meanwhile
the Allies are responsible for order and security in the
Province, but we have no troops there now, the Italians are
few, and the French will not oppose the Poles, who are

---

[1] He had been abolished.

their allies — a nasty tangle. English opinion seems to be almost entirely with L. G. At this rate the French Alliance won't last much longer. O! golden silence!

Monday, May 16, 1921. A Bank Holiday here. Went to the cathedral in the morning. A large Romanesque-Gothic pile shut in by houses built on to it almost all round. A certain simple grandeur within, but could not look over it, as it was full of little girls who were receiving, I suppose, their first communion. The cathedral was full and there were rows waiting without. The girls were all in white from head to foot with white wreaths and their hair down fastened with white bows. A great many men in the congregation. The Centre Party must be pretty strong here. It is the most solid and consistent of all the German parties. I wonder whether a State or a Church gains most from union and loses most by separation? I should say the State, in both cases.

Began to study the Ruhr.

Went off in the afternoon to see the Wiesbaden races. They began at the unusual — to us — hour of three and ended at seven, which is more convenient than Ascot hours except for visitors from afar. A very pretty course with the pleasant scenery of the Taunus foot-hills in the background and a lovely day. Spacious stands, in tiers like the Coliseum, and not in rows as in our stands. Nice lawns in front and a band. I should say five thousand people at least. Degoutte and many French officers and their families and men who all kept apart from the Germans. I saw no English there. There was flat, hurdle, and jump racing. The horses were quite good and the riding vigorous. Hundreds of cars were there, and masses of money poured into the totalisators. A good middle and upper class country attendance. Many brought their children, even quite young ones, a variation rather pleasant. Returned with Colonel Legros, of the Artillery, who is in charge of Army sports at the French H.Q.

Tuesday, May 17, 1921. Finished the Ruhr article last night and sent it off with that on the German Army, both registered. The political news to-day is bad. The French press unanimously falls upon L. G.'s speech and cannot abuse it enough. Briand has refused to meet L. G. at Boulogne and says that he must consult his Parliament first. He also says that any invasion of Upper Silesia by the Germans will be regarded as an act of war and that France will take action in the West. Generals Nollet and Masterman on May 13 called on the Germans to fulfil the requirements of their note of January 29 by May 20. This demand covers disarmament of land and air forces. But other reports say that the *Orgesch*, etc., are given till June 20, and that July 15 is the final date for completion of all satisfaction.

I had a long talk with General Degoutte in the afternoon. He is off again to Düsseldorf to-morrow to inspect the latest arrivals, but he has no fresh orders and is not informed of political events, though he naturally sees, as I do, what the Paris Press is saying. He says that the newly arrived troops are magnificent, but require a little calming as they are rather full of fight. He says that we must remember all that these men have seen in the ravaged provinces, in many cases their homes, and the indignities suffered by their women-folk. He mentioned the case of a young officer who had hustled some Germans at some place. His Colonel had come into D.'s office to plead for him. "Punish him, General, yes, but I wish you to know that his mother was outraged by the Germans and that the officer can plead extenuating circumstances." "How could I remain deaf to such an appeal?" asked D. It occurred to me that if trouble broke out in the Ruhr with the French on one side of the basin and the Belgians on the other, there might be some ugly work. I do not know which of the two people hates the Germans most, or feels the more poignantly that the German has never been repaid in kind.

We talked of yesterday's racing. D. told me that he had done everything possible to placate the Rhinelanders and bring them into a good spirit, mentioning many generosities, gifts, and help, but he did not seem to think that much had come out of it all. We laughed at all the throughbreds, the well-dressed crowds, the cars, and the *pari-mutuel* at the races, and did not feel very uncertain about the wealth of this country. D. told me that he hated war. He had not belonged to a military family or the aristocracy, but to a bourgeois stock who had never been in the Army, but he had come in to repay the debt of 1870. I told him that the general officers' list in France now aroused my enthusiasm. They were a splendid set of men and politics seemed utterly uncongenial to them. Yes, he said, time was when politics governed the upper ranks, but the political favourites had gone down in the war, and now only the real fighting Generals remained. It no longer sufficed to be an aristocrat, or to have been brought up by the Jesuits, or even to be in the pocket of some advanced Socialist Party. There were all classes represented now, and not only bourgeois-bred Generals, but some of inferior *provenance*. One General on the *Conseil Supérieur* was the son of a gendarme. Politics were absolutely barred, and were in fact detested by all. We talked of Pétain. D. agreed that he had three times saved the cause during the war, first at Verdun, secondly in the June, 1917, mutinies, and lastly after Gough's defeat when he had so rapidly taken over the whole English front during a disastrous battle between the Oise and the Somme and had held the enemy. D. thought the mutinies had been exaggerated. "Only" ten divisions had been affected by them! I did not know there were so many! His own command had come up to replace some of those who had given way and was absolutely unaffected by the bad feeling.

D. and others here find L. G. incomprehensible; — one thing one day and another thing another. "White to-day, black to-morrow, and red the day after," as one General said to me. What was really important, said D., was that we should keep together as we had need of each other. No one defends the Polish *Putsch* to me, but they ask how the French could be expected to shoot their Polish Allies and are amazed that L. G. should suggest as a possibility that the Germans should enter Upper Silesia to do so. The trouble, thought D., had come from the two months' delay since the plébiscite and no decision. If he and I had the affair to settle, we could do it in half an hour. The way to succeed was not to make flaming speeches, but to get round a table and talk it over quietly. He thought the whole affair very grave. No troops would go from here. As General Michel said, "We cannot be everywhere." We are all looking forward to the 19th when Briand meets the Chambers. Meanwhile D. is asking his troops to remember that they have only come to do police work, and not to become excited or vengeful. He thought that France wanted peace above all things and he was certainly not seeking adventures. A *coup d'état* by a French General in these days was absolutely impossible. The whole Army thought like that. I believe D. to be entirely sincere in his hatred of war and desire for peace. But he loves his troops and prefers to be always among them. He had a fine record in the war, and after our long talks I have learnt to appreciate his measure and moderation. He seems to me just the man for the present job, that is to say, if no military indiscretion is a desideratum.

I asked him whether the second Bureau belief in the intended triplication of the *Reichswehr* came from isolated cases or from something better. D. quite believed that the deduction was generally applicable. It was drawn from many hundred reports all leading up to the one conclusion. D. could not conceive on what grounds the Allies had allowed the *Schupo* to exist in its present form.

He talked a good deal of Hugo Stinnes and his influence. Stinnes seemed to him a type of dominator much more dangerous than Napoleon. He was a Napoleon of commerce and economics, and bent, or tried to bend, all the world to his will. It was a type that the world could not permit to endure, and a type likely to be the cause of future wars if it did. One man should not be allowed to possess such infinite powers for mischief. I said that Cecil Rhodes was on the smaller theatre of South Africa a prototype of Stinnes. Another might come in America or Russia, perhaps even in France.

Wednesday, May 18, 1921. No change here or in Upper Silesia. Our press calmer and see the harm done. The French press biting and very hostile. There are more poisonous innuendoes in Henry de Jouvenel's leader in to-day's *Matin* than in any article that I have ever read. Is it the old story repeating itself once more? We have no enemy in Europe except the dominant Power and France is becoming that Power. That seems to me the principle unconsciously behind L. G.'s outburst. And we are practically disarmed by the short sight and folly of our rulers. The French say that they have 100,000 men on the Rhine to carry out their policy and on the English side there is only a speech! A truly serious moment. Will opinion at home gradually form and harden against France? If so, we must look to ourselves, reintroduce the Registration Act of 1915, amend the Service Acts, and then pass and suspend them till we need them, as we did the old Militia Ballot. But we must realise that we cannot afford an anti-French policy with no army, with Germany in the dust, and with the French Army the only modern army in the world. A diplomacy unbacked by arms can never succeed.

Where is our French Alliance now? I hope that this fatal course will be arrested. France is not populous enough to dominate Europe when it recovers. It is a temporary and rather fortuitous superiority of an army. So we should keep our heads and mend the broken windows if we can. The next week or two may be rather big with fate. The *Frankfurter* publishes to-day the text of Nollet's calls on the Germans, with all the claims and the dates on which they are to be settled. Will the Germans, and can they, fulfil the demands? Went to Wiesbaden and ruminated over all the possibilities. Pleasant in the shady gardens of the Kurhaus listening to a good band. A very hot day.

By the way, I asked Degoutte yesterday whether he had ready a proclamation to the Ruhr population. No, he said this was the business of the Paris Government and he supposed that they were attending to it. He would declare the *état de siège*, as had been done at Frankfort during the brief

French occupation there, and later, law would be administered by a *cour martiale*. I asked him about the decision of the *conseil de guerre* in the case of the *tirailleur* who had killed his man. It was not over yet, but D. said that, except in time of war, all capital sentences had to go to the President of the Republic. He, Degoutte, would have no power to confirm a death sentence. He said that a French *conseil de guerre* was always severe. Noted to-day that Domitian and Foch seem to have had the same idea about the Mayence bridge-head. Both pushed out to the Taunus hills.

Thursday, May 19, 1921. L. G. sends out by Reuter a statement that he holds to his views on Upper Silesia and that opinion in Italy and America is with him.

Went to have a talk with General Claudon and Colonel Spiral, of the Mayence Military Administration, which is under the High Commission of the Rhineland. Claudon confirms Degoutte's opinion that the change of behaviour of the German administration towards the French was due to orders from Berlin. These orders were that the Germans were never to meet the French if it could be avoided and were not to reply to any invitations sent to them. The Rhinelanders, said General C., were good, friendly people, *bons enfants*, and only asked to live in peace and make money. Now they had been taken to task about their easy manners with the French and had been hauled over the coals. He now never saw the German employé who was working in his office at 44 Rue Schiller, though formerly they met constantly and were on quite friendly terms. It was the same everywhere. The German propaganda from Berlin had taken firm hold, and was directing all efforts towards Germanising opinion and preaching strong patriotism. All the old forces were still at work, the militarists, professors, and the clergy worked hand in hand, and the Rhinelanders were too easy-going to resist, though they were far from Berlin, and owing to the structure of the country had easier relations with the West than the East. He was not surprised. After all, they were Germans. It was like Bavaria and Prussia, who resembled a quarrelsome couple who threw the china at each other until a third person intervened when they combined against him and said, "We are at home, and can do as we please." He thought Germany very populous, rich, and strong. He told me how at a lunch given by Tirard, Pierpont Noyes, the American, had taken up a rose, which was withered, from the table decorations and had said that it resembled Germany, being faded and fallen. "Yes," interrupted a Frenchman present, "*la rose est fanée mais le rosier est fort.*"

In the afternoon went to see Commandant Philippi at the German Customs Office on the quay. A capable man, in uniform, a black beard, quick and sure of himself, about forty-five, a man to bear in mind. He is in administrative charge of the Mayence customs line and his rule extends to Worms. He has only a very small staff, but all the railways, the rivers, and the roads are held by small posts of six soldiers under one of his customs officers, and he thinks that he stops everything and that little can pass. He is organising a second line in rear to make sure. The whole line of the Rhine customs only takes three chief inspectors, fifteen inspectors, and about one hundred and twenty customs house officials to control the German customs officials who remain at their posts. He thinks that the takings on the whole of the new line under the tariff instituted by Rules 81 and 82 of the T.A.H.C. may amount to one hundred million francs a month, [1] and so over a milliard francs a year. P. says that it will take another month to fix the whole thing up definitely and he rather hinted at an increase of the duty which, for imports from Germany, is on the basis of only twenty-five per cent of the German customs totals, which are low, and I should say, approximate to a ten per cent *ad valorem* duty. An immense number of things under the existing German customs are allowed in free, i.e., food and coal and much more. On some of these free imports there is now imposed a registration fee of one mark a ton. "If you increase the tariff will the trade fall in

[1] Compare entry for May 22.

volume?" I asked. No, he thought it would not. The new customs people had been assembled in Mainz, but the duties were not set going till April and in the interval much trade had passed to escape the duties. There was a large trade, and some one hundred wagons of coal came in daily to Mayence. The administrative cost of the new scheme was slight. The Germans had thought that we could not find the personnel to run the customs, but they had been wrong, and perhaps they did not know that France had about five times the number of the Rhine customs officials ready to act in the Ruhr when it was occupied. "What will the Ruhr customs bring in on the same tariff?" I asked. "About five or six times as much as the Rhine customs now," he replied. Actually, payments are made in paper marks. But it makes the French mouth water, and P. said that France could not exist with the present Budget and something had to be done. He was sure that the Germans could and would pay. They levied much lower customs duties than the French did. The tax of ten per cent which the Germans imposed as a tax on the wages of workmen was merely to enrage these people against the French. P. did not believe that the German officials paid an equivalent tax on their salaries.[1] He felt sure that the Germans in the Ruhr would keep quiet. He had studied them. Yes they would attack France with passion when the time came, but meanwhile they placed trade first and patriotism second. They had large paunches and about ten metres longer guts than a Frenchman and had to satisfy the corresponding appetites. P. did not agree with me that the blockade was a more effective weapon to use than occupation. We had a good chat over the political position. I enjoy talking with a man who opposes one's views. It is a perfect tonic.

Walked back along the river. Examined some of the Rhine barges. One belonging to Hugo Stinnes had come from Ruhrort with coal. I had a talk to the bargee or commodore of the flotilla of six barges of which he was in

---

[1] This is denied. See later.

charge. A fine ship built in Holland and taking eight hundred tons of coal normally, but with the Rhine at its present low water it can only carry three hundred. He had his wife on board; very good quarters astern with kitchen, bedroom, and what he called the best room — a barge drawing-room, I imagine. All spotlessly clean: flowers in the drawing-room window! He has one or two "sailors" or other bargees on board. The other flotilla barges have two or three other bargees. The smaller barges had smaller living quarters. No women, I suppose? I asked. Oh! yes, there was one to each barge! There are chicken-houses flush with the deck as part of the barge. He had nine hens. A corresponding partition was open on his port quarter. I did not ask what it contained. Rabbits, perhaps. If so he was all self-contained. There was sand for his chickens and a wire netting prevented them from getting out when their hatch was off. What a placid life! No letters, no telephone messages, no politics, no worries, and no bills! The man ought to live for ever! He is the typical "lucky bargee."

French sailors in charge of a couple of Rhine gunboats. There were two small guns mounted forward, no shields. The quays are solid, of great length, with several lines of rail alongside. The various firms have their warehouses alongside the quays. A very substantial and well-organised river port.

Friday, May 20, 1921. The debate in Paris was carried on yesterday by the interpellators. Briand has not spoken yet. The debate continues. Went to see the cathedral again. Have tried to like it for a week because it is old, but I can't because it is a patch-work. It may interest the historian of architecture, but how far are we from the delicate unity of Salisbury and the Gothic glory of Cologne! I hate Romanesque and hate equally, or more, the flamboyant. To patch them with Gothic is to ruin all three. The interior is worthy, but the tombstones and altar pieces are depressing if varied. We get renaissance, transition, early-Gothic, baroque — of course, because the German is baroque — late-Gothic, rococo, wood and stone, odious mural paintings, and every sort of other abomination.

Walked on to look again at the monument of the so-called Gutenberg, the *soi-disant* inventor of printing. A statue erected to a highly reprehensible person who may have been named Gansfleisch and may have lived four hundred years before the statue was put up. Don't believe in him and less in his statue. Nobody knows who invented printing nor ever will know. If we knew we should posthumously burn him at the stake. He has been responsible for all the heresies, illusions, troubles, and wars of five centuries. He still perpetuates enmities by permitting every hasty word of some over-wrought politician to be placed next day before all the people outraged by it, and far from aiding or promoting civilisation he has debased it. He has allowed every village idiot who pretends that he possesses the truth to mislead others, whereas the definitive truth is already a dead truth and written history a cemetery. Life is thought, movement, action. The troubadour made it pretty and the printer made it ugly. The only true history is that little scrap of our own time which we can tell because we see it and feel it and know it. It dies with us, giving birth to a new history and new truths told by our successors to their contemporaries and lasting only their time.

I prefer the crowded market-place of Mainz to the cathedral and the imaginary Gutenberg. Here is life, truth and movement. The French are right. The Rhinelanders are *bons enfants*. There is simply nothing of the Prussian here. No stiff formalism, no bluster nor swagger, but the easy ways of would-be happy dwellers in their fruitful valleys. But what does it all amount to? These people count no more than sparrows. The crowds will die and pass away as endless other crowds have passed away. *Vanitas vanitatum!*

Saturday, May 21, 1921. The Paris debate adjourned till Tuesday. Briand has not yet spoken. L. G.'s second statement of the 18th on Silesia has aroused a fresh flood of opprobrium in France and has made matters worse. Saw

Generals Degoutte and Michel in the morning. No news and D. says that I can safely go to Coblenz, as he does not anticipate any change, though he admits that he can never say for certain. A good offer to go in a French boat Monday with the Paris Municipal Council who are joy-riding here, but on the whole think I will stick to the plan already made with Robertson, as the Frenchmen start very early and from Bingen.

In the afternoon went to study the working of the new Rhineland douane at Mayence passenger and goods stations. A sharp French inspector, second string to Philippi, handed me over to an entertaining brigadier of the douanes, a wag and a character, who showed me round and explained everything. He had been at Cannes when the war broke out, rejoined as a volunteer though over age, served with the Alpins, and was at last hauled back to the customs service because the volunteering of nearly one thousand of its skilled hands had quite disorganised it.

At the Passenger Baggage Office the thing worked simply. The travellers from Germany brought up their goods which were examined and taxed at the rate of twenty-five per cent of the customs duty in the German law of 1906. A German clerk had the text of the German tariff before him, for all goods, and in each case simply divided it by four. He was paid by the owner of the goods, and got a receipt of which a duplicate with the same number was retained. For instance a parcel of textiles about 3'x2' was charged thirty-five paper marks duty; a crate and a dozen larger specimens of aluminium watering-cans was charged fourteen marks: books were allowed in free, and so on. The brigadier kept a book to show the number of wagons in and out each day and duties charged. They were not much for these small parcels, about three hundred francs a day. The Germans hated paying the duty between unoccupied and occupied Germany and with difficulty controlled their wrath, which fact tickled the caustic brigadier enormously. All the personnel is German except the brigadier, who is alert and comes down where he likes, at any moment, to observe.

He does not know a word of German, but carries a sort of tiny pocket dictionary, smaller than a match-box, which he is very keen on using.

We went on to the goods warehouses which were pretty full of things from Germany. About three warehouses contained goods which escaped tax under the German tariff. The rest were taxable. A large quantity of household furniture. The furniture of a bedroom, which cost about four thousand paper marks to make, paid one hundred marks tax, and so on. The German duties are all low, and reducing them to twenty-five per cent makes them harmless. A vast quantity of goods escapes all tax. It is amusing that the tariff was aimed at France and was made specially high for goods in which France competed with Germany. So now the compliment is returned by using the German tariff against German goods. I suppose that the total German customs staff at Mayence is about forty. On the French side only my little brigadier, but my friend the inspector came on the scene twice.

I had the goods taxes added up for six days. They came to 172,027 paper marks, or about 30,000 a day for goods and baggage at Mayence station alone, and this does not include coal and iron and steel which goes elsewhere, the port, I think, to be examined. Does the German personnel work squarely? It seems so, because any lapse from duty or fraud means a *conseil de guerre*, and then fines, imprisonment, and deportation if necessary. The Germans work, but not actively. They work not mainly from fear, but from the national sense of discipline, I think. It is the order! The inspector agreed that by making a new tariff and suspending the free list we could quadruple the income from the customs without arresting trade. We could, of course, double it by charging fifty per cent of what the Germans charge instead of our present twenty-five per cent. This new customs duty has an undoubtedly good effect in one way: it makes the Germans sensible of their real position. But the Germans in unoccupied Germany do not feel it. Nothing but blockade or an occupation can bring it home to them. The brigadier draws double pay and gets 1020 francs a month. All the German State services here and elsewhere are over-staffed to an absurd extent. The former officers and N.C.O.'s swarm in them. One could restaff a national army from these people without hurting the various administrations. The result is that the railways do not pay, but many defend the system because otherwise the men would be on the streets. The longer peace lasts the more will all these men be weaned from militarism and become absorbed in their new trades. It is inevitable. Another good reason why the control should be maintained for some years to come. As to where all the money goes I must ask at Coblenz. It seems at present to be only equal to three thousand pounds a month for Mayence station at the present rate of exchange, to-day about 237 paper marks to the pound sterling.

Returning, was with two Algerian *tirailleurs* in the standing part of the tram. They were unpleasant-looking fellows and not civil. They pushed rather rudely against a better-class German as they got down. He brushed his jacket angrily where they had touched him and gave a look after them which for concentrated bitterness and hate was a model of expression.

Talked with Lieutenant de la Rivière, 14th Chasseurs, and an English lady after dinner.

Sunday, May 22, 1921. Visited the Museum. A large collection of Roman antiquities, chiefly household objects, tombstones, bas-reliefs, sculptures, etc. A poor picture gallery of which a Ruysdael, a Palamedes, and some other Dutch works are the best of a second-rate collection.

Note that on May 8, before the Germans accepted the ultimatum, the mark was 265 to the pound and the franc 49. On May 20 the mark was 237 to the pound and the franc 45, London quotations. Very little change, and both currencies have improved slightly. I begin to believe that European exchanges will never reach their old parities and that we had better discard the old standards as quite misleading. I live cheaper here in Germany than in Austria.

The mark when at its lowest had four times its purchasing power here that it should have had at its international value, and it still has more. Is not the true parity the purchasing power? I think so. Why do not our financial pundits give us their figure every week or month? The 1914 parity means nothing at all, not even the dollar or the pound when gold is only half its 1914 value — less than half, about forty per cent.

If we can only have peace, if nations stop inflation, work and produce, break down the economic boundaries set up by the Versailles frontiers and introduce free trade in place of them, things will improve, provided that Governments limit their normal expenditures to their normal income. If not, then not.

Coblenz, Monday, May 22, 1921. Travelled by river to Coblenz. Put up with Mr. Arnold Robertson, British High Commissioner. His wife returns in June. He has a delightful little son of three and a half, Donald, whom he worships. Years since I was in a Rhine steamer. As good as ever and decent cooking. A lovely day. The general aspect of the river scenery has not much changed — although there are naturally more dwellings — as the factories have, as a rule, been kept out of prominence. Many more vineyards, especially on the right bank. Quite Charlemagne's idea when he brought the vines to Rudesheim. The scenery between Bingen and Loreley particularly attractive. No English or Americans on board. Many towed barges met, but few steamers. The trains of coal wagons on both banks seemed very numerous. River low, but has only fallen one metre more than the normal. This, however, makes a difference in river navigation. We occasionally passed through very broken water. The current is at least seven to eight miles an hour and our friends at Budapest will have to alter their views on this matter. The skipper put it down at eighteen kilometres an hour, but this is an exaggeration. I was amused by the coquetry of the barge-masters — each tries to make his barge most spick and span. The men not steering were all washing the boats or painting or tarring them. The Dutch boats were on the whole the smartest. Talked to Robertson and walked and motored with him. In the evening dined with him and about a dozen men, all members of his staff, except Colonel Stone, the United States member of the High Commission. The latter sat next me and spoke exceedingly well on the subject of America's desire to help in allaying Europe's troubles and also about our Army in the War. He works hand in glove with Robertson and the two are cordially in agreement on practically all subjects.

I had a long talk at dinner with Captain E. R. Troughton in charge of the New Customs and with Captain W. H. Georgi who knows more of the Ruhr than most people. Major F. J. Quarry, Intelligence Officer, and for fourteen years a professional pianist in Germany, gave us some exquisite music on a Blüthner grand after dinner. These military titles mean nothing much. Only Ryan is a Regular. Talked to some others of the staff later.

R. has an excellent staff. Some of them were on Fergusson's staff at Cologne, and a more competent lot of fellows at their special jobs it would be hard to find. This staff could give the F.O. an admirable and reasoned opinion on almost every subject connected with Germany and the occupied territory, but I imagine that London has little notion of the competence of this organisation which is rarely consulted. As everywhere else I found our people critical of the French. The High Commission of Tirard (President), Robertson, Rolin Jaequemyns the Belgian, and Stone get on very well together, but Tirard's staff are often difficult. Tirard spends part of his time in Paris and is largely occupied with politics. R. J. is a good sound lawyer with moderate views. Robertson is broad and strong and a stickler for fairness and impartiality. Troughton practically runs the customs for him on a small Commission of three to which R. has refused to allow a President to be named. There is also a permit Commission at Ems. The wide experience of Ryan, Troughton, and Georgi in their departments is of great value to R. The latter now allows that the customs may bring in four to five millions a year and that a strike may not take place in the Ruhr if it is occupied, but he is dead against the occupation of that region and holds to his previous view that if the R.H.C. is implicated in it he should have another one hundred and twenty men to keep him accurately informed of what is going on there. He has still no policy laid down for him in the Rhineland. He does not pretend that the customs tariff is perfect. He was ordered to prepare it at the shortest notice, whereas a system of this sort should take six months to prepare. He had been against it, but had said it could be imposed if desired, and it had been imposed, but many blemishes remained. He was now for ending the system, as the Germans had surrendered.

Troughton gave me the English texts of the various ordinances of the R.H.C. which I wanted. I had a long talk with him at dinner. He thinks the customs now bring in ninety million paper marks a month and says that the French exaggerate the probable profits in order to make a case for the retention of the ¡customs and their extension to the Ruhr. I find him a most modest man of calm mind and considered judgement. He does not venture an opinion without being sure of his facts. He has worked before the war in various metallurgic and other industries connected with the Ruhr which he knows well and can translate the most intricate technical German.

After dinner had a long talk with Georgi. He is fiery, eloquent, enthusiastic, and a little extravagant, but he knows the Ruhr perfectly and is a great asset to R. He thinks that the Treaty of Versailles has so disturbed the economic balance of France and Germany that France had necessarily to endeavour to get control over German resources or sacrifice her own. Germany, he says, had built up the largest iron and steel industry in Europe based on coal and especially coke from the Ruhr coalfields, and on iron ore from Luxembourg and Lorraine which are the most extensive in Europe and yield ore called minette. This is oolithic hematite containing thirty to thirty-five per cent of iron mixed with a gangue of limestone which renders the ore easy to smelt. Minette ore produces pig iron with a high percentage, two per cent, of phosphorous, which is converted into steel by the basic or Thomas process, the slag obtained being a valuable fertiliser which we call basic slag. Some sixty-five per cent of the pig iron produced in Germany was smelted from minette of which thirty-two million tons came to the extent of two-thirds from then German Lorraine. Of these thirty-two million tons, twenty-one millions were smelted in the Ruhr and Saar and eleven millions in German Lorraine.

But geographically Lorraine deposits are far from coalfields possessing coking coal. The Saar is close at hand, but produces little coke — 1,700,000 tons a year only — and now much less. Germany did not encourage the iron and steel industry to concentrate in Lorraine, as it was too exposed. It was for this reason that they did not canalise the Saar and Moselle to give continuous river transport from the Ruhr to the minette fields.

After the war the German iron and steel industries in Westphalia were faced by a serious crisis owing to the loss of the minette ore. They were driven to use other native ores and to call for more Swedish ores, and took other steps to make themselves independent. They amassed credits abroad and acquired interest in foreign ore-producing companies, particularly in Sweden and Spain. As Germany's iron ore deposits are estimated to contain two thousand million tons of ore, her position is better than ours, and the now French minette is threatened with death.

France found herself after the war with about sixty million tons of minette yearly in theory, but only twelve millions were produced in 1919. To produce this quantity she needed twenty million tons of coke a year, and the bulk of it can only be produced in Germany. The Germans are still sending coke, but not a fraction of what France wants, and Germany is the only possible customer for her ore except Belgium which is also dependent on the Ruhr for coke. The Treaty imposed certain deliveries of coal to

France, but for ten years only. She sees this now and has to restore her position or find the minette a drug in the market. She wishes to become the first steel producer in Europe and can do so only at Germany's expense. It is in fact of vital importance for France to take the Ruhr basin and a bitter economic war is really raging now. The French policy is not one to cripple Germany, but to aid France, and Georgi thinks that the French iron-masters have converted the French Government to their views and hold that at least Germany's coal production must be internationalised in the interest of France and her friends, i.e., the Belgians, whose interests in this matter accord with those of France. Belgium used to take twenty-five per cent of the Briey ore, or five million tons a year, but is taking very little now as railway frieghts are so high. Belgium has also little coking coal.

In 1913 the Ruhr produced $114\frac{1}{2}$ million tons of coal. The proved coalfields in Westphalia and on the Lower Rhine cover 2300 square miles. The output dropped to 71 million tons in 1919 owing to the usual causes. It is now 300,000 tons a day, or about 100 millions a year. The coal is of the highest grade consisting of gas coal equal to that of Durham, long-flame coal for steel-making and household use, bituminous or coking coal used also as steam coal and making an excellent coke for blast furnace use, and lastly semi-anthracite coal. The coke production is now 1,900,000 tons a month — $2\frac{1}{2}$ million tons of coal coked. Average cost of production of Ruhr coal is 210 paper marks a ton or 17 shillings. The net selling price is fixed by the German Government at 227 marks a ton for unscreened and unwashed coal. It pays to the German Government an ad valorem tax of twenty per cent.

Georgi knows much about the iron and steel industry in the Ruhr and the statistics of it. Two-thirds of the whole German iron and steel comes from the Ruhr. The German output has fallen since the war to 550,000 tons a month of which 365,000 from the Ruhr. It is there also converted into finished goods such as rails, girders, and machinery. Over 25,000 trucks of fifteen tons capacity are loaded daily. The Ruhr created the industrial wealth of South Germany and France could control it by occupying the Ruhr. The Ruhr *is* Germany from an industrial point of view and is also Germany's arsenal.

Meanwhile in Lorraine only forty per cent of the blast furnaces are in operation, but even then iron-masters cannot get rid of their pig iron. Georgi thinks that if the French occupy the Ruhr, the balance of power of Europe would be upset to our detriment, but he does not prove this to my satisfaction. But that they would control the industry of Germany seems certain. He says that there are 17,000 German inspectors employed in the mines and quite as many more in the various iron and steel works, etc.

The Ruhr coal output at present is allotted: Two million tons a month to reparation; 900,000 tons a month to colliery consumption and workmen's coal; 600,000 tons a month to the occupied Rhineland; 800,000 to South Germany; 500,000 to Germany west of the Elbe and Berlin; and 2,500,000 tons a month are consumed in the Ruhr itself. Silesia generally supplies Germany east of the Elbe with coal. The German production of brown coal is mainly in the Cologne region. It is 2,800,000 tons a month. Also in Central Germany at Halle, 7,000,000 tons a month. It is converted often into briquettes for domestic use.

Georgi thinks that it is desired to place a flat-rate tax of forty gold marks per ton on all coal produced in Germany when France occupies the Ruhr. I have never heard of a bigger figure than twenty marks. It is quite certain that the forty marks tax would make German coal higher in price than American coal which can be placed at German ports at $8.50 per ton.

Tuesday, May 23, 1921. A talk in the morning with Robertson. We are both exceedingly vexed at a report that our four remaining weak battalions are to go to Upper Silesia, that Morland is to have French troops under him, that we are to have no force left in the Cologne area where there may be 1¼ millions of Germans. Moreover, R. is left to read this news in the German papers! I cannot conceive any policy more silly. All our administrative and customs staff left without a man to guard them, and R.'s staff as well as Morland's horribly lowered in prestige and dignity. Allen and his Americans are 17,000 here, good solid regular troops and very fine fellows. As for sending four weak battalions to Upper Silesia where the Poles, who detest us after L. G.'s campaign, are in practical control of the country, it is a most light-hearted proceeding. Our Government seem to think that the occupied territory is France and that the Poles will not resent our appearance.

Went to the office and talked over matters with the staff. Lunched with M. Tirard, President of the High Commission, and some of his staff and officers later. Tirard subjected me while we were alone before lunch to a public-meeting harangue on elementary facts about the position here. He seemed to me a nice fellow with good intentions. Spent the afternoon ruminating over what I have learned here. It seems to me that this is all a bigger economic problem than any of us have realised, and that Westphalia, Saar, Lorraine, and Upper Silesia are all parts of one great problem. I should not wonder if Schneider of Creusot and Hugo Stinnes got together one day and amalgamated all their interests. Said so to Troughton, who replied, "Perhaps they have!"

Wednesday, May 24, 1921. Empire day, and here we are with our Union Jack on a pole outside this house and soon not a soldier to look after it! Over a million Germans round us — loving us so dearly! — a huge territory for which we are responsible filled as at Solingen with large working populations with many Communist groups which may give trouble at any moment. Only our Kreis officers to keep them in order, and then there is our customs line, of serious length and a handful of customs officers and no British guard. Strange people we are, but I dare say that nothing will happen because our young Kreis officers have the habits of command and the Germans the instincts of obedience. It is really comical to think of the Germans also in charge of all the railways behind us! An occupation without occupiers! However, here at Coblenz, though Robertson may rage at the humiliation of it all, there is Allen and his 17,000 Americans, and a very large Stars and Stripes waves over Ehrenbreitstein!

Went to have a talk with M. Rolin Jaequemyns whom I knew at the Hague Conference and at Brussels twenty years ago. A very wise, capable, and agreeable lawyer who is a great favourite with the English and Americans. We had a good talk. He went through the whole situation admitting that neither he nor his Government desired to occupy the Ruhr militarily, but concluding that a civil occupation with the threat of military action in reserve might meet the case. He thought that it was impracticable to man all the Ruhr industries as Loucheur had suggested, and that it would be enough to have supervision at all the mines and to charge some figure like twenty francs a ton on all coal, with any necessary variation according to grades of coal, as a tax. This would be paid at the pit mouth. It would help English and Belgian coal, and the German owners could be left to distribute the burden of the tax among the consumers of the coal and its products. Not a bad plan, as it is simple and effective and leads to no interference with German workmen. He is all for doing it by agreement with the Germans, and says that things cannot be settled except by agreements. He spoke highly of Degoutte. We talked over old times. He was most sarcastic about the League of Nations which he said had become a centre of intrigues, and thought, as I did, that we had been on sounder lines at The Hague in 1899. He asked me to come again to Coblenz to talk at greater length with him.

Went on to the U.S. Headquarters to talk with General Allen whose opinion carries so much weight. A tall, straight man, with straight views and a strong face: a very worthy representative of the United States. He was a trifle sarcastic about the first speech of the new U.S. Ambassador in London, Colonel Harvey, and suggested that diplomatists were usually expected to be diplomatic. All Harvey should have done would have been to point out the position taken up by the Harding Administration at home and to have left it at that.

He tells me that he and Robertson never discuss matters in advance, but are in nineteen out of twenty cases in agreement. He thinks that if a U.S. Brigade had gone to Upper Silesia the Poles would never have risen. He would have taken strong measures with Korfanty and have told him that if he wanted to make trouble he could go somewhere else to make it. He had given the same advice to German agitators who threatened to vex him in his area and they had stayed away from Coblenz in consequence. He did not know what America wanted with a strong division in Central Europe and wondered how long they would stay. Service here was very popular; every man had his girl. I congratulated him on the appearance of his troops. Less on that of the girls.

He was not sure how far France would be able to go. The time might come when her friends would not follow her, and he is apparently not keen about the Ruhr and asked when France would leave it if she went there. I thought not for years until the old veterans and officers of the Imperial Régime had pot-bellies and were beyond the fighting age. A. did not seem to approve of this, though he said that he felt for France and was all for helping her to get her just rights. But I do not think that he will approve of any exaction or excessive claims. He takes up a broad, sympathetic, but just view, and it is certainly in the interest of France to *ménager* Allen, as he is a good friend and might become a bad enemy if any hanky-panky were played. I told him that the sight of the first American sentry on the Rhine had the same effect upon me as that of the first American Marine sentry at Chaumont in 1917. I was glad that they were still here and in good strength, for so long as they stayed they stood for what was right and just, and that was all we wanted. He called Germany France's bugaboo, and criticised the view that, because the German houses and factories were all standing Germany was not down. She was down, and had a great work to recover her own position, let alone to satisfy reparation claims. It was true that she had not much foreign debt, but she still had a great effort to make. A. thought it absurd to suppose that America was not interested in the recovery of one of her best customers, and also England's. This had to be borne in mind. He gave me not obscurely to understand that in case France overstepped all limits, America would regretfully have to take certain disagreeable steps. Like Jaequemyns he extolled Degoutte and thought he showed great tact and good sense as well as being a fine soldier. He also spoke of the excellent effect of the Americans meeting our soldiers whom they had never seen before. They paid each other visits. Our men came here to box, etc., and there was a good feeling.

General Allen asked me to come up the Rhine to Loreley with him this afternoon. Robertson and his staff were going. But I wished to get to Mainz to-night, so had regretfully to refuse and left by the 2.30 express boat for my destination. I have seen a great deal of my host. He is a delightful and very live man, with much strength and good judgement, while he has also a very charming and agreeable character. I am only afraid that his frank criticisms may injure him with the F.O. Nobody at that institution seems to take any interest in the High Commission. No one acts as father, mother, and family solicitor and watches over its interests. To take away practically the whole garrison from British-occupied Germany and not to tell the man responsible for it, is an outrage. Robertson is on the best of terms with all his colleagues and they all seem a happy family even if France's Allies criticise her a bit, and do not always follow her. But France's ways are not our ways or American ways, and even the Belgians resent French action at times, though they feel themselves to be in the French boat.

Robertson told me just before I left that some Reichstag Deputies and the Labour leaders in the Cologne area had come to Piggott and had offered to give him every possible assurance of good behaviour if he would prevent the relief of our British troops by the French! Reached Mainz about 10.30 P.M.

Thursday, May 25, 1921. Wrote letters and then read carefully the full text of Briand's long speech which took two and one half hours to deliver on Tuesday. His figures of the plébiscite in the Upper Silesian industrial triangle are different from those of our Staff at Oppeln directly after the election and quoted in my diary at the time. Briand gives a total of 343,485 Polish and 289,980 German votes in this area, and alters what we took to be a German majority of 50,000 into about an equivalent Polish majority. I must write to Percival or Bourdillon to explain the discrepancy,[1] but, after all, the term "industrial area" is vague and the French may have included in it some country areas to help matters out. Certainly there was no anti-Polish sentiment among us when we added up the figures at Oppeln, and we were, if anything, disappointed at what we took to be a Polish minority.

Briand made it clear that if France had gone into the Ruhr when the Germans surrendered, she would have stood alone. But he said that if the question of security came up, France could not hesitate. He was interesting when he declared that in view of the *enchevêtrement* of international interests in the conditions of the world's life, no isolation was possible for great nations. Has he realised that his Allies will not follow him? Have they all warned him? He may yet be forced into the Ruhr by German unwillingness or inability to fulfil some condition of the ultimatum, but I think it would be against his judgement, for he described the Ruhr as a "*gage inerte.*"

---

[1] Later it appeared that M. Briand had lumped all the coal area together and had included in the triangle the Rybuik and Pless area which is not yet opened up. It is a theory which can be argued, but the facts should be stated.

Wrote to Bourdillon at Oppeln asking him to explain Briand's figures.

Sunday, May 29, 1921. Busy these last days writing some longish articles on the Rhineland Commission, the new customs line, and the general question of the coalfields of Europe, which sounds dull, but is fascinating. All my other articles have now been published and Burnham writes a very encouraging letter about them with very interesting accounts of the political situation in London and Paris, the Poles, and our troubles with the French. According to to-day's French papers our first battalion was received at Oppeln with acclamations — by the Boches! Good Lord! Briand got a good majority when the Chambers voted at the end of the long foreign debate. I have never known him to speak better or to be better-informed and more precise. He was all solid argument and reasoned statement. A most convincing speech and not a word of heat nor mention of L. G.'s speech.

Monday, May 30, 1921. Saw General Degoutte in the morning; all quiet on the Rhine and he is of his former opinion that nothing will happen here now. I told him the nice things that Coblenz was saying about his tact and courtesy and moderation. We discussed the Anglo-French differences. D. thinks that things are settling down in Upper Silesia, but we both think that the re-establishment of order, which is the business of the Allies under the Treaty, must precede decisions, as otherwise they will not be carried out. We both want an English and an Italian division at war strength to complete Le Rond's force. D. suggests that France should not be held responsible for the anti-English speeches in the Chambers and the abuse of the Paris press. He thinks that the speech of Briand and his majority should be a satisfaction to England, and remarks how many concessions France has also made to English opinion. We agree in praising Briand's statesmanship. Told him that I thought of moving on as I had exhausted the interests here and thought of going to Berlin or visiting Alsace and Lorraine. He told me that General

Berthelot was at Metz and Humbert at Strasbourg. There was a civil commissaire at Metz. Nancy was the best place to study the Lorraine industries. D. told me that there was another division coming here because the 1919 Class was quieter here than in the interior. Punishments here had not gone up since the 1919 Class had come in to the Rhine.

I must register the fact that, though I like the Algerians and the Moors as troops, I find myself resenting their authority over the white population here almost as much as the inhabitants do. Racial prejudice, I suppose. The Americans feel the same. I have never seen a French soldier talking to or walking with one of the North African soldiers. They go about quite apart.

Had a talk in the afternoon with Herr Mayer, the Director of the Disconto-Gesellschaft Bank here, on the economical situation of Germany. He was immensely interested to hear of the broad results of the new customs taxes and evidently knew nothing whatever on the subject, but he thought, after all, that the profits to us did not amount to much, and that the permit difficulties were really killing trade. The clients all told him that this had stopped all business, but this is evidently not quite the case. Respecting the future he was pessimistic. He thought that Germany could pay her way, but did not see how the reparations could be paid unless Germany was entirely free to trade, as it was only in work that she could find a hope of paying. We discussed relative prices of goods here and in England, and he admitted that a tax of twenty-six per cent on imports from Germany into England would not stop German trade. I do not think it will either, for they can undersell us so severely. He admitted that, in regard to the 240 marks to a pound sterling, one could buy here three times as much for 240 marks as one could in England for the pound. But he did not agree with the English and French complaints that Germans were under-taxed, for it was not fair to say that we paid in taxes so many pounds and the Germans so much less. It was quite a high rate of pay for his employés in the bank to get 11,000 marks a year, but it was only £50, and the corresponding employés in England had £150 at least. Therefore if these grades were taxed, say, £25 in Germany, they would be taxed more in proportion to their income than the English employé if he were taxed £50.

All wage-earners had the ten per cent tax deducted from their wages and never saw it. All officials and State employés were in the same boat. He did not admit that any escaped, for evasion of taxes was not a German habit. As for the *capital levy* of 1919, it had been 11,000 marks on a capital of 100,000 marks and both reckoned in paper. An *income* of 100,000 marks was now taxed 45,000 marks to the State and also had to bear some 15,000 marks rates and taxes to the town in Mainz. The capital levy was 5000 marks for the first 50,000 marks, and 6000 for the second. He thought that the income tax, i.e., 60,000 marks on an income of 100,000, was as high as the State could go, for if a man threw all his capital and brains and energy into making another 100,000 marks of income, with all the risks attaching to it, and then found he had less than forty per cent of it left to spend, he would prefer not to risk his capital and to slave for so little profit. He also told me that people were allowed to pay their taxes in War Loan scrip which meant the repayment of much of the war debt. He could not understand why England destroyed her old notes. Germany kept hers in reserve when they came back. He admitted that all the State departments were overmanned, but this was better than to have these people in the street. This was why railways, posts, etc., were a loss instead of a profit and because the charges to the public were so low. Also there was still unemployment pay of which he disapproved. But on June 1 all railway fares would be doubled and unemployment pay was being steadily curtailed, so Germany was coming back to the straight path on State finance. The best business done was in coal. Iron was not doing well now. There were many obstacles to German trade. The eight-hour day was the rule everywhere, but was often exceeded and the cost of it met in some way other than regular pay. By law only one hour extra a day for four days in the week was allowed. The clerks at the bank worked from 8 A.M. to 12.30 and then from 2.30 to 6: on Saturday from 8 to 2 without a break except half an hour for lunch. These hours suited a town like Mainz best, but did not suit great towns like Berlin and were not copied there. I noticed that to-day, though a Saturday, there were many clerks still at work when I left at 6 P.M. Read a book of Rhine legends by Ruland.

I see that my war diary figures in the *Annual Register* for 1920. L. G. and I are the only people mentioned by name in the *Times Literary Supplement's* review of the *Register*. The writer says that some people think that I shall outlive my generation. I hope not. Rip van Winkle and Maurus of Heisterbach had rather a poor time. However, I suppose he means my diary. Yes, that may live if it be true that *veritas prevalebit*. After ten impressions sold out of two volumes dealing day by day with the most dramatic and contentious epoch of all time, I have not had a single letter to deny any statement made in it relating to the war. If my contemporaries cannot refute me, how can history do so? A few old cats have squawled privately. How ungrateful, when twenty years hence they will mostly be dead leaving no memory except in my pages and on a mouldy and neglected grave in some obscure churchyard! "Waverley" went through six editions in nine months. I went through ten in four months and larger editions at two guineas a set of each two volumes. I wonder if that has ever been done before?

Tuesday, May 31, 1921. To-day the German Government must send in to the Allies a list of the so-called societies of autoprotection — *Orgesch, Einwohner,* etc. — which they intend to disband. The Bavarian decision on this matter is not yet announced, but Commandant de Charry told me to-day that it was only Munich and South (Upper) Bavaria that were obstinate, and that North Bavaria was ready to agree.

M. Barthou, the War Minister, and General Buat arrived from Paris to-day. They were met by M. Tirard, who seemed a changed man, and by General Degoutte, and at two held a review of all the troops of the garrison in the Rheinstrasse. There was a small tribune erected. Barthou saw me and came to shake hands and made some nice remarks; so did Tirard who was very alert and bright. Degoutte invited me to the tribune, but I begged to be excused, as I wanted to take some snapshots of the troops with my new toy, a Goerz camera, and had an excellent place in front of the stand for doing so. The French Infantry came by first, in marching order, looking fine, and followed by their machine guns. Then came the Algerian *tirailleurs* and then the Morocco troops, all quite good and steady, but the Algerian *Tambour-Major* was not very skilled in chucking his stick in the air and catching it and I was constantly expecting him to miss it. The 75's on motor-lorries were very attractive. Then came the long 155's drawn by motors, then the cyclists, flocks of them, then tanks which looked most spiteful and were fast-moving little Renaults, not one man of the crew being visible; then the armoured cars, still with no protection for their tyres; and finally the various auxiliary services, while the aeroplanes hovered above. A very good show, the men looked well, and their officers and *sous-officiers* were ablaze with war decorations. There was a pretty fair crowd looking on, but mainly French, I think. Officers pretty well mounted. The Cavalry acted as escort to Barthou and looked well. I snapped all arms except the 75's and the cyclists who passed while I was renewing a film.

Lunched with an American Red Cross man called Lassiter; a nice fellow, on his way with his own car, a 50 h.p. 8-cylinder, to Strasbourg, to bring back to Coblenz some U.S. civil dignitary. He told me that the American Y.M.C.A. spent $60,000 a month at Coblenz and only got a quarter of the money back from the men. They supply papers, books, and magazines to the American soldiers for nothing, and also materials for all games. Many of the fathers and mothers of the Americans are natives of these parts, which L. does not like, but he says that the German-Americans are gradually being sent home. Of course it is very useful to have a few German-speaking Americans for Military Police, etc., but the fact of some parents of the men being here, combined with the habit of the Americans of walking out openly with the German girls, must affect American sentiment.

Went to see the Stadt Park in the afternoon. There is a café there which seems to be an attraction, and it has a terrace with a fine view over the town and down the river. In this quarter there are streets of villas built by the town for the French married officers, my jarvey told me. They would have cost some £1500 each in England.

I saw yesterday that the Saar Commission, or at least the French part of it, had gone to Berlin. Do not much like it. But when we buffet the French and L. G. talks so unwisely of "new friendships," we cannot complain if France begins to look after herself. I fancy that that phrase has given the deepest offence of all.

Wednesday, June 1, 1921. A piping hot day. Railed to Frankfort. Chiefly to see Herr Richard Merton of the Metallgesellschaft, to whom Troughton had given me a letter of introduction. He talks English well and had been much in England and the United States; a very fine office and they combine banking with their other business. I asked him for his views on the present position. He thinks that we are individually sane, but nationally mad. He says that France won about one-fourth of the victory and expects one hundred per cent of the profits. He agrees that coal is at the bottom of the present troubles. His own firm in the Lahn has suffered from the Ruhr partiality for Sweden and Spain, just like Lorraine, and he puts it down to cheap foreign prices. He wants us to remain in with the United States and to dictate policy together. We can then exercise such pressure that the German bonds in French hands will be unsaleable. He also wants us to let the Germans smash the Poles on Upper Silesia, but I said it would not do, as Poland would declare war and the French enter the Ruhr. He wants the customs duty taken off and the twenty-six per cent too. Germany can trade and pay by keeping her present resources and by having the frontiers thrown open, but if not, not. He criticised the Allies and thought that none of their statesmen dare tell them the truth. But he also criticised his own people and said that they must abandon all dreams of being a Great Power and set to work. They had been bad losers, he admitted. He had been reading Bismarck's memoirs over again and found that since his death the Germans had made every mistake against which he had warned them. R. M. is a strong Imperialist and says that there is no authority and that without it the State could not go on. He had been on Groener's staff in the war, and said that if Ludendorff had been a South German and Groener a North German they might have won the war. A pleasant fellow with a quick brain and reputed to be very capable in his business, but he gave me no suggestion of any real value.

Frankfort is a fine and interesting town. It is not too big to stifle the Main as London stifles the Thames. The banks of the Main are pleasant in parts of the town, as Goethe found them in his day, and like him I found it agreeable to cross the Main and contemplate the scene from the other side.

Fine buildings, some broad streets, with trees and shade, outside the busiest parts. Rather a fine statue of Bismarck and Germania. The theatre good, but makes a shameless and unsuccessful effort to pretend to be higher than it is by reducing the size of the higher figures. A fine art which this particular architect has not grasped. The old part of the town round the Römerberg quite interesting. Much that is really old, but there are some faked-old houses. The old nooks and narrow lanes round the Römer are the most attractive bits. The Kaisersaal has little to recommend it and is also mock-old, very largely. It was in the Römer that Goethe acted as a servant in order to see all the dignitaries who were assembled there on a great State occasion. And to think that only the menial of that day survives in memory and that all the great dignitaries who never noticed him are utterly forgotten! Truly a triumph of mind over things which do not matter! The portraits of all the Emperors rather good. I see that several of them had their moustaches turned up like Kaiser Wilhelm II. He probably took his fashion from them. Went into a few old curiosity shops and drew blank. Then remembered the number of Jews in Frankfort and did not look any more.

The shops and show places mostly shut from twelve to three, so there is not much time for a day-visitor to see the sights. But I went to the Stadel Gallery across the river in order to see Rembrandt's "Blinding of Samson" which used to be at Schönbrunn. I take off my hat to the Habsburg for selling this picture. A gruesome work, strongly and even superbly painted, of course, but I am glad it is not in London. It is frightfulness *in excelsis*. The Stadel who made and endowed this gallery had fine taste in Old Masters, especially Dutch. I liked immensely the two Franz Halses. Also Rembrandt's portrait of a woman, a Cuyp, a Vermeer, and a Ruysdael; nearly all the Dutch pictures are good. The mass of the German pictures might well be exchanged for one really fine Velasquez. There never was, there is not, and there never will be, a German school of painting.

But the Lenbachs, in a little end room by themselves, are fine. William I, Bismarck, and Moltke, most striking. They look so sad. Was Lenbach prophetic? Gladstone's portrait by Lenbach here too, most characteristic, but it is all too dark and dirty-looking, while there are not enough high lights on the face. Still, there is the old eagle, the greatest head of our times, in any country. The Bismarck portrait I have seen before, a replica probably, in the house of a German colleague at Brussels long ago. It is a tremendous thing, all character. Von Kaulbach's portrait of his wife is charming, a perfect pose. The Trustees of Stadel must have catholic tastes. Tischbein's portrait of Goethe in the Campagna I loathe, but it remains with one. There is one room for the most modern, filled with the *ne plus ultra* of childish futurist abortions. A man who loved his Vermeer and Hals could never have bought this ridiculous rubbish which must make Stadel turn in his grave.

Missed Gosling the Consul-General, and Goethe's house was shut. Think I will go again to-morrow.

Thursday, June 2, 1921. To Frankfort again. Saw Gosling and had a good talk; went to see Goethe's house: happily I have his autobiography with me: returned to lunch with Gosling, his brother and sister-in-law who was Hungarian, the Revd. Mr. Bullock-Webster, formerly a Master at Eton, and his daughter, a pretty and nice girl, and a pleasant American lady who married and then divorced a German officer, second thoughts being best. Then went to various shops and got some maps and books, looked at the statues in the town, and passed two hours with the editor of the *Frankfurter Zeitung*, Herr von Dewall, at Im Trutz 7.

Goethe's house, or rather his father's, interested me much. The career of the great poet, and especially the first five chapters of "Dichtung und Wahrheit," are lost upon us if we have not seen this his first home. It is as nearly as possible as it was in 1755 when his father restored it, and it breathes all the spirit of those days. A charming old town house with Anne written all over it, and inlaid walnut furniture all belonging to the period. We must remember that everything was modern in 1755, even the pictures, as Goethe's father was a strong supporter of contemporary artists and furniture-makers, an example which, if followed in England, would evolve higher art. A comfortable house with plenty of room. Goethe's study is at the top of the house, and here too is his writing-desk where his first poems were written on what I can only call an Eton "burry" or bureau. Hope for the Third Form at last! The light from the left, small panes about six inches square, all the windows opening inwards, both top and bottom, each in two parts, a plan to copy.[1] An older house opposite, and the paved street a good way below.

[1] If one needs no blinds or curtains.

I liked the corner fireplaces on the broad landings, each warming three rooms. Goethe's father's library a pleasant room with padlocked wire fronts to the bookcases and green silk hangings behind. All the paternal books still in their old places. A music-room with old spinets and other musical instruments, and a picture gallery with a lot of small and unimportant little daubs; black frames with gold edges inside, and all alike, as Goethe describes them. A jolly kitchen which also warmed the dining-room stove by a flue through the wall. Quite a good staircase, but stone, with fine iron and wood balustrades. Each storey projects on the outside above the one below it, as described by the poet. A new museum behind with much of interest. Evidently the whole has been preserved with religious veneration and there is nothing to jar. There used to be a view from the upper storeys out at the back, Goethe tells us, but the Kaiserstrasse has shut it all out; there is a little garden behind. The house of a very well-to-do German citizen of the eighteenth century.

It is well to recall the influence of Shakespeare on Goethe, which he so handsomely acknowledged, and that of contemporary English writers like Pope, Goldsmith, etc. The success of the "Vicar of Wakefield" in Goethe's house is interesting, also that of the "Rape of the Lock," but, strange to say, he nevers refers to Pope's "Essay on Criticism," and perhaps he never saw it. Had he known dear Easthampstead Park he would surely have appreciated the pastorals which were written in the happy valley where the old house stood. Strange to think how much chance has to do with our lighting upon books that influence us.

Mr. Gosling, our Consul-General, I found very pleasant and well-informed. His brother just back from Transylvania and bitter against the Roumanians, but admitted that the peasantry are Roumanian. Mr. Webster extremely well-posted in all affairs in Germany and in Europe generally. A man of intelligence with sound ideas. We had a great talk about taxation, commerce, the exchange, politics, and so on. This confirmed most of my views gained here, but added many details. Gosling takes what one may call views friendly to Germany. We were all severe on Korfanty's Poles. No one had any new solution for Upper Silesia. It is the opinion that the Germans keep down the mark, as it enables them to beat us all in trade, but Webster thinks that the United States regulates the mark value. Gosling and D'Abernon communicate by private letters. A pleasant house and a good cook. We all agreed that native troops in control of a white people were a mistake, but Gosling said that these troops had behaved well at Frankfort, and that the trouble which had arisen had been caused by the Germans.

Looked at the monuments. Gutenberg's does not resemble the Mainz figure, and I prefer the Frankfort conception because there are two other figures on the plinth representing the assistants who must have had a good deal to do with the business. Bismarck's statue rather fine, standing, with Germania on a horse behind him, and a dying dragon writhing on the ground. Behind is an extract from one of his speeches delivered on March 11, 1867:

> Setzen wir Deutschland so zu sagen in den Sattel.
> Reiten wird es schön können.

I thought that if the Boches followed that advice now instead of trying to create illicit military organisations, they would do better for themselves.

Found von Dewall expecting me, as Gosling had arranged our meeting. His pretty and intelligent wife gave us tea and remained during our long talk frequently joining in. Von Dewall belongs to the small nobility. He is a youngish man, a thinker, honest and moderate, who has made the *Frankfurter* one of the best and most reasonable papers in Germany. He thinks himself rather out of things here as his paper reaches Berlin twenty-four hours after the papers there are published, and there are no regular foreign correspondents here to spread his views. But, as I told him, properly organised Governments miss nothing, and his views reach the chief people if they want to know what Germany is thinking.

We thought the position highly dangerous and that Silesia was the storm-centre. Of course he wants it to be German. We went into the Treaty, and he made the suggestion, which at first seemed legitimate, that if Briand added on the Southern Poles and Kreise to the industrial triangle the Germans might claim and add the German Western and Northern Kreise to it.[1] He did not like my idea of an Inter-Allied control of the triangle for a period, he thought that it would leave a cloud hanging over the country. I thought the cloud better than a thunderstorm, and that it was our interest to gain time till people became calmer.

Von D. admits Germany's defeat — by starvation as his wife added — and admits the consequences, but the word "reparations" he considers a reflection on German honour. The German papers formerly used the word *Wiedergutmachung*, which was all right, but now they used the other word and it infuriated the Germans, as it had an offensive meaning in German and implied that they were criminals. I thought that they had only to go back to their *Wiedergutmachung*. It did not matter to us what word they used. I asked if he accepted the Treaty. He said that he did with one reservation, namely, the admission that Germany was responsible for the war. I told him that I thought this a serious matter coming from him. The English were, I said, absolutely convinced of Germany's guilt, and besides the Germans in signing the Treaty had acknowledged it. The reason for the severity of the terms was Germany's guilt, but his admission confirmed the Allied belief that the Germans were not in earnest and so justified all our actions now. He thought that the only thing to do in this matter was for neither side to discuss the question of responsibility which would be written about by our respective historians for ages to come. I asked him, if Germany was not responsible, who was? He said Austria, and then added

[1] But this would not do, as the Northern Kreise are not in the mineral area.

Russia. I said that Austria was Germany's tool and that Austria mobilised eight Army Corps before Russia mobilised. He thought that France had been in the making of the war, and I entirely differed. He made no charge against England, though his wife referred to the mobilising of our Navy, which of course brought from me the answer that it was assembled for manœuvres under arrangements made and known months earlier.

Then we talked taxation. He thinks that the income tax is nearly as high as it can go. He is paying thirty per cent on his modest salary. He excused the taxes not being all paid by saying that the German bureaucracy could not accustom itself quickly to new methods. The taxes were not all paid, but would come in soon. He admitted that many fresh taxes might be imposed and expected to see them affect coal, large estates, houses, etc. Dr. Wirth had talked yesterday of studying the increase of the coal tax to bring the coal up to the level of other European war prices. Germany had hitherto kept coal cheap to allow her industry to revive, as it has. The Germans had low wages and a low standard of living, but he admitted that the big industries and the banks made heaps of money. It was these people who owned the motor-cars which he met everywhere and I had seen at the Wiesbaden races.

I told him quite plainly that I saw no hope for peace unless we controlled Germany until the old Imperial officers and the veterans had become too old to serve and Germany had turned to the performance of civic duties in a chastened mood and in the spirit of Bismarck's speech of 1867.

He told me that if Bavaria was trying to accept the abolition of the *Einwohnerwehr*, there were many officers and the hill people in Upper Bavaria still much against acceptance. He approves of Dr. Wirth. We talked of many other subjects very frankly, and I found him a very reasonable man, with good knowledge of facts and anxious for a pacification.

Gosling told me to-day that the Germans had published

in pamphlet form their list of French war criminals and that it is very hot.

Saturday, June 4, 1921. Another gorgeously hot day. I am thinking of the Playing Fields and the crowds that must be there to-day. Decided yesterday to go to Berlin to complete my information, and secured rooms at the Adlon. Sent off various wires.

Went to say good-bye to General Degoutte in the morning and as usual we went on gossiping without regarding the time until a hungry A.D.C., Captain Boisseau, invented an excuse for disturbing us when we found that we had made each other an hour late for lunch.

I began by thanking him for all his courtesies and by telling him how happy I should always be to think of him here, as he seemed to me, without any flattery, exactly the man for the place. I imagined, I told him, from Barthou's speech on the Rhine — in which he had made the most charming remarks about England and the British Army in the war, and also about the need for Allies to keep together, and the intention of France never to annex the Rhineland — that we had reached the end of a chapter, and that provided the Germans kept their promises and no fresh incident occurred, we could regard the Ultimatum incident as closed. I regarded Barthou as a very loyal colleague to Briand, and besides, Barthou had spoken in the name of the French Government.

General Degoutte agreed. He saw no chance of any movement here now, but at the same time confessed that the future filled him with anxiety. He and all French soldiers who had been in Germany had been much impressed by the proofs of wealth and strength which they saw on all sides here. They had ruefully compared all this evidence of wealth, and the smoking factory chimneys, with the devastation in France. They could not help asking themselves what would happen when the Germans became eighty millions and the French were still forty millions. The teeming hordes of German children inspired serious thoughts, and then there was Austria whose desire to join Germany was a disturbing symptom. To this I replied that I agreed, but was of the opinion that each generation had to settle its own problems and should leave the future confidently to the next generation. We had beaten to the ground the greatest military monarchy of all time and had done our duty. It was no use trying to solve the problems of the next generation, first because it was not our business, and secondly because a host of changes were sure to take place, and these we could not foresee, so it was no good attempting to make cut-and-dried settlements of the unknown. It was really preventive war in another guise.

Degoutte considered Upper Silesia to be still the great danger of the present moment and asked my opinion about it. I said that I could find good grounds for all the proposals in turn; for that of the Germans that all Upper Silesia should remain to them, because in a plébiscite they had polled sixty to sixty-five per cent of the votes; for the Korfanty line, because I believed that there was a tiny Polish majority east of this line; for Briand's desire to treat the whole mineral region as one, because the exploited and unexploited mineral region included both the triangle and the Pless-Rybnik Kreise; and lastly for the Anglo-Italian thesis because the industrial triangle was really a region by itself, containing all the great agglomerations of people in Upper Silesia, where the Germans had a 50,000 majority. How can one reach any settlement then? asked Degoutte. I saw no solution except the continued control of the triangle by the Inter-Allied Commission and the division of the rest between Germans and Poles.

We talked of Poland and were both gloomy about its future and inability to govern itself. Degoutte said that the military opinion had been given to the Supreme Council that the maintenance of order required the presence of 36,000 troops in Upper Silesia. In place of that, though France had supplied 12,000 which was her share, there were only 14,000 troops altogether and it was not enough to keep order. Let the Allies make up their strength as they should! France was expected to do everything. The Watch on the Rhine was a joint Allied affair in which each Ally should share in proportion to her population, but this principle had here again not been adhered to. France practically supplied the troops and her Allies only criticised her. England did not understand France. There were two ways of opposing risings like those in Upper Silesia, or at Kaiserslautern in the autumn of 1919. One could either impose by a mass of troops, or one had to shoot. He viewed with the greatest repugnance any effusion of blood in civic strife and the whole feeling in the French Army was opposed to it. For example, at Kaiserslautern the strikers had fired on the French and the latter had not replied. There had been more casualties on the French than on the German side, but the French forced a settlement because they had the mass. Le Rond had not superior force and so could not be held responsible for not suppressing Korfanty's rising. To shoot was altogether repellent to the French in such cases. If it repelled them to do so against strikers in Germany, how much more would not the same feeling inspire them in the case of their Allies the Poles, who said to the French, "Fire and kill us if you like, but we shall still sing the Marseillaise while dying."

I turned to the French native troops in order to know his opinion about them. I said that I admired them as troops, but could not approve of their authority over a European population, and imagined that their presence on the Rhine helped to make even the Rhinelanders hostile, and in my view impaired the prestige of whites in the eyes of the native troops.

Degoutte replied that this was largely an economical question. He had 25,000 native troops in the Rhineland and some 60,000 French, normal garrison. France could not afford to spare 25,000 more Frenchmen from reconstruction. As to the feelings of the Germans, it did not matter a straw whether France sent white, black, or yellow troops here, as the Germans were implacably hostile and would cavil no matter what was done. Degoutte said that the principles of the French Revolution were those of Jesus Christ, namely, that every man was free, equal, and a brother. He thought that this was a much bigger ideal than mine which was too severely practical. I said that I acknowledged the superiority of the ideal, but saw no empire of subject races consistent with it. If Abd-el-Kadr was a free man, equal, and a brother, why did the French suppress this brother? It was a long time ago, said Degoutte, but now, if a people rebelled and wished to be free, the French would applaud. But you were fighting battles only this week in Morocco, I said, why? Because the tribes punished were incorrigible robbers, and besides there was a Sultan and nothing was done without his approval. I suppose that I must have smiled, for Degoutte added that he supposed I should say that the Sultan was in France's pocket, but there the principle was, and it accounted for the presence of the native troops here. I said that it seemed to me, in French Empires or ours, that to indoctrinate a mass of unintelligent and uneducated natives with the idea that they were as good as whites or better, when they were not, was to ask for trouble. One day France might find it so, with all this vast force of native troops in her new army, and I thought that war and peace garrisoning of an occupied country were two different things. We ourselves had fought against 30,000 German-led natives in East Africa, and in war-time Germany would never in future have a leg of logic to stand on if she howled about the use of native troops. Degoutte turned to the Malgaches to help him out, and said that a day or two ago he was with Barthou near Treves and that when he reviewed the Madagascar troops the German population had assembled in thousands and that a German youth had presented a bouquet to Barthou. This was because the Malgaches were Christians, and the Germans were astounded when they saw them in the cathedrals and churches, and asked, "How can these savages be Christians?" "But the Berbers are

not?" I replied. "No, they were Mussulmans of course."
It was no use pursuing the subject further. I shall watch
in future with some interest the application of the principles of the French Revolution to the French Colonial
Empire.

He asked me for my views on the Greco-Turkish question. I said that I meant to tease the authorities in Paris
and Rome before long. They had all told me that they
wanted to make Turkey a barrier against Bolshevism,
and would not listen to me when I told them that the
Turk would never be a barrier against anything. Sforza,
it was true, had warned me that Russia would be in Constantinople this year if we did nothing, but his policy of
pandering to the Turks did not postpone the loss of Constantinople, but rather promoted it. I told Degoutte that
France and Italy had only been out for loot, namely,
to get concessions out of the venal Turks, but Moscow
had bribed higher, and the Turks had flung the Treaty
with France back in her face. I was still convinced, like
Herodotus, of the eternal hostility of Europe and Asia,
and the question had become much complicated by our
Eastern possessions, but the heart of the matter was unchanged, and our business was to support the Greeks who
were in the forefront of the battle now as they were
twenty-three centuries ago. The Turks were just a warlike people, a scourge of Christians, who had lived and
would die with arms in their hands. The theories of Bolshevism were repugnant to them, but they wanted money
and arms, and these Moscow gave without conditions.
How could the Turks hesitate?

We parted with mutual expressions of good-will.

Am amused to read that Ormsby-Gore asked the P.M.
in the H. of C. whether I was with the Greek Army and
whether I had an official mission! The P.M. replied
that the Government had no information of my movements.

I also see that Mr. Harmsworth says that the Polish
insurgents number between 60,000 and 100,000, and "it

is hoped that the six British battalions now on their way will render the force at the disposal of the Inter-Allied Commission adequate to restore its authority." On what does this hope rest? On the chance that there is no fighting, I presume.

Took a last stroll round Mainz, but the intolerably oppressive heat drove me into a tram before long. This climate explains the Rhinelanders. It is like Cairo in August.

Sunday, June 5, 1921. What are the conclusions to be drawn from these three weeks on the Rhine? If we consider the French first we must extend a very sympathetic friendship and consideration to them. They were wantonly attacked in a most unprovoked manner and suffered fearfully in the war in men, money, and damage of all kinds. They did not get paid even such reparations as the Treaty allowed them until, two and a half years after its signature, an ultimatum brought the Germans to book. Had not France maintained compulsory service and her present large army, we should have found Germany by now rearmed and unready to carry out the Treaty. France bore the greatest brunt of the war, and after a war fought in common with her Allies, was left to bear the greatest burden of the guardianship of the peace. On the Rhine she finds the great bulk of the troops. The same in Silesia. She is alarmed for her future because of the large population of Germany, her almost intact industries and country, and her obvious intention to seek revenge at the first opportunity. The Anglo-American guarantee failed France and she had to look after herself. So she seeks to make alliances with the States round Germany, and this necessary policy compels her to be unduly lenient to Korfanty's bandits who flout Allied authority in Silesia. France cannot bear that the two great armouries of Germany, the Ruhr and Silesia, should remain in German hands, and those who force France to leave those districts in German hands will make themselves responsible for the consequences. France is in this fearful predicament, that if she leaves Germany all her resources to enable her to pay France, she *may* be paid, but Germany, the payments ended, will have all these resources to enable her to renew the war. If France takes hold of these resources, Germany cannot pay France and France will be financially broken. An Anglo-American guarantee of France against aggression from Germany will cover the whole danger, for Germany will never fight such a combination again, but there is no sign of such a guarantee, and therefore France feels bound, for her own security, to look after herself.

Belgium necessarily stands with France, since events have proved her to form part of the French front whether neutral or not. She has remodelled her Army. She is a valuable support to France, but has her own trade to look after, and does not like to see her fate so much in French hands. She would prefer an alliance with England, Italy, and France, and this quadruple alliance, which would hold the old frontiers of Rome on the Rhine and the Alps, would be wholly in our interests so long as it was strictly defensive. If an Anglo-American guarantee were a complement of the Alliance, Europe would quickly settle down. That is certainly our interest, and therefore indicates our right policy. But we must help France more to cause peace to fructify, and our miserable show on the Rhine and in Silesia is unworthy of us, even if everyone knows that our other troubles just now impede our action.

The present German Government seems honest and to want to carry out the terms of the Treaty. But it is weak, and the Right parties have quite other ideas. The German people want peace and are ready to work. Every good German naturally looks to a recovery of his lost territories some day, and most of the country has been implicated in these stupid secret organisations which we are endeavouring to break up. The old Imperial officers and war veterans are all for these organisations, but, as time goes on, they will apply themselves to other matters, and every year gained counts much. I think that Germany can pay if she keeps the Ruhr, and the Allies — not the Poles —

control Silesia. In this event the Rhine customs should drop so long as she pays. Germany can tax drink and tobacco more. She can tax coal more. She can apply the remedies of Hegedüs to landed estates and houses. With her low exchange, and in spite of paying reparations, she will largely dominate the markets of Europe, which we must fail to do while Labour demands higher wages than trade can bear, and completely disorganises business and destroys our markets by its strikes. Europe is on the way to recovery, but German reparations rule everything, and the Silesian problem affects not only reparations, but all Central Europe which depends on the Silesian coal. The nature of the Silesian settlement affords, therefore, the index to the future of Europe. We must, however, be prepared for a Germania Irredenta cry increasing in volume as time goes on and Germany becomes stronger. This cry, of which the *Anschluss* in Austria is a symptom, will require cool and firm handling or it will lead to great trouble hereafter.

CHAPTER X

BERLIN AND VIENNA

Arrive at Berlin — A talk with Lord D'Abernon — The Kaiser Friedrich Museum — Our German policy — A conversation with Professor Hans Delbrück — Emblems of imperialism — Mr. Finlayson on German State finance — Germany must double her revenue to pay reparations — The Chancellor, Dr. Wirth, at the Embassy — General von Seekt, War Minister — Their views on events — The Rodensteiners no more — How the Bolshevists plotted to invade Germany — A conversation with Chancellor Wirth at his office — Views on finance — Germany can pay — He wants us to help him — Militarist dangers — The Universities — He shows me Bismarck's rooms — An interesting figure — Lunch with General Nollet — We discuss the work of his Commission — M. Haguenin and his colleagues of the Reparations Delegation — A British view of disarmament — Colonel Thelwall's views — Uninspiring Berlin — The Embassy interior — A perfect hostess — American Embassy views on Germany — A conversation with Dr. Rosen, Foreign Minister — Return to Paris — An exchange of ideas with Lord Hardinge — Return to London — Off to Roumania — Munich — Some Bavarian opinions — Vienna — A provincial procession — Austria's mountaineers — A talk with Chancellor Schober — His first acts — Dr. Hertz's views — Austria a colony — How Austria obtained her best information during the war — The situation in Austria — Only a third of expenditure met by revenue — The League's financial plan — Vienna holds her own.

Berlin, June 6, 1921. Arrived here this morning after a cool night journey. Saw the Ambassador, Lord D'Abernon, before lunch. He tells me that the German armed bands in Upper Silesia are on a long line, Ratibor-Oppeln, facing east and part of it is not far from Gleiwitz. He thinks that the Germans have put themselves in the wrong by this advance. The German Commander Hoefer is to meet General Heneker at the latter's Headquarters to-day at 11 A.M. It is apparently the plan that three of our battalions should be strung out on this long line to keep the Germans out. Le Rond declares that he will evacuate all the industrial area if the Germans advance any further, but I do not see the logic of this declaration. Told D'Abernon, in reply to his question, what I thought the only peaceful solution to be and how utterly opposed I was to the despatch of our present weak force. D'A. is not opposed to the suggested solution of the United States Embassy[1] and said that he would not object to it. He thought that the Germans were putting themselves in the wrong by their advance which was much more forward than people had imagined. We are to talk to-morrow.

In the afternoon the text is published of an ultimatum from the Inter-Allied Commission to Hoefer telling him that unless he withdraws to a named line and begins to retire within twelve hours they will — what! attack him? — no, run away and evacuate the industrial triangle, and let the Poles back into it, a scurvy trick. We have fallen pretty low, I must say. Hoefer's reply also published. It is evasive and practically says that he has not the power to order the *Selbschutz* back. A ticklish position.

Saw Addison at the Embassy in the afternoon and had a talk on German finance, reparations, and taxes. Then went on to tea with Lady Kilmarnock — he is on leave at home — and heard about Berlin affairs. There seems to be a lot of gaiety going on, but chiefly in diplomatic society and in that of the various Allied Commissions. The old lot of the Germans seem to have retired to their estates as in Austria and Bohemia. Few Germans join the Allied society and those chiefly when they have links of marriage, etc., with Allied families. Officers who frequent this society are turned out of their German clubs. There is, in fact, no real friendship, but the little diplomatic society of a great capital is always self-supporting socially and does not worry about an embargo.

The Adlon a good hotel. But three-quarters of its clients are foreigners, largely Americans who swarm in Germany now. The replacing of paper table-covers by linen ditto is regarded as marking the close of a phase in the war! It is just completed, but linen napkins still unobtainable, the bread is not white, and cream is not to be had. The prices here are just treble those of Mainz. A delightfully cool morning, but it was very hot later again. The Germans here and in the Rhineland, especially if they are bald, make

[1] See entry for June 18.

a point of going about without hats in the most broiling sun. They must have precious thick heads. Perhaps this accounts for their actions in 1914.

Met Mr. Wilcox, the *D. T.* resident correspondent here.

Tuesday, June 7, 1921. Spent the morning at the Kaiser Friedrich Museum looking at the Dutch pictures only. A fine collection, the van Eycks most remarkable, the Rembrandts numerous, some very fine Vandycks, and the Rubens room filled with examples of this master whose female models were exceptionally expansive and repulsive. Nearly all the early Flemish and Dutch of any note are represented, but the pleasure a little spoilt by chattering copyists at work and by the horrible stuffiness and heat of the rooms.

Lunched at the Embassy with the D'Abernons; Mr. Edwards and Mr. Bunbury also there. Lady D'A. looking younger and lovelier than ever. I liked the Lenbach of her. It has never been exhibited, but is very fine indeed. We had a long talk about all the events of the day. D'A. thinks that the outlook is much brighter to-day than yesterday, so I suppose that Hoefer is not going to advance. It seems that we then propose to form a British line west of Gleiwitz and to tell the Poles to fall back behind the French who will form another line further east. If this succeeds the process is to be repeated until the insurgents have disbanded or crossed the frontier. At the same time the northern portion of Upper Silesia is to be cleared of bands. A quaint sort of plan, but it seems that French are also to be with British troops. It would be better to have one combined line and to sweep east. However, we shall see what happens. L. G. has gone away ill for ten days and H.E. thinks that by that time matters must be better or worse, he hopes and believes the former.

Generally speaking our policy seems to be one of moderation, and innocent of all vindictiveness. H.E. thinks that we have turned many worse corners, notably about reparations, and he hopes that with Harold Stuart and General Heneker on the spot matters may be arranged. The German Ministers tell him that Korfanty is like a bull and not easy to deal with. They understand and approve of the English policy. H.E. thinks that Wirth's Government may prove to have more stability than many people consider likely. He is all for Wirth and admires as I do Briand's clever handling of a very difficult crisis. He also thinks highly of the work of Nollet's Commission, and does not believe that any other people would have surrendered their arms as the Germans have done. But he says truly that when the control is removed, the Germans may rearm, and he thinks that the claim which the half-defunct League of Nations has to watch the Germans under Article 243 (?213) of the Treaty is a very poor protection to us. Therefore he thinks that more attention should be paid to the future guarantees for France than to minor affairs which we lay stress upon, and we are in accord that we shall have to come to an agreement with Germany on the subject, as we have so little right to a prolonged control under the Treaty. We are also of opinion that an agreed control might be maintained for some fifteen years until the old Imperial soldiers have forgotten war and Germany has returned to a civilian frame of mind. Will she ever? That is the question. But we can see.

H.E. advises me to try and see Wirth, Rosen, the new Foreign Minister, Finlayson, our man on the Reparations Commission, and Haguenin, a talented French colleague on the same Commission. I want to see also General Nollet, Hugo Stinnes, and Professor Hans Delbrück, and must see what luck I have. H.E. has seen Stinnes and says that he is considering the situation more in terms of business than of politics. Stinnes says that England and Germany must take Russia in hand together, but I am not anxious for such transaction. Stinnes tells H.E. that as a slump in industry is approaching, the French, if in the Ruhr, would soon find crowds of workmen out of work and would beseech Germany to take it back again. I told H.E. of the situation on the Rhine, and we discussed a number of other matters connected with all these events. Lady D'A. says that the attitude of German society towards us falls and rises with the feeling of the hour, but that almost all the old lot whom we used to know are away in their country houses, and that society is largely Jewish, when it is not diplomatic.

In the afternoon had a long talk with Herr Merton, who is here to visit his business friends. We talked about German policy, industry, and taxation for a long time. He thinks that Germany can pay her debts if she is left free to trade and the sanctions are removed. He tells me that tobacco is coming in to Germany cheaper across the Belgian frontier than into Germany direct, and that this trade was now deserting German ports and going via Antwerp. I told him that the new customs line allowed no such preference. He had studied the regulations and assented that in principle they did not; it was the way the Belgians applied the customs and discriminated and graded tobacco. I told him how I wished that there were one semi-official paper in Germany to give the Government view as the *Norddeutscher* and the *Cologne Gazette* had done in old days with their starred articles. The former, he replied, has been bought by Stinnes, and the present Government can scarcely use it. The *Cologne Gazette* is a good paper, but as it is in occupied territory and under Allied control, it is also unsuitable for the purpose. Merton thinks that the *Frankfurter* crabs the Germans too much and that it is not popular — because it is a Left and not a Right paper, no doubt — but he says that everyone has to read it, as it is well edited and its business articles and news are quite first-rate. He tells me that Stinnes is not a Jew, though he looks like one. He belongs to an old Westphalian family.

Dined with Wilcox at the Rheingold Restaurant and had a long talk over German matters. A hard-working, well-informed, and intelligent man who does not spare himself.

Wednesday, June 8, 1921. Telephoned to Professor Hans Delbrück, who was the last German to take a meal at my house in London before the war, on an occasion when he came over to lecture at the London University. Went out to see him at his house in the Grünewald, 4 Kunz Buntschuh Strasse, about twenty minutes by taxi. I said that I had come because he was one of the few Germans who had kept his head during the war and I wished to congratulate him on having, in all his articles which I had read, preserved his intellectual independence. What was he thinking now? I had his last book on my table, but wanted to talk of the present and the future and not the past. He has aged and is greatly saddened. He lost his eldest son in the war and is now badly off, but has a nice, quiet house and a good library. His second son had wanted to go to the University at Heidelberg. Delbrück had no money to send him there, so the youth worked as a common miner till he had saved enough money, and is now at Heidelberg. I congratulated him upon having such a son. D. is pessimistic about the future. What Europe could not understand, he said, was that Germany needed a strong Government to preserve the principle of authority in the State and he now saw no chance of getting it. German parties were not like the English which were mere clubs and not really divided on most principles. L. G., although almost a Unionist, could join the Radicals to-morrow without much loss of credit. In Germany parties were at deadly enmity and there was no real union in the Reich. His young people believed in Germany's future. He did not. He thought that the Crown Prince might come back some day, as he had a large following, but not the Kaiser. He said that all the same he regarded the Kaiser as a Pacifist and did not believe that he was responsible for the war. As for his desertion of the Army, which many Germans reproached him with, what else could he do? I should read, and make all my English friends read Rosner's "Der König," an account of the life at the Imperial H.Q. during the war and especially of the last month in 1918. Rosner was a reporter of little account, but had won the Kaiser's confidence and had written a story which was absolutely true of this period. Only some remarks about the Empress Frederick were incorrect, as Rosner did not know that side of history. D. said that if the Kaiser came back, some twenty-six other German Kings, Princes, and Dukes would also have to come back, and that was impossible. I did not see why.

I asked him about the state of opinion at the Universities. He said that they were nearly all Nationalist and so were the students. The Church too. But there were adherents of the Left in some educational centres.

D. is a Monarchist. He thought that a Hohenzollern could with difficulty return, as all his following would expect a restoration of their old prerogatives and this was out of the question, and the Crown Prince knew it. Moreover, the Federal States would not admit a German Kaiser unless they had their own chiefs back. He was rather for an Elected Prince and thought that Bavaria and Brunswick stood the best chance. He thought, like D'Abernon, that Dr. Wirth would last much longer than people expected, but D. raged about the position of Germany owing to the exactions of the Allies and was most pessimistic about the future, trotting out possible Bolshevism which I ventured to disbelieve in.

As for the future I said that the first thing for Germany to do was to give proofs of good faith, and, instead of bothering about becoming a Great Power, to set to work to re-create and reconstruct, leaving the question of military power to the next generation. It was no good for his generation and mine to try to solve the problems of the future. We had enough of our own, and I told him that our distrust was largely due to all the secret military organisations which we had been left to discover for ourselves. He scoffed at the *Einwohner, Orgesch*, etc., and said that people only laughed at them, while, as for arms, Germany had nothing of the great warlike machinery necessary, and even if the *Reichswehr* were prepared for triplification, which he did not admit, it was only a drop of water on a red-hot iron. He was an advocate of the balance of power, and now this had been destroyed with fatal results.

We had a long discussion about Upper Silesia and I told him my views, and Briand's theory, and all the difficulties so far as he did not already realise them. We discussed what history would say of these times. D. thought that history would fix upon the want of great men as the distinguishing feature. If Germany had had a Bismarck and a Moltke instead of a Ludendorff and a Tirpitz, things would have been different. If you had had a Bismarck we should have had no war, I rejoined. He has the lowest opinion possible of Ludendorff and Tirpitz and attributes to them and to the Revolution the collapse of Germany which he bitterly resents and cannot get out of his mind. He was moderate during the war, but now I think he hates the Allies with the deepest hate possible. But he impressed upon me that Europe was utterly wrong in regarding Germany as a danger. It could not be with her warring parties and without any semblance of authority and without an army. That view does not give us an incentive to promote the resurrection of either.

I branched to ancient military history, his particular sphere, in order to end the talk on a slightly more agreeable note, and presently we were immersed in Marathon and Salamis and had all the maps out to argue how the Greek and Persian armies and fleets were placed during the battles, and in this congenial exercise forgot present history and lived in the past. So we parted, with much the same formality and coldness as that during our meeting and our talk. He is not yet really resigned enough to talk. The iron has entered into his historian's soul. Between us and the Germans the war has killed even purely intellectual friendships.

Joseph Addison came to lunch and we had a change, or at least I had, in a most amusing gossipy talk about Germany, Paris, and our Embassy during the war, Lord Bertie and his peculiarities, and so forth. Addison's pet theory for reparations is to deduct a percentage of the cost of all German exports in all the countries to which they are exported — not only Allied countries — but I do not see how this can be arranged and he admits that D'Abernon does not agree with the scheme. He speaks very highly of H.E.'s ability and good sense in his difficult post.

Strolled round the Royal Palace which still flaunts the gold crowns, the eagles, the Cross — what would people say to a gold Cross over Buckingham Palace? — and all the rest of the emblems of Imperialism. Also looked at the equally deserted Palace of the Crown Prince, the statues of the Great Frederick, and the William I statue. It is so strange to see these places shorn of all the old pomp and glory. They leave us thinking and wondering. Cannot still, for the life of me, understand why the Kaiser built a renaissance cathedral just outside his drawing-room windows. The inherent defect of everything German is lack of taste. Even the really fine and characteristic statue of Frederick the Great would be far finer were it on a plain plinth with all the etceteras removed.

Went on to see Mr. H. C. E. Finlayson, the capable member of our Reparations Commission here. A shrewd Scot of cool and balanced judgement, trained under Sir John Bradbury. What I wanted to know was the precise situation of Boche State finance [1] and their chances of paying their way and paying us. It seems that their revenue and expenditure (ordinary) are made to balance at about 47 milliards of paper marks, but extraordinary expenditure still shows a deficit of 33 ditto to be covered this year, 1921. There are also 175 milliards of floating debt, paper marks, in the form of Treasury Bills. No real attempt has been made to arrest inflation. The actual fiduciary currency is 80 milliards of paper marks. The gold reserve is down to 1.090 milliards gold, or about £54,000,000 at present rates of exchange. There is also an anticipated deficit of $12\frac{1}{2}$ milliards of paper marks on railways expected in this financial year in spite of the doubling of railway fares, etc. This is not shown in the estimates, but has since been admitted. The sum owing for reparations this year is 40 to 50 milliards of paper marks — 3.3 milliards gold marks. [2]

[1] Note that eleven to fourteen paper marks equal one gold mark, the figure depending on the New York Exchange.

[2] Namely: 2 milliards of gold marks as per ultimatum, plus 1.3 milliards of gold marks = twenty-six per cent of exports on 1920 figures. Total, 3.3 milliards of gold marks.

Leaving aside the extraordinary deficit, which will be practically absorbed in the reparations, and the Treasury Bills, etc., the position is roughly that the revenue produces 47 milliards of paper marks and that the liabilities are:

40–50 milliards, paper, for reparations, a conventional figure on account of the doubt what the 26 per cent will bring in.
12½ "   "   " railways.
47   "   "   " ordinary expenditure.

Total 99½ to 109½, leaving a deficit to be made good of 52½ to 62½ milliards. In other words, the revenue of last year must be *more than doubled*, and this is the case when Silesia, the sanctions, depression, and the loss of the Russian market seriously hamper trade. Our old trade with Germany, 141 millions sterling in 1913, has been practically destroyed by all these things.

Can Germany produce a revenue of, say, 110 milliards of paper marks, and how? This really means can she find these 40 to 50 milliards of paper marks to pay the Allies the 3.3 milliards of gold marks a year? On the whole, if her trade is freed of hampering and encumbrances, and the mark does not fall too much,[1] she can. She can find 1.3 milliard gold marks (1) from deliveries in kind, notably coal, dyes, timber, ammonia, wooden houses, and as much German labour as she is allowed to use; (2) from the operations of the German Reparation Recovery Acts which are paid in to the Reparations Commission by the Allied Governments which may bring in 250 million gold marks a year, and by (3) fresh or increased taxes on coal, beer, brandy, tobacco, sugar, the turnover or *Umsatz* tax, the unearned increment tax, etc., which may give about 1.6 milliards of gold marks a year. All this means about 3.1 milliards of gold marks a year which is near to the required figure of 3.3.

Such a scheme includes neither increased income tax nor capital levy, nor would it mean a resort to such drastic

---

[1] By October it had fallen to 1200 marks = £1, or to about one-fourth the rate in June. This made Germany's task practically impossible.

finance as that of Hegedüs for Hungary. In fact, the land and the industrials would appear to get off comparatively lightly, and this may mollify the Right. Round this question will rage a battle, as the Left want direct taxation and the Right want indirect. It is a big thing to do and the deliveries in kind have of course to be paid for in Germany or may lead to further inflation. No. 2 is paid for by the Allies to the profit of their protectionists. No. 3 is paid for by German consumers mainly. So far as I can make out, a German revenue of 110 milliards paper marks amounts to some £400,000,000 in sterling, and, allowing for the twenty-five per cent depreciation of gold, means a call on the sixty million Germans of only half the amount of our present call on the forty-six million people in the United Kingdom. But Finlayson tells me that this comparison is unfair.

I have not included in the above the cost of the armies of occupation. The recording angel may know the figure, but no one else does. It is to be limited to one quarter of a milliard in future, or at least this is all that the Germans are to be answerable for.

Thursday, June 9, 1921. Cooler, some rain. Lunched at the Embassy and met the Chancellor Dr. Wirth, General von Seekt, the head of the War Office, two members of the German F.O., Dame Adelaide Livingstone, and Addison. The Chancellor is a tall and solid man of forty-one with high colouring and thickish brown hair and a moustache. He wears glasses. He was in a frock coat. He is of the Centre Party and was a schoolmaster. We found that we had both been students at Freiburg-i-B., and so had some common recollections of the town, cathedral, football ground, etc. He was through the war on the Russian front in Poland and Galicia as a private soldier, and said that this experience had enabled him to understand the partitions of Poland, though he thought them acts of injustice. He thought that the Poles were people who were only united in offensive policy abroad, and never in their internal policy. He said that there was a proverb that no Swabian became intelligent until he was forty, so he had reached an interesting age, as he was forty-one. He had known English and had read his Shakespeare, but had then got out of the habit and was now reading the English papers for practice. He also speaks French quite well enough to get on. He does not smoke. He told H.E. to-day that he was quite sure to get his taxes and he was even humorous about them. Lady D'A. thinks him solid and not easily put out. He is not nervous and on wires as Dr. Simons was. Dr. Wirth asked me to come and see him to-morrow. He was taken by my quotation from the Bismarck statue at Frankfort.

I talked with von Seekt, who says that he has all the volunteers that he wants for the *Reichswehr*. They were coming on well and great pains was taken to see that they got the right men. He admitted that the Police were fine fellows, especially in Berlin. His great trouble had been that it had fallen to him to reduce the officers from 16,000 to 4000. It was easier with the younger officers, who were soon placed, but with the older officers it was different. I asked about the *Rodensteiners*, to which society some thirty of us belonged in old days. It has died a natural death with the disappearance of the old lot. Waenke von Donkerschweil is dead, Dame is at Constance, among the old lot of the Nachrichten Bureau of thirty years ago. Von Seekt is a thinnish man who looks as if he would order one to be shot at dawn without embarrassment, but in conversation he is agreeable. Dame Adelaide Livingstone is here about war graves. There are 5000 of our men buried in Germany. She contemplates a visit to the Baltic states where some eighty of our graves are.

H.E. told me to-day that Hoefer and Heneker had fixed things up between them. Hoefer had told Heneker how many Germans there were in his Volunteer forces and where they were. Now the movement against the Poles was under way and Harold Stuart and Heneker had taken hold of Le Rond and had told him that if he did not play the game they would take their troops away. The Chancellor seemed to think that the crisis was over, but the real trouble is with the Poles and I am not reassured yet.

Talking at lunch, H.E. and one of the Germans agreed that the battle of Warsaw — where H.E. seems to have been of great service to General Weygand when the Poles would not take orders easily — was one of the most important battles politically in history, for if the Bolshevists had won they would have swept across Germany and would only have been stayed on the Rhine. They were very cunning, well-informed, and cynical plotters. They were coming into Germany under the National (German) colours with the pretext of re-establishing German nationalism, and when they had got a grip of the country they would only then show their hand and substitute the Red flag. I asked what the Germans would do now that Lenin seemed to be moving more towards the political Right. They said that their game was to support him, and they seem to want us to do the same. I do not believe in any entanglement of this sort. Better for us to keep out of it all.

Had another wrestle to-day with the German Budget, and was helped by Wilcox and Finlayson. Believe that I have got the general situation fairly well, thanks mainly to Finlayson's clear mind. I must say that I think the Germans have not been diligent in arresting inflation and that they ought to have paid off their floating debt and stopped the printing press by this time. Also one must conclude that they never attempted to find the money for reparations until they were brought to book by the ultimatum. Was all this floating debt and paper money deliberately kept going so that they might sham financially dead to the Allies? In the same way was not the cheapness of coal to restore their industries, and the cheapness of food, beer, etc., all part of the same game? However, it is ended now, but if they had made the effort necessary they could have done more before. It is a good thing to have D'Abernon here. He is known as "the doctor of sick finance." He is very active and quick at things and has vast experience in these matters. He is also a man of the world, and that means more, in every profession, than most people admit.

In the evening went for a short time to Dame Adelaide Livingstone's dance in the Lichtenstein's Allee. A very pleasant party and a capital reel by some young Scots officers in kilts, and Mackinnon with the pipes. No Germans, and mainly Allies, with the Dutch, all the Allied Embassies and Commissions, etc. Met Baroness Gevers whose husband, the Dutch Minister, was so intimately associated with the closing days of the war in South Africa. Lady Kilmarnock's girl, still in the schoolroom and with her hair down her back, looked a pet. Baroness G. had been in Berlin all through the war and the Revolution. What an experience and what changes! I asked her when they realised that the Germans were going to be beaten. She said that she could not give a date: the fact dawned on them all slowly. "Why do they say still that they were not beaten?" I asked. She laughed and said, "They may say that to you, but they all *know* that they were beaten."

Friday, June 10, 1921. In the morning went to the Chancellor's office at 77 Wilhelm Strasse, Bismarck's old Olympus. Dr. Wirth arrived a little late, apologising for having been detained by wrestling over taxation questions with the Federal representatives. He was in country clothes which suited him better than yesterday's stiff frock coat. He looked uncommonly well and fresh and full of go. A very good colour. He speaks clearly and not too fast. When he gets interested, he fixes his eyes on one with a penetrating glance. He is decidedly intelligent and perfectly honest and sincere, unless all appearances belie, and very easy to talk to. Quite nice manners and no side or *gêne* of any kind. He did not talk at me nor lecture. He looked like a well-to-do factor from North Britain, and though we alternately talked in three languages we got on quite well.

As he had begun on finance I followed up that line and

told him how interested I was in his present work as
Finance Minister. It was, he allowed, a heavy task. He
knew roughly the Hegedüs scheme in Hungary and said
that the Socialists wished him to follow it, as it was so
drastic and in line with their politics. But, as to the Hungarian land policy, he thought that the big estates of
Hungary were only found in few parts of Germany, and
as the Germans had many small and medium-sized properties,[1] the Hegedüs plan could not be applied rigidly. I
doubt whether he means to offend the landowners by applying it at all. It does not seem necessary at present. As for
the plan of a first mortgage on houses, this plan depended
on house rents being free. This they were not at present
in Berlin. Were they in Hungary? I was not sure, but
thought not. They certainly were not in Vienna. But the
Societies tax of fifteen per cent? I asked. He admitted
that it was now being prepared for use in case of need.

Then we came to reparations, and he told me that, contrary to the views prevailing in France, he thought the
Paris scheme more favourable to Germany than that of the
London ultimatum. I could not quite grasp the reasons.
But he said definitely that Germany could pay the two
milliards of gold marks a year. He had found more people
ready to help him than he had counted on. He had recently addressed a body of industrial magnates and had
found them much more amenable than he expected. Dr.
Stresemann, the leader of the *Volkspartei*, had been sitting
the other day where I was sitting and had given him the
impression that he would support him. Even Hugo Stinnes
had become much more moderate. Wirth thought it a
misfortune that Stinnes had gone to Spa and had made a
great political demonstration. An error had been made in
sending him and would not be repeated. Wirth's trouble
arises over the twenty-six per cent arrangement and over
the eighty-two millions which he described as the third
instalment of the reparations.

He told me that in the position in which he was placed

---

[1] About one-half of the land is distributed in this manner.

he required to gain a little political success in order to affirm his position with the young German democracy and increase the confidence of his Reichstag. He belonged to the Centre Party which he described as the real governing party in Germany.

He did not think that the Rhine customs were worth much to us and they severely injured German trade. The occupation of Düsseldorf, Duisburg, and Ruhrort is a sanction which he also feels deeply. I suggested that the dates of June 10 and 30 might be important in this matter, for if all the claims of the Allies had been met at these dates they would be much mollified. He thought that the disarmament was proceeding quietly and that there would now be no difficulty with Bavaria.

I told him my view about the need for vigilance on our side until all the old Imperial officers and veterans had been merged in the civil population. I also told him that there were two things which we had long desired for Germany in England even before the war, namely, real parliamentary government in the first place, and secondly, the substitution of the civic spirit for the old militarism. We had got the first, how about the last? Were not the Universities, the clergy, and the students the props of militarism, and how could a spirit change except by a change of methods and even of men in education?

This danger Wirth admitted. The professoriat had all spoken to the Imperial cue, like one man, and of course the students followed it. Germany had suffered terribly from the subservience of her high teaching staff to the Kaiser. So had the German Army, I suggested, by Generals telling the Kaiser what he liked to hear, and not the truth always. Dr. W. admitted it, but said that a change could only be made gradually at the Universities by selecting men of greater honesty and breadth of mind. The question was under study, and he agreed that all this question of the civic spirit was really far more important than anything else. As for the Rhine towns seized, he reverted to this more than once and said that it could be defended only on strategical grounds, and what was the use of holding these towns when Germany could be invaded anywhere and at any time?

We talked of my mission from Lord Burnham and he asked several questions about it, inviting me to come and have a meal with him when I was in Berlin again. Then he asked if I would like to see Bismarck's working room and the other rooms of the Palace. I accepted and he took me round. A comfortable and large house, with pleasant shaded and turfed garden behind, apparently quite private and not overlooked. The great hall where the Berlin Conference took place is double the size of the room at the Ballhaus-Platz where the Vienna Congress was held. It is large and lofty. Bismarck's old study is medium-sized, in the centre of the Palace facing the Wilhelm Strasse. The chief piece of furniture left in it is Bismarck's old writing-table, one of those mahogany so-called "pull-down" writing-desks which are my pet abomination. It stood near the centre window, probably sideways or Bismarck would have got no light. The advantages of the desk probably were that he could pull down the top and lock up secret papers when he went out of the room. For the rest, the only objects of interest were the portraits, one of Wilhelm I, another of Wilhelm II over the mantelpiece and a third full-length of Bismarck in his later days, by Lenbach. There was a sort of salon beyond with a kind of conservatory and a bear-walk further on. The Chancellor showed me the room where he, Wirth, held his Cabinets. It is at the back looking over the garden. Seats for about twenty people, with blotting paper, etc. A large map of Upper Silesia with the position of all the troops marked attracted my attention and we had some talk about it. There is a second larger council room where he meets the Federal people, but it only had green baize over it and nothing prepared for work. In general all this formerly occupied part of the palace has a disused and rather shabby aspect. The furniture a mixture of French, Venetian mirrors, some quite good, and some highly uninter-

esting Italian religious pictures which Wirth admired and
I did not. I could not help admiring the modesty of Wirth
in not occupying the historic rooms. A pleasant visit and
I found Dr. W. agreeable because he is totally without pre-
tentiousness and talks naturally. His own room where we
first talked is in the east wing of the house at the back. A
large writing-table, and in a corner near the door a table
and sofa and two armchairs where we talked. I keep on
asking myself whether the attraction of Dr. Wirth comes
from the character of the man himself or from the glamour
thrown over his office by Bismarck, and I cannot decide
what the answer may be. All that one can say is that here
is a man who fills Bismarck's place at the age of forty-one
and on his public form is an honest man who is striving to
do his duty by his country and the world without fear and
favour. He is simple, pleasant, intelligent, and strong,
without a trace of heat or prejudice, but, for the rest,
events will measure his statesmanship.

Got back to the Adlon barely in time to lunch with General Nollet, the very pleasant and capable head of the
Inter-Allied Military Commission of Control, his naval
A.D.C. Lieutenant Michelier, and another older member
of his staff. We sat from one to four talking and had a
most interesting and often amusing discussion. Nollet on
the whole will not commit himself about the result of
German disarmament on the fateful dates. He says that
he never believed in Bavarian intransigence, as he did not
see why it should differ from other parts of Germany.
Things appeared to be going well, but he could only conclude when the figures were in to show final results. It was
easier to conclude about material than effectives. I asked
about the discrepancy between his and Simons's figure
for guns, namely, 33,000 and 49,000. N. said that Simons
had given the latter figure and it included guns which the
Germans had said that they had destroyed. His own
figure of 33,000 was what he could swear to. Yes, the
German Army, like German industry, was powerfully
equipped; they spared neither pains nor money. It was

his object to break up all the Army, not only men and guns, but carts, harness, and the thousands of categories of warlike stores of all kinds in every arm and service. Then the rapid restoration of a modern army would be a long, costly, and difficult business.

I thought that he rather approved of my proffered solution for Upper Silesia, and at all events he did not dissent from it. The Germans, he agreed, were certainly champion informers, as the French at Mainz had told me. Their motives were first, money; second, vengeance; and third, an honest belief that they were serving real German interests. The money motive came first by long chalks. Much was given away out of spite and for revenge. If a man were kicked out of the *Reichswehr* for no reason given, he would probably come to the French and say where there were arms concealed, especially if he had been in charge of them. This is a state of mind unaccountable to us and the French.

He admitted that France could disarm had the Anglo-American guarantee stood. Germany would never have dared face such a combination again and the question of control would not have mattered. Now it was different. It was not a permanent safeguard to disarm Germany, but by strictly limiting effectives so far as was possible, and by destroying not only arms and guns, but also carriages of all sorts, aeroplanes, harness, saddlery, and all the thousand of stores of all kinds of war material, France would probably have warning of an attack, as it would take so long to build all this up again. But he is plainly worried still about future control, as there is no effective means for it in the Treaty. He would like the control to remain, but does not at present see how he can get it. I am not quite certain whether Nollet really believes that all the German promises regarding disarmament will be made good by the dates fixed. It may be, or it may not, that he pretends doubt so as not to let the Germans learn his opinion and believe that they have done enough. Perhaps he will just give the figures when all the returns are in and allow the Supreme Council to judge. He is a good steady man who inspires general confidence, and one can go bail on his conclusions. He tells me that his Commission have worked in complete accord all through and have invariably arrived at unanimous conclusions. Nollet admitted that the German Police were finer fellows than the *Reichswehr*, but said that the latter were the most valuable military force. He intended to see to it that the Police were real police like the English and not camouflaged troops as they are now.

Saturday, June 11, 1921. Professor Delbrück called in the morning to know my views about Churchill's speech at the Manchester Chamber of Commerce on June 8, briefly reported in the German papers, advocating an understanding between England, France, and Germany, and declaring that the German exports to pay reparations would make her the first industrial nation in Europe. D. said that it was a speech which he might have made himself. I had not read it. D. said that his difficulty was that he could not conceive how the Germans could come to terms with the French. We had some talk about it. I fancy that the French feel like D., but business is business and seems to ignore national feelings.

Met at M. Haguenin's pleasant rooms his colleagues, M. Beaumont, the Italian M. Brazziani, M. Berthelot, son of the General, and Mr. Finlayson. We had a good talk about finance, trade, industries, and reparations. Briefly stated, these experts of the delegation of the Reparations Commission do not believe in reparations. They say that Germany can pay only in gold or in goods. There is no gold to speak of, so goods must pay. Therefore goods must be not only exported but sold, for it is not the exported goods but the sold goods that produce the reparations money. So Germany will swamp all the markets which are open to her, depress our home trade by underselling it, and end with a dominant commercial position. On the other hand, the gold flowing into New York will affect the value of the dollar because Berlin will be buying dollars, and Germany might even seriously affect British currency. If protectionist tariffs keep out German goods, then Germany cannot pay. We cannot have it both ways, but we are trying to do so. Winston, whose speech I have now read, attacked the question from the other end, but they all agree with him. It is as simple as A B C.

Finlayson explained the Chancellor's views about the twenty-six per cent. It seems that the ruling agreement has two clauses which are contradictory, one making the twenty-six per cent to be paid by the owner of the goods, and the other leaving it to be paid as Germany likes. The Chancellor's other point must refer to the eighty-three milliards of bonds due next November, but the actual payments yearly do not seem to be affected. These experts speak again of the fact that Germany was the first in position to trade on a large scale after the war because she had cheap labour, mobilised industries, and cheap coal. Her exports had been immense in 1920, with indecent profits, and her shipping was booming. Haguenin all the same believes that when Germany is paying hard, and her exports bounding up, the mark will so improve that she will have a slump. It is all a mass of contradictions, and Finlayson calls exports a sign of weakness and not of strength. Haguenin told me that some French and German industrial magnates were already in agreement, but the thing had not yet included all the interests which they wished to rope in. They say that Wirth means to double the price of coal, i.e., to increase it to 450 marks a ton. It was eleven to fifteen marks pit-head price before the war! They expect that the industrials will soon discover means for using lignite more extensively. They also say that the Swedish and Spanish ore now used in the Ruhr is more expensive than minette. This wants looking into, as I have been told the reverse.

Sunday, June 12, 1921. Had a talk in the morning with X. He has been here eighteen months, but says that we must deduct some few months from that term on account of the Kapp *Putsch* and some other events when work could not go on. He tells me that it is physically impracticable to complete the disarmament by June 30, the date fixed by the ultimatum. The work will go on till the end of the year and possibly till next March, apart altogether from the question of post-war control later. He sees no reason to doubt the French idea of the intended triplication of the *Reichswehr*, and of the existence of arms and equipments for such organisation. I told him that Delbrück had told me that his friends said that the *Reichswehr* had only 50,000 combatants. X, and Y, who was with him, smiled. X said that they could not say for certain that there were not *more* than 100,000, because men might be away on leave and so forth, and there was no certainty that the strengths were restricted to the authorised figures. He said that Z believed that there was not a single gun left. X thought this opinion optimistic and considered Z credulous. The Germans had much flattered him. In regard to the Police, he said that in Berlin they were mostly old N.C.O.'s of the Guard. The Police were not local as with us in England. They were a single force in the hands of the Government. It would be a job to demilitarise them. They were restricted to one rifle for three men and one automatic pistol per twenty, but whether this was true was a question. He thought that a continued control was advisable and took no exception to my fifteen years.

The fortress guns were coming on well. The Germans had fallen into a trap here. The Treaty limited them to guns already in position. So they had collected all their heavies and had crammed them into the fortress, but had not placed many in position. So they were all rounded up and were now being destroyed. There was a hole in the Treaty about the Police. No term of enlistment was laid down and the Germans could take men and pass them through it. It was not certain what the actual terms of enlistment were now. Morgan said that the Commission worked well and in complete accord together. He said that I had probably found out for myself that nearly all the

British officers in Germany were friendly to the Germans from a bare sense of justice. I said, yes, but the Germans told us that they liked us and hated the French, and told the French that England was the only enemy. Probably they told the Italians that they hated us both and only loved the Italians. So it really did not matter what the Germans said. Morgan agreed with this.

Lunched with the Kilmarnocks. He is just back from home with the London news. Colonel Thelwall, the Commercial Secretary there, and the K.'s son and little daughter. A pleasant little party. Thelwall says that he agrees generally with the views which I mentioned to him as those of the Reparations people, though he works on independent lines. He said that no one could understand the twenty-six per cent scheme, for if it were levied on all German trade with us it would have to be imposed on many things we needed, notably dyes, which could not stand such a duty. We might leave the German Government to scale up the duties to *average* twenty-six per cent, or let them make some fresh proposal. He was much opposed to the new customs on the Rhine and called them wicked. I had told Morgan that I was sorry to hear that we could not give Germany a clean bill of health regarding disarmament by June 30, as the French were sure to make a row about it, and then the Ruhr loomed up again, and we should not be able to remove the Rhine customs and so give Wirth the little political credit which he needed with his people. Thelwall thinks that we are all still too unregenerate to adopt my plan of abolishing all economic barriers, and all customs on all frontiers, for a year, but says that undoubtedly liberty of international trade is the great aim to be kept in mind, and that only this liberty can lead to the pacification and reconstruction of Europe.

Note that all the people to whom I speak about the new Commission of Guarantees wish it to be quartered here, as Berlin is obviously the only place where it can do its work properly. But it hankers after the flesh-pots of Paris, so enchanting to so many other Commissions, and it ought to be ordered to stay here. Still, one must admit, Berlin is not an inspiring capital. It is not Imperial like Vienna, nor glittering like Paris, nor homely like London. It has really no points, and most of its public buildings are plastered or crowned with fiddling ornaments or statues which destroy a plan even in itself not ignoble like the Reichstag building. When you have said Brandenburger Tor you have just said all for Berlin architecture. Why? Because the Tor is Greek and simple. Those six massive Doric columns facing Unter den Linden, though not one hundred and fifty years old, are superior to all the rest of the public buildings in the town. Why do people design new things when there is Greek, Anne, and Georgian to choose from? If only the Berliners knew how vile their taste is!

But there are some good interiors. At the Embassy to-night, where we were some eighteen to dinner, I thought the plan of the ground floor, barring the hall staircase, quite good. The arrangements are excellent for entertaining and very dignified. We were all English or Americans, and the Ambassadress a very perfect hostess. D'A. has gone home for Ascot. The little circular room in the centre of the ground floor rooms is curiously Adamsy, and the ballroom is fine; furniture and pictures also good.

Monday, June 13, 1921. Wrote in the morning and then lunched at the American Embassy, at 7, Wilhelm Platz, with Mr. Dolbeare. There were five members of the Embassy including the Councillor and First Secretary. The Ambassador is away. Mr. Pennoya just arrived from London. We discussed Germany all the time. The only new suggestion that I heard about Silesia was that the Germans should keep all but the Pless-Rybnik bit and agree to open up a certain number of mines in Poland for the Poles. They do not think much of the Poles. In general I found that the Americans thought pretty well as we do about Germany and are to the same extent pro-German as we are supposed to be. They want to keep their German market. This is the leading thought. They strongly approve of Wirth, and say that Rathenau is the only other Minister who counts. They are dubious about the effect upon various currencies of the movement about the world of great blocks of reparation monies. They suggest that the Military Control should be continued at reduced establishments. They think that German Labour will never permit Monarchism to reappear. They regard the University professors, who are State servants, as the supporters of the reaction, and not the schools, where there are no new books owing to high cost of printing, but good men are chosen to teach and to inculcate the new ideas. They are inclined to believe that Germany was busy amassing credits abroad secretly during the last two years, and did not talk about them for fear that they might be confiscated. They point out that Germany was under no obligation to pay reparations until her total indebtedness had been stated to her on May 1. They fancy that Germany will try to open up Russia and will also control the trade of Central Europe. I found them all apparently pro-Hungarian. They are for the abolition of the March sanctions, and think that if Wirth taxes coal he will still leave the price ten per cent below the world value to give them a pull in the market. This tax will tend to raise German wages and prices all round. I asked about a tax on Societies. They say that a tax on Societies on the Hegedüs lines will give the State almost a controlling influence over most of them and will make it interested in their welfare. It will then be able to exercise a preponderating influence on the trade, whatever it may be, and on its world markets. They consider that the workman's wages in Germany are enough to support a single man decently, but not a family.

At 5.30 I went to see Dr. Rosen, the new Foreign Minister, at 17, Budapeste Strasse, near the Tor. A tallish, thick man of about sixty with a moustache and a bit of a beard; rather slow and precise in his conversation, an official type, not like a Jew, though they say he is one, and the conversation was a trifle stilted at first until we came to subjects of mutual interest. Then he kept on warming up and soon became quite communicative.[1]

I suggested that he was regarded as a Kaiser's man, in a Cabinet where all the rest were of a Left or Centre complexion. He said that all the members of the Government shared Wirth's views. If they had not done so, they would neither have joined him nor have been asked to do so. "All diplomatists before the war were Kaiser's men," R. continued with much truth, "just as all yours were King's men; and as the Kaiser reigned till 1918 only the youngest diplomatists are anything else."

We drank a lot of tea, and smoked a lot too, and it was just 8 P.M. when I finally left him. It was raining. I had come in by the garden gate and he insisted on going out with me in the rain with no hat or umbrella. There is a door from his garden which leads into the Chancellor's Palace garden adjoining. A pleasant enough place to live in, but R. complained that he never got any exercise now. He had sat with his back to the light in his study while we talked, leaving me facing it — an old trick of second-class diplomats — but as he came out into the garden I saw him better. I should say that Wirth means [to conduct his own foreign policy, and has taken Rosen for clerking on account of his wide experience, his reticence — though our talk scarcely bore it out — and his knowledge of the diplomatic ropes and routine. I thought that Rosen might be handled if he were taken the right way. He seems to me to be impregnated with the Japanese spirit. One must be prepared for a long pow-wow before things begin to come out.

Tuesday, June 14, 1921. X telephoned in the morning and I went to see him. I asked why Nollet had not helped the Germans by telling them what other illicit organisations he wished to be abolished. The answer amused me. Nollet was afraid that if he named them there might be a

---

[1] I am unable to publish the interesting and illuminating conversation which followed for two hours and a half as Dr. Rosen asked me to consider it confidential. I submitted it to him later and he allowed me to use only the paragraph which follows.

great many others which he had *not* named, and then the Germans would say that he had not named them! But X said that the next German statement was almost due, so perhaps all will be well. It does no harm that Nollet should have mystified and terrorised Rosen, but rather good. The great thing is to get the job done. X said that there were only 22,000 of the Bavarian rifles to hand yet. Left by the 2 P.M. Warsaw-Paris express.

Paris, Wednesday, June 15, 1921. Arrived 12.30 P.M. up to time, after a good journey. The devastated country *en route* is an ever-fresh reminder of stern truths. Had tea alone with X and we had a long talk comparing our respective experiences. He says that to-day the news from Upper Silesia is worse. He defends Hoefer's action, and says that Harold Stuart is up against Le Rond thoroughly now, and is in process of concentrating the British troops as a protest against Le Rond's intrigues. Le Rond had mischievously planned to scatter the British troops amongst the Poles and then to say to the Germans, See what your British friends are worth! X says that he knew Stuart in India and that he is a pretty stiff proposition when he is up against a man. X believes nothing of the accounts in the French press. He sees no light and no way out. I told him my view, and mentioned the American suggestion as interesting. He asked what it would mean, and I said I presumed sinking shafts, running headings, and equipping and organising some Polish mines in the Dombrova area for the Poles. The alternative to my plan and the American seemed to us to be arbitration.[1] X said that the French were determined to carry out their policy in Silesia. I said Yes, *it was a policy* as Poincaré had just naïvely admitted in *Le Temps*, but we all went there, not to promote a policy, but to do justice, and that point of view had never been accepted by the French whose idea of justice was to get what they wanted. I was glad that Stuart was drawing his men together. I said that such a weak

---

[1] It eventually came to this after the August Conference in Paris when the problem was relegated to the League of Nations.

force should never have been sent, and that I was for their coming away, and for giving the reasons openly. We could not go on with this dangerous fooling. We were risking our men's lives all the time.

I asked X whether Lord Hardinge had not had a pretty hectic time since last we met. He said he had had. He was just off on leave two days before L. G.'s speech on the 13th when he received a wire telling him to await an important despatch. It came, and Hardinge went to Briand and delivered it. It was pretty sharp, and H. had to tell Briand some unpleasant things, but he did so in diplomatic language which did not give offence, and all would have been well if it had been left at that. But then came L. G.'s speech, which took everybody's breath away.

I thought that X might know why Rosen was so disliked. He only knew that he was mistrusted and mentioned Tangiers without alluding to any particular incident. At The Hague the trouble was over a question of precedence, Rosen having become the doyen owing to the war. It was with such futilities that some diplomacy concerned itself.

What a strange experience all this has been! — London, Paris, Rome, Athens; then Rome, Paris, and London again; the Conference; Paris, Cologne, Düsseldorf, Berlin, Oppeln and Upper Silesia, Breslau, Dresden, Prague, Vienna, Budapest, Paris once more, Mayence, Wiesbaden, Coblenz, Frankfurt, Berlin, and now Paris and London again. What a kaleidoscope of scenes, places, events, people, and things! If only I can complete the series by Bucharest, Transylvania, and Sofia, I shall have done the bulk, and can then complete at leisure Poland and Jugo-Slavia which are not quite ready to be visited yet, and the western fringe of Europe, that is, the full cycle of modern post-war Europe. Many people will know their own corners better than I, but one must visit every seat of government and see all the leading men in order to judge the whole enchaining of circumstances and the relation of the various parts to the whole. I am constantly reminded of my old experiences in campaigns and manœuvres when I have gone round and have found people obsessed by their own little battle and quite ignorant of what was happening a few miles off. So it really is in diplomacy and foreign politics. The lookers-on see most of the game.

London, July 6, 1921. Three weeks of perfect weather and still more perfect company at home, and now I am off again to the East of Europe to complete my tour. We have got through the coal strike at long last and efforts are being made to make peace with the Sinn Feiners, so possibly home troubles may be sufficiently mitigated to enable us to pay more attention to the Near East, where the situation has grown worse on account of our weak policy towards Turks and Greeks. The position has worked out as it was bound to have worked out when France and Italy backed the Kemalists, and we feebly gave way to them and failed to help our natural allies, the Greeks. Now the latter have evacuated Ismid to concentrate their forces, and the Kemalists are profiting by their absence. There are 160,000 Russians of Wrangel's and Denikin's armies scattered about at Constantinople, in Egypt, in Serbia, and a plot by these gentry to murder Harington has just been detected. These Russians, being in a state of despair and destitution, are ripe for mischief, while Bulgarian plots have been recounted by the *D. T.* and the Kemalists allied themselves with Soviet Russia on March 16, and have since been in touch with them. There is a question of Roumania sending troops to Constantinople to help the weak Allied forces there. Sforza is out of office in Italy by reason of Giolitti's resignation after a vote which displayed lack of confidence in Italy's foreign policy. Philippe Berthelot is also in a difficult position by reason of his brother's connection with the now fallen Banque Industrielle de Chine. These two men were the great supporters of the pro-Kemalist policy of France and Italy, which has always been against sense. Where is the promised Turkish barrier against Bolshevism now? Barrier and Bolshevism are allied! All this comes from the Allied failure to insist on the ratification of the Sèvres Treaty and from our failure to take a strong line in a quarter of the world where our interests were much engaged.

Vienna, Sunday, July 10, 1921. Arrived here last night via Carlsruhe and Munich after various unpleasant worries with the German passport people who turned several of us out of the through *wagon-lit* for Bucharest at Kehl at 4.30 A.M., on the pretext that we had insufficient visas. With difficulty we kept our hands off the chief offender. This happens every day at Kehl, it seems. The result was that the train went on without us, and that I have lost three days. However, I saw a few people at Munich, and came by day through the beautiful scenery of Southern or Alpine Bavaria, which exudes riches and comfort, and where the crops look splendid and the pastures are greener than anywhere else in Europe. The Bavarian Tyrol must be a charming place for a motor tour. In general I found that the Bavarians frankly admit that they lost the war, and are not bothering much about the reasons why they lost it. The *Einwohnerwehr* have given up their arms with reluctance, but admit that the vast extension of the movement was an error. They had suffered so much in Munich from the Spartacists that when the *Einwohnerwehr* was started, every patriotic burgher joined, whereas what was needed was only a small special constabulary in groups of twenty to thirty men. The larger movement naturally looked to the Allies like a new and camouflaged army. As I reached Munich there came the news that the French had boycotted the High Court at Leipzig, where the German war criminals are being tried, owing to the release of the worst offenders, and that the Ruhr sanction is up once more. This makes the Bavarians mad, and they openly tell me at Munich that they hate the French so much that every man will march against them if he can only provide himself with a stick. Ought not this situation to have been foreseen? How could we expect that which is justice in French eyes out of German courts and procedure? As things stand, the worst culprits get off and a few wretched underlings get short sentences.

Respecting the Tyrol I find that the Germans are taking no action, at least outwardly. Their view is that this matter of the *Anschluss* will settle itself by the natural force of circumstances, and that any overt action by Germany now will rather prejudice the case than promote it. A wise decision from their point of view, but unless we can induce statesmen to deal with Austria on big lines, we shall have to make our political book on the basis of an eventual reversion of Austria to Germany.

This morning I went the rounds to see who was here and found that nearly all my friends and cronies were holiday-making, and no blame to them in this torrid heat. But Bundeskanzler Schober is at his post of duty, and Dr. Hertz is here too; I shall see them both to-morrow. Between them they can tell me all that I want to know. Lunched at Sacher's, and found it stuffy.

In the afternoon there was a great fête, called a *Trachtenfestzug*, to help the children. Deputations from all the Provinces assembled at the Rathaus in their provincial costumes and then formed a great procession, men and women, horses and decorated carts. There was every kind of queer device representing episodes in history, keepers hauling poachers to prison, men threshing, a sort of local Bacchus carousing, riders cracking great stock-whips, the noise of which sounded like a machine gun in action; heaps of women and girls, all very gay, riding, driving, and walking, some two and two with their swains — a long procession through the Ring Strasse and into the Prater. The crowds on both sides of the road quite thick and the windows well filled. These people have certainly the capacity for enjoyment. It was interesting to see all the local costumes, and as each Province was preceded by a flag or notice board with its name, it was easy to see who they all were.

I thought it a clever idea to unite all the Provinces at the Capital, as the fissiparous tendencies of this country must be arrested. I was particularly interested to notice that five-sevenths of the costumes were those of mountaineers. One might have expected it from the agricultural statistics, which show that two-thirds of the pasture land is Alpine, but here was the visible proof. It might have been all Tyrol so far as the men's and women's dresses were concerned, but I did not notice the Vorarlberg little black conical hat, to my regret. There were large straw hats with immense brims, from Carinthia, I think, and some of the dresses were quite pretty. The men were great bucks, mostly in shorts or knickers with stockings below the knee, shooting-boots, a light coat, and the Tyrolese or some other very similar head-dress; occasionally this was made of long feathers with foxes' tails dangling on each side. A likely-looking lot, mostly armed with sporting rifles, carried slung, and the women were strapping, upstanding wenches with a great look of health, and many pretty. The cries uttered were ear-piercing, and were often taken up by the crowd. There was no conventional yodling. A sort of running conversation went on between the procession and the crowd, and there was an endless waving of handkerchiefs and much good fooling. There seemed to be a jester with every deputation. In fact it was more like an English fifteenth-century show than anything else. The spirit was that of the Canterbury Pilgrim Tales.

It takes a German couple, however, to walk fifteen miles through crowded streets, holding hands all the way in this sweltering heat. I have not seen any people so festive since the war began. The Vienna crowd was very good-humoured and out for pleasure. There was no denying the military training of the armed bodies of mountaineers. They had Kaiser-Jäger written all over them. If L. G. had seen this show, he would no longer have thought it of no importance that Austria should go to Germany. I had no idea that I should see anything so interesting, or so instructive. It is good to see the spirit of nationality returning, even if each Province keeps its old customs, and is a bit more independent than the Central Government here like. In all seriousness one must remember that Schwaben and Ober-Bayern, Salzburg, Steiermark, Tyrol, Vorarlberg, and Carinthia produce as good and hardy races of mountaineers as there are in the world, and that all these people are Germans and will never be anything else. Nor will the Germans of what the Germans call German South Tyrol, now in Italian hands. They are a bit elementary, too, all these people, and will be a tough proposition to tackle in their native hills. I do not believe that the theories of our modern *illuminés* have touched the surface of this crowd. That is our fault, perhaps. We legislate or dream for a little circle of Western intellectuals while the mass of the people think in much simpler terms.

Vienna, Monday, July 11, 1921. Dr. Masirevitch, the Hungarian Minister here, gave me a diplomatic visa for my journey to-morrow. He talked of Hungary's troubles, and told me that some of the parties were assailing Horthy now, some because he was not Socialistic enough and others because he kept too great state, or that they wanted King Karl back. But, as M. truly said, no one would gain from Horthy going. He told me that the persecutions of the Magyars in Transylvania continue and that a Baroness Banffy had recently been bastinadoed. I asked where — meaning geographically — and he said, "on that part of the body traditionally reserved for the bastinado." I said that I should make inquiries. She belonged, he said, to the family of the Hungarian Foreign Minister.

The Bundeskanzler had a diplomatic reception at the Ballhaus Platz from eleven to one, and received me after the Nuncio had been in. Herr Schober the same as ever, cool, calm, and self-contained. I congratulated him on rising to the highest place in the Government, and said that it seemed to me that sense of duty had outweighed all other considerations with him. He had had a secure and popular post and now he was the predestined sport for intriguers. S. admitted that it had been a sacrifice, but if only the credits were granted by the League of Nations Commission he thought that Austria's position would steadily mend. He said that Italy's abandonment of the lien on Austrian resources was not yet final. Nor is that of Jugo-Slavia. He asked what my view was, and I said that

I was for the proposed credits. He seemed rather surprised, and asked if I really was. I said, "Certainly, it is the only way to prevent Austria from breaking up, and I had been in favour of Sir W. Goode's proposals too, which I thought were even better." L. G. had upset that apple cart, but L. G. could never tackle foreign politics closely when he was beset by internal troubles. Now things looked like clearing and then I hoped we might have an Austrian policy at last.

Had he read, I asked, Count Ottokar Czernin's article in the Wiener *Sonn- und Monntag's-Zeitung* of to-day on Austrian diplomacy? Was it all as bad as Czernin alleged? Schober — who is Foreign Minister as well as Chancellor — said it was not. He was quite satisfied with his representatives abroad. He found it perfectly easy to do the two jobs and the criticisms of Czernin on this point were not justified. He had seen Czernin only yesterday, and C. had said nothing about his coming article. He would see him again and have it out with him. But Czernin counts for little now. S.'s secretary had told me that he was not rated high, and I had replied that his book alone condemned him.

I then asked the Chancellor to tell me how the relations with the Provinces were getting on, whether there was any increase in the authority of the Central Government, whether he was reforming the Army, and how the *Anschluss* position now stood. He said that the relations with the Provinces had greatly improved. He had taken the initiative in getting into touch with them, and as soon as he was installed had written to them all a very frank letter saying that the State could only exist through the Provinces, and the latter through the State. He had told them that Vienna alone could supply them with the funds they needed for various reforms, and had made it clear that unless they played the game he would not retain office. It was probably a good letter, as S. is a man of great good sense, who inspires general respect, and the Provinces had all replied in very amicable fashion. He had further promised to go round and see them all on the first opportunity. This is all a good move.

As to the Army, the faults of which S. knows well, he was reducing its numbers and improving its quality. "As you did your fine Police," I remarked. Yes, he said, and he had his own man now at the head of the Army and things would get on. As for the *Anschluss*, he said that he hoped the phase of plébiscites was over. He had assembled the Great-German Party, and had plainly told them that government was impossible if they continued their propaganda and that he would sooner go now than later, if they would not give him an undertaking to be quiet. This they seem to have done, and if they keep their promise a great difficulty is removed. It will not alter facts, but will stop this dangerous diplomatic tension which made the Austrian Government look so contemptible.

I asked about Bulgaria. S. has no Minister at Sofia, and so did not know what was happening, but had wired to the Dutch Minister, who was looking after Austrian interests in Bulgaria, and expected a reply soon. The Bulgarian Minister here had stoutly denied the alleged intrigues with the ex-Tsar Ferdinand, and we both thought a rising of the peasants, yesterday reported from Bulgaria, to be most unlikely[1] with a peasant Government in office. The Bulgarian Minister had even gone so far on behalf of his Government as to ask Schober to forbid the entry of Ferdinand into Austria, and this had been done.

"If only we are left alone and are given our credits, the country will make progress and become *viable*," said S. He evidently has doubts about England's good-will in the matter, and meanwhile the crown has gone to the terrible figure of 2745 to the pound sterling, and prices here are no easier than they were. Coal is coming in again from Czecho-Slovakia, but to nothing like the amount needed. As for bread, the old prices and difficulties remain, but a law is in preparation to make rich people pay the full cost of the loaf, and others less than the full price, according

---

[1] There was not one word of truth in it.

to their means. This will improve the situation to some extent, if the plan prove practicable, but a total abolition of the bread subsidy is not yet in sight.

I asked about the customs and whether he had seen Benès and had any negotiations with him. Schober said that he had not, but would like to meet him. Meanwhile he had told his Ministry that Austria should not await proposals, but should make them herself. It was better for her to remove her own customs barriers, even if the neighbouring States did nothing. I told him that I thought both Benès and Banffy would meet him halfway if he set to work. We had a talk about the show yesterday and of other matters, after which I took leave of him, and he asked me to be sure to call and see him again if I stopped in Vienna on my return. He told me that he was sending Mensdorff to the League of Nations and that M. had only agreed to go if S. would defend him in Parliament which S. had promised to do.

I like Schober. He is the right type for the situation and commands general confidence. He has measure and experience with sound judgement, weighs his words, is not pompous, and seems very frank. I think that he is genuine and can be trusted. If he can get the Provinces to back him, I do not see why he should not remain, but Austrian politics are too shifty to permit of undue optimism.

In the late afternoon met Dr. Hertz at last, at an afternoon meeting of the League of Nations at my hotel, and was introduced to a number of League enthusiasts, notably Mrs. Philip Snowden, a pleasant, capable woman, who eulogised my War Diary, and is a fine speaker. Miss Marshall, who spoke capitally; Herr Dernburg, the well-known German Reichstag member, and his boy who is studying philosophy at Berne; Mme. Grünberger, wife of the Food Minister here; Mme. Hertz, Dr. Raditch, whom I missed when I was here before, and various others. Hertz came up to my rooms first and we had a little quiet talk. He approves of Schober, like others, but fancies that there may be an election in the autumn, and that afterwards the two strong parties may combine. He thinks that things continue to improve here, and although he admits the importance of the half-promised credits, he rates even higher the importance of clearing the decks of all the lumber of the Peace Treaties, and of giving Austria a *tabula* more or less *rasa* to work upon. It is the uncertainty of the future that hurts Austria most, and he says that foreign bankers would put down all the money needed if the situation were cleared up for good and all, and if there were no more talk of making Austria pay reparations if she recovered twenty years hence. He says that the Austrian banks are doing a vast business, and that hundreds of new banks have been started, but that it is largely fictitious business, and produces nothing, for the profits made come out of the people's incomes and help to paralyse European trade. We talked the whole situation over.

Dernburg is not a very attractive personage. His chief contribution to our brief talk was that Germany could pay in gold marks, but that the conversion of 132 milliards into another currency was impracticable. America had jibbed at the last conversion into dollars and the City of London would do the same if the conversion into sterling were attempted.

During my meal before leaving Vienna, Dr. Hertz came up again and we had some talk. I told him that all this part of Europe would never get on until some form of free trade were adopted, as all these little States were ruining themselves and each other by their tariffs. Hertz did not dissent, but thought that the whole trend at present was for States to impose higher duties to prevent Germany from swamping their markets with her goods. Even countries like Spain, Switzerland, and Holland were joining in the movement. This made exclusive action by a more or less dependent State like Austria very difficult. He thought Austria had become a sort of colony among the Succession States. But whereas England would not cut off supplies from Jamaica as a reprisal, this was practically done to Austria by her former Provinces.

Hertz told me a curious story of the war which had just come out from an examination of the Austrian archives, and it was as much news to him as it was to me. It was a well-known fact how well-informed Austria had been during the war, and the reason had only now appeared. It seems that the Italian Ambassador at Petrograd, being unable to advise his Government by the telegraph, was given the use of the Russian wireless every day and sent detailed reports of everything that was happening, including strengths and disposition of Allied troops. He sent them, of course, in cipher. But when Italy entered the war she had published a Red Book to defend her action. Owing to inexcusable oversight the telegrams published were not paraphrased, but were word for word as sent. The Austrians had kept the tapes with the Italian cipher messages, and the Red Book enabled them to discover the Italian cipher. So all through the war while the Russian wireless was utilisable, the Austrians read everything that came over it and obtained great credit for wonderful intelligence. Hertz thought that the successes of the German command assumed a different aspect in the light of this exposure, particularly the success against Serbia during which the strength and positions of all the Serbian forces became exactly known. Occasionally the information was wrong, as when the presence of a turning column round a German flank was inaccurately reported. The German General stopped his attack and threw back a wing to meet the column which was non-existent, and so failed to win a big success. One will need confirmation of this story from the Italian side, especially information concerning the Red Book messages, and an explanation whether the same cipher was used all through the war or not. It might have been so used owing to the time and uncertainty connected with the despatch of a fresh cipher to Russia, but the story, if true, is a fresh warning of the double-edged character of wireless in war, and shows clearly what precautions are required.

Left 11.45 P.M.

In the train to Bucharest, Tuesday, July 12, 1921. Meditating over Austrian matters including various data collected yesterday for reading *en route*. The contradiction, which I remarked in April, between the almost bankruptcy of the Austrian State and the growth of private profits has become still more glaring after the lapse of three months, and the publication of more statistics of trade, customs, bank profits, etc. Both exports and imports have gone up, but coal accounts, in weight, for two-thirds of all imports in 1920, and foods for a large part more. Czecho-Slovakia and Germany remain Austria's best clients, delivering forty-five per cent of Austria's imports between them. England sends goods of only 144,600 cwt., and takes only 50,000 cwt., while America, under harder conditions of distance, sent 2,900,000 cwt. With all the great activities of Austrian business, it is not satisfactory that we are left in the lurch like this. I think that Austria is moving more rapidly on the Benès lines than other States round. Austrian customs officials may now grant licences for imports of large classes of goods without special application, and I am much struck by the opinion of the Special Commission of the iron industry, in which agriculture and labour took part, that Austria's industry being dependent on exports, a protectionist customs policy did not suit her. This may have been in the Bundeskanzler's mind when he spoke to me.

However, the horrible fact remains, and is confirmed by the Budget for the second half of 1921, that the revenue is 24.1 milliards of Austrian crowns and the expenditure 49.5 milliards, or a deficit of 25.4 milliards. Only a third of the expenditure is met out of revenue. As before, the main causes of the deficit are the food subsidies, 10.3 milliards, the service of the debt, loss on railways, and the necessarily increased salaries of officials who can barely live now, as they are paid but half the wages of skilled workmen. The bed-rock fact remains that Versailles created a State and deprived it of the means of existence. Whether the mistake was due to malice or ignorance is no matter now.

Will the plan of the Finance Committee of the League of Nations secure acceptance by the Powers and will it be effective? I do not feel sure. There has been no suggestion yet how to end the Budget deficit, though Austria has done much by raising her revenue sixty-three per cent above the previous half-year, and by doubling receipts from income tax. Customs duties have also been doubled. The Committee fusses about the currency reform, but it is the Budget deficits and the stopping of the printing-press that should be taken in hand first through foreign credits and internal loans combined. Currency reform is necessary, but all the world must share in it.

If relief action is not applied here, all the rest is financial dilettantism. The Committee puts the cart before the horse. Sir W. Goode was wiser and more practical. The crown has steadily lost ground from the moment that the League of Nations plan came out. It is also indefinite as to time and amounts of help from outside, and to ask for control of Austrian finances while the Committee seems prepared to do little to help is rather absurd.

However, Austria continues to hope, and her private business continues to develop. There is great activity. Everybody is busy doing or trying to do something. The bank profits are large and branches are being started everywhere in the Provinces. Styria promises well in coal and mineral oil at workable depths. Many companies pay good dividends. New ventures are constantly being undertaken. The hotels give us a hot bath every day in the week except Sundays, and white bread has returned at last, though not yet for the ration bread. Vienna holds her own. Her grandeur and her charms are enhanced by the fact that she is so adaptable, that she is the gateway of the East, that her railway network is first-rate, and that her great banking competence attracts clients from all sides. Vienna is genial and broad-minded in pleasure as in business, and I do not think that any of these self-isolating, ultra-nationalist States around can take her crown of usefulness from her.

CHAPTER XI

NEW ROUMANIA

Country and crops — A first talk with M. Take Jonescu — Summer nights in Bucharest — Mr. Millington Drake — Mr. Peter A. Jay and Colonel Poillon, U.S.A. — People to see — An audience with the King of Roumania — A talk on current affairs — The question of Transylvania — MM. Jacovaky and Grigori Jon — Complaints of Bulgaria — Bucharest architecture — The butterflies — Roumanian statistics — M. Filaleki on Russia — The opposition on strike — Views of M. Nedkov, the Bulgarian Minister — Answers to Roumanian charges — A conversation with the Prime Minister, General Avarescu — His account of 1916 — His views on the Straits — A talk with M. Goga — Religions in Transylvania — Roumanian resources — Wheat, maize, and timber — Foreign capital — Industrial concerns — Railways — Foreign trade — Banks — Public finance — Public debt — A talk with General Nikoleanu on the police — Mme. Lahovary on the agrarian reforms — A talk with the Minister of Communications — A talk with the General Staff — General Gorski and Colonel Palada — The strength and distribution of the Soviet armies — More complaints of Bulgaria — A conversation with the War Minister, General Rascano — Roumanian Army organization — M. Garoflid, Minister of Domains, on the agrarian laws — Colonel Dundas — Consul Keyser — Mr. Guest on the oil industry — A dinner at the Take Jonescus — The Foreign Minister on Roumanian policy — Mr. Alexander Adams — The Decree Laws — An investigation at the Roumanian Foreign Office — The complaints about Bulgaria — The oil industry — Statistics and observations — Trammels of the industry — The export tax — Astra-Romana and Steaua-Romana — Mr. Charles Spencer on the future of our trade — By motor to the Danube.

Wednesday, July 13,1921. A piping hot journey yesterday, more like India than Europe. The Magyar customs subordinates at Vienna were perfect boors, threw and tumbled things about and made themselves as unpleasant as they could. Reached Budapest about 8 A.M. and the Roumanian frontier at Curtici at 3.30 P.M.

The corn is mostly cut. As we travelled east the ricks were already made. Nearly all the reaping by hand. I did not notice a single modern agricultural machine; neither reaper and binder, nor anything else. There must be a big opening for these things in Eastern Europe. In general, the cultivation is in strips and patches, denoting a peasant proprietorship and a division of the land. Am not sure that this will help wheat export.

We reached the valley of the Maros — they pronounce it Muroche — soon after passing Arad. A broad valley, highly cultivated, bordered by hills and woods, with a winding river as broad as the Thames at Maidenhead. Through the night into Transylvania and climbed the Alps about dawn by the Prédeal Pass. Very beautiful, both gaunt and wooded peaks, with masses of wild flowers in the clearings and valleys, the houses built chalet fashion, of wood with balconies for each floor. The streams were fairly full and there must have been recent rain.

We passed fashionable Sinaia about nine and reached Bucharest at noon. Dering is away, but Millington Drake, the First Secretary, sent his car for me and recommended a lodging which I found miles better than the hotel, and so put up there. We passed to-day through the Ploesti oil area where there was much activity both at the wells and the refineries.

I went to the Legation to thank Millington Drake for his kindness and afterwards had a talk with M. Take Jonescu, the famous Foreign Minister, at his house. I have come here at an interesting moment, for to-day the Treaty with Jugo-Slavia is published and it has the definite and expressed aim of keeping Hungary and Bulgaria quiet. T. J. made a long speech on it and on other foreign affairs on Saturday last. I hastily scanned both before seeing T. J. Our talk covered the Treaty, the complaints of the Transylvanian Magyars, Austria, the intrigues of Stamboulisky, the Russian question, free trade in Eastern Europe, the agrarian laws, and other matters. There is not much to be said about the Treaty, as the text is clear, but the military convention which issues from it will not be published, and this seems to follow the precedent set by France and Belgium on the military side. T. J. had the report of the Unitarian padres on his table, so he must realise its weight. I said that I wanted the Roumanian answer to it. T. J. said it was full of inaccuracies, and besides said that it was impracticable for Roumania to do everything in a hurry. I shall have to keep T. J. up to giving me the necessary reply, but as we are to meet again I did not dwell longer on this subject. T. J. is very suspicious of Stamboulisky, as he says that S. has tried a feeler with Roumania, and then with Jugo-Slavia, and has now sent the mission to Kemal because there was no one left to intrigue with but the Soviet and the Turks. T. J. thought that Bulgaria was out for revenge. S. was inordinately vain. S. had flattered T. J. more than the latter had ever been flattered in his life and he was rather sarcastic about it. He had told S. that Roumania was not going to have the Treaty of Neuilly upset. But three times a week he still received love-letters from Stamboulisky, and I said that I could not understand S.'s attitude, as the Little Entente made it impracticable for Bulgaria to move without being overwhelmed. We do not seem to possess the key of S.'s intrigues yet. T. J. said that Ferdinand constantly wrote [1] to his son lauding S. to the skies, and the son showed the letters to S. T. J. thought that Ferdinand wanted to come back. I replied that I could not conceive why. Coburg was a much more pleasant retreat than Sofia. T. J. was not sure about Schober; he appears to me a little jealous of all the other Eastern Europe diplomatists, and I judge that most of the accusations against Bulgaria have reached London from T. J. Does he too enjoy the lime-light? He was slightly sarcastic about our trade agreement with Russia and did not expect that we should get much out of it. I said, Yes, we have a trade agreement, and no trade. I said that I wanted his views on Russia and would like to talk to those who knew most about it. T. J. said it was an error to suppose that Roumania's propinquity brought her any better information about Russia than came to other States. Such as his news was, it told of famine and persecutions. But the frontier was hermetically sealed and no really good news came over. Surely, I said, there must be infiltration across the frontier. He admitted that there was a little, but it only brought local news from just over the border and nothing of real value to enable him to estimate the future.

[1] See King Boris's denial, entry for July 29.

He admitted that he did not expect anything from Russia in our time, but also said that Russia was a strange country and that no one understood her.

He does not think anything like free trade in Eastern Europe is practicable. I imagine that he will block the Benès ideas if he can, but I expected nothing else from Roumania. I realise why Benès gave ten years as the period for carrying out his plan. I asked him about the new agrarian laws. Was the compensation to expropriated landlords to be really forty years' purchase? How could the State find the money? How could he find the farmers? Would not the amount and quality of production greatly diminish? Yes, it would, replied T. J., but the division of land was a social necessity and the men had been placed on the land by a Decree Law before the laws were passed by Parliament. There were three agrarian laws, one made by Bessarabia for herself, one for the old Monarchy, and one for Transylvania. The calm and unity of the country was due to these laws, and without them there would have been Communism and Bolshevism. As things were, he had obtained, as I had seen, a unanimous vote for his last Treaty and the country was contented. The forty years' purchase meant little, for the amount was based on pre-war valuation, and, in view of subsequent loss on the valuation, an owner really received only one-quarter of the value of his land at the date when the valuation was made. "Do you call that justice?" I asked. It was a social necessity, he repeated. There would be no great difference between the Transylvanian laws and the others. We talked general politics a bit, and he laid stress on the different policies incumbent on victors and on vanquished. Dined with the Millington Drakes at the Châteaubriand. A boiling hot night. The dogs made too much noise for sleep.

Thursday, July 14, 1921. The dogs barked till 4 A.M. The cocks crowed all night and sounded a general reveillé at 3. There was a diocesan conference of sparrows at 4.30 A.M. At 5.30 there concentrated three Army Corps of flies in my room. Then the street cries began. One must do in

Roumania as the Roumanians do: Rise at 6. Work till 1. Remain in a comatose state after lunch till 5, when people reappear at their offices, see people till 7, and dine in the open somewhere about 9 or 9.30 P.M. It is India without Indian compensations against the heat. Won't come here again at this time of year.

Lunched with the Millington Drakes — she is a pretty woman, daughter of Lord Inchcape — Mr. Jay, the U.S. Minister, Mrs. Devereux, who is travelling round to write another book, and a King's Messenger — at the Jockey Club. Dined at the Châteaubriand Restaurant in the open. Mr. Peter A. Jay and the Poillons dined with me. Lieutenant-Colonel Arthur Poillon pronounces his name Polion, but of course the French do not. She is a very agreeable lady. We had much talk to-day of the Roumanians and their affairs. I do not gather that the foreign missions here are wildly in love with the Roumanians. Such cases as the Reschitsa affair, which is making a great scandal in Parliament, are much too common, and in fact this country has not got into its stride administratively and is very far from being immaculate or efficient. But on the whole, when one recalls that these people were almost in subjection up to 1866, and when one considers all that they have been through since, especially in the war, and of the recent doubling of the size of the country, in which there was not even personnel enough to run the old Monarchy, one must be lenient. But we must have it out about the treatment of minorities, as this is a matter of good-will and principle. Mrs. D. has just been staying with Baroness Banffy, and says it is true that she was beaten, but she did not lay claim to the reported bastinado! I suspect she was aggressive and was just a little hustled. She says that the report of the Unitarian padres is absolutely accurate. At Châteaubriand's, which is a sort of Château de Madrid of Bucharest, we had quite an agreeable dinner and the three Americans were very pleasant and entertaining. I was much amused, and almost consoled, to find that the German bandit of the Kehl customs had treated the Poillons as he had treated me and had bundled them out of the train at 4 A.M. too, though Poillon is Military Attaché, and was on an official mission, and had a *laissez-passer*. He is furious about it still, especially as he was carrying a lot of his Embassy bags which had to go on by themselves! We had a good talk. Jay has only just arrived here. Poillon has been here a year, and though he admits Roumania's potential wealth, he thinks Mexico is richer, and he would rather put his money into the latter country, as one day or other the United States will have to regulate her proceedings. Got home quite late. Another broiling night. The street cries are as numerous as those which Wheatley recorded of old London. A really charming place for insomnia. A damp, enervating, orchid-house heat, and no cooler at night.

Friday, July 15, 1921. Went to the F.O. in the morning to talk with the Directeur du Protocole, M. Alexandre N. Jacovaky. Told him of the people I wanted to see and the things I wanted to know, and he was most helpful. I must see the Minister of Finance, M. Titulescu, about public finance; Delyanu, Secretary-General of General Avarescu, about trade and oil; General Valiano about railways; Filaleki about Russian affairs (he is intended for Minister at Warsaw); General Rascano about the Army; M. Groja, or M. Goga, about the Government of Transylvania, and General Nikoleanu about the Police.

I have to ask Avarescu to request these people to see me, by the Secretary-General Chrenichavo. A good many Generals appear to be in charge of departments under Avarescu. Went with Millington Drake to Avarescu's Bureau on the chance of seeing him. Drake has to tell him something rather stiff, as he said that the Roumanian Government had let us down about something. I did not ask what it was. We were both fobbed off, and promised appointments by telephone. The Secretary-General talked to us while we waited. I asked him whether the President of the Council here stood in the same position towards the other Ministers as the P.M. usually does in England. It seems that he is a real chief, and can dismiss any Minister when he pleases. But as a matter of courtesy he usually consults his colleagues first. We were also told that the agrarian law had been altered at the last minute in the Lower House, and that the indemnities to dispossessed landlords were now to be paid half by the new peasant proprietors and half by war profiteers. I thought this was rather a good joke, but asked how they could be sure that the profiteers would stump up. The Government had certain rough statistics which showed that they could, we were told. The constitution has to be changed, and there is a regular procedure laid down for such changes. So a modern constitution does not resemble that of Medes or Persians. Then we were also told of a new law which compels all officials — including M.P.'s — to justify their income, i.e., to show whence it comes. If they cannot justify it, they are to be deprived of eighty-two per cent of it, this figure being fixed merely to avoid total confiscation, which is not permitted by the constitution. Great fun if this law were passed at home, but I should say that culprits could easily get round this new law, and send their ill-gotten gains abroad. They have only to buy cheques on London. However, it is a step in the right direction, and a proof of good intentions.

Went to have an audience of the King at the Palace, 4.30 P.M., and we talked for an hour and a half about Transylvania and the Hungarians, Monarchy and the state of Europe, sport in Roumania, the King's cure, personalities in Europe, Russia, the agrarian law, Lloyd George, the war in Asia Minor, Constantinople, the Allied representatives at Athens, the Queen's writings, Bulgaria, and many other subjects. They have in mind my visit to Hungary and my articles on that country. The King began on my visit there at once, and I told him frankly that I liked the Hungarians, and that they were English in their point of view, and that the directing class mostly spoke English. They had been harshly treated, but now had made an end of their propaganda in Transylvania, and I hoped that the King would meet them halfway. Benès had adumbrated to me some sort of reconciliation with the Magyars on his side, I told him, and perhaps H.M. would be able to make some concessions to them also for the sake of peace.

The King said that the propaganda had only been stopped officially and evidently thinks that it continued unofficially. He must insist that the Treaty should be loyally accepted first of all, for otherwise it was an impossible situation. He could not grant special advantages to Transylvania. To constitute the new kingdom solidly he had to lay down a common principle for all State services, such as posts, army, gendarmerie, etc., and if this was not done at once it could not easily be done later. The Magyars made all sorts of difficulties. They had even received their regulations in the Hungarian schools in Transylvania from Budapest, and he could not admit such interference from outside. He, too, liked the Hungarians, and wanted the best elements to remain, as they would have a good influence. All the Bishops, Orthodox, Catholic, and Protestant, had come to swear allegiance. He had told one particularly distinguished Magyar prelate, who was a great nationalist, that he trusted him because he was a Bishop and a gentleman. All troubles would end if the Magyars would cease their intrigues against the State. He said that the report of the Unitarian padres was full of inaccuracies. They had consulted only Magyar and not Roumanian authorities. He knew whom they had consulted. I said that hostile reports upon Roumanian bullying continued, and told him the story of Baroness Banffy and the bastinado. The Baroness was a fighter, he said. She had been tried, had pleaded her own case, and had simply said that she was a Hungarian and had done and would always do her duty towards Hungary. She was successful and was acquitted. The King thought this a worthy procedure on both sides and I agreed. The King said that he must have heard if anything like beating had occurred, and believed that she had only been a little hustled on one occasion. I told H.M. that nothing was more calculated to arouse fury against the Roumanians in England than the report that they had beaten a woman like Baroness Banffy. Yes, or any woman, interposed the King. I agreed, and asked him to remember the case of the Austrian General — was the name Haymerlé? — in the fifties who had whipped Polish ladies and had been chased and hunted in London by Barclay & Perkins's draymen, on his visit to that brewery. Our people would listen to no excuses in a case like this and would simply see red. The King thoroughly understood and was not annoyed by the plain speaking.

We went on to the question of Monarchy in Europe. He thought that all the Monarchies should support each other, and I said that I agreed and thought Monarchies were more efficient than the new Republics, most of whom could not even form a regular parliamentary government. The King thought that there would be a revulsion of feeling soon and that Monarchies would return. I agreed and said that Germany and Hungary would have Monarchies to-morrow if they could have their way. He evidently fancies Rupprecht of Bavaria for the German Crown; but he thought Karl's act stupid. One only took a step like this, he said, when one was sure of succeeding. I told him of the difficulties in the way of Rupprecht's return. He thought that France was almost as good as a Monarchy, as she was the most conservative country in Europe. As for Poland, she needed a King because of her traditions. "There are plenty of young Princes in Europe for the place," I suggested. "Yes," said the King, thumping the table, "but he must *avoir du poing.*" "Yes, a Poniatowski," I said; but I admitted that I did not know the Prince fit to play that rôle. But possibly this was only my ignorance, as I did not run after Princes like London hostesses, and there might be a *beau sabreur* of a Prince somewhere.

The King said that he wanted Poland to keep Galicia so that it might form a barrier.

The King talked of Bulgaria and of Stamboulisky, about whom he shares T. J.'s views. S., said the King, is a Bulgar, looks like a bull, and talks nothing but Bulgarian.

This entails a translator, and S. has Stancioff's daughter with him, a nice clever girl.[1] "Oh!" I said. "Why do you say, Oh?" "Because I see better where Stancioff comes in." "Yes, but I brought Nicolas Misu with me," said the King, "and he speaks fourteen languages, so I was quite secure." S., he said, thought that he had the monopoly of ideas which everyone possessed. He was a little King of the castle of the children's nursery rhyme.

H.M. then discussed Constantinople, and the Turco-Greek war. He said that the Greeks had gained an important success. He wondered why we had not backed the Greeks, why we had objected to the Greeks bringing back their King if they wanted to do so, and why we boycotted him when he was doing the job we set him to do. I said that I wondered too, but an allied policy was usually a weak compromise, and made the Foreign Ministers seem as feeble folk as the conies. There was some talk when I left England, I continued, of a Roumanian re-enforcement at Constantinople. The King smiled and said that he thought it was best for Roumania to keep out of it all. I fancy he did not want to share Greece's fate and be deserted as she was. I laughed and said that I should be of the same opinion in H.M.'s place. But the King made it clear that he could not afford to have the Straits closed again, and we were both in full agreement on this point. The talk ranged over many other subjects. He agreed that the agrarian laws might reduce the wheat output, but hoped that in a few years things might right themselves. We talked of the sport in the country, especially in Transylvania, and he told me of a drive in which fourteen bears had been killed, which he thought a record. I was rather sorry for the bears, which are good creatures and will be exterminated at this rate. Much talk of personalities, some of whom want exterminating more than the bears.

The King seems a well-informed, kindly man. He was in white drill naval uniform.

Dined in the evening at the Jockey Club with Jacovaky

---

[1] Mlle. Stancioff has since given up this delicate rôle.

and M. Grigori Jon, another F.O. man, from the Banat. They poured into me a stream of facts to show that the Roumanian administration was all it should be, and the Magyars perfect terrors. They beg me to go there and see for myself. I said that I could not afford the time now. I had come to have the official replies to the charges and meant to leave it at this. Sir Willoughby Dickinson is due here Monday, from the British Union of the League of Nations, to examine into the cases of minorities and confessions, and I did not consider it my business to do this work unless Lord Burnham definitely so instructed me. I should be *brulé* with one side and perhaps with both if I did. What I wanted was definite replies to definite charges. I undertook to state the main charges and they undertook to answer them. We had a long talk till late, of all the affairs of this part of the world. I approved entirely of their views about the Straits. They will never accept that they shall be closed again, and on this point Roumania will be our firm support if she be handled properly. They are a trifle suspicious of the attitude of the H. of C. towards Hungary, because a few independent Members spoke up for her when the Treaty of Trianon was discussed, and the Roumanians weave this into an imaginary English web consisting of Hungary and Bulgaria. I tried to dispel these illusions. Jacovaky says that Stamboulisky behaved well at the Council when Ferdinand of Bulgaria raised the question of joining in the late war. All the Council, except S., said that F. knew more than they did and that they would follow his lead. S. alone told F. to beware, as he might be risking his crown. "And you might be risking your head," replied F. In effect S. was thrown into prison and remained there till the smash came, two and one-half years later. Only his fine physique kept him alive. But the old ambitions prevailed, and in two years the Bulgars might wish to renew their old attempts. They were Turanian or Slav according to the policy of the moment, and now seemed to have an idea that the Turco-Soviet alliance would serve their ends. I said that I had not the key of

S.'s attitude and did not believe the Roumanians had.
That was why I was going to Sofia to investigate. It
seemed to me that, according to their showing, S. had a
double dose of original ineptitude, which seemed to me
unlikely, but I did not believe that England would have
any weakness for Bulgaria if she recommenced her old
games. They suggested that the future revival of Germany
might be at the back of it all, but I thought it idiotic of S.
to show his hand at this point of the game, if this were so.
Perhaps, I said, he has been misconstrued. I should see.
Stancioff's daughter, they said, had a French mother. I
said that I attributed much of the Near-Eastern trouble to
money-hunting originating in the I. O. Bank, and its clients. Directly money touched politics you never knew
where you stood. They feel this, too, after the debates in
Parliament here on the Reschitsa case, in which eighty
Deputies and thirty Senators received shares to support a
formerly alien concern. They admit that the Roumanian administration is bad, but declare that their Army
and judges are above suspicion. This is noble. The High
Court Judge gets sixteen pounds a month, and the Lieutenant about four pounds.

Saturday, July 16, 1921. Had a talk with M. Pavlovich,
Chargé d'Affaires of Serbia here. He tells me that Pachitch
is ill and when well will go to Marienbad. Also that all the
other Ministers and chief people will be scattered and
away from Belgrade till the end of August. So I see no use
in going there now. I will see M. Nedkov, the Bulgarian
Minister, to make sure of Stamboulisky before I start for
Sofia.

Have had a look round Bucharest now and find it impregnated architecturally with the German spirit. It is all
modern, baroque, and rather pretentious. The people have
not developed a style or an art of their own as yet. Taste
always comes from above and filters down into a people.
There has been no "above" in Roumania owing to the
serfdom of sixty years ago, and there is not much in the
way of aristocracy, or leisured classes, to select between

styles and tastes. There is no traditional national taste. The country is politically ultra-national, dislikes the pretensions of foreigners to run its affairs, and so will advance much more slowly than it might. Typical examples of the defects of administration in small things at the Capital are the absence of pillar-boxes, and the ignorance of the jarvies of the geography of the town. There must be no examination of them before they are licenced. I never find a carriage driver to know any address, or to speak any language but Russian. The jarvies are mostly Russians who do their little horses well, but otherwise know nothing. They wear long black or blue velvet coats. Even at the F.O. there is no one at the door who speaks anything but Roumanian — which is unknown to nearly all the foreigners here. The best thing in Bucharest is the feminine portion of the better classes in the community. These are decidedly pretty, well and simply dressed, and in good taste. Their manners are very French, and France has still a great position here, though German is still the most popular language in business circles. If one asks one's way in the street the reply is usually in German. The ladies have good figures, features, ankles, and eyes; a little inclining to the harem style sometimes, and with a certain Eastern appearance, but they are quite attractive. They are the butterflies of the Roumanian garden, and do not really represent its products.

Looked into various facts and statistics. There are some sixteen to seventeen millions [1] people in the new Roumania of 316,132 square kilometres, of whom some eighty per cent are peasants and sixty-five per cent illiterate. The density of the population is fifty-seven inhabitants to the square kilometre. The national unity has been accomplished in the recent settlement which has created a country of nicely balanced rotundity, well-placed, with the advantage of access to the sea, and with every sort of wealth, but with six States abutting on its frontiers, three of whom are unfriendly. With $12\frac{1}{2}$ million hectares of

[1] 17,393,149.

arable land and nearly five millions of pasture and grass, with immense forests, and with her gardens and vines, Roumania is, or at least should be, the chief granary of Europe. The sailings from her ports in 1920 were 2,557,000 tons of foreign and 171,000 of national shipping. Her oil output can be taken at a possible 2,000,000 tons. She is sure to tend towards industrialism before long, and the field is open for repairs of rolling stock and bridges. With a doubled area she has only one-third the locomotives she had before. She needs heaps of things that we could supply — machinery, tools, textiles, clothes, linen goods, soap, stationery, type-writers, motor-cars, rolling stock, pottery, china, and glass. Her industry is practically non-existent, and her new rural small proprietors will soon develop greater needs.

She is the largest wheat-producing country in Europe. Her minerals are largely unexploited. Her coal is but little developed. So is her copper, asphalt, ozokerite, mica, and asbestos. Her sub-soil is as rich as the soil itself, while the population is enduring and sober. Her surplus of wheat, maize, wood, and oil is already large. She is a natural complement of industrial England. But she is without organising capacity, is short of agricultural machinery, and is on the whole committed to a selfish tariff which retards her rehabilitation; and she has done little for irrigation as yet, though the potentialities are great. She admits free only articles of primary necessity, places a fifty per cent ad valorem duty on articles of secondary necessity, and bars luxuries, even Lyons silk. She is sensitive and dislikes semi-foreign enterprises. She wants long credits. Her area has been increased from 137,000 square kilometres to 316,000 by the addition of Bessarabia, Bukovina, the Banat, and Transylvania, but she has still a very elementary railway system, has a merely embryonic goods transport system, and her main lines must be speeded up, as the trains are intolerably slow. The endless customs barriers prevent free communications. She has divided some three and one-half million hectares among the peasants, and this, together with universal suffrage, is the basis of her social reorganisation. One is struck in Roumania by the remoteness of the country, by the long time taken to receive letters from London, and by the indifference generally shown to Western European politics, which seem to us here like the affairs of the moon.

To-day I talked with H.E. M. Filaleki, who is named for Minister at Warsaw, to discuss Russian news. In general I gather from him and others that the Soviets have spread a web over Russia, with Moscow as a centre, and that at points in the web where the circular and transverse lines of the web cross, that is to say mainly at the larger towns and railway junctions, there is a strong Soviet rule which holds in its hands communications, supplies, and such administration as there is. But both in Russia and the Ukraine the distances are great, and the intervals between the Soviet posts broad. In these intervals the peasants and villagers form societies of their own and do as they please. The peasants grow only enough for their own use, and it is said that in some districts not over ten per cent of the arable land is cultivated. It is impossible to foretell what will happen. Lenin seems to have admitted the rights of private property and enterprise, but this is against Soviet principles and Trotsky holds to the old theories. Helsingfors is the best centre for Russian news now, but we have no good intelligence nor really trustworthy agents. On all the Roumanian front no visas are given for passports on either side, and officially the frontier is closed, but many people slip through by bribes or evasion. There were 100,-000 Russian troops on the Roumanian frontier, but they have been sent into Asia — no one knows where.[1] It was desired to demobilise the Russian Army altogether, and in fact the numbers have fallen from 2,000,000 to 500,000, but the others refuse to leave, as they would lose their rations which alone keep them together. They are a rabble, and in Poland simply took to flight and threw away their arms, at least all the infantry. The Roumanians are not

---

[1] See entry for July 20.

afraid of them, but think the situation grave at Constantinople, as the Wrangel-Denikin Russians are all Bolshevists and practically occupy Constantinople, while they are also infecting Serbia with their poison. Much will depend on the success of the Greeks, but no end is seen to the Greek campaign even if it be successful. Filaleki thinks that the Bulgarians are hoping much from Russia and he dreads a big Slav movement in the future. He thinks that the religious question separates the Croats from the Serbs and is not very sanguine about the success of the Jugo-Slav cause hereafter.

The dog-days continue. Everyone who can escape is escaping. The nights are almost insupportable and the days not much better. The proper kit for this season is a bathing-suit with sandals and a Japanese parasol.

The Millington Drakes dined with me at the Château-briand. The Government here are in a fix over the Reschitsa case in which several Deputies and Senators are involved. One of the Ministers made a very crude remark in the debate, and though Avarescu apologised for it, the Opposition withdrew, and the Government does not dare to submit the Bill to the King. Everybody buzzing about, and I cannot get on with my investigations until they have regained their balance.

Sunday, July 17, 1921. Went to call upon M. Nedkov, the Bulgarian Minister, who has been for twenty-three years in the diplomatic service, including sixteen in Turkey, and knows Balkan affairs by heart. After we had fixed up my visit to Sofia, I opened the question of the accusations against Bulgaria, and we discussed in turn reparations in kind, the affair of the frontier bands, the supposed mission to the Kemalists and to Russia, the reported intrigues with ex-Tsar Ferdinand and the Turks, the general question of Bulgarian conduct and neutrality, the conduct of Bulgaria's late enemies in the Balkans and here, Jugo-Slavia's proposed "sanctions" against Bulgaria, and sought for the key-explanation of all this pother.

As to the reparations, he explained that the census of

animals to be delivered up took time, that they were all now assembled on the frontiers for delivery, and were merely waiting to be taken over. It was a terrible thing for a country in Bulgaria's state of exhaustion to make such a delivery, but they were keeping their promise. He said that the comitaji system was applicable only to the old days when the Turks and their suffering Christian subjects were in question. Then the bands found help from these subjects, and they had done much to create revolution in Turkey and to drive the Turks out of Europe. This system was not applicable now and there were no bands officially organised. But there still were bands, he admitted, especially on the Dobrudcha border, because the Bulgarians in the Dobrudcha had retreated with the Bulgarian Army and had left their families behind. These families were in sore straits and attempts were being made to help them. But the men who had crossed over wished to return to their families and with them there joined many Turks, Tartars, and Roumanian deserters. These men gave much trouble in the Dobrudcha and certainly behaved ill on many occasions, taking part in looting and other excesses. If the Roumanians would join in regulating the situation of the Bulgarians in the Dobrudcha, the trouble would cease. I was not to count the bands as having any official character whatsoever, and it was to be remembered that the war had produced much moral and material demoralisation, in Bulgaria as elsewhere, and had made many people desperate.

Regarding the supposed relations with the Turks, the Bulgarian Government neither has nor had sent any mission to them. A tobacco merchant called Grozkoff, with one other man and a clerk, had gone to Constantinople, and after making a contract had passed into Asia Minor. Among the Turks who came to Sofia was one young man who had attracted some attention (Djevad Abbas) because his object was not clear. He lived at the Bulgaria Hotel and spent much money. But the Bulgarian Government knew nothing about him and did not see him. There was also a Bulgarian officer called Nikolaieff whom the Bulgarian Government wished to send to Russia to negotiate in favour of the Bulgarians still detained in Russia. He had got as far as Prague when the Allies made a fuss about him and he was recalled. This man was acting for the Red Cross and there was no other object in his mission. Neither with the Soviet nor with the Turks did Bulgaria desire to intrigue. It was absurd for her to do so, with a population of five millions surrounded by strong and jealous neighbours.

Ex-Tsar Ferdinand was living quietly at Coburg, and had no influence on Bulgarian politics. The only Bulgarian who might have visited him was Radoslavoff, who was in Germany and was the man, next to the Coburg Ferdinand, most responsible for the war. But Ferdinand hated Radoslavoff, to whom he attributed his fall, and was unlikely to have seen him. F. was disliked in Bulgaria. He almost openly showed his contempt for the Bulgarians, and he had no motive in life but personal ambition and the desire to rule a great country. With these reports there had also come — about a week ago when I was at Vienna — the report of a peasant rising against the Government, of the closing of all banks and telegraphs, as I had known, and Nedkov said I had only to inquire in Sofia to discover that there was not a word of truth in all this stuff. Ferdinand had happily not bequeathed either his character or his ideas to his son Boris, who took after his mother, was a good democratic King, and much liked. The Bulgars were democrats and very independent, but they like discipline and the principle of authority represented by a King, and N. was sure that a Republic would not work so well.

Then I said that I wanted to hold the key to all this mysterious series of accusations, especially those which aimed at Stamboulisky, as he had displayed courage and good sense in the Council before the war, and was not a man whom we should condemn unheard. "If you want the key of all these charges you must not seek it in Sofia, but in the countries round Bulgaria," said Nedkov. "Bulgaria only asks to work out her reconstruction in peace and not to be attacked. But her enemies are jealous of her." If I knew, he said, the mentality of some of the people in this part of the world, I should understand to what base means they descended to secure their ends. They were afraid of Bulgarian industry and jealous of her superior education — some fifteen per cent of illiterates compared with eighty per cent here. Their object was to cry down the credit of Bulgaria and all her works in order to create a prejudice against her, and so to prevent her from profiting from a revision of Sèvres, and possibly of Neuilly. Athens, Belgrade, and Bucharest were all concerned in this plan of campaign, and perhaps personal jealousies entered into the second rank of causes. They did not wish Bulgaria to regain her old popularity in England and France, and so these tales were invented, supported by every kind of suggestion and innuendo. They did not want Bulgaria to have her Treaty rights at Dedeagatch which would help her exports and British imports so much, as Bulgaria would become too formidable a competitor with them, and so they used all the bogeys of the day, Turk and Bolshevik, comitajis and Ferdinand, in order to create a hostile feeling against Bulgaria. That was the real truth of all this matter. "Have you said as much here?" I asked. "Yes, I have told them the truth," replied N. And has Stancioff done the same in London? N. did not know, nor had he heard of the initiative at Vienna before I told him of it.

The Bulgarians were a quiet, hard-working folk, he thought. There was only some dogmatic Bolshevism in certain speeches, but nothing at all *agissant*. A race of peasants would have nothing to do with Bolshevism, as he said I must have observed here since the agrarian laws were passed. The Serbs were trying to profit by the delay in reparations in kind, in order to threaten Bulgaria with sanctions and to occupy the Debnik mines within twenty-five kilometres of the frontier. These mines were the Bulgarian Ruhr and all their industry depended on them. So that is the answer of this reformed Bulgarian lamb to the charge of troubling the water up-stream. Not finally convincing in regard to the missions to Kemal and Russia, but, as a whole, worthy of careful consideration, and certainly given by Nedkov with an air of sincerity and with considerable feeling.

At seven went with Millington Drake to see General Avarescu, the Prime Minister. M. D. had to see him on an unpleasant matter. An Anglo-French combine had received the signed contract for the repair of Roumanian rolling stock, etc., a very big job and most important for Roumania. The Minister of Communications had signed an undertaking to present a Bill on this subject to the Parliament by June, but now the Reschitsa case had frightened them off. That is their story.

I found General Avarescu dug into a corner of his room. He was sitting in the corner, and a large writing-table was planted across the angle. A tallish man, just like the typical Don Quixote, as Princess Bibesco had told me in 1916. He was very pleasant. I told him that I had come to make one request to H.E. the President and two others to General Avarescu. The first request was that he should instruct six Ministers, whom I named, to give me all the information I wanted about Finance, Commerce, Army, Police, the Government of Transylvania, communications, and oil. This he very kindly undertook to do and made a note of it. Then I asked him, as a General, to enlighten me on a point of history. I said that I had never felt completely informed about the Roumanian plan of campaign in 1916. Who made the plan? Why was it made? What advice did the Allied General Staffs give? Did they fail the Roumanians in any particular, whether in regard to troops or war material; was their advice wrong, and did the Roumanians attribute any part of the responsibility of their defeat to us, the French, or the Russians?

Avarescu replied that to answer these questions fully he would give weapons to his political enemy Bratiano. Unfortunately he could not separate himself, one half General, the other half Prime Minister. But he would tell me how the whole thing came about. I could rest assured that no responsibility whatsoever attached to the English and French, nor even to the Russians, who had kept their promises. The truth came out by chance at a meeting of the King, Bratiano, and some twenty Generals, when it was a question of expanding the Roumanian divisions to twenty-four before Roumania came in. Avarescu had opposed the plan, as it gave numbers before quality, but Bratiano, speaking as Prime Minister, overruled him, giving as his reason that there were only weak forces in their front. This showed the whole bent of Bratiano's mind; his plan was to wait for the eve of the collapse of the Central Powers and then to appear in the field with a huge force and impose his own terms. But the Central Powers concentrated a superior force, while the Roumanian columns traversed the Transylvanian Alps in many columns widely separated, giving the Germans the opportunity of which they took full advantage.

Avarescu had been with the Second Army, but after the disaster of Turtukai on the Danube, he had been sent down to restore matters in the south. So he had not been in the advance, nor responsible for the plan, which was that of General Iliesco, Bratiano's Secretary-General, an old retired engineer who blew his brains out when the plan failed. It was a political plan, directed to a political objective. He, Avarescu, on September 13, 1916, had drafted and submitted a plan for recalling all the Army from its forward march, for crossing the Danube, rolling up Mackensen, and marching towards the south to set free our Salonika armies. I remarked that on that same day I had told the Italian Ambassador in London what would happen if the advance across the mountains continued, and he had telegraphed my opinion to Rome, whence it was sent to Roumanian G.H.Q. Sir William Robertson had given the advice to attack the Bulgarians. Had Avarescu been made aware of these warnings? No, he had not. They would have reached Roumanian G.H.Q., but at that time, and until after the smash beyond the mountains, he had been in the south. So this campaign is just one more — and a very typical instance for our Army schools — of the disastrous effect of political interference with strategy.

Then I asked the P.M. if he would give me his views about the general situation at this moment in the regions round Constantinople, as it seemed to me grave, or might become so unless the Greeks won their war handsomely, a consummation which the Allies had done nothing to promote. Where had the Russians gone from the Bessarabian front? What was Avarescu's view about Constantinople? Should not we Allies have a plan to meet contingencies? He replied that the situation had not yet developed enough to offer complete data, and there was still much indecision, and many matters indeterminate. But he considered the liberty of the Straits absolutely vital for Roumania. So do we, I replied. Yes, here our interests are entirely identical and we must help each other, he said. He could not tell what would happen to the Greeks. They had miscalculated once, and might again. They had not much gun ammunition, and could not afford to squander it. Was the Greek discipline good enough to prevent this? As for the Russians, they had left his front in June, but the preparations had begun some time before, and though some of the troops had been sent to Siberia, the greater part had gone to the Caucasus. About May 15, I suggested; the usual time for the opening of active operations in Russia, and in the summer they could march all the way. I supposed that it was a bit over one thousand miles to Angora from the Dniester by land, with the railways to help, and some could go by Odessa and coastwise. Certainly they might be filtering in by now or very soon, if the communications were of any service at all. Avarescu said that he would put me in touch with the Army Intelligence and I could learn their views and hear their reports. That will suit me well. The P.M. told me, as others have done, that the Army was the most solid asset of Roumania.

It was now nearly 8.30. We had both intended to talk

for ten minutes and had spun it out to an hour and a half. The P.M. had a most important engagement at 7.30. But, he said, when people who are soldiers, whether in plain clothes or not, begin to talk soldiering, time is forgotten. An interesting figure, cool and shrewd, not liable to be stampeded, and with great knowledge of Russia, which he constantly visited before the war. He told me that the only thing he found fault with in our General Staffs during the war was their failure to strengthen him with fifteen divisions in August, 1917. Had we done so the Eastern front could have been kept going.

Monday, July 18, 1921. Went to see M. Goga, Ministre des Cultes et des Arts, in the morning. A youngish man of marked capacity and intelligence, a Roumanian of Transylvania, poet and writer, who had often been in prison for preaching liberty for his fellow-subjects. He told me that the various religions in Transylvania were now on an equal footing respecting subventions, because their heads had taken an oath of allegiance. On the material side they had nothing to complain of. They were the Roman Catholics, the Reformed Church, and the Unitarians, and they had of right six seats in the Upper House. He allowed perfect liberty of public worship and even that the Magyar hymn should be sung in church, though it was not sacred music. He made a rule that Magyar schools should be established wherever there was a Magyar majority, and even talked of a Magyar University in the Czekler district. Some seventy-five per cent of the personnel of the railways and posts was Magyar and the Roumanian wish was to make the people happy, but the strong nationalist sentiment of the Magyars made it difficult. The gendarmerie and the troops were Roumanian, but universal service was being applied without difficulty. (The King had told me that he had found and spoken to a Magyar soldier in his guard at Sinaia.) The real trouble was that the Magyars would not accept the Treaty. He admitted that the Roumanian personnel was very inefficient and not large enough, but they were doing their best and everything he said seemed to show that the Minister himself was for a broad liberal policy without which, he said, he would deny all his past. He was willing to give me or anyone facilities for going where I would and speaking to anyone alone, and he had just given Mr. Tudor John (?) permission to address public meetings there. He would certainly give Sir Willoughby Dickinson every facility if he wished it. It seems that there are not more than 1,500,000 Magyars in Transylvania, but of these a solid block of 500,000 in one district. Everything was normal there now, and the country thriving. It only required national antipathies to die down and in a few years the situation would be quite satisfactory.

He was having a fortnight's Congress at Bucharest in September to receive all the artists — writers, poets, musicians, painters, sculptors, etc. Each branch would have a two days' discussion and then there would be general meetings. By these means he hoped to unify the artists and to learn their needs. They were all coming from all parts, he thought, and he said that the Magyars in Transylvania had decided to take part in politics and to form a party. At present there were only five Magyar members, but they had a right to twenty-five seats when they wanted them. There was universal suffrage, but not female suffrage yet.

Mr. Grigori Jon lunched with me, and I acquired the certitude that some of the F.O. here think that it is England who is standing behind Bulgaria and Hungary, and is responsible for their assumed contumacy. They think that England desires the support of these States for her particular ends. I told him quite crisply that England did not need nor seek the support of any State for her own ends and could look after herself. He said that they had been much impressed in Roumania by some statement of Count Bethlen, to the effect that English opinion was with the Hungarians. I replied that the English thought themselves free to express their individual sentiments as they pleased, but that the Government held to its friends and allies so long as they played the game. We had always had individuals who attacked the Government, and even sometimes supported England's enemies. It was part of our tradition, and perhaps a pose. Grigori said that the Roumanian press here was very second-rate and that no one paid any attention to the views of any paper.

I saw Sir W. Dickinson afterwards. He is here with his wife and daughter and goes on to Geneva later, after a look round. He has been filled up at Budapest with all the Hungarian criticisms of Roumania and thinks that the persecutions of minorities and creeds are the greatest danger to the Treaties. I hoped that he would see Goga and then have a good look round. A trustworthy man of a fine type with a pleasant daughter. I shall be curious to learn his appreciation of the Magyar minority question later on.

Looked deeper into Roumanian resources. I should certainly place agriculture first in spite of the oil. With the new territories there are 14½ million hectares of arable land or forty-five per cent of the total surface of the country, so it may be able to double its wheat export if no other circumstances interfere. The weight of the grain runs from 77 to 84.2 kilogrammes to the hectolitre, and the Bessarabian wheat seems the heaviest crop. The mean production is 15.7 hectolitres to the hectare. As 4,150,000 hectares are cultivated for wheat, this may give 65 million hectolitres of which half may be exportable. Maize is a huge crop because the people eat a maize polenta now, though they may go in for wheat when better off. The weight of this crop is 72 to 83 kilogrammes to the hectolitre. It covers four million hectares, and requires no expensive plant and manures. Its culture prepares the land well for wheat and produces 74 million hectolitres a year, of which a fifth may be exportable, chiefly in an industrialised form such as alcohol, glucose, etc. The Roumanians thoroughly understand the due rotation of crops. Galatz is the chief port of exportation for cereals, as the Danube and the Pruth lead down to it. The capacity of export of the New Roumania in cereals of all kinds may be 550,000 wagons of ten tons worth 5½ milliards of lei. Cattle, sheep, horses, and pigs are part of the produce of the country also, but the war made fearful ravages in the live-stock and there is now only half the head of 1916.

Wood is another large source of profit, and the forests cover seven million hectares; the best wooded region being Bukovina. About two-sevenths of the trees are resinous. The river system is very favourable for transporting wood to the mills for foreign markets, and also offers large sources of power as yet very partially utilised. The raft business is managed by gangs of men who take contracts for the work. Here again Galatz is the principal port. Everyone is nominally compelled to follow certain rules of the Forest Code, and only a fixed quantity per hectare may be cut each year, in all some ten million cubic metres, of which half is needed in the country, and thirty to thirty-five per cent is available for export, representing 150,000 to 200,000 wagons of ten tons, value $2\frac{1}{2}$ milliards of lei. Almost every description of wood is grown. Rafts, funicular and Décauville light lines, chutes and canals, are used for transportation. There are numerous sawmills and other factories for dealing with wood produce.

In oil, the total annual output capacity is placed as high as $4\frac{1}{2}$ million tons, but not the half has yet been obtained in the best year. The losses in the war, the destructions, and the *crise des transports* which still continues, have depressed the industry, but there is no doubt about its resources, into which I must look more closely. All these figures disclose the potential resources of Roumania, but the actual exports are at present far below the figures stated.

Tuesday, July 19, 1921. One of the most exasperating things here is the absence of trustworthy statistics, and the sheer impossibility of separating them, for the new Provinces, from the Austrian figures. But here and there one picks up an interesting indication. For instance, in the Old Kingdom before the war, 1000 million lei of paid-up share capital were placed in industry, nearly all in limited companies with larger or small foreign share capital. Oil companies represented half of this amount of foreign capital invested in Roumania, and ninety to ninety-one per cent of it was foreign, Germany, Holland, and England heading the list. Sugar industries were mainly Belgian. In textiles only an insignificant British capital was engaged. Chemical industries were German and Austrian, cement and porcelain mainly Belgian. In all, out of 511 million lei of foreign capital invested in Roumanian industries, Germany came first with 121 million lei, the Dutch second, and England third with 97 million, or 18.8 per cent. It is curious to note that more than half of the Roumanian industries were worked with foreign capital, the percentage in separate industries being 91.9 per cent in oil companies, 95 per cent in gas and electricity, 72.3 per cent in chemical industries, 74 per cent in metallurgic industries, 69.61 per cent in wood, and 94 per cent in sugar. It is difficult to get at the figures for the new Provinces, but it is thought that in the New Roumania there are 734 industrial concerns with a total capital of 2536 million lei, excluding Bessarabia, Bukovina, and the co-operative societies which may bring the figure up to $3\frac{1}{3}$ milliards of lei. It is curious that a country with so little coal makes such little use of the driving power of its many mountain rivers and falls.

Roumania was fearfully backward in railways even before the war, when she had some 5.3 kilometres of railways for every 10,000 inhabitants, compared with 36 kilometres for Sweden. This most important economic factor has been seriously neglected. In 1916 she had only 3600 kilometres of railway with about 1000 locomotives, of which half were useless, and 20,000 carriages and trucks. The greater part of this was destroyed or fell into the enemy's hands. A large programme was needed with an estimated cost of 1546 million lei, which would have given, in all, 14,871 kilometres of railway. The system also had to be reversed and lines led to Jassy, Galatz, and Bucharest, instead of to Vienna, Budapest, and Odessa. The State could not carry out the work alone, and had to resort to the banks. But want of coal, difficulties of transport, and the potential motive force of Roumanian "white coal" made it necessary to study this latter source of energy in order to electrify Roumanian railways. The fall of the exchange makes this an expensive prospect, and in effect very little progress has been made.

As for the foreign trade of Roumania, one cannot make out that New Roumania had a much larger export trade value than 1318 million lei in 1913, the imports nearly balancing, but if she can export five and a half million tons of cereals and the ten million tons of wood, which she is capable of doing, as well as work up her oil to the maximum figure, it is thought possible that her exports may rise to seven milliards of lei before long. Intensive and more scientific cultivation of the soil, rational exploitation of forests which are still far behind the German efficiency, good work with the oil, and, above all, a large increase of railway rolling stock, are the only radical means of cleansing Roumanian economics and finance so heavily hit by the war.

If we look at the banks there were 197 in 1913, with 215 million lei of paid-up capital. Since then, new banks have been formed, and many old ones have increased their capital, so that last year there were 277 banks with a subscribed capital of 1355 million lei, not including private banks. Adding the numerous banks of Transylvania (654) and those of Bukovina and Bessarabia, there are in all 927 banks with a subscribed capital of 1523 million lei, and a paid-up capital of 1398 million lei. The popular, co-operative, and village banks in New Roumania also number 8883 with a total capital of 621 million lei. The great credit banks are 13 in number, and for 8 of them their united capital and reserve rose from 179 million lei in 1915 to 1174 millions in 1920. In great part it is due to inflation.

Public finance is less engaging. The Roumanian Budget for 1916–17 showed revenue and expenditure to balance at 640 million lei, and the consolidated debt before the war was 1795 millions. Roumania's situation was among the best in Europe. The war profoundly changed this situation and in the Budget for 1919–20, there was shown a monthly deficit of 256 millions which could be met only by further loans. The revenue was 816 million lei and the expenditure 3900 millions. The war policy had been one of Budget deficits and of consolidated long-term loans, but in the main, of floating debt contracted at the National Bank. In the course of the financial year 1920–21, the Government unified the currency and established a normal ordinary Budget, leaving over till the autumn the extraordinary Budget destined to cover reconstruction, reparations, and pensions. The normal Budget showed 6090 million lei of revenue and 6600 millions of expenditure, in which the Army figured for 900 millions and communications for 1163 millions. The indirect taxes were very heavy in comparison with the direct. An income tax might bring in a milliard and by so much reduce the indirect taxes. But this Budget did not include a capital levy, nor a tax on war profiteers. This year's Budget includes both.

The general total of the public debt on June 1, 1920, was 11,329 million lei, including 7234 millions of floating debt all contracted during the war. Adding the increase of the public debt by the aggrandisement of Roumania and by the unification of money, the general total debt is 25,000 millions. Per head of population it is 1470 lei compared with 6395 francs for England. It was thought last year that with a rational Budget, unification of the currency, and a foreign loan, the public finances could be restored. The fiduciary circulation is 13,371 million lei including roubles and crowns still in circulation compared with 40 milliard francs in France. I have seen the national wealth of Roumania computed at 153,336 million lei. Depreciation and the instability of the exchange, together with the absence of succession duties, and up to this year of income tax, make all calculations dubious, but if the wealth is 153 milliards, a debt of 25 milliards is not deadly. I think that there is a great future for English trade in Roumania, and that if we use our banks to take the financial place formerly filled by the Germans we should have a larger share in the future profits from Roumanian resources. It was on their banks that the Germans based their successes in Roumanian trade.

The Serbian Minister had asked me to call this morning. When I went he was ill. He might have telephoned to spare me the trouble. A young secretary talked a bit of Bulgaria, and showed great distrust of her. Afterwards I saw M. Paul de Jurjewicz, Councillor of the Polish Legation, who advised me to go to Warsaw by Czernowitz, and promised to arrange for me on the frontier. As this route will take me through Galicia, it will be well to adopt it. J. made a point of the idea that, when Russia began to be opened up, Poland would be the best jumping-off ground, because it was near, and many Poles knew Russia well. He was rather sarcastic about the supposed evolution of the Russians. He doubted that they had the capacity to evolve. He said that I should find the Poles working hard, and thirty per cent more workmen busy.

Saw General Nikoleanu, the head of the Bucharest Police, a man with clear views and a rapid, incisive manner of speech. He has only 2600 men all told, including 1000 gendarmerie who belong to the Army. He ought to have many more, but as the pay is only 400 lei a month, and it costs a couple and a child ten lei a day for food, they are resigning fast. He has detective brigades, and *sergents de ville*. Some three hundred men are always on duty in eight-hour shifts. He wants much, but cannot get it. In winter the lamps are all put out at 1 A.M., so the burglars have a fine time. All prisoners are brought to the Prefecture to be tried, so the Police become acquainted with them. Bucharest has now 800,000 inhabitants and wants many more police, he says. The town is divided up into inspectorates, radiating out from the centre of the town, and the inspectorates are divided into circumscriptions. In the provinces there are 5000 police and 12,000 rural gendarmerie. All the system is one, under the Minister of the Interior, and there is no difference in the new Provinces.

Lunched with the Millington Drakes at the Jockey

Club. Mr. and Mrs. Sproull Fouché, Mr. Greene, all of the U.S.A., Miss Stuart, Mr. Baggallay, and Mr. and Mrs. Napier. The Fouchés touring the world and have just been to Bessarabia, where they say the Jews cross the frontier nightly at a cost per boat-trip of two hundred lei. In the winter they cross at night on the ice. They all want to get to America, but the new U.S. immigration rules will stop them. Went to call on Mme. Lahovary, wife of the Roumanian Minister in Paris, in the afternoon and discussed the agrarian laws with her. She thought that the ultra-democratic reforms had all come much too quickly. The division of the land should have been gradually made, not in a hurry, and then, when education had gone further, universal suffrage might have come later. A largely illiterate electorate was not ready for it now. Instead of handing the lands over to the State, it has been so arranged that the new peasant proprietor had to be confronted with the original proprietor before the tribunals, making them as it were rival and hostile contestants and creating bad blood. She thought that the old proprietor would be able to keep 330 hectares, while houses, grounds, gardens, orchards, and vineyards — in fact any plots whose production was entirely due to the old owners—were not included in the 330. The peasants in some cases received only five hectares. The distribution of the lots was all done locally. How can a man and five hectares make a farm? I asked. What about capital, farm buildings, plant, cattle, seed, and so on? She said the peasants had made heaps of money before and during the war. The Germans behaved well to the peasants and villages, but sacked the towns. The peasants had hired their wagons to the Germans at high rates. They bought seed, and the cattle came to them from the captures in Hungary. They were contented, but would all farm the fields in patches, as indeed they are doing, and the result in exportable surplus wheat might show a loss. Roumania would get a large conservative class through these changes. The King had set the example by giving up the Estates of the Crown.

Mme. L. was on the whole in favour of these changes, but would rather that they should have been presented as a social reform than as a reward to the people for their conduct in the war. She pointed out that everybody was working for the State and doing something for the country.

Later met M. Caius Brediceanu, head of one of the F.O. departments, who drove with me to the Athene Palace Hotel where we talked Eastern Europe. I try to make them see that the attitude of Hungary towards the Trianon Treaty is perfectly natural, and that some of us keep our personal preferences for the Hungarians without in the least failing towards Roumania. B. is in charge of Hungarian affairs and I explained fully my point of view about it all. Then I raised the question of the future of Slav sentiment in Eastern and Central Europe, and what it all meant. B. said that the Czechs were the only Slavs with education and capacity for organisation. They had inherited the natural leadership of the Slav people. It was they who had stampeded the Northern Jugo-Slavs at the close of the war. I said that I had been impressed by a recent speech of Benès in which he had described his country as the Western advance guard of the Slav people. What did this mean? He could not be in both camps, and previously he had based all his policy on the Entente. Had it failed him? Had L. G.'s statement that he did not care whether Austria went to Germany angered him? Was he seeking a more solid basis for an anti-German combination? B.'s views on this subject are as unformed as mine, but he promised to think it over and write to me.[1]

The Government passed their Budget to-day. It is 7,660,594,452 lei, and the public debt has risen to 27 milliards. An internal loan for 100 millions is projected. It seems that the Roumanians have made arrangements with Germany for a first credit of 450 million marks payable in merchandise. This is where we are hit. Reparations seem

[1] He did not. Roumanians are not remarkable for keeping promises or appointments.

a less blessed word for us than Mesopotamia, and that is saying a good deal.

Wednesday, July 20, 1921. Saw General Valiano, Minister of Communications, in the morning. He said that he had 1300 locomotives now in use, would have 2000 by next April, and 4300 in all at a later period, the date of which he seemed uncertain about. He has 80,000 wagons and carriages, of which 20,000 cannot be used, and wants 100,000 in all. He is hoping to make a contract for 500 English locomotives and describes the terms as favourable, because payment, including interest, can be put off till the autumn of 1922. The locomotives actually ordered are 50 Baldwin from America, 80 from Skoda, 50 from Oonsten Koppel (Berlin), 75 from Henschel John of Cassel, 176 from the German consortium, and 300, nominally from Bruthnel (Canada). I am to get the maps and programme of construction. He told me that the Anglo-French contract for repairs "might" come up again in the autumn, but that it could not be passed now as opinion was hostile to it.

Went on to visit the General Staff. I found the Sub-Chief of Staff and head of the Intelligence, General Gorski, at the G.S. building in Stirbey Voda Street. A good modern staff officer with sound views. We had met in Badoglio's office in Rome earlier in the year. Later he introduced Colonel Dimitrie Palada in charge of his Russian section and we had a good talk over the whole position. They gave me all that I asked for and made no mystery about anything.

In general, the Bolshies now have 70 divisions of infantry, each of a mean strength of 5000 with 24 guns, and 20 divisions of cavalry. The total strength is 300,000 to 350,000 infantry and 50,000 to 60,000 cavalry. These troops are divided into three main groups, namely, Western front, Caucasus front, and Reserves. The Western front runs from Archangel to the Black Sea, and is in three commands. The Petrograd Command has only three divisions of infantry and extends south to the Libau-Moscow railway. The Mohilev Command continues the line southward to the Pripet and has one cavalry and ten infantry divisions. The Kiev Command completes the line down to the Black Sea and has four cavalry and fourteen infantry divisions. This latter command faces Bessarabia and the Roumanians.

Taking the Reserve next, it is now distributed over a large area of which Kharkov is the approximate centre. The area covered is an oval 700 kilometres by 500, and here are eleven to twelve divisions of cavalry and seventeen to eighteen of infantry. This reserve is available for the defence of the Crimea, and is also suitably placed for re-enforcing either the Roumanian or the Caucasus front.

ı The Caucasus front has the Ninth Army, so called, with one cavalry and three infantry divisions from the Sea of Azov to Sukhum Kale. The Central Caucasus Command or Terek Group has five divisions of infantry and reaches south of Tiflis. Further south the Tenth Army has three divisions of cavalry and five of infantry, includes Baku and Erivan, and reaches down to the Persian frontier. Note also five divisions of infantry in the Orenburg district and five in Transcaspia. Assuming the general totals to be correct, there is little left over for Siberia.

For the actual Bessarabian or Roumanian front I was given another map which shows the Russian front opposite the Roumanians to be divided into four sectors. The places and numbers of all the divisional headquarters are shown. Gorski and I both think the general dispositions very reasonable and that they show that someone who knows his business has made the plan. There has been a general movement latterly towards the Caucasus and the south. The centre of gravity is now Kharkov. They think here that a movement by sea is open to the Russians, and also the re-enforcement of Kemal by sea and land.

But Gorski declares that, though the Bolshies have not abandoned their pretensions to stampede Europe, they are incapable of much harm owing to want of food, communications, and money. He says that their experiences have taught them that they cannot stand up against regularly organised troops. So he thinks that they may pursue their plans in Asia or Asia Minor where they are likely to meet softer military material. The position of the Bolshies facing Roumania must be difficult, as the Ukraine is full of armed bands all across the Bolshie communications. These bands run up to 15,000 strong, and all the villagers are armed. The Russian break-up led to the desire for local independence, and the Ukraine was not backward in this movement.

The Dniester front is held by the Roumanians and the Bolshies on the opposing bank. It is impossible to launch a boat without it being fired upon. Bessarabia is full of vineyards, and the produce used to have a great sale at Odessa and in South Russia. Its means of transport was the Dniester, from July to September. Later on by sledge. The land has been divided as in other parts of Roumania, and the great proprietors retain their vineyards, as these have not been expropriated. On arable land their holdings are limited to one hundred hectares here. There is a difficulty in marketing produce, as the Dniester used to be the main line of traffic. So the Roumanians are prepared to treat, and the projected meeting on board a ship in the estuary of the river may come off. Bessarabia is stiff with wheat [1] and the chance of Bolshie irruptions for the sake of food may be on the cards. But generally Gorski thinks that ten Roumanian divisions can take on the thirty-two Bolshie divisions of the Kiev Command and the Reserve.

I find them much incensed against Bulgaria. They say that it requires a whole division in the Dobrudcha to keep out the comitajis, and if they pursue the bands they are fired on by Bulgarian troops and may let themselves in for a regular war. They say that they have captured correspondence from Bulgarian sources with Russia, and ditto from Bulgarian Deputies who had embarked in a boat on the coast for Odessa. They say that the mission to Kemal is correct and also the Nikolaieff mission, and that

---

[1] Later reports showed that the Bessarabian wheat was partially scorched by the sun.

the Bulgarians are Philo-Russian and Slavs, and will not change their character. I only wish they would give me definite proofs, for at present I have only statements. They also say that Bulgaria has many more men than they allow and heaps of hidden arms.

Had tea with the Fouchés. I liked her story of the musical Bessarabian peasant of whom she had taken a snapshot playing the flute. He was asked why he had not married. He replied, "My flute is my love, and wine is my joy." Fouché tells me that he is experimenting with a patch of cotton crop on the Queen's estate. It is doing fine, and he believes that huge crops could be had. It has never been grown here before. He is a cotton-grower, and says that he has never seen any land like this of Roumania. His view is that wherever maize can grow, cotton can grow.

Thursday, July 21, 1921. In the morning saw General Rascano and M. Garoflid, Minister of Domains. Called on Colonel Dundas, our Military Attaché, in the afternoon and had a talk. Saw Mr. Keyser, our consul here, in the evening, and Mr. S. Guest, Secretary of the Astra-Romana Oil Company, the biggest in Roumania. Dined with the Foreign Minister, M. Take Jonescu, at 9 P.M. A busy day.

General Rascano is a pleasant and capable man. He has followed my writings for many years and knew all about my views. He tells me that New Roumania has a contingent of 140,000 youths of twenty-one, but he will take only 120,000 for two years' service, and will train the other 20,000 for a few months as specialists, and then place them in the Reserve of the Army. They are to be trained as railway men, telegraphists, postmen, carpenters, and other useful trades, so that on mobilisation, or in case of civil troubles, the State may have under its hand a militarised personnel to run the utility services. At present the Army has twenty-one divisions, besides two rifle divisions on the Hungarian frontier. The new organic law is coming out in April and will be on the basis of nine Army Corps. He said that Roumania had to anticipate a war on two fronts at present, so I presume the idea is an army of three expanded corps on each front and a reserve army. They seem pretty well off for war material, but are very short of aeroplanes, having only two to three hundred.

General Rascano and I thought, that in view of the situation on the Black Sea Littoral, we ought to have a closer understanding. They want a lot of ships and two thousand aeroplanes or more, and can supply any amount of troops. I should like Greece to be in this arrangement, but the liberty of the Straits demands an international garrison. It is foolish for us to be taken unawares by events on the Black Sea Coast. With Roumania and Greece we can control all this front, besides preparing a check on Bolshevism if it moves east. The Black Sea is a much more suitable theatre for suppressing Bolshie intrigues and operations eastward than it ever was in Russia's Imperial days. We can here put a stopper upon Lenin and company. That is why Bolshies and Turks will spare no efforts to get hold of the Straits.

Rascano tells me that he is dividing up the men of the different new Provinces on the Italian system so that the whole Army may become homogeneous. There will be the same proportion of the various races in all the regiments. This is worth trying. He says that the Hungarian officers will not serve, but Saxons and other races will, and the Saxons he describes as very dependable. I fancy that the Disarmament Conference at Washington will not arouse much enthusiasm here, unless the U.S.A. takes over the Dniester and the Dobrudcha fronts! We talked for an hour of Roumania's various military interests.

Later I saw M. Garoflid to talk about the agrarian laws. He gave me a succinct account of their origin, application, and future development, and is also going to send me the text.[1]

He said that this question had been debated in Roumania for forty years and could no longer be evaded when

[1] He never did. Nothing comes in Roumania unless you fetch it.

the neighbouring Russian, Ukraine, and even Bessarabian peasants had all taken the land. It was a question of staving off an agrarian revolution here, and the Bill led to a great struggle of six months in Parliament before it became law. The King had taken the lead and had given 100,000 hectares of the Crown estates to the people. The law was in application now in the Old Kingdom. In Transylvania they were proceeding by short leases and the law would be applied in the autumn. Bessarabia had joined Roumania on the condition that her new land laws held good, but she had been persuaded not to expropriate the great landlords altogether, but to allow them to retain a portion of their lands. The old proprietors' share for the whole New Kingdom was one hundred to three hundred acres of arable land, and the peasants had two to ten acres according to the local conditions. There was no cast-iron rule. The peasants were well off. Many had worked with their own teams and wagons for the landlords, and had their own traditional working tools, and also their houses. It was easy for them to exploit their new lots. Yes, it was intended to give them full possession and all the titles, as well as the right to sell the land. But anyone could declare fifty per cent of his property to be inalienable and then could not draw back. This property then remained in the family. Gardens, woods, and vineyards were not included in the expropriations. The proprietors received about one-third the pre-war price of their land. It was an immense sacrifice on their part and they had behaved admirably in consenting to it.

I talked with Colonel Dundas afterwards. He commanded the 61st Division at the end of the war and spent four winters in the Ypres salient, which must be a record. He spoke enthusiastically about Allenby and Jeudwine, but thought that in many cases the initiative had been pressed out of our officers by too much ungumming. Like South Africa, I said. He is a hard, conscientious Scot, and is neither pro nor con Roumanian. A good type. He agrees with me that we neglect Roumania and her importance. Joffre and Badoglio have both been here and we have sent no one of importance. He thinks that the officers here are not very contented, as a subaltern gets only 1400 lei a month, and it is not enough to live upon. D. has a house in the Banat for his family, and so gets in touch with the common people. He travels constantly and knows this country well. He tells me that at present the mayors and *notaires* are having a gorgeous time, as they have the power to allocate the land. He tells me that Constantinople is in a great state of mind about a Bolshie attack on Bessarabia, but D. does not seem to worry about it. Nor do I very much, since someone — Rascano, I think — described the Bolshie communications behind the Dniester through the Ukraine bands as resembling tracks cut through a primeval forest. So it appears on the map given to me, though the strength and possibilities of these bands are on the vague side. We had a good talk, and later met again and discussed our own Army affairs. He is off to Budapest again to meet Thwaites and Gorton. He writes a fortnightly account, and a weekly letter giving all the news. A good man to have here.

I had a talk with Consul Keyser in the afternoon. He has been here eight years and speaks Roumanian pretty well, it seems. He has not a high opinion of Roumanian energy, and says that most of our business houses have lost money here owing to the fall in the exchange and refusal of the people here to pay the price of goods contracted for. But this is nothing new, nor is it peculiar to Roumania. Yet nobody ventures to tackle this vital problem of the exchanges. Saw Mr. Guest in the evening, and we are to dine together to-morrow. Apparently the Astra Company's one hundred per cent dividend means nothing, for it is in the depreciated currency as against the original gold value investment. He says that a smaller dividend than about one hundred per cent now means that a company is on the rocks. One may be here, he says, for months and never hear of the legion of small companies which fill our financial papers at home with reports of their doings.

He regards the whole oil industry as highly speculative, and most uncertain, and thinks that an enormous capital has been sunk in it with disproportionate results. The export tax of three pounds per ton on the light benzine is crippling. His difficulty is the constant fanciful experiments made by officials here who do not understand the industry. He is inclined to doubt whether bribery is very rife. The lack of transport, the export tax, and strong foreign competition are among his worst troubles, but he considers the Roumanian oil the best in the world.

There was a good deal of Bolshevism at the workings at one time and the men threatened to take over the wells. The Government at last acted drastically and made wholesale arrests. This stopped the trouble dead. They could do things here that would not be possible in England. Roumanian labour had not the wit nor the experience of our Trade Unions.

Dined with the Take Jonescus at 9 P.M. A nice house of the Cairo type, very suitable for entertaining, with good rooms and good modern furniture. An excellent and cool balcony for sitting out on these hot nights. The second Mrs. T. J. is a tall good-looking lady with very fair hair. Also there were Prince and Princess Grigorie Ghika, Mme. Falcoyanu, and Mme. Mavrocordat. I had a good talk with T. J. during the evening. I told him that my difficulty about Bulgaria was that I had only statements against statements, and that I could only give the two without drawing conclusions. If he liked to give me proofs of Bulgarian duplicity, and they satisfied me and were not refuted by what I learnt at Sofia, it would be different. In the end of the talk he asked me to come to the F.O. on Saturday morning and he would show them to me. I had told Millington Drake that I proposed to take this line and he had approved. Now we shall see what it all means. T. J. quite understood my difficulty.

I had a talk with him about the Slav renaissance. He is the ally of the two Slav people in this part of the world, and thinks that Jugo-Slavia will never trust the third Slav

State, Bulgaria, again. But he allowed that Roumania was very isolated, a Latin island in a more or less Slav sea, and told me that he was ready to admit Greece into the Little Entente. He had acknowledged King Constantine by accrediting his Minister to him, and thought with me that the situation of the other Allied Ministers at Athens was supremely ridiculous.

T. J. is, of course, a strong Ententist. His main complaint against us all is over the reparations, in which Roumania figures for only one per cent as the result of the Spa Conference, while there are large sums claimed against Roumania for her depredations in Hungary. But one per cent on 132 milliards of gold marks is a pretty big sum after all. He does not think that he has been treated fairly in this matter. I opened up the question of a closer understanding between England and Roumania on Black Sea affairs and he seemed to favour it. He told me that, though want of money had prevented Roumania from proceeding with the naval plans recently suggested by one of our naval officers sent here, he had accepted, and was just about to sign a contract for the training of Roumanian naval people by ours. This will help a good deal.

He also said that his representative at Constantinople had recently sent him a wire telling him of the various rumours current with regard to Roumanian intervention in Greco-Turk and Constantinople affairs and had asked to be told what the policy was. T. J. had replied by five points. First, that Roumanians would not take any part in the present hostilities between Greeks and Turks. Secondly, that in case Bulgaria intervened and initiated any action against Greece, Roumania would proceed to *taper* at once. Thirdly, that Roumania would assist in the defence of Constantinople if her aid were needed. Those were the main points. The others have escaped me [1] and I think were of minor importance. He had stated this policy to the King of Roumania, who had entirely approved.

[1] One was that no request of any kind for Roumanian intervention had reached Roumania from the Allies.

T. J. seems to have a very free hand in foreign politics and to be in complete control of it. He said that his man at Sofia, M. Rascano, was excellent, and kept him well posted with timely information. This Minister is on good terms with Sir Arthur Peel. He did not ask how his information was obtained, but it was very good.

T. J. thought that our diplomacy was not active enough. He was not talking of our diplomacy here, but of it generally. He did not include Millington Drake. The latter was very active and alert and he liked him very much. He had seen him on a variety of matters. The German Minister here had presented his credentials and since then had not been near the Foreign Office, nor had had any communication whatsoever with T. J. I am not very surprised. The Germans sacked T. J.'s house when they were here, leaving nothing but the walls, so a German Minister can scarcely regard himself as a *persona grata*. It was a silly, spiteful thing to do.

I asked T. J. whether he was forming any school of foreign politics. He seemed to me to have initiated, and in fact created, the whole foreign policy of New Roumania, but if this were to be an enduring work he should train up the best young men in his ideas and then they would carry it on. Bismarck had made the mistake of not forming such a school, with the result that when he left office he was succeeded by one imbecile after another, who accumulated blunder on blunder, and led up to the disaster of 1914. Moltke had formed his own school. It had been beaten, but had been damnably efficient, and its fall was due mainly to the horrible political inefficiency of Bismarck's successors, and to the fact that a Chief of Staff had been nominated in 1906 because his name was Moltke. T. J. had not thought of it, but seemed much interested and asked various questions about it.

We also discussed the Poles, and he told me of various conversations which he had had with L. G. about them. T. J. had admitted to L. G. that the Poles were considered abroad to be inefficient, and that they were neither liked nor trusted. Well, then? asked L. G. Yes, said T. J., but can you, he asked, conceive a peaceful Europe without a Poland? Can Poland stand unless the Allies support her? Is not a Russo-German combination certain eventually if we do not cultivate a strong Poland? L. G. admitted all this. Well, then? asked T. J. He told me that the great defect of Poland was her want of leading men. Certain influence had compassed the political ruin of every man of any importance who had risen, out of jealousy. The sure hall-mark of the second-rate man, I replied; the big man likes competence and seeks for it. Poor Sapieha was the last victim. Where is Roman Dmowski? I asked. Ah! a very good man with great *esprit*, intelligence, and competence. He is vegetating at Posen apart from affairs.

T. J. asked me much about my visits to other countries and I told him my views about personalities and things. I did not raise the question of his *sûreté* or *sicuranze* service, as I believe it is called. It is very active and pretty vexatious. T. J. is said to have agents everywhere and to look after the press, especially in France. But for Roumania, with so many dangers round her, and a somewhat elementary civilisation, the system can be understood. We had quite a pleasant evening, and talked till midnight.

Rascano told me in the morning, by the way, that they meant to suppress the Dobrudcha troubles with a strong hand. They had declared martial law there and had a whole division on the spot. The bands came by narrow tracks through the forests and the Roumanians were making them into broad tracks so that troops could pursue more rapidly. They had armoured cars there, and wireless telegraphy, for their wires were regularly cut. T. J. told me that they would have only 500,000 tons of wheat this year for export from the Old Kingdom, while in Transylvania and the Banat there was only about enough for local needs.

Friday, July 22, 1921. Sent off some wires to Constantinople and Prague. The lady at the Post-Office made very heavy weather over them and covered sheets with rows of figures to calculate the cost. Mr. Alexander Adams, Commercial Secretary at the Legation, is back and he lunched with me. An intelligent young-looking Scot, aged forty, highly trained, and skilled in economics. He has known Roumania for many years and we talked of his reports. He was not surprised that Guest did not give me what I had asked for. All the oil companies were like that. A. did not take jaundiced views of the oil industry, and said, in reply to my inquiry, that I might justly place the potential output at 2,000,000 tons a year. But he admitted the fearful transport difficulties and the competition and falling prices. He was amusing on the subject of the visit of Mr. X, who had been in Bucharest five days, had not seen Transylvania, and had cursed the Roumanian administration of it. A. employs a man in running round and comparing figures. A.'s chief difficulty is not only that of inadequate statistics, but of the inaccuracy of official data. He is against any international policy for England. France has always had one and has always been at war. A. preferred our system of meeting a situation when it arose. He had not brought his 1920 Report with him, as it was not published when he left London. He had dealt largely with economics and declared that the Roumanian debt of twenty-seven milliards was really over fifty milliards. He had thought it necessary to take up the whole question of the exchanges which were affecting our trade so seriously. Hardly any politicians understood it, nor even many experts in economics. He thought that last year's harvest would give an export of one and a half million tons of wheat.

Dined with Guest and we talked oil and then branched to diplomacy. One of his troubles is this strange Roumanian habit of passing "Decree Laws" suddenly, which take effect at once and are rarely thrown over by Parliament later. It is necessary to have a British Minister here who will act at once on his own responsibility in some cases to protect British interests, and to prevent a Decree Law from seeing the light when it harms these interests. A Minister who will not act without F.O. authority is of no use in these cases. He told me more of his Astra-Romana Company, of the attacks of the Standard Oil people on the British, and of the attempts of a German group backed by certain politicians here to *accaparer* the oil industry. I think that we may have trouble over the ultra-national sentiment here when it is used as a cloak for expropriating the oil industry as it may be some day. Our interests seem to lie with the Conservatives of the present Government.

Saturday, July 23, 1921. Went to the Foreign Office in the morning. Take Jonescu was punctual. I first showed him for his approval a short wire which I proposed to send to the *D. T.* on the Middle-East policy of Roumania, based on his message to his man at Constantinople, which he told me about the other night. He initialled it to avoid reference to the censor and to save time. I did not know before that there was still a censorship. Evidently T. J. looks after the press. The lady at the Post-Office knew his hieroglyphic of initials at a glance.

Then he handed me over, after a brief talk, to M. Derussi, the Secretary-General of the F.O., and to his Minister at Sofia, M. Rascano, who is here on short leave. Derussi has also been Minister at Sofia for three years, so they were both well-posted. T. J. had also taken out of his own portfolio numerous despatches for me to read. We then adjourned to the next room and had a good investigation. For actual proofs of Bulgarian duplicity or evil intentions I was shown orders informing certain commanders that if the Allies came along they were to give them certain returns, forming enclosures in the Bulgarian official letter of instructions. The returns were marked "A" and "B." One was the correct one, the other destined for the Allies, if they asked for one. Photographs of the originals were attached. I was also shown alleged Bulgarian postcards with Kemal's photograph on them. There are also sets of stamps, one lot bearing the heads of Lenin and Trotsky and the other the head of ex-Tsar Ferdinand, with pictures of Bulgaria, including the Southern Dobrudcha and Macedonia, and other possessions not now Bulgarian. I was also shown numerous official reports, and one of Stamboulisky's own despatches to the Allies, answering the charges against him.

I think that there is a strong presumption, assuming these reports to be authentic, that the Bulgarians have been, and are, in constant correspondence with Moscow. I saw no captured despatches, in fact nothing in writing on the subject, but was told of various Bolshie visits, the last being of the Soviet Commissary, Lippovitch, ten days ago to Varna. He complained to the Préfet next morning that a million had been stolen from him, and he is supposed to have had four millions — I suppose roubles. The great enemies of Roumania in Russia are Rakovitch and Bela Kun. Rakovitch is a Bulgar who had Roumanian citizenship for a time. He is the Soviet representative at Kiev, and is very active, as well as dangerous, for he knows Roumania. Bela Kun is in the Ukraine, and Bessarabia is his special province to work up.

With Grozkoff there went Lieutenant Pissaroff, late of the Bulgarian Army, and a trader named Entcheff. Stamboulisky had given different accounts of this mission to everyone in turn. At one time it was a private party, at another, a tobacco contract, and at a third, a meat deal. They have no doubt here that S. is in constant touch with Russians and Turks, and that both these people send men to Bulgaria constantly. One is the Djevad Hassan[1] who is cutting a dash at Sofia now. They think that if the Greeks had not won their battle — as they have in the last few days — the Bulgarians might have been in the field with 200,000 men, but this, of course, is only an opinion. It seems probable that high Bulgarian officers have been in Constantinople to harmonise the operations of Turk and Bulgar comitajis. One high Staff officer went there and the excuse was that he went on account of some property left to him. Then Sofia was asked how another happened to be there at the same moment, and Sofia said that he was ill and had gone to convalesce.[2]

[1] Djevad Abbas is his real name. See later.
[2] This must have been some time back.

They regard Stamboulisky and his Bulgarians as ready for mischief at any time. They will all do anything they can to advance the interests of their country, and S. has publicly proclaimed himself the disciple of Lenin. He is utterly ignorant of the elements of foreign policy and thinks that the old games can begin again. The Bulgarians, they say here, have twice the number of men allowed by the Treaty and heaps of hidden arms. They have also a system of compulsory labour for all, men and women, for two years, and the men, who number some 200,000, wear a sort of uniform and have been seen drilling and doing musketry. They live in barracks most of their time. The Bulgarian excuse that they cannot pay for a Volunteer Army is absurd, for the cost of the compulsory labour system has been reckoned up and costs more than a Volunteer Army would.[1] It is necessary that this system should end, as it is merely an astute means of turning the Treaty of Neuilly.

I am told that Peel has resigned, but that he, the Serbian and Greek Ministers, and the Roumanian, Serb, and Greek Military Attachés, can give me full information, photographs of documents, etc. M. Picot, of Syria, is the French Minister. He makes flowery speeches lauding the Bulgarians and displaying a tenderness for them which facts do not warrant. Our military man on the Inter-Allied Commission, Plunkett, they consider Bulgarophil. He would not allow the Serbian Military Attaché to give evidence before the I.-A. Commission, because he had no orders to that effect from the F.O. The Roumanians say that some people positively resent the presentation of proofs of Bulgarian ill-will.

In fact, it is the cumulative effect of much evidence, all pointing in one direction, which leads to a deep suspicion of Bulgarian bad faith. With complete mendacity Occidentals might not be taken in, but it is the infantile character of Stamboulisky's goings-on that disarms them. For instance, he went one day to the Serbian Minister and made a

---

[1] I think it only costs one-fourth.

statement to him. Afterwards he denied that he had made
the statement or had even paid the visit! We were really
dealing with Old Bulgaria and the old elementary conditions, which few Westerners could understand. Mendacity, intrigue, short-sight, hate, and violence were among
the Bulgarian arms. There was a lot more told, but as I
am off to Sofia on Tuesday, I can examine things better
there.

But I can find no proof of any intrigue between the ex-
Tsar and Stamboulisky. Each hates the other cordially.
Derussi agreed with me about this. Possibly Ferdinand is
fool enough to want to get back, but there is no proof of this,
and, for the rest, what could he do? I don't think poor
King Boris can have a bed of roses. The two Roumanians
say that the most dismal thing in the whole affair is the
disunion of the Great Powers, whose representatives do
not pull together, and often it is enough for one to take a
line for the other two to take two other lines. They think
that an Allied warning to S. would do good. My own impression is that Kemal has been bucking to Sofia of what
he will do in order to help himself out by getting the Bulgarians to threaten Thrace, and the simple Bulgar has believed him and has begun to get ready for a Balkan ram-
page. The Turk probably knew that he would be beat if
Bulgaria did not force Greece to recall some troops to
defend the home territory.

Sunday, July 24, 1921. I have been dipping into the oil
question. I find here, as in many other countries, that the
oil-fields are nestling under the mountains and generally
on the eastern side of them. The Boyars, I suspect, took
the rich lower-lying ground and left the poor foot-hills to
the peasants, thus inadvertently giving them the richest
parts of the country. It is on the eastern and southern
slopes of the Carpathians that all the oil is found here and
I expect that it is more or less continuous from the Danube
to Galicia.

The Bashtanari, Campina, and Moreni fields were
among those first developed. There was one single well in

the latter field which yielded 400,000 tons of oil in the period of maximum prices! The real headquarters of the industry is Ploesti, where there are the great refineries, and I was to have motored there to-day, but Guest is ill and I have other guests at lunch. Hither lead the chief pipe-lines from the important fields, and other refineries are at Campina. From Ploesti there now runs a five-inch pipe-line to Constanza on the Black Sea, which I am told has a fine oil port, specially designed, with ample storage. To that extent the transport difficulty is overcome, but I found lines upon lines of tank wagons all round Ploesti and right up to Bucharest, and there are, of course, masses of material required on the fields or near them for building, drilling, refining, and storing. The industry is much hampered by the lack of transport facilities. Also, petroleum-mining must be as speculative as other mining. It is cheaper in its plant and shafts than coal-mining, but less sure in its results afterwards, for one never can say what an oil sand may produce till it is tested. But when the old Columbia well in the Moreni field produced oil worth £1,200,000 in eighteen months after costing at the outside £5000 to sink, we cannot be surprised at people being willing to take chances. It is not at all uncommon to find pioneers drawing as much per day from a well as they have spent in sinking it. There has been, all the same, a wealth of money spent in over-capitalisation of most uncertain ventures in which the distinguishing feature has always been lack of working capital, which has disappeared in the capacious pockets of promoters. If intending investors came here and examined the industry on the spot, they would soon discover which was good and which bad. The equipment and sinking of wells which had transport facilities within reach were formerly comparatively small affairs financially. They have since become more costly. It now may cost £20,000 to sink a well. But here, as elsewhere, title is everything, especially as many small owners may have to be handled. Here people take mineral rights under leases, leaving to the owners the surface rights. The old term of a lease was usually twenty-nine years, but now varies, payments being by royalties, rents, or both, or by lump sums down. By legislation of 1914 no oil leases may remain unworked for more than ten years. This still holds good.

Commercial supplies of petroleum, says a high authority on this industry, are restricted exclusively to strata of sedimentary origin and to those of comparatively recent geological age, the Tertiary, which yield the bulk of the world's oil to-day. Except coal and iron, mining areas rarely coincide with oil-fields. Enormous quantities of sand are extracted with the oil. Guest says that he often has hundreds of men working all night to remove it. Sands are often thrown up for many days before the oil appears. Gas often comes up for weeks or months before oil in good quantity appears. But Roumania has some wonderfully rich fields. An area of one hundred and thirty acres at Moreni gave 4,000,000 tons in ten years, and in one single year (1913) gave nearly a million tons or 7000 tons (52,500 barrels) per acre.

One indication of oil is the poverty of the top soil when petroleum exists. Vegetation seems sterilised. There are injurious compounds in soil containing oil which have a very marked effect. But it depends on climate and geography. Much rain may counteract the effects. Where the rainfall is small, the vegetation is usually stunted or non-existent. The expert, as a rule, sneers at surface indications, yet most of the wells here and in Galicia were started on surface indications and against geological advice. Oil prospecting, like the higher finance, seems to be an art which nobody understands — though many think they do — nor can learn by textbooks. As for the engineering and geological science needed for the industry, this is of the highest order, and here in Roumania a General Manager who cannot speak Roumanian, German, and French, is of little use.

The petroleum industry cannot complain that it has been neglected of late, nor that 1920 was a bad year, even if the conditions of the silver market brought large profits which were alien to the industry in itself. Oil has been a political and commercial interest of a first-rate kind. It has figured in the Supreme Council; it has become of vast importance to navies and armies; it is being generally adapted to mercantile shipping. The tens of thousands of motor-cars turned out every week, all rely upon it: many railways — here for example — make use of it. The oil supply of the world seems below the demand. The life of the best well is not long. The calorific value, the saving of space, labour, and dirt, as well as cost, implied by using oil are great advantages. So, even if there is now a fall of prices, a good company, run by men of known integrity and competence, with good reserves of potential oil-fields, and a good specialised staff, is still worth following. The others are not.

The greatest trouble to such companies at present is the stupidity of Governments. All being short of money, and oil companies of the best class being rich or at least producing riches, it seems obvious and natural and just for Governments to squeeze them dry. But it is uneconomical. It is killing the goose that lays the golden eggs. The way to make use of the goose is to get hold of the golden eggs. These are the income of the share-holders, i.e., the profits of the companies, and the more the industry itself is assisted and freed from hampering restraints the more eggs there will be. The Governments are really saying to the goose, you must lay no more golden eggs, and we will take precious good care that you don't. One can draw more taxes, from a people taxed up to a certain point, only when they have more income, and, so far as regards oil, the more the companies are hampered the less the income. When one sees a company, like the Royal Dutch, taxed in 1915 some 8,000,000 florins and in 1920 80,000,000 florins, as well as forced to pay heavy export taxes in some countries, including Roumania, one can understand why there are fewer golden eggs in the possession of the tax-paying investor; why he is less inclined to speculate, and why the country which owns the wells eventually loses all industry. A fixed export duty is wonderfully silly and unjust. It is silly because it does not make allowance for prices, and forces curtailment of production. It is unjust because it is a subsidy to other companies working in countries which have no export duties. There should be an agreement between Governments on this subject, but they are too busy pouring out money on unproductive expenditure to care.

The best way for great companies to get on is to have holdings in all parts of the world, and to spend much money on research. The Royal Dutch understood this early, and the Americans late. It is an expensive business to send surveying parties far and wide, and to set the best engineers, chemists, and geologists on research work, but the companies which have done so have profited. Only companies with large means could afford it. Political troubles upset all calculations, as we have seen since 1914. Here in Roumania the social and economic conditions have had a disturbing influence upon oil. Transport difficulties alone have proved a serious obstacle. Extension, production, and refining have all suffered. The want of materials, especially for drilling and of electric power, have contributed to this result. The generating stations for electricity are in progress, but not completed. The large damage done in 1916 is not yet all made good, nor has a penny of indemnity yet reached the companies, four years after the harm was done to them. If the Government released its control of petroleum exports in July, 1920, there remained restrictions on the amount that might be exported, and also there were very high export duties. They have since been reduced and should be abolished owing to the fall in prices. The more stable the conditions of politics and trade the better the outlook for oil.

If, in a country exploited for oil, this industry enters the political arena; if certain parties in the State are known or supposed to be interested in one company rather than another, and if there are large State holdings in oil-fields which may be allocated to some favoured company, then the game is not a fair one, and an honest company may be playing against another using loaded dice. However, the Dutch at home and in the East Indies are as hide-bound about the economics of oil as anybody else. One should ask Deterling!

The American Minister and the Millington Drakes lunched with me under the trees at the Châteaubriand. We talked Eton — where all of us had been — Roumania, and diplomacy. Jay rather irate because the Roumanian F.O. here had said that they could not accept letters in English, which is the American rule, and Jay has no one who can draft a really good despatch in French. Drake told him our practice which was to write in French. Jay said that out of one thousand or more Americans at the Peace Conference in 1919, there were only two who could draft a letter in really good French. He thought that the best way of doing business was that of a certain American Minister at a Central American Capital. He went into his balcony with a police whistle and whistled once for the President, twice for the Foreign Minister, three times for the Minister of Commerce, and they came running round to him. I thought that Curzon and Hughes should agree to send all notes and despatches in English and let the foreigners write in their own languages if they liked. The sooner all the world spoke English the better. It had to come. French was splendid for lying or for love letters, but only an infinitesimal fraction of Anglo-Saxons were good at it. Millington Drake is one of this fraction and he learnt French as a child and talks it with a beautiful accent. I like him very much. He is active and energetic, very clear-headed, most industrious, and with the saving sense of humour. If only the F.O. would keep staff enough to let their young men — one at a time — travel in the country and get to know something more than the Capital and the *corps diplomatique!*

Mr. Jay told us to-day that the Standard Oil Company were not exporting from Roumania, owing to the export tax. Jay is an uncommonly nice fellow. A big, robust, active American with strong English sympathies, who could not be anything but straight if he tried not to be. He is in the regular diplomatic service and has been at Cairo and Rome, as well as in Salvador.

By the way, if I were a Roumanian, I would, in the conditions of to-day, take *"ense et aratro"* as my motto. It corresponds with facts, and recalls Trajan.

Had a talk with X after dinner at the Athene Palace Hotel. I begin to feel that the main danger to our large capital sunk in oil here is not from difficulties of production, increased cost of labour and materials, or even lack of transport and low prices, but from the uncertainty about the action, if not the honesty, of the Government which might declare oil a Government monopoly, or grant some rival companies large areas of oil-producing State lands, or in other ways make money by devious ways out of the companies. It is only by such means as this that political groups can reward their followers, for Governments have no money to throw about. I asked X about the Steaua-Romana Company. It seemed to me the mine which nearest rivalled the Astra-Romana. But was it not a German concern, and why had it not been expropriated? It had been by law, replied X, as all the enemy-owned mines were supposed to be taken over in part payment for compensations due from Germany. But then X gave me details of what followed, and I was highly entertained and enlightened by the story. X also told me that the Government were handing over some twelve hectares each to various small Roumanian companies, more or less as a gift, so one never quite knew where one stood, and this uncertainty about Government action was the main danger to British investors here. The French have a large holding in the Astra-Romana, both private investors and banks; in fact a larger holding than in their own companies. He told me to-day that he sent two trains a day to Constanza for export — eight hundred tons. The royalties paid to the peasant proprietors are ten, fifteen, and up to twenty per cent on profits. The boring tests have been little applied and it is probable that much more oil may be found further into the plains.

Monday, July 25, 1921. Hotter than ever. Spent two hours getting some money from the Bank of Roumania, and had a talk with the English Manager who is not an optimist. Changed my lei for lewas. Got my hair cut. The other men there were being manicured like ladies.

Lunched with Mr. Charles Spencer, Chairman of the Sheffield firm of Cravens Railway Carriage Company, who is here with his allied French group after the repairing contract. A very shrewd man with a good wit and judgement. He has been here since December, and was interesting as well as entertaining on the difficulty of doing business here. He has had a good look round and agrees with me that a large system of barter is the only means[1] of causing our trade to revive. But he would not give our Government the control of it, only the supervision. He would place it in the hands of business men of the Associated Trades, with a strong Labour infusion, and finance it through the banks, as big business abroad used to be financed. He thinks that the future of our trade is nearly hopeless unless this idea is taken up. Spencer has big and sound ideas. He told his French group that if there was any question of bribery here, he would take the next train home. He says that once you begin this practice, you have to bribe everybody down to the office boy, and that it breaks you in the end, apart from the immorality of the proceeding. He says that the Roumanians think that anyone — a plumber or a motor-car mechanic — can repair a locomotive, whereas it is one of the most technical jobs in the world. It is the same for bridges, and one must know the exact effects of the extreme heat and cold here. I think that his firm will remain here to advise and finance the repairs and that he will get his contract in time, as he does not like failure. He tells me that a 104-ton locomotive costs £14,500 in England and the same article £8500 in Germany. He thought that the German low prices and

---

[1] Later on I discarded this opinion.

long credits mean Government support. I thought that it might be so, but that cheap coal and food, and the German acceptance of low wages and standards of living, were enough to account for it all, while the low exchange in Germany was a fearful handicap to us. He did not see how we were to make money by exporting goods abroad now, nor how we were to lower the cost of living in England if we did not. We had a long talk over the commercial deductions from my tour over Europe. He was sick about the drastic cutting-down of the Oversea Trade staff in London, and said that they were invaluable. They could, at any moment, present our traders at home with any facts and figures needed, and they had all the reports from men like Alexander Adams here, whom Spencer rates highly and calls a ticket index. He introduced me to two of his French group who were lunching near us. One was a very nice fellow, Colonel Lebert, who was at the French G.Q.G. most of the war. Another was a shrewd and amusing M. Strauss, a Portuguese Frenchman, who described the Roumanians as *livresques*, saying that they had read everything and were very intelligent, but could *do* nothing and were not practical. It was the same in Rio de Janeiro, of which Bucharest much reminded him. Spencer had hoped that the twenty-six per cent duty on German goods would enable us to compete with them. I told him that it would not, and his own figures for the locomotives proved it. I was even dubious about a fifty per cent duty. We must get our coal and labour cheaper and hours longer or the Boches would win the Peace. Spencer thought that the elimination of waste was a leading advantage of the German system. He asked me if the Germans were keeping down the exchange on purpose, and I said that it looked like it, but I could find no evidence of it. Spencer thought that the only people here who were all right were the peasants. He thought that there were many men in the highest posts who could not be bribed.

Tuesday, July 26, 1921. Started 5.30 A.M. by car to Giurgiu (Giurgevo). A horrible road full of holes choked

with dust, a beast of a car which, after bringing its only
spare tyre into use, broke down again soon afterwards.
Crawled into Giurgevo and transferred to a carriage.
Only a few minutes to show passports and pass douane.
Crossed the Danube on the steamer. The river eight
hundred yards broad. Found myself stepping ashore in
Bulgaria.

CHAPTER XII

¦BULGARIA

THE Roumanian Consul was very attentive. He and Mr.
Wincer, the British Vice-Consul, lunched with me, and in
the evening Mr. Wincer, and Mr. Coates of the Shell Company, dined with me at Frank's Restaurant. Coates
brought his Polish wife. Much talk of the situation here.
Coates has been at Varna, where three weeks ago there
came in from Odessa a motor-launch carrying seven persons, under the red flag, and transferred money to one
Brons-Boroevitch, who is possibly running the Bolshevists
here. They say that he was Lenin's secretary in earlier
days. They say that the Bulgars spend their time discuss-

ing politics. Coates is organising the Shell business in Bulgaria. A smart and pleasant fellow. He puts down the sale price of gas oil at three to four pounds a ton, and the Roumanian export duty on it at one pound a ton; kerosene (lamp oil) — market price six pounds a ton, export duty two pounds; benzine — market price twelve pounds a ton, export tax four to five pounds. It will thus be seen how heavily Roumania hits this trade, when the cost of production is considered.

I went to look at the headstones of the graves of the two British officers who fell here in 1854. They were William Meynell, 75th Regiment, and James Burke, R.E. The graves were in good order. There are nearly eighty of our men of the Salonika Army buried in the cemetery here. Part of the price of that odious Salonika strategy. I think that troops of more nations must have passed up and down the Giurgevo-Bucharest road during the war than over any other in Europe. Wincer does not think much of the various folk in this part of the world. He says that they usually lie, and always lie about each other. There are 40,000 people in Rustchuk, and 10,000 of them are good Jews of Spanish origin, who practically possess the trade of the town. Had to spend the whole day at Rustchuk, as the train does not start till midnight. No attempt has been made to suit the convenience of travellers between the two capitals.

Wednesday, July 27, 1921. A strange day. Very hot, of course. We traversed Bulgaria. Not so naturally rich a country as Roumania, but fairly well cultivated. More wheat than in Roumania. It is mostly cut and carried. The straw ricks are massed by battalions, ricks varying from ten to fifty tons; a fire would destroy each group. A few agricultural machines at work. The main standing crop is maize, but vegetable marrows are popular, and I think that they are cutting a second crop of hay. I saw some large herds of cattle, trek-oxen mostly, I fancy, handsome, upstanding, grey beasts; and herds of pigs; mostly near water. There were also some herds of black-

and-white cattle. In some cases there were pig bathing-
places cut out by the side of streams and fenced in. Here
the pigs were revelling in the mud and water, almost entirely covered and lying in crowds. I can't recall that I
have ever seen pigs so well looked after or provided with
bath-houses at home. There are also large flocks of sheep.
More black sheep in the flocks than I have ever seen anywhere. But then we are in the Balkans.

Plevna interested me. So far as I can recall the to-
pography, after the lapse of all these years, we passed
through the centre of Osman Ghazi's fortified camp, and
saw the positions so long assailed in vain by the Russians
in 1877. Skobeleff, the Grivitza redoubt, and the Roumanians who saved the situation, all come back to memory.
A fine tactical position such as the Turk would never miss,
but one example the more of the truth of the Napoleonic
maxim that he who remains behind his entrenchments is
beaten. As we approached the mountains — Balkans
mean heights — the ground became poorer, and finally we
threaded the gorges of the Isker with no other communications in the valley but the line, and with all the rest taken
up by the stream itself. The hills gaunt, severe, and repellent, but apparently passable anywhere by infantry and
mules, and covered with rough vegetation and scrubby
trees. We were ascending all the time, and finally de-
bouched upon the plateau where Sofia stands at a height of
1600 feet, surrounded by higher and distant mountains on
all sides, and fell into the city without any appreciable
warning at about 4 P.M., after a broiling hot, dirty, and
dusty journey, with nothing to eat or drink all the way.

An emissary of the F.O. Press Bureau, M. Achtardjieff,
met me and we drove to the Union Palace Hotel, where a
room had been taken for me. He told me that Stamboulisky had decided to leave for Switzerland to-morrow for
his holiday, and that my only chance of seeing him was
to-night. So I hastily made a toilet of sorts, despite the
fact that water had failed in the hotel, and then I visited
the head of the Press Bureau for an instant, transferred

into an elementary motor-car, and drove off to S.'s country house a few miles outside the town. A new place, recently built, cream-coloured with red tiles, consisting of farm house linked by a row of cowsheds to S.'s own house, a two-storied quite small building, with no window on the ground floor on the outside of the court, and I should say not more than two rooms on each floor. There was a small guard in one of the rooms below, orderlies, perhaps. Sir Charles Stewart Wilson, of the Reparations Commission, was just leaving and we exchanged a few words agreeing to meet again. With him was M. Boris P. Kissimoff. He is Minister designate for Athens, and seems to be S.'s chief man. I was shown up at once to the top of the little house, up wooden steps half covered with a drugget stair carpet without stair rings or rods, and met S. at the top. A big burly man nearly six feet high, with tremendous muscular development, inclining to fat, a large strong face with a little turned-up black moustache, ruddy complexion, brown eyes which often flashed fire, and a mop of curly black hair. I was interested to find myself with the *bête noire* of the Little Entente. We sat down at a table in the centre of the room, which seemed to be bedroom, study, dining-room, and audience chamber all in one. There is a bed at one end, a hanging place for clothes on the wall; a sideboard-cupboard with a few plates, dishes, and bottles; and four chairs. In this room is a window built out where S. can survey arrivals at the farm. There are two other windows. We sat down at the table. S. at the end with his back to the bed, I on his left, Kissimoff, who translated, facing me. Mentally I compared Chequers with these humble surroundings.

After a few formal remarks I opened the conversation by observing how much interested I had been by the story of S.'s conduct at the Council before the war, and that it was of historical interest, so I wished to hear S.'s own account of it, as his courage on that occasion appealed to me. He gave his account. It was on September 15, 1915. Yes, he had told Ferdinand that if he led the country into a disastrous war, he would have to answer for it, not only with his throne, but with his head. F. had almost fainted at the threat and his Ministers had crowded round him to support him. Danieff had told F. that the voice of Bulgaria spoke with S. F. had recovered, and glaring at S. said that other people might lose their heads as well as he, that S. was young, yet might lose his head before F. who was old and to whom life had not the same value as for youth.

But then Stamboulisky said to me that a higher test of his own courage came when the tribunal before which he was tried — a real Balkan tribunal it must have been — had caused him to be informed — or maybe the message had come direct from F. — that if he would recant and send a message to the Bulgarian Army that it should march unitedly under F. in the good cause, his life should be spared. He took an agonising half-hour to weigh his reply. He was young and loved life and activity intensely. On the other hand was his personal and political honour. He decided to refuse, but came back into the dock with a pistol concealed about him, determined to take his own life in the court if he were sentenced to death rather than trust himself to his executioners. But F. must have feared to murder the peasant's favourite at such a moment, so he had him clapped into prison for life by the judges instead.

He had seen F. only once since, and this was when the Revolution had begun and F. was about to leave the country. F. had asked him to go and calm the Army. At this last talk with F. he had told the fallen monarch that Bulgaria could get on with Boris because he would make a good constitutional monarch which F. could never be. That was his last communication with him and Boris was present.

Now that the ice was broken and I had found S. in an expansive mood, I asked him if I might speak quite frankly to him. Yes, he replied, the pleasant and the unpleasant. I laughed and said that I was coming to the unpleasant. There was a strong suspicion that he was negotiating with the Soviet and the Turks of Kemal. I asked him to explain to me the Nikolaieff mission and that of Grozkoff; the arrival of Commissaries at Varna; the presence of Djevad at Sofia, and to give me his own views on these events, and on the general situation in Russia and in Turkey.

S. said that Nikolaieff's mission was as Nedkov had already explained to me.[1] But the sufferings of the Bulgarians in Russia were much on his conscience, and he could not desert them. He therefore hoped that he might attain his object through the good services of the Czecho-Slovak State which was in relation with Russia and aspired to the leadership of the Western Slavs.

"Do you reckon yourselves to be Slavs?" I asked. "How do your people generally regard the Russians to-day apart from the Soviet régime?" "We are Bulgarians first and Slavs only afterwards," S. answered. "In the days of older men like you, Kissimoff," he went on — and I asked to be included in the Kissimoff generation category — there was strong pro-Russian feeling. There was all the story of 1877–78, the statue of the Tsar-Liberator which I have since seen before the Sobranje, and the subsequent history of that period. But now Bulgaria was emancipated from leading-strings. Events, and particularly the doings of Generals Kaulbars and Skobeleff in 1882 and the succeeding years, and the Russian design rather to use Bulgaria as an instrument of policy than as a friend, had embittered many, and last of all came the war in which the Bulgarians had fought the Russians. But, yes, certainly the Bulgarians were Slavs, though it did not supersede the fact that they were Bulgarians first.

And the Soviet, how long would it last? S. was of opinion that it could not last long. He had reports that Trotsky had been arrested and was in prison. Lenin was becoming more moderate and the peasants generally were bitterly opposed to the Bolshevist régime. But what would follow was a problem. It might be chaos or there might be a constitutionalist-monarchist revival or even absolutism. He inclined to think that a federation might come out of

<hr>

[1] See entry for July 17.

it, as all the various parts of Russia stood for their own
autonomy. But no one could say. The Soviet had hoped
that the Turks would be beaten by the Greeks, as then the
Turks would call upon the Reds for men as well as for arms,
but their hopes up to a recent date had been disappointed.
Did I know that the Soviet and the Kemalists were allied?
Yes, since March 16. "Well," S. went on, "then you may
or may not know that Kemal has forbidden Red propaganda in Asia Minor and has even hanged six Red propaganda agents. It is only extreme need that could ever
make him accept Red help as such. He wants, and accepts
readily, money and arms."

Grozkoff had returned and S. had seen him this morning
at the little house where we were talking. G. had no political mission from S. He had gone off on a contract for
tobacco and supplies, had been to Kemal's H.Q., had seen
and heard many interesting things, but had no political
negotiations. Kemal had told him that the Greeks might
beat him, but that he did not mean to be rounded up. He
would retire to regions where the Greeks could not get at
him and would continue the war until the Greeks gave in.
He said that Kemal had 200,000 men. The Bulgarians
took a certain interest in this war because it was between
neighbours and it was generally known that there was no
love lost between Bulgarians and Greeks. Yes, I said,
everybody here has plenty of enemies. There is Roumania
with three hostile people on her borders and Bulgaria with
at least as many. But between that and disturbing the
peace of Europe was a wide gulf, he said, and he went on to
assure me of Bulgaria's good intentions.

Yes, money had been sent to Bulgaria. It had come
from Constantinople in Turkish pounds. He professed not
to know much of the Soviet missioners to Varna, and not
to know Brons-Boroevitch's name. I gave him the details
which I had learnt and he neither accepted nor rejected
them. Some Reds had come to Varna, but had immediately gone off again (after depositing their cash, I imagine). But the Bulgarians were not intriguing with any

people and only asked to be left in peace. That is his attitude.

I remarked that after what S. had told me of his past relations with the ex-Tsar Ferdinand, I need not press him about his supposed intrigues with F. No, indeed, he said, after what has passed all Bulgaria is against him. "I wonder what the old villain ["sinner," *greishnik*, Kissimoff translated it alternatively] is doing now!" S. did not mention the initiative of his Minister at Vienna, as he certainly would have done had he felt reason to plead good intentions, so I said nothing of it either.

As for Djevad — he is Djevad Abbas, not Djevad Hassan — he was still here and the Government had had no communication with him.[1] He was under the surveillance of the Police. The Bulgarians were always being accused of things that they had not done. The War Minister here (Dmitroff) had been charged with visiting F., but he had not done so. Whom did S. wish me to see while I was here? I asked. "You can see whom you like," he replied, "but be pleased to remember that the Government is always attacked, and be sure to realise the motive of criticisms."

"The great thing in life is to be prepared for death," he said. "Every time I go out I ask myself if I shall ever return to this house, and so I place in order and on record the Government business for the next day so that the functions of Government may not be suspended by any fate of mine. Yes, one must be prepared for death," he mused, "and then one can·face events calmly." I was not much taken aback by this insecurity that the head of this Bulgarian Government feels. There have been too many murders in the past to wonder. But I think S. is jumpy. Kissimoff said that S. had built this house and now lived here because he felt the need of being often alone to ponder over his problems. I think, too, that this great Samson of a man — he reminds me of Rembrandt's picture and his biceps would turn Dempsey green with envy — has assassination on his

---

[1] Kissimoff had received him as a private person. D. had asked to see S. and had met with a refusal. So M. Kissimoff told me later.

nerves. When anything drove up to the farm he hastily looked out of his built-out window with unconcealed uneasiness, and when anyone came upstairs he was palpably anxious and went out to see who it was. I expect that governing Bulgaria is a fairly wearing duty, and that iron muscles may ill-conceal very distraught nerves. He told me, as one of his reasons for living here, that he felt the need for an hour's gymnastics every day, and I do not wonder when I think of his exuberant physique and masculinity. This curious contradiction in him — his love of combat and yet dread of personal consequences — perhaps explains partly his position. He is a peasant born and bred. He is a Balkan Highlander whose theatre of action for preference is the mountain, and with target and broadsword would be an uncommonly ugly customer. He would fit perfectly into the picture of Scotland in Mary Stuart's days. But steel nerves are better than muscles in these days, for the bomb and the pistol make no account of muscle and the smallest imbecile may bring down his Goliath. The particular psychology of S., combined with the fear of some countries round of the fighting powers of the Bulgarians, who are indeed the Prussians of the Balkans, explain much here. Kissimoff told me that they knew well whence came the hostile reports of Bulgarian intrigues. So do I, but I merely said that they did not originate in British sources. No, they did not, K. replied, but they were repeated in English papers. "That is why I am here to make an independent inquiry," I answered.

In a dramatic fashion when S. had reached this point of his story to me, the King (Boris) was announced. S. did not go down to receive him. He just let him come up, *sans façons*. The young King came in. A most striking contrast with his Prime Minister. The King is twenty-seven, slight and slim, quite good-looking, with good features, grey eyes, and a charming, gentlemanly manner. He sat down facing S. and we went on.

After a few civil remarks from the King, who said that he had come on the same mission as I had, namely, to see

S., before his departure, I rose to go. But S. had more that he wanted to say to me and kept me there for some time longer, talking of many matters. He particularly asked me to deal with the question of the reparations which perhaps were on his mind after Sir Charles Stewart Wilson's visit. S. said that he thought the work of a Reparations Commission ought not to interfere with the internal affairs of an independent country. I replied that it was difficult to know where to draw the line since the whole duty necessarily interfered with every part of the internal administration and had done so in Germany and was doing so. King Boris expressed his agreement with this point of view. Then S. went on to plead for time in payments and gave his arguments in support of his desire, mainly pleading the fall of the lewa. He made a third point of the need of Bulgaria for the economic outlet on the Ægean which the Treaty had promised her. The conversation went on for about a couple of hours and covered so many subjects that I think I will ask Kissimoff to give me his recollection of it to check mine.

I had the curious feeling, on leaving gentle King Boris alone with his large and robustious peasant Premier, that I was leaving him rather unprotected! However, I chaffed S. and told him that in the Swiss mountains he could double his hours devoted to gymnastics. "Yes," he said, "and as I steam out of Sofia I shall lift my arms to heaven and thank God that I am a free man!" I thought — *patriæ quis exsul* . . . and took my leave. What a strange experience! Surely I have been living these two hours in Anthony Hope's Ruritania!

Dined at the hotel. Was famishing, having eaten nothing for thirty-six hours. Bulgarian sour milk with compote is a dish for the gods. Bulgarian caviare is almost in the same category. From the sublimely fantastic to the ridiculously material!

Thursday, July 28, 1921. Captain J. W. Collins, *Times* correspondent, called before I was dressed. A nice young fellow. He thought that Grozkoff had really gone on a sort of contraband mission, in the profits of which members of the Government might have shared. He thinks Djevad has left, and says that Reshad Pasha is a more dangerous person and is here in the Kemalist interest. There is also a Bulgarian who seems to be called Atchkoff, who is said to be an agent of the Opposition, here with the Turks. Grozkoff's constituency is close to the Turkish (old) frontier. C. thinks that Stamboulisky did well in seeing Bulgaria through her troubles, and says that there has been no trouble at all since the Armistice, but that S. has a bad attack of swelled head and often makes violent speeches which go beyond what he intended to say. So the irreconcileables are out gunning for him, and party feeling is very bitter. Collins thinks that there is very little in the accusations against Bulgaria.

Went to the Legation to deliver a letter for Sir A. Peel, but as it was Bag day and the Chancery was in the condition, customary in these cases, of a household expecting an addition to the family, I did not ask for H.E. with whom I am dining to-night. Saw Kissimoff again and we agreed to compare our recollections of the interview of yesterday. Tried to see M. Picot, but he is away for a month. A pity, as I wanted to size him up. Drove round the town, which is not large, but has attractions. It is well situated, and the view towards the Rhodope Mountains, over the red roofs, and gilded domes of the Orthodox churches, is quite fine. There are some good public buildings, notably the Sobranje, the Theatre, etc., and they are not pretentious nor over-large. Most of the houses are two-storied, the main streets are broad, with a good deal of shade. One gets out of the town in any direction in ten minutes and can then apparently ride anywhere. There is a club and good tennis courts, while the British Legation is quite a dignified building, very creditable to the Board of Works, far superior to that at Bucharest, at least outside. I am told that all Legations are to be built on the Sofia model [1] in future. But this must surely depend on climate, and I

---

[1] The Stockholm model, I am told, is even better.

hope that they will choose better sites than they have here. The provision of furniture by the Board of Works is a great benefit, and I must congratulate Sir Lionel Earle upon his handiwork. There are not the Bucharest crowds here, and in the best part the streets are broad, well-paved, and clean. Whether one can say much for the roads elsewhere I am dubious. But on a first impression Sofia makes its mark. The great and fine equestrian statue to the Russian Tsar-Liberator Alexander dominates all the *Place* in front of the Sobranje. How the Bulgarians can have had the face to take up arms against the Russians with this memorial in front of them is one of those mysteries that seem almost unfathomable. And with the portrait of Gladstone, it is said, in every peasant's house, they fought against us! Now they have to *payer les pots cassés* and they do not like it.

Spent the afternoon at the Roumanian and Greek Legations with M. Panourias, Greek Chargé d'Affaires, M. Trandafirisco, Roumanian Conseiller de Légation, Colonel Filimon, the Roumanian Military Attaché, and his colleagues, going through the list of Bulgarian iniquities and estimating the values of their present military organisations and forced labour conscription. I received much evidence of the Bulgarian intention to pursue the policy of Prussia after Jena. The Bulgars are trying with almost a minimum of camouflage to do what the Boches have failed to do under French activity and constraint, namely, to keep up their old Army. They are said to have 60,000 men all told instead of the 20,000 agreed under the Treaty; they have concealed their war material; and by this labour conscription they practically have the call to the colours of the whole population in their hands. The training of the men is said to go on from 1 to 3 A.M.! The Military Attachés tell me that Bulgaria, by her own figures, has a contingent of 40,000 men a year, and a total of 856,000 liable to serve. All this ought to be suppressed with a firm hand, but the Inter-Allied Military Commission under the French General de Fourtou is said to be trifling with the question, and the Council of Ambassadors in Paris seems to be poorly informed. The Bulgarians are only allowed, for example, three cavalry regiments. They have turned the rest of their eleven cavalry regiments into a so-called mounted gendarmerie. The gendarmes are allowed aviation, machine guns, and carrier pigeons! The class is divided into 20,000 men who serve regularly and 20,000 more who do nominally three months' service and are supposed to be part of the conscripted labour. One way and another Bulgaria is capable of placing a large number of men in the field, and I do not think that any soldier can read the Labour Conscription Law without seeing that it is compulsory service thinly veiled. I was also told of Yakovlaff Lippovitch and of the Soviet Commissaries Boris Tomski and Moes Voleinsk, from Odessa, and who had come to Varna in the Tamara motor-launch which left on its return journey July 10. One Prodkin, formerly Bulgarian Chief of Police, and now Inspector of National Navigation, is said to have made many visits to Odessa.

I told them frankly that their military case seemed to me proved, and they gave me photographic copies of reputed actual Bulgarian orders showing the spirit that prevails and how they are trying to hoodwink the Allies by false orders. De Fourtou is accused of being bribed, but I rather think it is the policy of his Government to take the place of Russia and pose as the protector of Bulgaria. This accounts for Picot's fatuous speeches. But, on the political side, there is only a lengthy series of accusations with no direct proof of actual negotiations with Kemalists or Reds. The ill-will and deception which seem proved on the military side show up the political charges, which are numerous, in a fierce light, and the least we can believe is that the Bulgarians have been playing with edged tools.

Dined at the Legation with my old friend Sir Arthur Peel, and Colonel Baird, now Military Attaché here and at Constantinople. Peel gave us an excellent dinner with good wine. We discussed the Balkans all the evening and they both threw a flood of fresh light upon the subject. Much talk of personalities and events here. Later Baird went off to a dance and Peel told me of his experiences in Brazil during the war. Home late.

Friday, July 29, 1921. Met Baird at the Legation in the morning and talked of the Bulgarian Army. He says that the Army is down to 20,000 men, but that the Compulsory Labour Law will give 36,000 to 40,000 more for a year's service which will be passed in barracks, and while he supports the Bulgarian contention that they cannot raise a Volunteer Army, he regrets the consent of the Supreme Council to the Compulsory Labour Law. He is more or less philo-Turk, and would give Constant[1] back to the Turks, Dedeagatch to the Bulgars, and make an Allied-rule zone in Thrace. He does not count the Allied garrison at Constant as more than one and a half divisions, and would like four to make the thing safer in case of crisis. The Russians, he says, are a great danger. They will not work and will not go away because they have nowhere to go. Wrangel is still with them.

He says that Atchkoff and Fuad are the chief Kemalist agents here now. Protogueroff, a Bulgar retired General, is chief of the Macedonian bands. Djevad probably knows most of the Thracian bands. There is undoubtedly co-operation between these various bands, but not with Government initiative or even approval. He thinks that there is a regular conspiracy against Bulgaria, and says that in these regions a Treaty is merely regarded as a jumping-off place for fresh adventures and intrigues, not as a permanent settlement. A very true judgement, I think. He deplores our propaganda at the end of the war. He has some of the leaflets dropped by our airmen, and says that they told the Bulgarians that if they stopped fighting they would be given the territory that was Bulgarian, whereas, what with Macedonia, the Dobrudcha, Tsaribrod, Thrace, and other places, nearly as many Bulgarians were now under alien rule as there were in Bul-

---

[1] One gets in the habit of calling Constantinople by this abbreviated name in these parts.

garia herself, and unfortunately all the people in these parts were totally devoid of the faculty for conciliation, and not one of them could rule over another. We had made an old-fashioned peace under false pretences, and he would much rather have said *væ victis* and parcelled out gains to the victors without professing high-flown sentiments which facts had refuted. The chief result for us was that we had totally lost the prestige which we had gained here before and during the war. Baird is like Dundas, a soldier who says what he thinks and does his duty without fear or favour. These people are an honour to us and it is a pity that our Government does not attend to them more.

At 11 A.M. went to the Palace to see King Boris and remained with him till 12.40 P.M. A good-sized house, much overcrowded with ex-Tsar Ferdinand's inartistic furniture and pictures. His talents seem to have been confined to architecture wherein atavism must have helped him. The room on the stuffy side and H.M. did not suggest smoking during our talk. We discussed in turn the Soviet and Turkish accusations, the state of parties here, the question of ex-Tsar Ferdinand, H.M.'s father, of the King himself, the internal state of Bulgaria, the bands and refugees, the Army, the need for a policy of prudence, the distrust of which Bulgaria was the object, the question of union with Serbia, and much more. H.M. began in English, but soon branched into French in which language he prefers to talk.

The King throughout talked with good sense and displayed a greater character and competence than I had expected of him. His good looks, rather fragile appearance, his diffidence almost amounting to timidity, and his superficial airs of a *petit-maître*, are not the real man. He is no drawing-room King, and while he has charm, good manners, and a deprecating modesty, I should say that he is working with sustained assiduity to master the rôle of sovereignty and will soon be superior in statecraft to any of his Ministers. I suspect that there is the stuff of a hero behind the courtly manner of the gentle King, but I am not quite sure. Time will show.

He told me that Stamboulisky had described to him our talk. He assured me again that all the charges against Bulgaria with regard to the Reds and the Turks were false. There had been no negotiations. Tobacco and cheese were Grozkoff's motives for his trip. With regard to Nikolaieff's mission there were a great many Bulgarians in Russia before the war and always had been. Many were caught there by the revolution and had been subjected to all the pains and penalties of Russians themselves. He wished to get them out, and I hope that Benès may help him to do so.

He asked me to consider the position of Bulgaria which had suffered dreadfully in a succession of wars and was much exhausted. He regretted that at such a moment a regular campaign of misrepresentation had been opened against her. He said that Bulgaria's enemies conducted this propaganda with a thoroughness, pertinacity, and absence of measure which Bulgaria could not rival, as she had neglected this side of statecraft and had not the means of her enemies for conducting it. Bulgaria sheltered 500,000 refugees from Macedonia, the Dobrudcha, Thrace, and Tsaribrod. She was the corridor through which passed from West to East and inversely all the uneasy spirits of the day. A regular *bouillabaisse d'éléments louches* had descended upon her and she was not an island like England and could not keep them out. From times immemorial fighting had gone on in these regions. The wars had increased the savagery of the people, and those without work or homes took naturally to fighting as the only trade they knew. The bands had even just recently attacked in broad daylight a Bulgarian town of 15,000 inhabitants — either Shumla or near it — and had then retired into the forests with their booty. He deplored the Dobrudcha raids, but his Army was so reduced that he could not cope with them. The Roumanians had posts of twelve men, whereas his posts were only two men.

He meant to carry out the Neuilly Treaty, but said that a Volunteer Army of 33,000 troops and police could not be raised for twelve years' service in Bulgaria, and still less the officers with twenty years' service. He would follow the counsel of the Allies, but hoped that they would understand the position. I said that I thought no one could unless they came here. The course of events, the facts, and the psychology of personalities here seemed to me closed books to our Occidentals.

He agreed, saying that nothing here resembled the conditions in Europe. He had a good, laborious, naturally quiet people, but the elements of disorder remained. A Volunteer Army could be recruited only from ne'er-do-weels and then they might become a Pretorian Guard, and act for one party or another, probably for the Communists like Austria's Army. A Bulgarian peasant would come out for a national training for a short time, but not for twelve years. Bulgaria had 80,000 men in peace before the war and now had to keep order with 20,000, and with many more imported disorderly elements in the country. I asked how the parties stood in Parliament. He said that Stamboulisky's Agrarian Party had about 120 members out of 240. The next largest were the Communists, then came the Right or Nationalist Party of Gueshoff and Danieff combined, then the Democrats, and lastly the small groups of Socialists, Radicals, and Democrats. He advised me to see not only Gueshoff and Bouroff, but also Stainov who was not a Deputy. I asked the King if he had any Council of the Crown or elder statesmen to advise him. No, he said, he stood alone. I am told that he goes to see Ministers instead of telling them to come and see him, because he likes to catch them unprepared with set speeches. He knows that this attitude is considered servile, but it educates him by making him conversant with the machinery of the departments. Later on he will assert more regal authority, and as Governments change he will naturally inherit authority as the only stable element and the depositary of traditious and consecutive policy. He told me that he was endeavouring to see Opposition leaders from time to time, but it was difficult, as all sorts of rumours at once flew about, and the practice was not much liked by the Government.

Then I told H.M. that I was going to be indiscreet. I had not said much to Stamboulisky about H.M.'s father, but I wanted to tell H.M. that the dragging of his father's name into the list of supposed iniquities of Bulgaria prejudiced her cause and should be glad if he would explain to me how the case stood. The King's manner at once changed and he displayed deep feeling. He told me how much statecraft he had learnt from him. He had been allowed to see all that went on from the *coulisses* and it had been a great education to him. When the break came, he felt that the only course in Bulgaria's interest was to make it a real break, and had consequently had no more direct relations with his father. This had been a great grief to him, but he felt instinctively that F. understood. He would have heard in some roundabout way had it been otherwise. He had only broken the rule when his Uncle Philip had died. Then he had sent a telegram of sorrow and condolence. He had not signed it Boris, but some other name which I did not quite catch. F. had replied to him in a kindred spirit and had signed by the name which he used when travelling and when he wished to remain *incognito* — the Marquis de Something, I think. There it had ended, and there had been no direct communication since. Even greater was the deprivation of the companionship of his sisters. He was devoted to them, and they always looked up to their elder brother for advice and guidance.[1] He spoke of them with deep feeling and came near to tears. The whole of this part of his conversation was most impressive and dignified, as well as pathetic. I could not help saying that his sentiments did him honour, and that I wished that the world could have listened as he spoke since the burden of kingship would have appealed to the hearts of all.

[1] I saw a portrait of one of them at Vranja later. She must be quite lovely. Her name is Eudoxia, I think.

After a little pause he went on to say that he well knew the distrust which Bulgaria inspired. It could be met only by fair dealing and a policy of great reserve. This was not much in the manner of the Bulgarian who in political affairs was a plain speaker, and a hard hitter, even violent at times. But people here were beginning to come round to him and to adopt this policy. As for any attempt to flout the Treaty or attack neighbours, he considered it madness and it could only be regarded as *harakiri*. There was Serbia with a million and a half of soldiers, Roumania with as many, and Greece with 800,000 or 900,000 mobiliseable men. What could Bulgaria do against them? I said that she could do nothing, and would only imperil her destinies and her existence if she tried to fight them.

There had been much talk, he said, about a union with Serbia. But there were memories and hates that rankled deeply, and he said that before union with other people came up, it would be well to see whether these same people could effect their own unity. I said, Yes, the Serbian Constitution has been fudged, but nearly as many members opposed or did not vote as supported Pachitch. There was never such a thing known in the initial vote of a Constitution of a country. Also it must be remembered that there is the dynastic question to be considered.

The King invited me to visit Vranja and asked me to telephone to the Maréchal de la Cour Courtoklieff when I wanted a car. There was an English gardener there called Delmar and he would show me round. I accepted with thanks. He also suggested other trips, but I said that I was leaving on Monday night and had so many people to see that I could only hope to see a gallery and museum or two. He telephoned to the F.O. to get the directors of these places to show me round. He also explained the stamp episode to me. An order for stamps given to Germany before the war had only recently been executed. They had the ex-Tsar F.'s head on them, and several had pictures of places now Serbian. Owing to the exigencies of finance, and by the thoughtless act of a P.-O. subordinate, these stamps had been recently placed in circulation. They naturally seemed to justify all sorts of rumours, but they had been almost immediately withdrawn. H.M. had not seen the Bulgarian postcard with Kemal's photo. An interesting talk which left a most favourable impression on me. A sympathetic figure and a great asset to Bulgaria.

After lunching with Captain Collins and his Bulgarian wife I took this diary to the F.O. and went through my Stamboulisky conversation with M. Kissimoff. His recollection of it required me to make only two or three minor changes in my text. He went on with me to the Museum where are most interesting Thracian sculptures, including many of the "Rider of Thrace," a sort of legendary St. George; many little bas-reliefs of the Three Graces, all showing Greek influence; icons and iconostases; many Roman, and also Bulgarian antiquities, with strong evidence of Scythian, Byzantine, and Ionian art; a fine set of coins, some fair bronzes, and a wonderfully fine hard red sandstone bas-relief of a man feeding a dog, dating 500 B.C. If only Bulgaria would keep quiet for a few years, her artistic history would be of great interest. It is in the churches and monasteries that one will best study it.

The Director of the Press came to see me at 5.30 at the hotel and we had coffee and a talk. I told him what I thought of the position here. There is a censorship of the press, but not of foreign telegrams, he told me.

Then went on to call on General de Fourtou whom I found to be quite a different person from what I had expected, and his information destroyed my best hope of being able to confirm English criticisms of Bulgaria on the military side. De Fourtou is not a Le Rond by any means. He is a bright, intelligent, and very alert Frenchman of a good type who declares that he is not a Frenchman here, but an Inter-Allied General who proposes to tell the truth as he sees it and to endeavour to administer justice impartially. The Little Entente States assure him that Bulgaria has 64,000 men under arms. He is positively convinced that she has not more than 33,000 soldiers and police and at the outside may have 3000 more to keep her numbers filled. The Reparations Commission can check exactly all expenses, and men could not be kept without being paid for.

We happened to get on to the subject of the papers which I have on misleading the Allies by false returns, and on the subject of Bulgaria's supremacy in the Balkans which is the main cue of another supposed paper by the present Bulgarian C.G.S. De Fourtou had received copies of both, as I had, and had showed them to the Bulgarian War Office and asked for an explanation. They promptly and decidedly declared them both to be forgeries. The paper about false reports dates from 1919 when Lupcheff was C.G.S. He was in Paris at the named date. The paper is not recognised and is countersigned by an officer who was never at the W.O. and is described as not of a rank conformable with that of an officer who would countersign a C.G.S.'s orders. The paper of July 12, the W.O. say, is not of a serial number known at the W.O. here, who offer to open their archives to any inspection and demand production of the original. Further, the heading given of "Chief of the General Staff" is never used. The heading used is "General Staff" only. They also say that *no* papers are signed on fête days such as was July 12, the date of the order.[1] This seems pretty damning, and I shall have to talk to the Military Attachés very straight when I meet them at the Greek Legation to-morrow. They are sure to have acted in good faith, I think, but if the W.O. are right they have been deceived by a forger.

I said to de Fourtou that this was a very serious matter, and that if the Allies did not look out they would land themselves in another Dreyfus case which would be hell. F. said that he had made the same remark to his Chief of Staff yesterday, and that the cases much resembled each other. F. had told them that he could not produce the

---

[1] I later inspected the original again with the Little Entente people. The date was in Bulgarian and rather blurred. We were not agreed whether it was June or July.

original, and admitted a mere copy or a photo was no proof. I said that I had seen the original, but did not know whether it could be produced, as the production might give away the agent who had abstracted the paper, or said he had. This wants a bit of thinking over. Will tell Peel in the morning, and then, if the Little Entente people have not already been told, will tell them and see what they think of the matter. We must put ourselves right in this matter, and promptly.

De Fourtou is already convinced that there is a dead set by the Little Entente against Bulgaria. I have been gradually reaching an identical conclusion. He says that his proposal to Paris about voluntary *versus* compulsory service has been a *via media*. He thinks that Bulgaria can get some 3000 volunteers out of her present Army, and perhaps 5000 a year thereafter. So in six years she *may* get her 33,000 men. He proposes to fill up the first year with men drawn by lot for four years' service. I told him that I agreed with this plan which I thought good and suitable. But Paris wired yesterday — the Council of Ambassadors — refusing the plan and tying down Bulgaria to a Volunteer Army. Moreover, Paris has foolishly accepted the Forced Labour Law with minor modifications in Articles 10 and 12, which do not change the main lines of the Act. De Fourtou and I agree that this is a serious mistake. So do all the Little Entente people.

As for war material, F. admits that some twenty guns may remain hidden — not more — but that the rifles will never be given up and there may be 80,000 to 100,000 left. The Serbs say 140,000. F. thinks that "sanctions" to extract them may be a remedy worse than the disease, for the Little Entente may enter Bulgaria and never leave. Each State wants something and who will put them out? I agreed, and said that I did not think that the rifles mattered. Even if they were given up, the Bulgarians could import them again later, as all Eastern Europe was stiff with rifles. It is a great pity that Baird went off to Constantinople to-day. Only yesterday he thought that the first of the secret papers was the most damning evidence of all of Bulgarian duplicity. There is hardly a leg left to stand on in the case against Bulgaria now, so far as proofs go. There is little left but suspicion and prejudice. This conviction stole over me after my examination of the F.O. *dossier* at Bucharest, but I have been insensibly trying to make it all accord with the English charges. These supposed forgeries, if they are proved, ruin the case on the military side, even if it remains true that Bulgaria wishes to retain compulsory service and has hidden many arms.

F. said that the atmosphere here was highly charged with electricity and that we were "*en plein pays balkanique*." Yes, I said, in the mountains of the moon, and the psychology could not be understood unless one came here. He had told Foch the same thing. We agreed that the Bulgarians were trying to camouflage their forces and arms, but also agreed, as others have agreed, that we should do the same in their place. He said that directly he received a report of concealed arms he sent it on immediately, straight from his desk, to his Italian colleague in charge of the armaments branch, but the latter always found the Bulgarians warned before he could act. It had been necessary to employ Bulgarians in the Commission and these people doubtless warned their friends. As for rifles, he could not deny that many were needed to protect peasants and farmers against bandits and wild beasts. Everybody was armed in this part of the world. I said that it all resembled a Drury Lane melodrama, and that as one emerged from the gorges onto the Sofia plateau one really entered a different world. Yes, and two hundred years behind ours, said F.

Saturday, July 30, 1921. In the morning went off for the Little Entente Conference at 11 A.M. Met at the Greek Legation M. Panourias, the Chargé d'Affaires, and the Military Attachés of Roumania, Serbia, and Greece. Of these a new hand to me was Colonel Néditch, the Serbian whom I had heard of as a capable man and so found him to be. His assistant, Commandant Vaféas, was also there. Colonel Joanidis, the Greek Military Attaché, I had also not met before. I told them all at once that there was a *fait nouveau* and informed them of de Fourtou's action and of the Bulgarian reply. It seemed to me that the only thing to be done was to test the accuracy of the incriminating reports and to abandon trust in them if their falsity was proved. It was impossible to build up a charge on forgeries, and I reminded them of the Agram trials and the Dreyfus case. Néditch at once said bluntly that a forgery would ruin the whole case, but neither Filimon nor Joanidis committed himself. Panourias, however, declared that of course the Bulgars denied everything. They always did, he said, and he began to bring out a lot of other papers on new subjects. I would not listen to him, and insisted that we should have out the two queried papers and examine them. We looked over the 12th July paper and there was a difference of opinion whether the Bulgarian original was June or July. I thought it was June, but opinions differed. We had a discussion, and then I begged Panourias to forgive me for saying what, as an old Intelligence officer, I should do. I should see my agent safely over the frontier and then place the original of the document before the Bulgarians and play a straight game by them. The inquiry which they had offered should be facilitated. The other document P. could not find for a time, but it is really in the same category. Copies of these papers were both shown to me at Bucharest where naturally they had influenced opinion. It seems that four agents — one French — have been murdered here in the last ten days for spying, so the game is a little warm.

P. packed me up a lot of new papers which I said that I would call for later and then excused myself for having to go off to see M. Dmitroff, the War Minister, who had fixed 12.15 for a talk. I asked Panourias what he was going to do. He said that he would do nothing. I said that it was not my affair, it was his, and I excused myself for speaking so plainly to him. He was the best judge of what action he should take.

Met Dmitroff with the Chief of the Press Bureau to translate. I forgot to warn him that I had not come for official replies. He knew nothing of the papers — de Fourtou must have taken them to the Chief of Staff — said that he was reducing the Army by another 4000 men, and hoped to keep order with the rest. He expressed himself determined to put down the bands and said that he had been condemned to death by the Macedonian Committee[1] for the action which he had already taken. Political life in the Balkans can be many things, but can never be dull. He only allowed that a few arms might have been taken by the peasants during the retreat, and on the whole was too precisely official for the conversation to be worth continuing, so I took my leave. None of this peasant Government can speak any foreign tongue. We cannot speak theirs. So all the materials for misconceiving each other's minds exist.

I was due to lunch with Panourias at the Union Club, and there found Filimon and Néditch with him again. P. informed me at once that after my departure they had discussed their course of action and had unanimously decided to meet my views. He was going to take the original of the document to de Fourtou to-day, as they had decided that it was the correct step. I said that I was very glad. We discussed the general situation. Panourias said that the withdrawal of the Compulsory Labour Act was of primary importance and I said that I agreed. The way these representatives of the Little Entente hate Bulgaria is a caution. They detest her for her past political crimes from which they have all suffered, and abominate her for the cruelties and indignities which her men heaped upon their prisoners during the war. Néditch said that the Bulgars had exterminated whole districts which they had intended to Bulgarianise and annex. They had killed all the intellectuals and men of mark and one hundred and eighty priests. The mere idea of being friendly with Bulgaria would make ev-

[1] Dmitroff and all his companions were murdered in October.

ery Serb's hair bristle. Panourias had already given me a very long list of recent Bulgarian raids into Greece. Filimon was no less hostile, but they all said that the Bulgar was a brave soldier in attack and defence and wonderfully obedient. They all agreed that the term "Prussian of the Balkans" was a true one. I asked why they seemed to fear such a little people. "We could, any one of us," they replied, "crush her now, but this is not the question. What we all know for certain and by tragic experience is that on the first occasion that we are engaged elsewhere Bulgaria will be stabbing us in the back. So it is our duty to render her harmless."

I happened to mention that I hoped to motor out to Vranja on Sunday. Filimon said that the wife of his Minister had two bombs thrown at her car as she drove there to see the King about ten days ago: joy-riding with compensations. Néditch told us a story to exemplify Bulgarian ferocity. In one of the wars the Serbs and Bulgarians were acting together against the Turks. Two columns, one Serb and one Bulgarian, were advancing together on parallel roads, each covered by cavalry which were in touch. Néditch was with the Serb Cavalry on the left. It was a strict rule of the Serbs that no rifle was to be fired on service except against the enemy. He heard many shots on his right and rode off to see what it was. He found that the Bulgars had coolly shot down every Turk — unarmed civilians — whom they met on the road. This happened constantly during the march, and at last Néditch rode over to expostulate. "Why make a fuss? There is one Turk the less," was all the answer he got. At last on the thirteenth occasion he rode over and told the Bulgars that they would be banned by Europe for their shameless murder of harmless civilians. "What do you expect?" was the reply, "we are making war, and to make war is to kill your enemies." I do not feel sure that the Bulgars deserved to be the special pets of our Radicals for so many years.

Dined with Peel at the Legation. He had kindly asked Drs. Gueshoff and Majaroff to meet me. The former was formerly Prime Minister, and the latter Foreign Minister and also Minister in London where we had met. Both are steady and experienced men and talk English fluently. They are among the most prominent members of the Opposition groups. Gueshoff is quite old. If Stamboulisky had taken Majaroff into his Cabinet to manage foreign policy he would have done better. We had a most pleasant give-and-take talk on Bulgarian affairs. They think Stamboulisky will not last long, as he is too violent and his speeches too unrestrained and braggart. His party are said to be tiring of him. Gueshoff contemplates an alliance with the Democrats and expects a great change of votes at the next election. Peel does not think that a Ministry can last long when it has all the intellectuals and the brains of the country opposing it.

The two Bulgarian authorities both affirm that Stamboulisky knows nothing of foreign political affairs and is rash and adventurous. He has probably not intended to make treaties with the Turks or Soviets, but has been playing with fire, desiring to pose as a great Panjandrum, and has been quite surprised at having alarmed Europe. We discussed the Grozkoff and Nikolaieff missions. It is quite possible that the former was only sent for loot by some of his friends here. As to Russia, there are some 200,000 Bulgarians there and the interest of Bulgaria in their fate is legitimate. The Bulgarians could all understand Russian. They were small traders, market gardeners, professional men, etc. Gueshoff asked me how Bulgaria was thought of by the countries round. I said that a frank answer to that question would be that the Bulgarians were detested by the neighbouring States on account of their cruelty and indignities to prisoners, and that they were feared because it was believed that they would seize the first opportunity to attack their neighbours and stab them in the back when they were engaged with some other enemy. Gueshoff said that he had been in charge of the Red Cross, and had constantly urged the importance of the kindest treatment of prisoners. Bulgaria had even demanded an inquiry into the treatment of prisoners, but the States round her had rejected the proposal.

It seems that Bulgaria is still under the influence of the change made during Ferdinand's time in Article 17 of the Constitution. This change enables the Government to sign a Treaty without submitting it to the Sobranje unless it contains financial clauses. Peel says that this change, when made, caused much distrust of Ferdinand in Russia. Some talk of the older Balkan times and Gueshoff promises me his book [1] about the period. They are dubious about Serbia's new Kingdom, and consider that the difference of religion of its main components, the desire of the parts for autonomy, and their dislike of the Belgrade centralisation, will hold things up. They do not much believe in a Bulgar-Serb combination, on account of prevailing bitterness, but do count a pacification with Roumania as among things open to them. The possibility of the marriage of King Boris with a Roumanian Princess is frequently discussed. Majaroff said that Boris would probably look first to the political interest of Bulgaria in his marriage and I think he will, as his sense of duty appears so strong. M. said that Boris's qualities were those of his mother. But I cannot refuse a tribute to Ferdinand for his judicious architectural and other improvements at the Capital. I like Sofia. The position is really wonderful, and there is a great charm about the little place, even if, off the main streets, one gets into impossible roads and shambling houses, almost bazaars. The climate is far preferable to Bucharest and the nights are cool. There are few flies, and though our Legation is in the dog-barking zone, my hotel here is out of it. Sofia, to Bucharest, is what the hills are to the plains in India and I am hating my return to the plains.

After Peel's guests had gone, we talked of the application of "sanctions" to Bulgaria to compel her to adopt voluntary service and disarm. Peel was against sanctions and said that Colvin, head of our Reparations Commis-

[1] He sent it to me next day and I found it very interesting.

sion, would deplore them.   I said that I agreed.   The conspiracy against Bulgaria by the Little Entente was obviously continuing in London and Paris and seemed to me a real danger.   If the Little Entente entered Bulgaria, they would arouse all the uneasy spirits of the Balkans, and would then each take its slice of the Bulgarian cake and eat it.   We should never get them out, for they were allies and would support each other, so the remedy was worse than the disease.   I thought that de Fourtou's plan for the Army here was serviceable, and I did not think that we should worry about the concealed arms, as it was really quite a trifling matter.   What really mattered was the Compulsory Labour Law and I supposed that the F.O. did not understand it.   There is, however, some indication that France is behind Bulgaria, as Picot's speeches have proved, and that France's object is to use Bulgaria for the rape of Thrace from Greece in order to support France's designs and finance in Turkey.   This was troublesome, and complicated the situation.   I thought that the Great Powers should issue a warning to all concerned that they intended to see the terms of the Treaties carried out with rigid precision and would not permit any changes in existing territorial arrangements.   Our real trouble in these parts seemed to me the failure to enforce the Sèvres Treaty. This weakness had allowed every confessed and unconfessed ambition in the Balkans to revive.   Peel is to talk it over with Colvin in the morning.   He leaves for home August 15.

Sunday, July 31, 1921.   M. Petco Stainov, son-in-law of M. Majaroff, and the man whom the King wished me to see, came round this morning, bringing a copy of Gueshoff's book on Balkan affairs.   I asked him to give me a brief sketch of the situation as he saw it.   He told me that the news was out this morning of the decision of Paris about restricting Bulgaria to a Volunteer Army, and that it had created great anxiety among the best people, for they did not know how such an army could be formed, nor the gendarmerie which was at present also on a compulsory basis, and, failing these, they did not know how order could be preserved in the country. The position of the King, he thought, would become very difficult. I agreed that it might be hard to raise the Army, but said at the same time that not much real effort to raise the Army had been made. Stainov writes in the *Mir*, Majaroff's paper.

Turning to the general situation, he said that Bulgaria was suffering from an exaggerated fit of democracy. The mass of the people were extremely Left, almost Sovietic, but obviously the extreme Bolshevist ideas, including expropriation of land and goods, could not be applied to a nation of small peasant proprietors. The people were tired of war and disillusioned by its results. They were finding that their political ideals could not be carried out and they owed the Agrarians and Stamboulisky a grudge in consequence. The Agrarians had definitely excluded all people from government except themselves, and so the Opposition had all the brains, culture, experience, and knowledge. Except the Minister of Commerce, no Minister could speak a word of any language but his own. Even at the Foreign Office there were only four or five men who knew any foreign language. The best men dropped out because they found that their knowledge and aptitudes were rather sneered at than esteemed. There was therefore no call to them to stay when their pay was only some one thousand lewa a month — say four pounds.

He regarded Stamboulisky as having passed the zenith of his power. His influence was now on the decline. The best peasants had seen that they wanted more than their leaders could give them. The party suffered from lack of experience in all walks of political life, and this was particularly noticeable in foreign affairs of which they did not know the rudiments. Stainov did not dislike Stamboulisky, and thought that his aim was sincere. He did not imagine for a moment that he had intended to make a treaty with the Kemalists or the Reds. Had he so intended he would have selected one of the very numerous Bulgarians at Constantinople who went about with a fez in almost Turkish dress so as not to suffer at Turkish hands, spoke Turkish, had many Turkish friends, and could have slipped over to Asia Minor without attracting any notice. Grozkoff was a peasant and wore peasant dress with baggy trousers and a broad red scarf round his tummy. It was enough to look at him and speak to him to realise his unsuitability for his supposed mission. But he was rather proud of the stir that he had made in the world, and it seems that he crossed in a boat which took over to Kemal a French political agent formerly with General Wrangel. S. thought that Grozkoff had really gone on business, as he was a leading light of the Consortium.

Stamboulisky, thought S., was a most quaint character. He was highly strung, could never sit still, and never looked one in the face.[1] He was afflicted with manias. One was for travel, and he had been all over the place at home and abroad. The question was now less whether Stamboulisky would fall, but rather who would succeed him. However, we have heard this often about other P.M.'s, and they are not so easily displaced when they have a working majority.

I went on to see M. Panourias and to get the rest of the papers from him. He has, to my vexation, ratted since yesterday, and did not take the original of the dubious paper to de Fourtou. I made no remarks, as I had already given my views, and Sir A. Peel had approved of them last night. P. went on to say that Allied officers had been killed here, besides several agents, and that sixty persons were on a list for assassination, so it was a serious matter to put himself forward. There was nothing to be said in reply to this argument. He has quite a mania for secret reports and thinks more of their damaging effect than of their origin and authenticity. We had an hour's talk over Balkan affairs. Panourias has been very active and useful and I am much indebted to him.

The King's car came for me in the afternoon with his Private Secretary and we motored out twelve kilometres

---

[1] This is not noticeable when one converses with him through an interpreter.

to Vranja, the ex-Tsar Ferdinand's creation and favourite abode. A park some few kilometres square, with woods, ponds, gardens, and farm, all created in the last fifteen years. A house in old Bulgarian style, specially attractive at the back, as the front is much shut in by woods, and the front door has a hideous glass and iron hot-house sort of a place for entrance. Mr. Delmar, in general charge of the place and gardens, whose mother was English and father Spanish, met us and kindly took us round. There is a Tyrolese Alpine gardener who has had many successes. Some good rock-gardens. The cows turned out to be Swiss. Bulgarian cattle are poor eating and the cows give little milk, they say. I am told that there are some white water-buffalo, very rare, but we did not come across them. The inside of the house very German. Each room a different style. The most successful is the Russian dining-room all in light wood resembling rosewood. A portrait in icon style of the King's mother, large in size, was a striking and even superb work, and there was a good deal of interest of one sort or another. The Victoria Regia house, with its huge water-lilies from the Amazon and the Ganges, quite a feature: the tray-shaped leaves some six feet broad. Going back I was pointed out the many empty spaces in the town where various fine public buildings had been planned, but not begun owing to the wars. Sofia would have been quite a fine town by now had peace reigned since 1912.

The P.S. told me that the King did not think that marriage festivities accorded at all with the sufferings of his people. He is twenty-seven, but prefers to wait. He led a lonely life. There was only his small personal staff at the Palace. He drove himself out to Vranja most evenings about 6 P.M. Ferdinand preferred to live at Vranja. Bulgarian was the King's mother tongue. He was popular with the people, sharing in all their life and visiting their cottages. He was a real democratic King and much more popular than Ferdinand who would never condescend to be near his people.

Monday, August 1, 1921. Made some farewell visits, and

amongst others saw M. Raditch, the Serbian Minister, with whom I had a fruitful talk. He told me that he had been much impressed at first by Stamboulisky, who was much more interesting to talk to when one knew Bulgarian, as he was a fine speaker with a happy faculty for phrases and seemed sincere. He was rather brutal than mealy-mouthed, in order to give the full effect of his meaning. But in time R. lost faith in S.'s sincerity and thought it only a pose. S. had endeavoured to come to some arrangement with Belgrade, and had visited R. on the subject. S. had later denied that he had had the conversation or had even visited Raditch, though witnesses had seen him there! What S. had said to R. was that the Black Sea ports alone were no good to Bulgaria nor the Adriatic ports alone to Serbia, and that the two States should combine to sweep down to the Ægean. That was S.'s view, but Raditch could not recall on word favourable to Serbia and was persuaded that when Bulgaria had gained Thrace she would then turn against Serbia and attack her.

Yes, S. had nerves, and the Macedonians, who secretly ruled Bulgaria, were the cause. There were some 200,000 in Bulgaria, but the really dangerous part of them was the extreme revolutionary party which numbered some 10,000 men. They influenced all Bulgarian life. They thought nothing of murdering a man. They had murdered ten people during the past month, and not in one case had the murderers been caught. S. had told R. that he meant to dispose of them in a month or two. "How will you do it?" asked R. "By knocking some thirty of the leaders on the head, then the rest will keep quiet." Kemal, by the way, had asked the comitajis to concentrate upon Thrace and not Macedonia. Very sound from his point of view.

S. did not hesitate to strike when it was in his interest. He had addressed a Congress of his party this year and had told them that they had overcome some of their enemies. "We have knocked the Army on the head [*assommé* was the word used by R. to me] and then the Church in this Sodom and Gomorrah of a town Sofia. We have turned the priests out and sent them up the mountains to be nearer God. But there is still danger, and at the first warning you must enter the village, seize your enemies, and then 'the stick to the head'" (a Bulgarian saying, but for a Premier a trifle terse).

R. did not consider that the Government was really constitutional. It was a tyranny and S. mocked at the Constitution and did as he pleased. The famous Article 4 of the Law on the National Catastrophe was a political weapon in his hand. So long as his enemies kept quiet, nothing was done, but directly they gave trouble they could be arrested under this article, thrown into prison, and their goods be sequestrated. It was no wonder that the Allies had protested or that the money of richer men had left the country and that the lewa had fallen. R. thought that S. would probably meet with a violent death. The Agrarian Party was organised better than any other except the Communists. The bourgeois parties were less well-organised and fought among themselves. When S. had asked the Reparations Commission for time to pay, owing to the fall of the lewa, the Commission had agreed with the proviso that Article 4, and the Consortium which was hampering commerce, should be withdrawn or suspended. The Consortium was a Government buying and selling machine. It was useful to S., as he rewarded his political friends by posts in it. But they knew little of commerce and so found much wheat unsold and so on. The system was a handicap to the country and was best left to merchants who understood it. S. survived, for one reason, because he never let it be known where he was going nor when. It was his chief precaution, and he was well-guarded. M. Raditch gave me copies of the Kemal postcard supposed to have been officially printed here, and Colonel Néditch, whom I saw afterwards, showed me the distribution list for the copies of it which were sent out, or to be sent out, by the Ministry of the Interior. There were 300,000 to go to Western Thrace and so on. The cards were to be sold at a high price to sympathisers and the money was to go to

Kemal. I wonder how much cash would ever have reached the latter! I think the matter was arranged by Atchkoff and Djevad Abbas. I gave one copy to M. Kissimoff who wanted to trace the *provenance* of the card, and asked him to send it on to King Boris who had never seen it and to whom I had promised a copy if I got hold of one. He also told me the story of the quinine reported stolen from Bulgarian stores and traced to Kemal. Raditch is a competent and well-informed Minister, well worth consulting.

In the afternoon I saw Sir Charles Wilson. He said that the Reparations Commission could not balance the Bulgarian Budget if Voluntary Service were introduced, as it was too costly. I found that his ideas and mine were in accord, and he says that Colvin has identical views. The only difference between us is that Sir Charles thinks that the Bulgarians have made a serious attempt to introduce Voluntary Service and that I am not sure that they have. They made a great splash about it some time ago and sent deputies round to propagandise. There was a statement that 6000 offers of service had come in. What happened then is uncertain, but from one cause or another the returns of men enlisted grew smaller and smaller, until it appeared that only three hundred men had actually joined the Army. Sir C. thinks that a Volunteer Army may be formed some day, but is at present contrary to the custom of the people. It would make it possible for *coups d'état* to take place, and even for Communism or Bolshevism to develop. The situation here was evidently not understood at Paris. He thought the Bulgars a good steady people, not attractive, but very well-behaved to foreigners. The Agrarian Government are babies; not clever babies, but cunning babies. They walk straight into any traps set to catch them. They had tried to keep a thick mattress between the Commission and the facts, but had been forced to give up this practice.

His view is that no permanent peace will result until Thrace is returned to Bulgaria and Macedonia is made independent. He has been in Thrace and says that the country is full of Greek troops, but that no people have an absolute majority there. He declares that the French can no longer be considered our allies. They are always working against us. He says that the Bulgarians want our support and would prefer it to any other. There are three Frenchmen here and they are all antagonistic, Picot the French Minister, Cérisey on the Reparations Commission, who is senior to Picot and finds the latter above him here, and a third, whose name I forget, who did a curious service for some highly placed person at home and has been rewarded by a sinecure here, namely, the patronage of French holders of Bulgarian bonds. They unite only in opposing de Fourtou, who has the best house of the lot and gives himself airs, they say.

Left for Bucharest at night and arrived late on Tuesday evening. A motor-car met me the other side of the Danube and jolted me back safely. Bucharest uninhabitable on account of the curiously exhausting heat. This part of the world is not a white man's country during July and August. Irak and the Sudan are refreshing in comparison.

Wednesday, August 3, 1921. Managed to get tickets and sleeper for Paris for to-morrow. They make one pay in French francs, and the amount much exceeds what one is allowed to take out of France in French money. So one has to buy French money from the smugglers or get no seat! A new and amusing form of robbery, but the traveller gets fleeced at every step in the East of Europe. Lunched with Colonel Terbutt, Colonel Lébert, and M. Strauss, who are pretty sick at the failure of their mission here, and are most severe upon Roumanian dishonesty. However, Mr. Adams, our Commercial Attaché, told me in the afternoon, during a visit which I paid to him and his wife, that he could give a dozen good reasons why they failed, of which the Reschitsa case, though the chief reason, was only one.

Adams says that even if the different price of the English and German locomotives were as 14 to 8, it still remained true that the English loco was twenty per cent a better article. It was for this reason that the English had almost the monopoly of railway construction and plant throughout the world, and it would not pay us to cut costs if it entailed reducing the quality. A sound view, I am sure. I talked to Adams about my favourite barter scheme and he said that others desired it and that if anyone could manage it the Co-operative Wholesale Association in England could. But they and others had failed before the practical difficulties of getting the Roumanian goods — wheat, timber, etc. — on board a ship. Adams says that if you can overcome this difficulty, then money and not goods is the best medium for purchase. In theory, yes, but, with exchange at the present figure, I think not. He admits that most of the Bessarabian wheat will be unexportable this year owing to the difficulty of getting it down to the sea. Then how can we expect the peasants to grow it next year? Adams admits the cereal wealth of Roumania, but says that the transport difficulties block everything. But matters are improving elsewhere than in Bessarabia. There is little bribery now, he says, only two francs for a ten-ton wagon to the Traffic Manager, and that is a trifle.

A good Clemenceau story, if a trifle premature, at lunch to-day. Clemenceau reaches heaven and is taxed by St. Peter with not having confessed his sins. "But, holy saint," replied Clemenceau, "since I reached heaven I have been searching high and low for a priest and cannot find a single one!" Another story of him after his operation for appendicitis. He was asked how he felt without it. "Quite well," replied the Tiger. "There are only two perfectly useless things in the world. One is an appendix and the other is Poincaré!"

Dined pleasantly with Mr. and Mrs. Guest at the Châteaubriand. Must remember to get the plan of the Sofia Legation for them out of the Board of Works. The site they think of buying here will just suit it. Guest thinks that a tax on profits is the best and the right means of taxing the oil industry here.

Thursday, August 4, 1921. The journey home requires many formalities, all those countries which I have traversed requiring that I should obtain their visas before returning. As there are four different coinages, and as the *wagon-lit* people have to be paid in French francs, one is absorbed in abstruse calculations. A little lunch party of the Millington Drakes at the Athene Palace Hotel where I met one of the partners of the Marmarosch Bank and should have enjoyed a longer talk with him. Two nice Americans from the U.S. Legation, and Colonel North, King's Messenger, whom I shall find on board the Orient Express to-morrow. Sent off some wires. M. Kissimoff looked in while I was dining early before the start. He had brought with him the Chief of Staff's reasoned statement why the papers were forgeries. It was in Bulgarian and K. translated it to me, promising to send it in French to London.[1]

His remarks pointed to a forgery and gave strong reasons for so believing. Why would not the Allies accept an inquiry and submit the originals? he asked. I could only say that I had advised it. I gave him a copy of the Kemal postcard and he will investigate its origin and let me know. He will send the copy to the King from me. Kissimoff is a useful man to oil wheels at the F.O. He is practically the only civilised being there and he translates for all the foreign representatives. He is honest and without passion, but feels things deeply, though he keeps great calm always. He also told me that the policy of the Bulgarian Government could be compressed under four headings:

(1) The loyal execution of the Treaty of Neuilly with the help of the Reparations Commission and the Inter-Allied Military Mission.

(2) The avoidance of everything likely to cause trouble in the Balkans, such as support of comitajis.

(3) The maintenance of good and friendly relations with neighbours.

(4) Compliance with the counsels of the Great Powers.

My last conversation with Raditch came to mind, and also the sarcastic remark of Panourias — *ils nient toujours* — but I said nothing. Left for Paris 8.15 P.M.

---

[1] It never came.

Paris, Sunday, August 7, 1921. Arrived Paris 10.30 A.M. after three days and nights in a hot train. A disagreeable affair on the way. At 3 A.M. on the morning of the 5th a bandit crawled through the window of my sleeping-car while I slept and stole my coat which was hanging up. It contained my money, gold cigarette-case and pencil, wrist-watch, pearl pin, amber cigarette-holder, etc., as well as my luggage tickets. The affair happened at the station of Homorod in Transylvania. My door was locked. I heard a noise as the thief escaped by the half-opened window, and I jumped up half-awake. I looked out, but the night was dark and I could see nothing. Then I discovered my loss and called the *chef de brigade* of the *wagon-lits* and made him report to the police. It was little consolation to hear that this was the twenty-eighth raid upon the Orient Express in two months. I was quite penniless, but the *chef de brigade* financed me on to Paris, and got my heavy baggage seen to.[1] Colonel North and I spent the days of the 5th and 6th August playing a good game of patience, for two, and so killed the time. It was very hot. The gradual return to civilisation through Hungary, Austria, Germany, and France was very striking, and each hour it became a shade cooler, or rather less devastatingly hot.

Saw at the Ritz King Manuel and had a talk about his plans, Sir Lionel Earle whom I congratulated on the Sofia Legation which is a credit to the Board of Works, M. Vlasto who was full of Greek affairs, Rupert Higgins who told me the latest news of people, and a few others.

Went off after lunch in reply to a message from the Embassy and found Lord Hardinge in his cool garden. With him was Mr. Arnold Robertson, my host of Coblenz, whom I was glad to see again. The Supreme Council meets again to-morrow and has a pretty heavy agenda paper. Curzon comes to the Embassy; Lloyd George and his forty satellites to the Crillon as usual. I told Lord H. my experiences

---

[1] After all, I was perhaps lucky, for a few weeks later brigands held up a Bucharest-Budapest express, chloroformed the passengers, and cleared the whole train!

in the East of Europe and how I differed in two respects from the decisions of the Council of Ambassadors about Bulgaria, giving him reasons with all indispensable details. As usual, I find that we are substantially in agreement. The Paris decisions of the C. of A. were taken during his absence on leave. H. knows Bulgaria, where he was for three years, practically in charge, in O'Connor's day, and he was also Consul-General. He thinks that the Bulgars are the sturdiest race in Eastern Europe. He was under the impression that the Compulsory Labour Law in Bulgaria had been knocked out, but I told him that it had not been, and that only two minor changes had been insisted upon. I also explained the question of voluntary and compulsory service and defended General de Fourtou's position. I think that H. will now act to put these affairs to rights. He is most keen on helping King Boris.

After talking round these questions, H. told me the story of his recent and successful intervention here in the Anglo-French dispute. He had been in England on three weeks' leave, and on July 27 was asleep in his garden at 3 P.M., when his butler announced that Lord Curzon wanted him on the telephone. He went in and C. told him that a break with France was imminent and that both sides were talking in such a strain as to render a rupture almost inevitable. The French were set on sending another French division to Upper Silesia and were prepared to act without a Supreme Council if we opposed them. C. then asked H. to come up to London at once, to talk it all over with him, and to go over to Paris with a despatch for Briand. H. duly arrived in London at 7 P.M. and at once saw Curzon. After taking stock, H. said that there was no cause for alarm; that he felt sure that he could settle the whole dispute with Briand in twenty-four hours; and that he proposed to come back to England on the Sunday to finish some work that he was doing. He added that all, of course, depended on the instructions which he received, but if they were moderate he might pull through. He left next morning for Paris. The instructions followed him, and he spent two hours reading them and converting them into French before he saw Briand. He had also thought of a formula to help Briand out, and thought that it was more a face-saving business than anything else.

When he saw Briand, he attacked him at once. "Well, you are nice people to let me go away and then send bombshells to London. Of course if you *want* a break you can have one. *We* are not going to allow a new French division to go to Silesia — if you do not continue on the Supreme Council *we shall*" — and so on. Then he read his instructions, which were moderately worded and presented his formula for which, he said, he had no authority as yet from our Government. This formula was that a joint representation should be made to Germany by England, France, and Italy asking the Boches to prepare transport for *Allied* (not French) troops. I think that there was also something about the Supreme Council. Anyhow, Briand accepted the formula and said that he preferred to put it forward as his own to his Cabinet. Which he did, and they accepted it unanimously, while our Cabinet at home accepted, too, and H. got home again for the conclusion of his holiday. A sound piece of diplomatic work.

Now, however, he would doze in his Paris garden while the war of words went on, as he was not asked to the Council. H. does not believe in "sledge-hammer diplomacy," especially with Frenchmen. H. said that the agenda of the Council was a long one and included the Near-Eastern question which H. did not think was ripe yet. I told him that Avarescu's views accorded with his on this point. Also I warned him of the suspicious *provenance* of the secret papers which were being bandied about in the Balkans, and rather suspected that the Triple Entente meant breaking up Bulgaria on the first excuse. H. said that he had known his T. J. for thirty years.

Rupert Higgins was at the Ritz and we went for a stroll in the Champs Élysées before dinner in the Ritz garden, which was an agreeable change after the last month of enervating Hades. We happened, during our walk, to pass the Crillon where we found a small crowd waiting to witness L. G.'s arrival. Five minutes later L. G. and Horne drove up together. L. G. threw himself quickly out of the motor and entered the Crillon rapidly, looking exceedingly cross, and not turning his head to right or left. There was not a single cheer, nor did I see any hat raised. One man only, near the hotel door, clapped his hands. Horne followed, beaming most amiably, and making a Fontenoy bow to the crowd who paid no attention. Not a very pleasant introduction to the assembly of the Council to-morrow!

Tuesday, August 9, 1921. Returned to London. Crossing the Channel cogitated what prescriptions I should give for Europe's ailments. I would cure exchange and currency first by redistributing the gold now so largely, unnaturally, and uselessly hoarded in American banks, by withdrawing unhealthy units of European currency, and by substituting others on a gold basis. The United States would have to initiate this radical reform and name her terms. She is, after us, the greatest sufferer from the present currency chaos, and has the largest number of unemployed resulting from that chaos. I prefer this to the scheme of asking the United States to forgive us our debts as we forgive our foreign debtors. Also I prefer it to the Ter Meulen scheme, or barter on a large scale, or export credits, which, however useful, are actually only palliatives. We and America must put this reform through, otherwise European export trade of each is dead and our unemployment will not end. I should say that we could simultaneously insist upon greater freedom for all international trade by the reduction to their lowest terms of passports, tariffs, permits, and export duties.

To cure the political illnesses of Europe I would ratify the Anglo-American Guarantee of France against German aggression, or, failing American approval, would make a defensive and offensive alliance with France, Italy, Belgium, the four States of the Little Entente, and Greece, to preserve all the Peace Treaties intact. The interminable Franco-German friction and the Anglo-French bickerings are all due to the unrest of France in face of the lapse of the promised Anglo-American Guarantee; and the uneasiness of Europe is mainly due to the unrest of France. I would place Sèvres among the Treaties to be maintained, and take stern measures with any Soviet-Kemalist combination that resisted.

I do not believe in disarmament as the best or even the right cure for Europe's ills. Armaments are symptoms of a disease and not the disease itself. I believe in obligatory arbitration when the Powers, and above all America, are great and wise enough to accept it, recognising as all should that an arbitral decision given against the claims of any one of us is nothing compared with the catastrophe of another world war. No State will keep up armies for anything but police work when obligatory arbitration becomes the settled rule in disputes, for no one will pay for armies which have no employment. Cure all the above evils and armaments cure themselves.

CHAPTER XIII

THE WASHINGTON CONFERENCE

October 19, 1921. Made an early start from Waterloo to catch the *Adriatic*, which sailed from Southampton at noon. On the platform met H. G. Wells, who was being seen off by his wife, and M. Chaliapine, the great Russian singer, both on their way to America, the former for the *New York World*, the latter for his manager, who will dispose of him as he sees fit. Expected breakfast on the train and found none. Nothing on board till 1 P.M. Chaliapine and I both like ravening wolves in consequence. He was full of his Queen's Hall success this week, but empty in other respects. Wells great fun. He had an amorous couple in his compartment who spent their time embracing each other. Wells said it was as great a protection as a baby in the carriage, and no one else would come in.

This White Star liner is twenty-five thousand tons, and reputed a good sea boat. Most comfortable, not to say palatial. I had a good cabin, but the White Star man came in and promised me a better. Went to look at it and found it bigger than my own, with a private bathroom attached, and a brass double bed, not to speak of an electric stove. Also, it was amidships, so I transferred to it and unpacked. Made my number to the skipper, Captain Hambelton, a hale and rubicund sea officer, who looks competent. Found myself at his table with Wells; Mr. and Mrs. Butler Wright, from the United States Embassy in London; his mother; Mr. La Vie, from New York; Dr. Mussen, a much-travelled Canadian; and Mr. Edward Palmer, of Boston, who all seem pleasant. Wright called over for the Conference. Talked most of the rest of the day to Wells and Chaliapine. The latter was detained at Petrograd during the Revolution and has only recently been allowed out. He has dominated Russian opera for twenty years. He is a native of Kazan. It is his fourth visit to England, and he loves the country, where he has many friends besides his musical admirers. A great, tall, masculine, cheery person, and even his talking voice is musical and of a beautiful timbre. Very much of a personality. He told the Soviet that he could not sing if he was unhappy for want of food and drink, so he got both, and now he can make his fortune again, judging by the delighted applause of London. Also the White Star cuisine will cheer him up, as it is excellent. A calm sea to Cherbourg, where we put in at dark for our French passengers and mail. A lovely sight with the lights and stars. What memories of old times as we anchored inside the famous breakwater!

After dinner talked with Butler Wright about the Conference for over two hours. We compared notes and ideas about Pacific questions and the limitation of armaments. I am not sure yet that the Americans have grasped the full significance of Japan's policy since 1915, but one will judge this better at Washington. It seems to me that the Genro [1]

---

[1] The elder statesmen.

have been in charge up to a recent date and that Japanese parliamentarism is a farce. Japan seems to me to have constantly infringed both the letter and the spirit of her alliance with England, and has been almost openly aiming at the protectorship of China, whereas we stipulated together in 1902 for the independence and integrity of China and Korea and the open door. Cannot reconcile Japan's action with the spirit of our treaty, and as we have let Japan know since 1911 that we shall not be drawn into hostilities with the United States, it is not clear that our alliance is anything more now than a drag upon Japan. But the alliance stands for a year after it is denounced, and it is not denounced yet, so if we all fall out at Washington we shall be in a quandary. The United States cannot attack Japan successfully at home, nor can Japan attack America at home. The distance across the Pacific and the want of local and properly defended bases in each case, not to speak of submarines, seem to me to prohibit grand operations without years of preparation.

China will be against Japan at the Conference. It is a matter of vital interest to Japan to expand in Asia, and I heard before leaving London that she might refuse to discuss the China question, and risk the disapproval of the Western Powers. But Japan will probably accept a standstill on naval armaments, as she is already powerful enough for defence, and may not want to continue an onerous competition at sea with the United States, which has such far greater resources. That may enable President Harding to obtain a *succès d'estime*, but one cannot expect much change in land armaments owing to the position in Europe, not to speak of Russia and Turkey.

I have written in the *D. T.*, and in the coming number of the *Atlantic Monthly* in America, that obligatory arbitration in all international disputes, and an attempt to reform the exchanges and unsound currencies of the world, are the real aims which should be pursued, but President Harding cannot be expected to cumber his Conference with fresh problems at present. The real danger is the plain and obvious design of Japan to rule in China, the weakness of the Chinese Central Government, and the collapse of Russia. We and the United States must not push our policy to extremes or Japan will challenge us both. She knows all the cards in our hands. Can we exercise enough moral and economic pressure on Japan to mitigate her ambitions? Butler Wright half believes it. I am not sure without deeper investigation. The whole question seems to me extremely dangerous, and if the Genro think that their time has come to throw off the mask, and are further alarmed by a Republican China, and by Soviet Eastern ambitions, they may consider that the destinies of Japan require serious decisions. An immense deal depends upon the tact of American statesmen, and much also upon the question whether Japan is ready to compromise. Butler Wright thinks that even the limitation of naval armaments will be a great gain. So it will be, but can it come if Japan prove contumacious about China? And will all the other States of the world accept a permanent inferiority at sea which a standstill in building will impose upon them?

Butler Wright does not think that obligatory arbitration will be in conflict with the so-called Monroe Doctrine. He spoke very well to-night on all these questions, and it is useful to clarify one's ideas by getting well-informed men to dispute them.

An ex-film fairy came on board at Cherbourg. An American lumberman millionaire married her and spent huge sums upon her, but is now divorcing her or she him. My pet on board is Betty Hamilton, aged ten, a delicious little American girl with a sweet nature, and very winsome.

Saturday, October 22, 1921. A good voyage up to date. Big rollers and a bit of wind, especially last night, but to-day lovely weather. We are making some four hundred miles a day. Sent off some wireless messages. Little news from the outside world and few ships met. Occupied myself these three days with running through all the China and Japanese literature which I brought with me. The only hope for East Asia seems to be that England, America, and Japan should agree to co-operate harmoniously, but we shall each have to give up some vested interests in China if we are to do so, and we must admit Japan's special interests in Manchuria and Mongolia or we shall not get on. In what manner will our American hosts present the case? Which of her two faces — the Eastern or the Western — will Japan present to us? If the Western face, will she follow up promise by performance? Or shall we find the Black Dragon militarist society in full charge, and what then? How can we consolidate the power of the feeble Central Government of China?

I have an uncomfortable feeling that the Black Dragon clansmen may think that their time has come to throw for the overlordship of Asia, and that the Genro may stand behind them and issue such instructions to the Japanese delegates that they may be unable to compromise. The whole policy of Japan in China since 1915 has been one of aggression and acquisitiveness, as well as unfriendly to England. The more I study her secret twenty-one demands of January, 1915, on China, and all her press campaign of 1916 against England, and her subsequent secret loans and alliances forced on China, the less I believe in the virtue of an alliance which Japan has broken in the letter and the spirit time after time. The policy of our Government in the face of this unblushing hostility is not yet apparent to me. There can be little doubt that Japan in 1915 and 1916 thought that we were going to be beaten. She did as little as possible to help us, and practically turned against us in our worst days, whereas in 1904–05 we were solid for Japan in her days of greatest danger. There is apparently a considerable civilian body of opinion in Japan which believes that the power of their militarists is diminishing, but I can place no trust in it while the Genro and the clans are in power and probably with a settled policy which will not be to our liking.

It seems to me that Japan was surprised at Russia going Bolshevist, and by China turning Republican. Japan's ruling circles are alarmed lest the infection may spread to their Left parties. They would like to secure Siberia up to Lake Baikal, first, for strategical reasons when Russia shall have recovered, and secondly, to provide her factories with the raw materials which they need. They are practically in possession of Russian Eastern Asia, and China is in their power if they stretch out their hand. Are they likely to abandon their predominance in Eastern Asia at the bidding of Powers which may be unable to coerce them? Will they be content with Manchuria and Mongolia, and shall we definitely admit their acquisition of these regions? Also, even if we have got to know some of their secret intrigues with China, how many more are there which we do not know? A *prima facie* case has been made out for denouncing our alliance with Japan, but she must be given a chance of explaining her position and of coming into line with us and America.

Tuesday, October 25, 1921. There are many pleasant people on board this liner, and some interesting figures. Mr. Elliot Goodwin, the Vice-Chairman of the American Chamber of Commerce, and his wife, are the most representative of the Americans on board. I like them both very much and shall find him later on at Washington. In character and qualities, as well as in judgement and measure, he represents what one values most in leading men. We have had some good talks and also play my favourite game of patience together, a game which he calls Russian Bank. Major Henry Whitehouse, another American, well known in England, is also an agreeable companion. Mr. E. J. Metcalfe is the brother of my old comrade of that name. Mr. F. A. Nash is a wide-awake and capable American commercial man, keen, young, and observant. The ex-film fairy has attracted some admirers. It seems that she is allowed three thousand pounds a month for dress, and wears ornaments amounting to the value of some score of thousands. She is rather pretty, undistinguished, and overdressed. Wells is always a great interest, full of jokes and quaint ideas, but most retiring and keeps in the background. He has been to the United

States only once before, and he hates life on board ship as cordially as I do. We become indolent, overfed, incapable of solid reading or good writing. I asked him if any good book had ever been written at sea. He knew of none except one novel by Conrad. The hypnotism of the sea, the throbbing of the engines, the eight hundred passengers on board and crew of five hundred and fifty, and the want of exercise, real peace, and good books are all a fatal bar to literature. It is a form of imprisonment, even if everything possible is done to make one's voyage agreeable; as it is on this beautiful, friendly, and admirably conducted ship.

We have on board Dr. Richard Strauss, the composer of "Salome" and the "Rosencavalier," a Bavarian by birth, director of the Vienna Opera House; Mme. Schumann-Heink, the singer; Mlle. Lucrezia Bori, another fine singer, who changed her name from Borgia so unnecessarily; Miss Kathleen Parlow, the violinist of great talent; and of course that strange, emotional, artistic Chaliapine, who receives wireless messages daily from his admirers in London. In Dr. Schuloff we have a competent caricaturist, while Chaliapine and Wells are competitors in this branch. Caruso had the same gift of dashing off impromptu sketches.

The weather has remained fairly good, with occasional relapses into pitching and rolling, but the ship is very steady and the temperature not too low. We hear news daily by wireless, and before dinner a little paper comes out with the gist of it all. Yesterday we heard that Wirth's Government in Germany had resigned over the Upper Silesia award, to my great regret, and that that deluded idiot Karl had reached Hungary by aeroplane, regardless of the dangers which he is bringing on the Magyars and of his promise to the Swiss Government. The fate of the Irish Conference still hangs in the balance. Poor Dmitri, the Bulgarian War Minister, has been murdered with several others. The Macedonians have got him. He told me [1] that they had condemned him to death when I met him at Sofia.

[1] See chapter on Bulgaria.

To-night we had a great concert on board. A little committee got it up and made me act as chairman for the evening. Chaliapine made excuses for not singing; so did Mlle. Bori; but Dr. Strauss was splendid in taking over the work of accompanying, and Miss Parlow with the violin and Mme. Schumann-Heink in singing were quite excellent. The dining-saloon was very full; practically everyone came. Our ship's band opened, and then we had Miss Parlow and Mme. Schumann-Heink, who were both immensely applauded. Chaliapine had come to look on, and when Mme. Schumann-Heink had finished, I went over to him and made a last appeal to him to sing. To our joy he accepted. Strauss accompanied him, and he gave us Beethoven, "Alla Tomba Oscura," or some such title, followed by a love song. He is indeed a marvel, complete, tremendous, and the finest dramatist imaginable. He seems one mass of sensibility and emotion and his bass voice is gorgeous, of great volume, range, and feeling. He was rapturously applauded.

Then I had to make a little speech to explain that the concert was for the benefit of the seamen's orphanages in England and America, but of course I began by asking for a vote of thanks to the great artists. Then four pretty girls made a collection which produced eighty pounds, and finally Miss Carruthers, an American lady journalist — her real name is Mrs. Margaret C. Deyo — sold our pictures and caricatures made by Chaliapine, Wells, Dr. Schuloff, and Dr. Frick. There were also signed photos of various celebrities. This went well, and produced a hundred and fifteen pounds, so we had nearly two hundred pounds to send to the fund, which was a good result, and I doubt whether a ship's concert has ever produced more talent.

Wednesday, October 26, 1921. Wet, cold, rough, and squally. The lounge, which is heated by hot air, is the warmest place on the ship.

Thursday, October 27, 1921. A fine sunny morning and a calm sea. I was surprised to hear from a passenger who constantly crosses the ocean that he had never known a rougher voyage. If he had said the exact contrary, I should have been less astonished. We made a good run to-day and were able to make New York docks by evening. The somewhat archaic methods of picking up our pilot and of undergoing medical inspection provoked much sarcasm among the passengers, especially the Americans. The view of the harbor is fine. There was much smoke over the city and some huge sky-scrapers, including one of forty-six stories, appeared like fairy castles at an immense height above the pall of mist. Here, in August, 1664, there sailed in my forbear, Admiral Sir Robert Holmes,[1] and captured the city, then called New Amsterdam, from the Dutch. It is a pity that he did not peg out a few claims while he was about it. He let in the English colonists who renamed it New York. The capture of New York is a feat unlikely to be repeated, I imagine. But I am not forgetting 1664.

A dozen destroyers passed us heading out to sea. At the Quarantine Station Mr. Percy Bullen, the *D. T.* correspondent at New York, very kindly came aboard and we had a good talk. Then had to go up to the sun deck to be victimised with Wells and Chaliapine by seven or eight photographers, and subsequently the same number of reporters came to examine me. Mr. Bullen dined on board with me at six. I asked my steward if he could get Bullen a whiskey and soda. "No, Sir, no whiskey, Sir; we have just passed the Statue of Liberty," replied the steward quite severely! Tied up at seven-thirty. The system of parking our baggage under the first letters of our names was good, but the examination by the customs people was uncivilised. Have rooms at the Vanderbilt Hotel. Mr. Ferris Greenslet came in later and we had a good talk. A bad night. The noise of trams continued uninterruptedly all the time and the room was stifling from the radiator. It does not do to be on the lower floors in this town — I beg its pardon — this city.

[1] It is from the Admiral that the elder branch of the à Courts take their name of Holmes à Court.

Friday, October 28, 1921. A fine morning. Read all the papers. The railway strike here is off, thank goodness. Comments on the Conference various. Opinion has not settled down yet. There is no material as yet to guide people. The *Atlantic Monthly* has made a feature of the Conference this month and has articles by me, Pitkin, Bland, Powell, Sidebotham, and Bywater. A good number, and I must congratulate Ellery Sedgwick, the editor. But he makes me write "honor," "guaranty," "labor," "defense," and "traveler." I prefer our spelling.[1]

Went off "down-town" as they call it — i.e., to the business quarter of Broadway — and called at Bullen's office, where his assistant and his son were at work. We went to the Equitable Assurance Society Building, from which there is a fine view of the town. We were fired rather than carried to the top by the elevator. Not exactly impressive, but weird, fantastic, and extraordinary. The greatest skyscrapers have grown up within the last twenty years. They are necessary owing to the restricted space on this tongue of Manhattan Island and are possible because they are founded and rest on volcanic rock. But no one knows quite how they will be affected by corrosion of steel or pressure on mortar, so no higher buildings may now be made.

Large crowds in the streets at the luncheon hour. We lunched at the Bankers' Club, a very agreeable institution. Then to see the crowd in Broadway to receive Marshal Foch, who arrived to-day, and was given a great reception which equalled that when he came to London in 1918. Streets and windows full. The public have a way of displaying their regard by resounding noise, and by dropping showers of little bits of paper from the windows of the huge buildings. It is like snow, and on Armistice Day was two feet deep in the narrow streets, they say. At three was again interviewed, and at four went to the *New York Times* office and had a good talk with the Assistant Editor,

---

[1] Mr. Sedgwick told me later that Webster had superseded Worcester as the authority for spelling, but admitted that his magazine had a list of about twenty words which were not in accord with Webster.

Mr. Van Anda. Very amusing to hear the veridic history of the Steed-Northcliffe despatch which has set all the press of Fleet Street and New York laughing. Van Anda thinks that little will come out of the Conference. Went for a walk to see the transparencies and advertisements by lights in the streets and studied the Fifth Avenue shops. The sky-scrapers oppress me. Dined with Ferris Greenslet at the Century Club, Seven West Forty-Third Street. The Athenæum of New York, well and tastefully furnished in the best English club style; very restful and pleasant. Met some nice people there after dinner and had a good talk about personalities and events. I find that the big papers here have a circulation of about 350,000 and the best magazines 120,000 or thereabouts. The *New York Times* is generally conceded to be the best paper, and the *World* and *Herald* next. The *Kansas City Star* has a good repute. So has the *Chicago Tribune*. Expect that generalising about America will be dangerous owing to the size of the country and the different interests of the States. Public sentiment is not expressed or perhaps we should say created, by the big papers at any one city, as it usually is by London and Paris.

New York has the effect upon me of meeting an ichthyosaurus in Berkeley Square. I have transferred my rooms from the second to the fifteenth story to try to escape the noise. A wonderful view over the city, twinkling with innumerable lights. But it is all amazing and gargantuan and I cannot imagine anyone wanting to live here. It is one perpetual roar and rush of people and vehicles; surging masses of humanity and trams, cars, taxis, and carts without end. A hateful place. Nothing great in the realm of ideas can ever come from such a restless spot.

A story of Admiral Sims. He was asked what the Supreme Council would do about the freedom of the seas. Sims replied that he did not care so long as they did not interfere with mixed bathing.

Saturday, October 29, 1921. A course of reading New York morning papers would exhaust the entire day if one did not learn how to skip. Each paper is of huge size and all employ horribly small type, trying to the eyes. But one soon sees that the mass of the material is worthless to a foreigner, as it consists of local gossip and sensations. It is enough to read the headings, which are conspicuous, and then to select the subjects of real interest and a few leaders. Then one can polish off the papers in an hour or so. They throw little light on the Conference as yet. There seems to be no mass interest in it, but I suppose it will come when the five hundred correspondents expected at Washington settle down. The foreign telegrams here are fairly good and keep us posted in outside news. There seems to me no definite attitude taken up by American opinion about the Conference. There is a mild interest in limiting armaments, and a vague suspicion that Pacific questions may prove difficult to settle, but no national policy nor partiality for nor dislike of any foreign nation. It may come, but the initial sentiment is rather Laodicean. I am told that one of Harding's private memos began, "America does not want a darned thing," and that about represents the preliminary popular indifference. But Harding and the United States delegates have had many meetings, and are said to have a definite plan of action and line of policy. Hughes, Root, Lodge, and Underwood are a strong team, and the work will be left to Hughes in the main, it seems. Harding is increasing in popular favour. Hughes said to be broader and more internationally minded than he was. Public opinion in the street resents our alliance with Japan. It will not be with us till it ends and the Irish Conference proves successful. These are our two stumbling-blocks, but I fancy that there is a fairly large section of this people which is incurably hostile to us.

Had a talk at the National City Bank of New York about finance and exchanges. They gave me their last excellent monthly summary on economic conditions, governmental finance, etc., and I am studying it. I wanted to see Delmonico's, so lunched there with Bullen. In London we should call it a fair second-class restaurant. Neither the

company nor the waiting nor the food was above the or·
dinary, but the prices were about double ours. I suppose
that Prohibition may have hit all the fashionable resorts by depriving them of their best source of profits.
Went on to the Metropolitan Art Museum to see the pictures. A very fine but most heterogeneous collection. Rich
in Rembrandts particularly, and some of the finest quality.
Rubens's Holy Family about the best example of that master that I have ever seen. Treasures of all schools, and some
notable modern works like Meissonier's 1807 and Rosa
Bonheur's Horse Fair. The Library seems to me better
organised than ours at the British Museum. An immense
reading public here, it seems. The huge reading-rooms
were very full. It is a pity, by the way, that no old
master ever tried to paint a Holy Family in Palestine.
Rubens's Virgin is a pretty Dutch woman with a complexion obtrusively Dutch. However, the Americans are to be
congratulated upon their public and private art collec-
tions of all kinds. As trade follows the flag, so art treasures
follow the money. That is one merit of public galleries,
for the gems remain. Found a good bookseller's shop in
Fifth Avenue, Brentano's, rich in all sorts of literature,
and exceedingly well arranged. Bought a few books on subjects relating to the Conference agenda.

Two "nigger" stories: Two blacks were disputing
whether the sun or the moon was of most value to the earth.
Finally they agreed that the moon was, because it shone
when it was dark. Story II: A black up for trial for stealing a chicken. *Judge*, " Have you a lawyer to defend you,
prisoner?" *Black*, "No, Judge, I wanter keep dis chicken."

Sunday, October 30, 1921. Ordered all the Sunday papers published here. It took two strong men to carry them
in. The *New York Times* alone was about the size of ten
copies of the *D. T.* The others on the same scale. They
were all encyclopædic, a sort of series of supplements on
news, politics, gossip, sensations, sport, art, theatres, and
so on, each paper representing a heavy day's reading. Met
a New York publisher to-day who disputes my notion that

the American public are great readers and great book-lovers. The crowd which I saw at the Library, he says, meant nothing because of New York's seven million people. He says that the public have the "spirit of acquisitiveness about books, but are not really book-lovers." He says that they prefer the papers, the cheap magazines, and the bad novels. So my first pleasant illusion vanishes. Or ought to do so, but I am not quite convinced. There are surely the gallant few who bear the torch in the gloom.

There were some things of interest in to-day's papers about Japan. First a *New York Times* cable from London quotes Baron Hayashi[1] as saying that the question of China would be brought before the Conference. But an Associated Press cable from Victoria, B.C., quotes Prince Tokugawa's personal hope that "the questions between China and Japan will be kept out of the Conference because it is better to solve these questions directly between the countries concerned." Admiral Kato, in the same cable, is made to say that a naval understanding is the great issue before the Conference. He also says that "Japan's basic principle is her desire to maintain a navy sufficiently strong to engage any naval force that any naval power might be able to send to her waters of the Far East." So, Kato goes on, "if American Eastern bases were so enlarged as to manipulate the whole navy, Japan would want to strengthen her own fleet in proportion." Again, the *Chicago Tribune* has asked a string of questions of Premier Hara of Japan at Tokio, and the answers were submitted to the Cabinet. Japan desires, according to this statement, that "an equitable reduction should be based upon a sole consideration of national security, having due regard not merely to the area or population, but the length of the littoral lines and geographical and topographical conditions." Asked about a standstill in naval armament, Hara replied that the paramount duty of the navy was defence against foreign aggression, and that Japan was only prepared to accept a reduction if and so long as the exigen-

---

[1] Japanese Ambassador in London.

cies of the national defence were thereby duly satisfied. The *New York Times* in another communication from Washington quotes a declaration of September 20 by the State Department which shows the line to be taken about Siberia. It says that "in the absence of a single, recognised Russian Government, the protection of legitimate Russian interests must devolve as a moral trusteeship upon the whole Conference." A pleasing task to become trustee for a lunatic!

These things are all very illuminating, especially Kato's warning that if the United States fortify her bases Japan will increase her fleet. Rifts in the lute of the concert discernible already at a distance. The United States is warned off the fortification of her own possessions!

In general I gather from the United States press and private conversations here that the American public regard the Conference with some indifference, want nothing, and are sceptical of success. But they do not wish the Conference to be a patent failure, and Senator Borah is already threatening fire and brimstone to all and sundry if no limitation of armaments ensues. Japan will apparently oppose a discussion on China if such discussion infringes any acquired rights of Japan, but it seems now that the China question must come up and that United States diplomacy has shown Japan that no trap is laid for her. There are one hundred Chinese already at Washington for the Conference and they had a good reception.

In the afternoon went for a motor drive up the Hudson, came back to tea at Claremont, and then dined later at a certain restaurant. Also inspected the Central Park in the afternoon. A heavy fog hid the distant view along the river. Some warships displayed their misty shapes. There were thousands of cars out. They went by in flocks and herds wherever one went. Saw Columbia University which boasts twenty thousand students, and I hope proportionate luminosity. The Central Park is well laid out, but the trees are most scrubby specimens and refuse to grow. Was given a cocktail at dinner, in a teacup. It was of gin and bitters and oranges. I hate gin, but there it was. Everybody drinks here. One wants to drink mainly because it is forbidden. My hotel valet says that all his colleagues can get all drinks at three or four places close to their lodgings. The workmen all drink too, generally vile stuff. A bottle of whiskey costs twelve 'dollars. A cobweb of bribery covers everything. They say that it would take ten years to clear off the cases down for trial. Drink is a curse, but Prohibition does not seem to be a successful cure in a free community.

Monday, October 31, 1921. More photographing visitors. This time they elected the roof of my hotel for my martyrdom. Went off to lunch down-town with Mr. Otto Kahn, the well-known banker, at a select little club where we had a good gossip in a private room. I found that he entirely shares my view that the restoration of sound currencies in Europe, and the acceptance of obligatory arbitration, are the real cures of the world's ills. I approached rather gingerly the question of utilising America's hoarded gold as a basis for new currencies. He was all for it, and thought that a third of the gold in the United States banks could easily be used in this way. The amount of gold cover could be under twenty-five per cent of the note issue. It would almost be enough to give out that the scheme was afoot to cause the currencies to bound up. Would not some States like Germany perhaps oppose? He feared they might, but should be compelled to toe the line by methods of constraint. It was the only way out, he agreed. He has spoken to Harding on the subject, and only last night to Mr. McKenna, who was dining with him. He praised Harding and said that he was not the mere figurehead that people had at first esteemed him to be. He was sound and patriotic and had greatly grown in the estimation of leading men. We both praised McKenna. The worst thing in the situation, my banker friend said, was that though foreign trade was vital for England it was less so for the United States. Therefore an administration might hesitate to touch such a thorny subject, as it might be bitterly attacked. Should we try the scheme on one State at a time or deal with all at once? Otto Kahn thought that it would be best to do the whole thing right off and he thought it would be easy. He would like a small committee of three good men from England and the United States each, and as few of other nations as possible. But they must have some sort of assurance that their Governments would back them, as the thing could not be done without Government support, and besides, real good men would not lay themselves out to construct an academic scheme, as their time was too valuable. All this is on the lines of my *Atlantic Monthly* article.

He advised me to see certain members of the Senate whom he named. They were very representative and of high intelligence and character. They suffered like the rest of the people here by being provincial and uninformed, and many were untravelled. He thought the Japanese raw. They might make mistakes because they lacked experience and foresight in diplomacy. He lauded the English and the manner in which they had conducted their affairs in past days. They must still continue the Atlas business for a time because the United States was not yet ready to replace them, but the Conference was a beginning. In view of the last Presidential election cries, Harding has to ride with a very light hand, but obviously the well-being of the world was an American interest and all must understand it at last.

Caught the 3.25 P.M. Congressional Express to Washington. A fast train, but more shaky than ours and the carriages not up to our Pullman cars in finish, comfort, or convenience. The country flat, desolate, unfinished, and without merits. But I was so glad to be quit of New York that nothing mattered. What a town! The highest, lowest, cruellest, cunningest, noisiest, of all great cities. But the great stations are fine and the railway system cuts out ours. We are best on the sea roads and the Americans on the land ways. Reached Washington 8.35 P.M. Pouring, and very warm. At the Washington Hotel I have pleasant but fearfully expensive rooms. They charge me twenty-five dollars a day for two rooms on the eighth floor! All the windows have mosquito net tin coverings and one cannot look out or allow the air to circulate freely. Ran into Major-General Squier, formerly Military Attaché in London, and we had a good talk about old times and the Conference. He told me an extraordinary tale, namely, that when Harding speaks on Armistice Day his voice will be heard for half a mile round, louder than in the building itself, and that at enormous cost it will be heard at Chicago and in San Francisco. It is a new invention, a sort of sublimated megaphone, and there is a huge and complicated mechanism of telephonic apparatus and amplifiers where Harding will stand, but there will actually be visible only a small reading-desk on which will be a box nine inches square. Every few hundred miles the message is treated to a process of magnification. One Colonel Carty, a genius, has worked it all out, and has a staff under him trained to the hour. Nothing but the cost prevents the speech from being heard, louder than in the hall itself, in every city in the United States! I was rather appalled, and said that oratory, with such an instrument at its hand, would become an awful power. The secret was being well kept. Nothing had yet appeared in the press. Squier knows all about it, as he is at the head of the Signal Service, which is helping Carty.

Washington, Tuesday, November 1, 1921. Rain and thunder. Warm. We are evidently going to live in a diplomatic glass house here and there will be little secrecy. All the American system is against secrecy. Harding and Hughes constantly see all the press representatives and things are all done *coram publico*. It is as if any press man at home could see the King and Curzon every week and ask any question! It is evident, for example, from press notices to-day that our hosts are finding as great difficulty in discovering a formula for the reduction of naval armaments as we found at The Hague in 1899. The Americans are out for a navy equal to ours at least. Their navy estimates are $400,000,000 and the number of men to be voted 126,000.

These estimates should come before Congress in December, but Harding has not yet reviewed them, and before December much may happen.

The American delegation cannot discover a satisfactory method of limiting naval strengths by agreement, irrespective of the extent of the limitation. That was exactly our quandary twenty-two years ago. Considerations of national defence come first with America as with Japan. The Americans think that a fifty per cent reduction during the next twenty years, taking the expenditure of the last five years as a basis, would be a grave menace to their safety, but it is suggested that much depends on the continuance or ending of the Anglo-Japanese Treaty, for while it lasts America has to regard the implied possibilities of the alliance. They have evidently not studied the 1911 treaty and the 1914 papers very closely or they would not put forward this plea.

The Americans also suggest that, even as between America and England, a fifty per cent reduction would be in our favour, since our naval bases and merchant navy are superior, and besides the higher price of American labour would tell in favour of England and still more of Japan. So they wail that every plan has its drawbacks, and yet here is the limitation of naval armaments standing as the first item of the American agenda and it is up to America to suggest something. There are also joint American Army and Navy plans for the defence of bases in the Pacific, and we have seen what Admiral Kato has said [1] about this.

Went round to our Embassy and after a talk with the Councillor, Mr. Chilton, First Secretary, Mr. Craigie, and Mr. Peterson, saw the Ambassador, Sir Auckland Geddes. He was looking well and was very much satisfied with the change which had come over American opinion regarding us during the last few months. We were regarded like mud when he came and only recently things have mended. He has stumped the country like an election agent and hopes that he has done some good. I am sure that he has, from

[1] See entry for October 29.

opinions expressed to me. He can now go anywhere without the old police escort. He is not told much about our policy, but is occasionally asked what our policy should be. The idea that the stay-at-home Americans may come some day to understand the real England fills one with a new hope.

Had a talk later with X, who does not think that Harding's and Hughes's policies are quite alike, for Harding sees neither black nor white in a case, but only greys, and is a man of compromise who feels his way. He is without vanity. Hughes is a Baptist and his father and grandfather were Baptist ministers. He is of Welsh-Nordic extraction, less known than any other statesman, resembling Wilson in certain points, and always liable to mount to the skies with his principles and to bring us in touch with the Deity. Hughes stands for the open door, for the integrity of China, and for the trusteeship of Russia in Siberia. But, says X, what is China and what is the open door? Does China include Manchuria, Mongolia, and Thibet, or not? He thinks that Manchuria is definitely controlled by the Japanese and must be so accounted. If Hughes finds it necessary to state a case against Japan, it will be damning, but if Japan is placed in the dock she will quit the Conference. Hughes is a good lawyer and will get up a case well. But, being a lawyer, he cannot think. You are either innocent or guilty. There are no greys; only the black or the white. X thinks that we shall all have our difficulties and must go warily especially at first, and study the whole situation before we commit ourselves. He thinks that the Japanese are less intransigent than they were, or were supposed to be, when I left London. They may be afraid of being left isolated and thrown back upon Asia without a friend. We discussed the naval question and he gave me Beatty's views. He hoped that a good sound Anglo-American understanding might result from the Conference, and perhaps an exchange of notes which would not have to be submitted to the Senate.

Lunched with Major-General George O. Squier and

Brigadier-General Lassiter, Squier's successor in London, and now Director of Operations here. We had a good talk on the state of Europe and the remedies for it. The Metropolitan is a very pleasant club with fine rooms, a good library, and good food. Most of the important people here belong to it. Lansing, to whom I was introduced; Hoover; Weeks, the head of the War Department; ex-Ambassador Wallace; and various others were there, including Mr. Elliot Goodwin. Squier interested me by saying how hard it was to become, and even still more to remain, a national character in the United States. It was so different in England, where all the public men were known and went on being known and their qualities being understood. Here few people could name six governors of States out of forty-eight, yet many States were larger than the minor European monarchies. Governors and ministers were unknown nationally, and after leaving office they disappeared from sight. Some Americans tried to name four national figures the other day, and of those selected one was the champion baseball player and the other Charlie Chaplin! The country was so big, and only figures like Roosevelt or Wilson stood out. The governors might be great men in their States, and their States very progressive and efficient, but the renown was local. The cabinets when formed were composed of quite unknown men, and one could go on naming other cabinets of the same type *ad infinitum*.

Washington is a pleasant, quiet, well-laid-out city. It is a capital and nothing more. There are scarcely any factories and few banks. The governing people are constantly meeting each other and the circle is relatively small. There is nothing of the noise and racket of New York. People can work and think. The distances are slight. I called at the White House to leave a card. "Walk right in," said the darky at the door. A most pleasant, dignified house of a good date, about 1800. Very public, as the grounds are small and there were no guards or sentries visible. There is just one minor sky-scraper in a corner of Lafayette Square which the White House faces. It offends the eye, but most of the other houses are homey and of quite medium size. Not a few from 1800 to 1830 by appearance. The Government offices seem well arranged and the architecture is good. I expect that it is a town that grows on one.

Called to see Mr. Oulahan, the correspondent of the *New York Times* at Washington. A competent man. He eulogised the American delegation team, which is indeed a strong one. He told me, to my regret, that England was not in good odour in America generally because her action at Versailles was considered selfish. The man in the street regarded us, in relation to Japan, as we should have regarded any ally of Germany in 1914. The people did not look into things closely and only regarded simple things such as the fact that we were the allies of Japan. Meanwhile Foch is making a triumphal progress through America and is being acclaimed by vast crowds. Looked in at the War and State Departments and made some appointments. I have been made a member of the Metropolitan, which seems to be one of the best clubs here. The Cosmos Club also hospitably opens its door to us all. Boodles and Athenæum please note.

Wednesday, November 2, 1921. Called early to have a talk with Major-General Harbord, sub-Chief of Staff, whom I was glad to see again. He was commanding a division on the border and had the reversion of a corps area, but when Pershing asked him to come he had to accept. From what he tells me, the limitation of land armaments will not figure at all prominently at the Conference, and this is confirmed by my reading of all the preliminary correspondence about the Conference between the State Department and foreign Powers. Harbord has, however, little notion of what his delegation will do. He meets their indents for information, but otherwise is not consulted and says that he probably knows less than I do. He is not at all sure that a standstill in naval armaments will suit the United States, yet such idea stands in the forefront of the American invitation and it is difficult to escape the consequences now. Harbord has a useful coloured chart of the Pacific hanging up with all the mandated and other territories in the Pacific marked in colour according to the nations now owning them. Guam is isolated in the midst of the Jap Caroline and other islands and one must regard the Philippines as an aim of Japanese ambition when one studies the chart. Harbord wonders whether his Government has seriously considered all the problems which it has stated and has any solutions for them. We discussed whether any form of economic pressure could bring Japan to her senses if she broke with us all here and reverted to a Pan-Asian policy. It is uncertain. Japan wants the resources and raw materials of China for her growing industries, but also the markets of the world for the sale of her finished products. It is no use to make goods if you cannot sell them.

Lunched at the Metropolitan with Frank Simonds, who is about the best writer in American journalism on world affairs. He now syndicates himself and has a varying number of papers — forty to eighty according to the interest taken in events — which he supplies. So he is not worried by "the policy of the paper" when he writes, but finds some disadvantage in not having the support of a special paper, as he would have if he wrote for only one. We had a long talk over the business of the Conference and exchanged ideas thereon. Like X, he thinks that everything centres round Hughes, and was most illuminating on the past and present character of the Secretary of State. He thinks that Harding is capable, but willingly leaves all the foreign work to Hughes, who runs everything. But if trouble comes, Root may restore matters, as he is a skilful negotiator and can bend while Hughes can only break, as compromise is antagonistic to him. Simonds thinks that the Japs have softened in the last few weeks and may not willingly face the consequences of a break with the West. I said that they were certainly creating an atmosphere to lead us to think so, but that the vital interests of Japan were unchanging and that it was not a question of what the Japs said, but of what they did. Simonds dilated on the hostility aroused here by the Anglo-Japanese Treaty, and imagines that Hughes will be as well prepared for a slap at England as at Japan. He agreed that Hughes reproduced with singular fidelity many of the characteristics of Wilson, and thought it arose from similar Puritanical upbringing. He would enter upon a war without hesitation if his conscience impelled him to do so. *Fiat Justitia . . . !*

Simonds wants China to be defined as the territory within the Great Wall. He thinks that another great war would pull down the whole edifice of civilisation. I agreed, but said that we could not afford to adopt too conciliatory an attitude in the face of excessive demands. Simonds thinks that war with Japan will come within five years. The Japs are going about saying that we shall not find them the people of the twenty-one demands of 1915, and they even profess to admit and regret their errors in 1915 and 1916. But I have not yet heard that they propose to abandon anything. For all the calm on the surface of things, and notwithstanding the amiable professions of everybody, there are many dangers in the diplomatic navigation. A fact to remember is that a failure will ruin the political prestige of the Republicans here.

Looked in at the Press Bureau to pick up some papers and found Mr. Hughes addressing the correspondents, who hung upon his words. An amusing affair. An example of how to talk diplomatically with apparent frankness and to tell an audience absolutely nothing. They all wrote frantically, but might as well have spared their paper. Hughes a tall, thickish man, vigorous and vital, but strikes one as a trifle fanatical in his outlook, and has the fierce twinkle in his eye of a bull before he charges. I put him down as dangerous. They say he has no weaknesses. What a tragedy, if true: However, he is assuredly a male man and that is much, and there is no duplicity about the man at all. It is not in him.

Met Philippe Millet and asked him to dinner after he

had made a joking and slightly malicious remark about the pleasure it gave him to find the Anglo-Saxon cousins at loggerheads. I did not know that they were, and said so. It is a strange revelation to me that he should arrive with such an odd Paris-made idea. He came in the evening and we had a good talk. Every discussion discloses new features of the Far Eastern question. Here is Millet saying that no one knows the number of secret agreements made between the Chinese and the Western Powers or their nationals, exclusive of Japan! Not even China knows them all, because many were made with local Chinese authorities who made too much money to blab about them. He finds the subordinate officials at the State Department very mysterious and also anti-Japanese. He says that his Ambassador, M. Jusserand, has a good moral influence and is more esteemed than any other ambassador. I believe he actually is an authority on English literature. Millet considers the Americans very little instructed in great State affairs. Another point made by Millet was that no agreement made by any Power with the American Executive was worth anything until countersigned by Congress, which is jealous of its rights. The iron and the irony of the scrapped Treaties of Versailles have eaten into Millet's French soul. The American Constitution in fact confers an altogether unfair advantage upon an American Executive, who can sign an agreement, perhaps profit from it for years, and then have it scrapped by Congress, and especially by the Senate, when it becomes inconvenient. No country can deal with America on such terms. Set myself to discover when a treaty is not a treaty, according to the Constitution, but could get no clear light.

Thursday, November 3, 1921. It seems that the Government here are harking back for a policy to Mr. Secretary Hay's principles of 1899 which affirmed the need for the open door in China. Mr. Hughes seems disposed to reaffirm those principles and adapt them to present conditions. In this case all the annexations, spheres of influence, leases of territory, and concessions acquired by

Powers in China may possibly come under review. Most of the Powers accepted the Hay principles. Few acted upon them. There will therefore be an anxious examination of consciences and troublesome hours.

Lunched with Maurice Low, *Morning Post* correspondent here, at the Shoreham Hotel. An amusing talk of American personalities and things. Low has been here twenty-five years. Very shrewd and well informed. Had a look at the shops. Bought some books at Brentano's. The shopman, when he heard my name, told me of the rush for my book when it appeared and how unfortunate it was that it was out of print at the moment of greatest demand. A representative of the International News Association, which feeds six hundred papers, interviewed me for a long spell.

I must record Simonds's story of the American Senator who had been attacked in an anonymous book. He thought he knew the writer and wrote a venomous and truculent letter to a man who was not the author. This man replied:

Sir,

In reply to your letter:
    A. I did not write the book.
    B. I wish to God that I had written it.

                Yours respectfully

———   ———

Dined with Philippe Millet and M. André Geraud (Pertinax) at the Willard Hotel. We told each other many tales of personalities and things and discussed current events. Is there any other category of persons who know so much over so wide a field as successful journalists? Very amusing that not one of the French delegation can speak one word of English and that Viviani thinks that his dramatic oratory makes him understood by all and the equal of Balfour! Why did not they send Barrère? These Frenchmen who are accustomed to their pleasant wines are much upset by the Prohibition laws here. I think it makes them regard life and America with more gloomy sentiments than if the flowing bowl circulated. We had a good talk over China and Japan, and were all somewhat Blandian. Bland's "China, Japan, and Korea" is certainly the best of the many books published this year on this aspect of the work of the Conference. It is a pity that he is not here. Sir John Jordan is coming with Balfour, so I suppose that our delegation will know what they are talking about, but Bland has more recent first-hand information.

We have a galaxy of journalistic talent. Wickham Steed, W. F. Bullock, and W. H. Lewis for the *Times*, Maurice Low for the *Morning Post*, H. G. Wells for the *New York World*, Bonsal for the new morning *Westminster Gazette*, and J. A. Spender is coming. H. W. Nevinson for the *Manchester Guardian*, P. W. Wilson for the *Daily News*, Philippe Millet for the *Petit Parisien*, Geraud for the *Echo de Paris*, F. D. Williams and P. Weir for *Reuters*, W. A. Crawford and M. Buckley for the *Central News*, and I. G. Hamilton for the *Daily Chronicle*. Some of these are syndicating their articles over here. I have the *New York Times*, which syndicates my articles to a number of good papers at Boston, Pittsburgh, etc., and have been asked to write by the *New York Herald*, so I shall have a satisfactory platform, I think. There are fifty-one Japanese journalists, eight Chinese, and many Canadians, Australians, Indians, and Frenchmen. It will not be the easiest thing in the world to send cables to the taste of England and America. The respective atmospheres are so different.

Friday, November 4, 1921. I sent off yesterday the news that the American naval plan was ready, and followed it up to-day by some rumoured details and some tentative observations. Saw the Ambassador in the afternoon and told him what I had said. He thought that I was on the right lines. We discussed China, Japan, and other subjects. We agree that it is absurd to attack the Government here about the secrecy of the meetings of the delegates. The American Government are most anxious for full publicity, but to disclose all the necessary and inevitable differences of opinion on plans as they develop is a frank absurdity and would make free discussion a farce and a successful issue impracticable.

There was an afternoon party going on when we left the Ambassador's sanctum, and crowds of people came in for tea and talk, especially ladies. Geddeses and goddesses. The Ambassador and his wife are very popular and successful hosts. Lady Harcourt turned up, but is only passing through. I was introduced to a great number of people, so many that I forget their names, all but pretty Mrs. Bliss, whom I was glad to see again. Her husband is at the State Department. Nearly everybody said they knew all about me and had read my last book. Met Commander Brown, our assistant Naval Attaché, who attracted me and looks a good man.

Saturday, November 5, 1921. Went round to the Embassy for a talk with General Bethell and Major Bridge, of our Military Attaché Staff, and also saw Commander Brown again. Talked with Simonds at the Club. He does not think that America will commit herself to any responsibilities in Asia any more than in Europe, and that we shall be leaning on a broken reed if we think the reverse. Lunched with Mr. Goodwin. We walked round to his Chamber of Commerce, which now has fourteen hundred and fifty affiliated local branches and an income of $750,000. The map showing the branches is most illuminating. If one draws a north-and-south line through the centre of the United States, practically all the great commercial area is east of the line except a few widely scattered districts on the Pacific seaboard. The Middle West, with Chicago for industrial capital, contains the bulk, and then there is the Eastern Coast block with New York for centre. One must convince the Middle West if one wants to enlist American business enterprise in any great scheme. Between the Mississippi and the Pacific littoral there is a vast region which is almost arid commercially, but of course there is all the life-giving agricultural part of the country besides.

The Chamber has a good sound organisation and Goodwin is the resident Vice-Chairman. It was begun under Taft only nine years ago and is constantly extending. It is very influential and steers clear of politics. Its purpose is national and it patronises the International Chamber of Commerce which met in London this year. It publishes a little magazine monthly called *The Nation's Business*, and I read the November number to-night. Goodwin has a taste for perfecting office equipment. I saw a room for sixteen typewriters in which all were silent machines. Wondered whether the typists were too. In another room were three automatic typewriters. One presses a button and the machine begins to type furiously, the keys moving rapidly as though touched by fairy fingers. It is fed from below by a scroll punctured in advance. Three machines can work at once under only one supervisor. A little piece of magic, admirable for duplicating circular letters, orders, etc.

I was photographically victimised again and then went off to Mrs. Bliss's house in Massachusetts Avenue. Found another tea-fight going on and another large assembly. Was introduced to heaps of people. They all seem a very friendly and sociable set of folk here, and life must be agreeable. But in the summer it must be very hot, almost too hot for heavy work, I suspect. The Jap reception was put off to-night on account of Mr. Hara's [1] assassination in Tokio. We do not yet know what political effect this sad event may have.

Monday, November 7, 1921. Lunched with the Goodwins yesterday in the Georgetown district. A pleasant old-fashioned house with many nice old things and the whole atmosphere was English country house. Most charming people with two jolly children. We had much talk of things here and of Americanisms in literature and

[1] Japanese Prime Minister.

conversation. Then saw the garden and went for a walk round the new quarter where stands a fine equestrian statue of Sheridan at what the French would call a *rond point*. A lot of fine houses growing up round. Saw a lot of people and read a mass of literature.

To-day went to Riggs's Bank. No one can live here in a hotel under sixty pounds a week. A ruinous country. This bank declared its last dividend to be twenty-six per cent. Heaps of little banks grew up like mushrooms during the war, but are now being absorbed for branch offices by the big banks. Ran against Lady Annesley in the street. She was looking well, and I was glad to see her again.

Attended a lunch to all the foreign journalists at the Shoreham. Oulahan presided right well. Many English, Dominion, French, Italian, Japanese, and Chinese journalists. A friendly meeting. After lunch we all got up and announced our names and papers. One Jap said his name in English was "high mountain and swift river," but that he was not so high as a mountain and his English did not flow so swiftly as a river. He was a little chap.

Wednesday, November 9, 1921. Much occupied these two days in seeing American officials and foreigners and in learning the regulations for Friday's ceremony and the Conference. But I slipped away yesterday afternoon and motored to Mount Vernon, across the Potomac in Virginia, to see Washington's home, distant sixteen miles. I was disagreeably impressed on the way by the slatternly, unfinished, and unkempt appearance of the land and the hamlets. It is so untidy that it looks as if an invading army had traversed it. I suppose that it takes a few centuries for a country to arrive at the garden aspect of England. The chief objects in the scenery were huge glaring advertisements on every side. It was only in the woods that one felt at home, and there the soft autumn tints were both varied and beautiful.

Mount Vernon stands on a commanding position over the river. It is of wood painted creamy white to resemble stone, has a high piazza on the river front twenty-five feet high with square pillars and tiled floor. Over the piazza is an open balcony. There is a cupola over the centre of the house surmounted by an old vane. In the house are some six sitting-rooms on the ground floor, with most of Washington's old furniture, pictures, china, etc. These rooms open direct upon the river and entrance fronts of the house by doors — there is really no back — and they must be uncommonly chilly in the winter, and draughty always. Above are the bedrooms, of which the room where Washington died is the best, and above again darkish attics, labelled guest-rooms, with dormer windows opening through the sloping, red-tiled roof. It is Anne merging into Georgian.

At each end of the house are colonnades sweeping round towards the back, right, and left, where come the kitchens, offices, and a succession of house and farm buildings. Each stands by itself, I suppose to diminish the loss by fire. Smoking is forbidden. The grounds are good and the lawn front sloping towards the river quite attractive. It is all very well kept up and with as great veneration as Goethe's house. I suppose that some of the out-buildings were for slaves. The roof is covered with demurely red tiles, and the effect on the whole is pleasant, Old-World, and home-like. The central part of the house is ninety-six feet by thirty and the rooms are not large. The date of it, they say, is 1743. It is an agreeable gentleman-farmer's Virginia home and it is a place of which an owner might become very fond. Washington seems to have been a good business man and to have made a good deal of money in real estate, etc., in his business days.

Going back I branched off to see the National Cemetery at Arlington, the scene of next Friday's ceremony when the unknown American soldier from France will be buried with all the honours. Arlington House was the home of General Robert Lee when the Civil War broke out. The estate fell into the hands of the Government and was made the national resting-place for soldiers and sailors who have died for their country. A fine site on the undulating and wooded Virginia hills. Many thousands of graves of men who fell in 1861 and subsequent wars. About ten thousand of those who died in France have been transferred here. There is a great white marble Greco-Roman amphitheatre — it is actually a complete circle — to the southern part of the cemetery to hold some seven thousand people who will witness the culminating part of the coming ceremony. I saw the grave for the unknown warrior close to the southern entrance in a very conspicuous and isolated position. I register a very fervent wish that our dead warriors may some day have such a beautiful and noble resting-place so accessible from the capital. The tombstones, or rather headstones, are usually quite small, of marble or granite, and bear the name, number, and State of the dead warrior. Whichever way one looks at the headstones, they are in line. The presence of Confederate dead, and a fine monument in the midst, are touching. I know nothing like it anywhere.

I found Pershing and the General Staff when I called to see them more fussed about the ceremony than I ever found them to be over a battle in France. They have no precedent, and everybody keeps on interfering and wanting alterations. Pershing told me how much impressed he was by the simple dignity of the ceremony in London, where he attended a fortnight ago to lay a wreath on the corresponding grave at Westminster.

I also saw General Buat yesterday. I think the French delegation has come with some cherished plan of resuscitating the Anglo-American guarantee of France, but I fancy that America will not look at it, while France's recent action, whereby she has made peace with Kemal to our detriment, does not encourage us to help her out. Curzon seems to have sent them a stiff note about it, but Buat truly says that the trouble has all arisen because we would not make up our minds to back the Greeks or to oppose them. That has been our vacillating policy all along.

I am contracting the iced-water habit. It is more pernicious than drink. Who said that America was the land of cold water and hot air?

This evening there was a dinner at the British Embassy to the British press representatives here, and some thirty or forty people responded to Sir Auckland Geddes's invitation. I sat on the left of the Ambassador and Wickham Steed on his right. We had a good dinner and it was all very well done. Steed opened the speeches and I summed up after Steed, Maurice Low, H. P. Wilson, Bullen, Hamilton, and others had spoken. We had a really good lot of speeches, each man putting forward his own views. Then I summed up, going through the points and covering the questions of China and Japan. Lord Lee also spoke and Sir Robert Borden was present. Most of the Embassy were there, including Chilton the Chancellor, Craigie the First Secretary, Commander Brown, and others. I teased H.E. upon extracting from the correspondents all their views and having given nothing in response. The sense of the meeting was against the continuance of the alliance with Japan, and Lee, in his speech, was very keen on drawing closer to America, but he was very reserved. Wells came in late, but did not speak. He told me that he was astonished at my sanity! I ended up by eulogising the Ambassador's service during the war, as I had long promised myself to do at the first opportunity. I was sorry that Geddes was present, but I could not let slip the opportunity. A good, attentive, and appreciative audience. The first wine that I had tasted since leaving England, except some good old sherry at one friend's house. A good talk with Geddes and found him as interesting and well informed as ever. I hear golden opinions of him from resident English and Americans. He does not play for safety. He occas'onally errs. That is one reason given to me by Americans why they like him so much.

Thursday, November 10, 1921. Busy getting tickets and making preparation for the Conference. Lunched at the Metropolitan with General Squier, who told me of his work in the war, when he was given a billion dollars and told to produce enough aeroplanes to darken the sun immediately. There were not four men in America, he said, who knew one end of an aeroplane from another and the difficulties were stupendous. But he got his Liberty engine through and it was a huge success. To posterity Squier's most instructive contribution may be his diary of 1914 in France, a copy of which is now in the State Department. He went there at Lord K.'s request, which Ambassador Page in London and Herrick in Paris supported, not informing Washington. He was allowed to see everything and to go where he pleased. His diary tells everything. I recall meeting him at the front that year. I am sure that he will be a very frank and trustworthy chronicler of that period.

To a tea-fight at the *Baltimore Sun* office in the afternoon. In the evening to the Press Club, which has been most hospitable in throwing open the place to us strangers. There was an entertainment, but chiefly speeches to tell us all the ways of Washington during the Conference time. At the end I was asked to speak, and after me spoke "the silver-tongued Bryan," who is an accomplished orator of the old stamp and made a sincere speech full of charming sentiments.

Friday, November 11, 1921. Third anniversary of Armistice Day. The unknown hero's remains left the Capitol early and at 8.30 the guns announced the departure. Motored to Arlington and had a seat in the top gallery with some colleagues, including Wells, Wilson, and Nevinson. The amphitheatre is round and open to the skies. There is a colonnade of two rows of marble pillars round it, over which is the gallery. The centre contains rows of marble seats and the place filled up gradually. The apse or stage had its front entirely covered with masses of flowers behind which the coffin was eventually deposited. The President, chief officials, and foreign delegations were all there, and in the boxes of the colonnade tier were all the diplomatic missons here. There were hymns, prayers, a solo, and the President's address. The amplifiers were turned on. One could see the President speaking, and note his rare gestures, but not hear his voice as he spoke. But the amplifiers made his voice heard all over the amphitheatre and to the waiting crowds outside too. The extension to 'Frisco worked all right. The voice seemed to come from the skies. All very dignified and impressive. A fine day with a good deal of sun, but still autumnal. The photographers on the topmost parts of the building were an odious, regrettable, but I suppose necessary, incident. The masses of people outside could be seen by us through the colonnades. Everything went well. Beatty and Cavan laid the V.C. on the grave, and Cavan in a most dignified manner spoke a passage from Corinthians [1] only, instead of imitating the usual florid utterances of European dignitaries on these occasions. The hero was finally interred outside, and the last act before the close was the approach of the Crow Indian Chief, who deposited his war bonnet and *coup* stick on the tomb. The Chief and his followers were all in full war paint. I believe that there were one or two black soldiers with colours at the grave, but I saw no blacks at all in the amphitheatre. P. W. Wilson called it all the apotheosis of nonconformity. Going back, the roads were so blocked that my taxi took three hours to cover three and one-half miles. I would have walked, but there was no footpath. I felt myself back at the Flirey cross-roads at the battle of St. Mihiel. The control of traffic is not America's long suit. Dined with Mr. and Miss Mary Wiborg, Mr. and Mrs. Wilson, and Mr. Pulitzer at my hotel. A very agreeable talk. Washington was lit up at night.

Saturday, November 12, 1921. This has been an astonishing day, indeed. The Conference met for the first time at 10.30 A.M. in the Continental Memorial Hall, otherwise known as the Hall of the Daughters of the American Revolution. A fine central hall, somewhat like a large theatre without a stage. A big parterre where was placed one large table and two at rgiht angles to it with a few others and a table opposite the Chairman for translators and stenog-

---

[1] Cavan told me that the King commanded him to repeat this text, which was on the King's floral offering to the dead hero.

raphers. The press was well looked after on the floor under the galleries. There were galleries on three sides of the hall, and behind the Chairman were four small boxes. The Ameircans were on the right at the top table, English on their left, and Italians at the cross-table to the left of the English. The French sat at the other cross-table on the left of the Americans and the Japanese on the French right. The French seemed furious that they should not be at the top table and Jusserand was white and clenched his fists. The top table was purely Anglo-Saxon from end to end. The Chinese, Belgians, and Portuguese had seats lower down. All the delegation staffs were catered for and the arrangements were good. The galleries were filled by Congressmen, Supreme Court Judges, officials, etc., and the boxes by the President's wife and friends, I imagine. We all saw and heard everything perfectly. The place was prettily decorated with palms and flags and was well lighted, mainly by electricity, as the natural light was not strong.

The President arrived when all the company were seated, and made quite a good address of welcome, simple, dignified, and in good taste. Then Balfour in a graceful speech, much cheered, proposed Secretary of State Hughes for Chairman and he was unanimously elected. Hughes then rose to make an historic statement. We found out soon enough that he had a concrete plan to suggest, and a very drastic one too. A simple, straightforward, business-like address with nothing to indicate its dramatic conclusion. He suggested a naval holiday for ten years during which there was to be no shipbuilding, and for all to scrap numerous ships amounting in all to some 845,740 tons for America, 583,375 tons for England, and 448,928 tons for Japan. These included all the post-Jutland new ships building and projected and also many old pre-dreadnought ships. If America and Japan are hardest hit in new ships, it is because they have been building most lately. Hughes gave the scheme quite clearly and will describe it further in a written memorandum. The total of ships to be scrapped by the three Powers is 1,878,043 tons, and within three months of the agreement we are to have: England, twenty-two capital ships of 604,450 tons; United States, eighteen of 500,650; and Japan, ten of 299,700. The age factor is said to have been taken into account in this estimate. We are all bound over not to replace ships for ten years and then to limit replacements to an agreed maximum of capital ships, namely, 500,000 each for England and the United States, and 300,000 for Japan. Subject to these conditions we are not to replace battleships till they are twenty years old, nor to make them over 35,000 tons each. Auxiliary ships — i.e., cruisers, destroyers, submarines, and aircraft carriers — are to bear definite relation to the number of capital ships.

We were all astounded at the far-reaching character of the plan, of which our delegation had no knowledge when they entered the hall. But the plan, however drastic, seems fair and sincere, and America is offering to scrap ships upon which she has spent $330,000,000 already. It is true that there are rumours whispered that the new American ships are failures owing to their electric propulsion having failed, but I disbelieve this, and even if it were so it is to everyone's advantage to arrest naval competition. I saw the Ambassador and some Japs in the afternoon. The latter do not seem opposed in principle, and their technical experts sitting close to me in the hall were all one broad happy smile when Hughes announced what America proposed to scrap. Our real anxiety is for the dockyard towns and for Sheffield, Vickers, Armstrong, Birkenhead, and so forth. The Clyde will also be hard hit. Naturally we must make sure of France and Italy, but in view of our financial position, and the need for ending the American-Japanese competition, we can be fairly contented. If we had sprung such a plan unheralded upon the Americans, I think it would have been rejected. Mr. Secretary Hughes sunk in thirty-five minutes more ships than all the admirals of the world have destroyed in a cycle of centuries. More, he appeared to me to condemn by anticipation all the armaments of the globe. The armies of the world seem to me beckoned towards the cell of the condemned. Teaching by example, America makes a great renunciation and the most magnificent political gesture of all history.

It is an audacious and astonishing scheme and took us off our feet. We seemed spell-bound. The few men to whom I spoke babbled incoherently. What will they say in London? To see a British First Lord of the Admiralty, and another late First Lord, sitting at a table with the American Secretary of State telling them how many ships they might keep and how many they should scrap, struck me as a delightfully fantastic idea. Yet I cannot see any real danger in it if all States follow suit, especially as I believe that the mastodons can never cross an ocean to attack people the other side of it, and in any case we are all three in the same position relatively and with much smaller naval estimates both for building and for maintenance. But a lot of our naval personnel will have to go, and that will be troublesome.

The Congressmen in the galleries took charge a bit to-day. They seemed to regard the Conference as a Republican Convention, cheered as they liked, and even called upon Briand for a speech and made him and other chief delegates rise and speak. This cannot go on or no more open meetings can be held. We cannot have an American claque which might groan instead of cheer, or make some other undisciplined inroad upon the liberty of action of the delegates. However, it is their way and they were enthusiastic. So Hughes wisely let them have their way, even if he seemed rather taken aback by their unexpected frowardness. I had never heard Briand speak before. He is a firm, clear speaker with a clarion voice of a timbre that carries, and he held himself stiffly and did not go in for animation or gestures. He dominates a sitting at once and is masterful. But he has not L. G.'s range, I think, nor particularly his humour. We came out in a trance, not quite sure whether we were walking on our heads or our heels. Something had cracked. The helmet of Mars, perhaps.

Spent the day reflecting over it all and then cabled to the *D. T.* giving an account and some comments on the proceedings of an eventful day which alone made coming here worth while. But though I admired Hughes's courage and plain speaking, we have yet to see his spirit of conciliation and compromise. He spoke harshly at times. He has strength, courage, driving power, and he will have great prestige if this Conference succeeds, but we have yet to learn whether he has the necessary art of conciliation. All the same the American proposal has tremendous import and may go through, though we may have to be stiff about France, as she has a great army and we have none. I hear from the Ambassador that the American Government finally adopted their naval plan only late last night. If it had not been so, they would scarcely have concealed their plan from some of the sharpest eyes and quickest ears in Europe and America.

Sunday, November 13, 1921. This morning came out Mr. Hughes's memorandum which says a certain number of things which were not in his speech. It gives the names of the capital ships which America will keep and which we and Japan are graciously permitted to keep also. It lays down the law about replacement of all types of war vessels. We may replace ships lost by accidental destruction. Of Hughes's so-called auxiliary ships, including cruisers, etc., we and America are allowed 450,000 tons and Japan 270,000, but we are not asked to scrap surplus ships of these classes. We and America are to have submarines up to 90,000 tons and Japan up to 54,000. This is more than we have ever had, and not what we came here for. Generally, all auxiliary ships whose keels have been laid down before Armistice Day can be completed. We and the United States may have 80,000 tons of aircraft-carrying ships and Japan 48,000. The life of cruisers is fixed at seventeen years, of destroyers and submarines at twelve years, and of carriers at twenty years. No auxiliary ship is to carry guns over eight-inch. More important, perhaps, is Article 27, which says that the limitation of naval aircraft is not proposed. We also are to bind ourselves not to sell combatant ships to other Powers nor to acquire them.

The plan meets with the general, even frantically enthusiastic, approval of the American press, and the Japanese appear to be satisfied. Our people seem to acquiesce in the principle of the plan. But the secondary navies must be roped in or some one of them may become a rival of our greatly reduced navy. Also our Government will have to decide about the auxiliary ships, in which branch we shall or may be too weak for our oversea stations if the fleets are to be properly accompanied. There are a few dissentient American voices which say that the United States plan is too generous, but on the whole all opinion is a trifle stampeded by the grandiose and startling character of the plan and does not look into its after effects very much. I am not thrilled by the ten-year period. We are likely to be compelled by experience to recognise many flaws in the plan, and I should like a shorter agreement till we see how the plan works. Also one must observe that America is saved by her isolation, size, population, and resources from risks of attack, and Japan by her great army. We are not self-contained as is America nor armed as is Japan, so we are in a different position and no account is taken of the fact. There is nothing as yet in the plan to prevent secondary navies from becoming rivals to ours, and we must protect ourselves against such risk. Again, an alliance between secondary navies might equal our reduced navies, and we must secure ourselves in this matter too. Neither America nor possibly Japan is in any way constrained to support us if we get into difficulties after signing.

Much reading and work. Heaps of letters and invitations, all requesting replies. As I am off home in a month, I am limiting my engagements to the minimum. Went to Frank Simonds's house in the afternoon and made his wife's acquaintance. A large gathering and many interesting people. Looked in at the Jap reception at night. Was introduced to the delegates and to General Tanaka. There seem to be two Admiral Katos. Spoke to Kato I, a man of marked character and distinction, a slight figure with a mask of a face. He gave the surprising news that last Saturday's Conference was interesting. Tanaka told me that he knew nothing of army plans. Burdened with this weighty information, I hastily left, having remained there five minutes. But the Jap Ambassador seems a human being and I shall look him up again. Note that correspondents now come to interview me at dinner. Think I will send them on to the Japs. They deserve it. Both.

Monday, November 14, 1921. On thinking further over the plan, I am still more for modifying the ten-year period, in the sense of granting power to build during the period. Our capital ships are much older than the American and will mostly be scrap iron in ten years. No armament firm will keep going its plant uselessly for ten years without orders, and there will be no one to build the replacing ships when the ten years are up. There will also be a tremendous lot of replacement building required at the end of the term. I should also like to see, every four years — that will make it just *after*, and not before every Presidential election — a formal consultation of the three Powers to consider any alterations which experience may suggest in the scheme. Further, I believe that, though Balfour has only suggested a limitation, this is an unequalled occasion for proposing the total abolition of submarines, and I half believe that it might be carried on the top of the wave of enthusiasm. We came here to limit naval armaments and are actually asked to increase our supply of submarines.

To-day the commissions or committees are distributing themselves for the sub-committee work and wrangling about secrecy *versus* publicity. Went off in the afternoon and had a pleasant talk with Mrs. Marshall Field, Mrs. Harriman, and another lady who was there, and then went to Mrs. Grafton Minot's house, where I found Miss Mary (Hoity) Wiborg, Lady Beatty, the American Admiral Law, and M. Geraud. Another pleasant talk. By the way, Mrs. Marshall Field said that our diplomatic people knew only Washington, Boston, and a few fashionable resorts, and little of the Middle West whence she comes. Yet there was the real, active, palpitating life of America. I told her that it was the same in every country and would continue to be so until the F.O. sent orders to change things. When a Foreign Minister runs round to see places that I have seen this year, he would know something. Meanwhile, as it was in the beginning . . . amen.

Geraud good fun about the French press and their much-missed wine. They sent a deputation to Briand to demand some of the champagne that he brought over and offered to pay for it! It is odd that the French are the *only* nation who speak French at the Conference. So they seem to be the only foreigners here. The boredom of having all the speeches translated into French after delivery, and of hearing all the French speeches translated into English, is simply intolerable.

Lord Riddell is here as the unofficial mentor of the press with Sir Arthur Willert acting for the F.O. as publicity agent. Not much love lost between them, I guess. Riddell called to see me and we talked for an hour. We covered pretty well the whole ground. A sane man with insight and experience. We gave each other a number of notions. Bullen is down again from New York. We are distributing the work here between us.

Tuesday, November 15, 1921. To-day at 11 A.M. the second plenary session of the Conference took place in the Continental Memorial Hall under the same conditions as the first except that President Harding was not there. Mr. Balfour rose to continue the discussion on the Hughes programme and made a good speech which was received with much hand-clapping after its main periods. He stated that last Saturday would be celebrated as a date imprinted upon grateful hearts and that he counted himself to be among the fortunate of the earth in having been present on the memorable occasion. After some graceful compliments to Mr. Hughes, he pointed out the peculiar position of the British Empire in comparison with that of the United States. He expressed his approval of the scheme and said it would receive full, loyal, and complete co-operation on his part. He did not go into details, but suggested reduction of the total tonnage and size of submarines, and briefly alluded to questions of replacement, but said that the structure of the scheme was clear and firm and would remain as it was presented by its original architect. He considered that it made idealism a practical proposition. A good passage led up to the conclusion that the opening day of the Congress, as he called it, was one of the landmarks in human civilisation.

Admiral Kato spoke next in Japanese which was clearly and loudly translated into English by another Japanese. Premising that he had no gifts of oratory, Kato said that Japan deeply appreciated the sincerity of purpose evidenced by the plan, and was satisfied that it would materially relieve the nations of wasteful expenditures and could not fail to make for the peace of the world. Japan accepted the proposal in principle and was ready to proceed with a sweeping reduction in her naval armaments. But he said that a nation must be provided with such armaments as are essential to its security and that this requirement must be fully weighed in the examination of the plan. He proposed to suggest some modifications respecting the tonnage basis for replacement.

Mr. Schanzer (Italy) also spoke, and after expressing gratification referred to the question of the French and Italian navies and said that he did not think that they could be excluded from the general question and felt sure that they would be considered. Briand spoke last. He did not refer to Schanzer's proposal except to say that France was perhaps too weak for the necessities of national defence. So I doubt whether the supposed Franco-Italian agreement to co-operate here is very close. Then he turned to land armaments, and said that France demanded that the question should be raised and that he intended to state publicly the position of France so that all might see that she harboured no thought of disturbing the peace of the world. After Hughes had proposed an adjournment, Briand moved that the next public meeting should be at the call of the chair, and this was agreed to.

Balfour was very effective to-day. He spoke extempore, very slowly, even haltingly at times, but was extremely good and the speech reads uncommonly well. He consulted a few words on a tiny sheet of paper when he came to the details, such as they were, and he addressed the Conference once as "ladies and gentlemen," which was natural as the galleries contained as many women as men. The house rose to him on several occasions, applauding loudly, and once standing up, though the speech made no appeal to any special springs of American feeling.

I don't think that the French are very happy. They have not got on much. One of the sharpest of the Frenchmen here tells me that all Briand's information was at fault and that he expected to find England and the United States at loggerheads, when he could play Bismarck's old part of honest broker. He finds us cordially in unison and is non-plussed. I do not think that he wants France's fleet reduced, and as there is no sign that Hughes will suggest any plan of land armament limitation, Briand wishes to bring out France's position clearly, when he should make a great speech and evoke much sympathy. But the time has passed for an Anglo-American guarantee or for passing a sponge over French debts to the United States.

Frank Simonds had a lunch for Hughes after the morning session and I went there. Glad to see J. A. Spender, who left London just as the old *Westminster* was making its bow as a new morning paper. Hughes made a little gem of a speech after lunch and was much more human and less stiff than at the Conference. I carried away the clear impression that he has larger views for the future than he is given credit for. He said that he first wished to accomplish the work of the day which was actually before him and then, when he came to other questions, the fact of his first success would be of advantage to him. So he has the future in mind and both he and Harding are accepting the responsibilities attendant to power, as every great Power has had to do in the past. He spoke well and appealed for our confidence in his sincerity. I told him that he already had it. It has never been in question. He is not going to stop at the first Washington Conference. That seems a certainty. This opens up a very wide horizon.

Wednesday, November 16, 1921. Attended Riddell's press conference, New Navy Building, in the morning, and Balfour's conference at the Embassy at 6 P.M. Interesting to see how these things are done. Riddell is a distinct asset here in liaison with the delegation and the foreign press. We do more for the world press than any other delegation, and I think it is appreciated, as it is all on American lines. But I did not much care to see A. J. B. with his gentle suavity of manner heckled by every sort of person of various nationality. He did his best to reply to all, but when asked how many people there were in the British Empire, he was quite nonplussed and had no idea. He also suggested that the Anglo-Jap Treaty had no relation to China! I was relieved when the fire of questions ended. The foreigners seem quite astonished to find that an English statesman need not be encyclopædic.

The first quiet day. No plenary session. The real business has begun and the delegates are busy. Saw a number of people. Am impressed with the multitude of motor-cars which crowd the streets and are always ranged along the pavements or parked in the centre of the broad streets, almost always without a chauffeur, as the owner drives. There can surely not be a housemaid in Washington without a car. I believe this town has the second worst record for street accidents in America. I do not wonder. The streets are mainly asphalt, the cars very noiseless, and the horn is rarely sounded. The chauffeur does not *pounce* on foot passengers as in Paris, but the foot passenger has no rights, and if he gets run over it is just his own darned fault. The streets are very broad, the traffic confusing, and the cars move very fast.

There is enough current work here to keep one busy all day. The Chinese memorandum with its ten principles comes out to-day and will be the basis for the discussion in committee. With these hot houses here I wonder any American survives.

Thursday, November 17, 1921. In spite of the understanding that the proceedings in the Far Eastern committee were to be private the *Washington Post* comes out this morning with Hughes's preliminary statement in that committee. It makes him say that his proposal of the open-door policy is advantageous to Japan, which would be on the threshold when the door was really opened. He is said to have brought up the question of mandates in the Pacific, and then to have sagely observed that in Eastern problems the first thing which suggested itself was China. He is said to have lauded China's ancient civilisation and intelligence, the industry of her people and her great dotential wealth, but to have added that China was now in difficulties and to have suggested that these were due to her recent change of government, which he compared with the delay which took place in American history before all the States agreed to the present Constitution. He is also said to have touched on other questions such as the mandates in the Pacific and trans-Pacific communication.

Studied the Chinese memorandum and went to talk it over with X. It is practically a notice to all foreigners to quit China and to let go of her. The ten points are all principles, and Admiral Kato, whom I also saw to-day, said that if inquiry went into all the concrete cases arising out of those principles the Conference would last a considerable time. Yes, indeed! All the same there is considerable sympathy on the British side with much of the memorandum. The Chinese are clever to have launched it in the press. It gives them the initiative and saves them from the need of demanding an open session to announce their views. From internal evidence there has been American help in preparing the plan. This is shown particularly in Article 7, which talks of the "well-established principle of construction that grants shall be construed in favor of the grantors," a principle of American law, but one not acknowledged by English law, which determines a dispute over a grant by the text of the document itself.

Admiral Kato, who made the reservation that he spoke only for himself, said that he regarded armaments as the main question before the Conference, and I do not think that his people are best pleased at seeing the whole Chinese puzzle thus thrown before the Conference for solution. He did not wish personally for the question to be debated in open session. He did not speak English well, and felt at a disadvantage. I gather from him that he is not in favour of abolishing submarines, while as to Balfour's suggestion of reducing the total submarine tonnage, he says that it depends upon what amount will remain for Japan, as he considers this arm indispensable to her. In short, we shall probably have no support anywhere if we raise this question, but all the same I am for raising it and for proposing prohibition, leaving the responsibility for the future use of this vile and unchivalrous arm to those who wish for it.

Lunched at the Embassy. A very pleasant party including Captain Little and Commander Brown, two competent submarine officers, and Captain Domville, a very shrewd sailor. Little came on board the K–7 when I was visiting her during the war. Domville was also on Tyrwhitt's flagship when I paid him a visit during the war. It is thought that the real trouble of permitting submarines to be built will come when some petty State gets hold of a few and holds others to ransom or blackmails them with this arm. Geddes is entirely of my opinion and personally is for total prohibition.

It is suggested to me that, on the basis of the Hughes proposals, France's and Italy's ratio of capital ships should be under 200,000 each to our 500,000 and the Japanese 300,000. Our first question in committee seems to have been to ask America for her estimate for these Powers, but no answer has been given yet. It is also necessary that power should be taken by us to denounce the agreement if States like Russia or Germany begin some great naval programme hereafter. We need to take infinite precautions. Several points have had to be submitted to the home Government, and our naval staff out here has not sufficient representation of the construction branch or shipyards to enable them to test the full consequences of the American proposals.

Various unpleasant cables from France, shrewish on the whole. It will be time enough to complain when the French allowance of ships is definitely allocated. It has not been done yet, so why this fuss? I suppose the French at home, like their delegates here, were totally misinformed of the real position and it will be interesting to learn hereafter who conveyed to them a false notion of the situation. Jusserand has been here for nineteen years and on Count Sforza's principle [1] should have been moved on long ago, but some vow that he must know too much to have misled his people. Others say that his fine taste in English literature has not aided him to comprehend the Anglo-Saxon spirit.

Sent my first general appreciation of the position here, based on Hughes's little private speech at Frank Simonds's luncheon. I am told to-day that the *Washington Post's* account of Hughes's remarks in committee is substantially correct. Got Bullen to raise the question of "privacy" at the press conference this morning. Some Americans must confuse privacy with privateering. But I only want to know where we are, and whether honourable understandings are made to be kept or to be broken.

Many delicious stories at the Embassy to-day of the methods of evading drink prohibition laws. It seems that some small British island called Bimini, forty miles from the coast of America, is one of the main centres of the illicit trade, which comes chiefly from Scotland. People

[1] See diary for Italy.

say that the British should not hanker for the cancelling of their debts to America as the latter has already paid Scotland an equivalent sum. The greater part of the American customs service seems to be in the business. Price of a bottle of whiskey anything from twelve to fifty shillings. It is obtainable anywhere by anyone who will pay for it. There is almost a minimum of concealment.

Friday, November 18, 1921. I have been sending off a cable daily to the *D. T.* in the morning and it appears in the *New York Times* simultaneously with the publication in London. It is syndicated by the *Times* and their group of papers here. Went to Mrs. Mark Sullivan's in the afternoon and then on to the Embassy, where I was glad to meet Mrs. Lawrence Townsend, an old friend of Brussels days, when her husband was the U.S. Minister there and she was one of the most popular hostesses. A very large party and many nice people. Our Ambassador and his wife keep open house and all Washington responds. In the evening a few of us gathered to hear some words of wisdom from a good authority. It seems on the whole that the Conference has been getting on to-day, but that the disarmament plan of Hughes has displayed some strange results on being microscopically examined by the naval experts. It is clear that first one and then another Power will in turn control the seas — provided battleships control anything — and again that the conditions for replacing auxiliary ships laid down in the memorandum are twice as favourable to the United States as to us and that Hughes never grasped the fact until our experts pointed it out to him.

Saturday, November 19, 1921. To-day the Japs seem to have been friendly to the Chinese memorandum when it was discussed by the Far Eastern Commission. The armament people also met and continued to dissect the Hughes plan. A report that some United States naval officers have incurred reprimand for criticising their own Government's plans. President Harding told the press last night that he was gratified — the awful but convenient Royal expres-

sion — at the progress made, and did not anticipate any
trouble with Congress. He said that reduction of naval
armament would not require sanction by Congress, but
that the latter might have to approve a naval agreement.
Anything in the form of a treaty would have to be ratified by
the Senate. But mere understandings regarding either the
limitation of armaments or the Far East — that is to say
an agreement not taking the form of a treaty — would not
necessarily require Congressional sanction. Perhaps not,
but the partitions between understandings, agreements,
and treaties seem pretty thin, and after our illusions at Versailles we can consider nothing valid unless ratified by the
Senate. I must take an American legal opinion upon the
question — when is a treaty not a treaty?

Visited Mrs. Townsend and met many nice people and
some pretty ladies. Wanted to pay a call on Commander
Brown and his wife in Chevy Chase beyond the "Million
Dollar" bridge. Found my taxi had to go back for different "tabs" to be carried fore and aft on quitting the inner
circle of the town. Got there late. A pleasant and quiet
wooden house well out of the town. The Naval Attaché
and some younger men from the Embassy and others, including the Third Secretary, Arthur Yencken, an Austra-
lian who strikes me as a young man of intelligence. I like
the Commander. A real good man with sound judgement.
We had a lot of talk about the naval plan and all agreed
that we might have a reaction after the ebullition of sentiment, or "slop" as one of them called it, during the past
week. But our official sailors, from Beatty downwards, are
displaying a partiality for the American plan which I
should not have anticipated.

There are, however, symptoms of hostility already manifest, here and at home. The American Navy does not like
losing its best ships. The great *West Virginia* was launched
only yesterday and is due for scrapping. Some high naval
officials are said to be criticising the plan very forcibly in
private. The Hearst papers are out to wreck the Conference. At home the *Saturday Review* discovers that at a

certain moment the control of the seas will pass to America. So it will, and afterwards to us. You can't put navies on a bed of Procrustes. You cannot make necessarily unequal things equal. The *Morning Post* at home attacks the stopping of work on the four improved Hoods, which act is having a good effect here. A little food for national jealousy and some country may flare up. Sentiment and religion and love of humanity are great compelling influences which have stampeded all this country and apparently most of the world, but sooner or later nasty cold reflection and national antipathies may change the situation. If Hughes does not end by throwing out the proposal of compulsory arbitration as the final aim and by dealing with currencies, I doubt whether this plan of curing a symptom of disease and not the disease itself will win through. A few people in America have taken up this leading theme of my *Atlantic Monthly* article, without acknowledgement, but the idea has not penetrated the people nor visibly the Government. There will be no lasting good done until it does. But perhaps it is best to postpone this part of the plan till we get through economics, land armaments, and Russia.

A strange thing, this American Constitution. Framed by a set of Colonial country squires with strong conservative instincts, and at the close of the eighteenth century when modern ideas had not the force which they have now, it is a strange medley of old and new, giving the President all power and yet almost none, and allowing the State to be governed by any wave of generous or spurious sentimentalism which may sweep through the country. The increased rapidity and facility of communicating news aid the rapid march of the prairie fire of thought. The tendency may often be not to do what the leading men know is right, but what the people wish, whether they be well-or ill-informed. I am persuaded that the men ruling here at present are sincere, high-minded, and well-intentioned. In the people the minds of the more intelligent are very clean and there is a hatred of unfairness. But there is also a mass of very uninstructed opinion which has to be reckoned with and only sees simple and visible things. This mass may be manipulated by bad people, especially those controlling a large number of newspapers.

The authorities here are as accessible in a broad sense as ours are inaccessible. Any representatives of any paper can see the President once or twice a week and the Secretary of State daily and ask them any questions they like. That gives pleasure and satisfaction, though the amount of news to be gathered by these interviews is comparatively slight. The actual area covered by each big paper is not large, nor consequently is the circulation. But the syndicate business spreads the influence of the best papers far and wide, and some of the best writers now syndicate themselves and do not belong to any paper. These voices carry farthest. One of the men who are doing this tells me that he has thirty-four million readers daily. Divided by four to allow for the sanguine American temperament, it is still large. Still the country is vast, the interests varied, and local talent considerable. So the big papers all over America do not always speak with the same voice, except in a case like this Conference where every paper draws its opinion from the Capital. It is less the press than the real and fundamental interests of each quarter of the country which ought to be studied before one can foretell what opinion will be given in any given case. The Presidential election is a temporary outburst of political insanity, and no one can count on anything at that time or for six months before it. Ambassadors ought to go on leave at that time. The parties are then searching for political weapons and any weapon will do.

Question: Why do American country roads have no "sidewalks"? Apparent answer, Because Americans never walk.

Sunday, November 20, 1921. A report on the Far Eastern discussion by the Commission yesterday shows that all Powers protest their great friendliness to China and undertake to do the most beautiful things for her. The Japanese statement is perfectly satisfactory. But handsome is as handsome does. A mass of reading. Then to Mrs. Hamilton Wright's to meet her brother, Stanley Washburn, who has done so well for the *Times* in many parts of the world. He and his sister know China and Japan well. He is now working on Elihu Root's secretariat. Low and several other people were there, but we had a good talk and exchanged ideas. Little difference between Washburn's views and mine. We think that Japan will use mellifluous language, but will never remove her claws from China and that we cannot make her without a very long and costly war. So in trying to help China to stand alone, we can carry Japan only as far as persuasion can take her, and I am strongly against a break with her in any case. Mrs. Wright a fervent advocate of China. Dined with Mrs. Marshall Field. The house looked well at night and the lighting very good. Some thirty-six at dinner, including the Beattys, Cavan, the Dutch Minister Van Blokland, the Vice-President Coolidge, Bethell, the ladies Vanderbilt, Harriman, West, Bliss, and a great many more. The table gorgeous with silver, roses, fruits, etc., and some of the guests infested with diamonds. An agreeable hostess who has a houseful of beautiful things. A good talk with the Admiral over the naval scrapping scheme. It is quite clear to me that the ten-year holiday is economically unsound. At the end of it we shall have twelve ships building and there will be periods of immense activity followed by others of atrophy. The Admiral likes the submarines no more than I do. He goes home at the end of the month, leaving Admiral Chatfield here. Mrs. West, a Californian widow, and very good company, was my dining partner. We leave the table here *à la française*.

Monday, November 21, 1921. We all assembled at the Hall for the discussion on land armaments. Very full house and heaps of ladies in the galleries. Hughes made a short speech, and then Briand took the floor, speaking from the end of the high table on the right of Senator Underwood. He broke his speech into three parts and after each part

the interpreter translated it with ability. The breaks
marred the effect. Briand showed us a France all for peace,
explained how she has reduced and was still further reducing her army, and then trotted us over all the old ground
of German wickedness, fairly and truthfully on the whole,
but sometimes forcing the note a little, and making too
much of Ludendorffian extravagances. He asked for no
guarantee, aware that it would be useless, but pointed to
France's isolation and hoped that no one would try to barter away the French Army when it stood between France
and threatening Germany.

Brilliant, of course, rising to heights and flights of eloquence when with his two hands, turned into claws as it
seemed, he convulsively tore the air on each side of his
head, frantically and St. Vitusly, as he brought some particular Boche iniquity to notice. A speech, it must be said,
that required a French Chamber for audience. Not one out
of ten of his audience understood him, and had they done
so they might not have been in sympathy. Living here
how can one visualise Paris, the Rhine, the Ruhr, Silesia,
Berlin? It is all so very, very far away, while every day
from Germany arrive sarcasms at French expense. The
applause was good. It was for the visible and audible eloquence, for France; something for the man, not much for
his case.

Balfour followed, admirable, measured, dignified, serene,
full of compliments for the masterly eloquence of the
French Premier, then branching to the thought of the
tragedy it would be were France morally isolated. It was,
he thought, because there had been no moral disarmament, and this did not permit the changes in land armaments that were visible here in relation to war at sea. From
this he turned to recount our losses in France — of which
Briand had not said one word — a million dead, two million wounded. We deplored the losses, he went on, but
did not regret them, nor had we changed our opinion that
the war was just, nor should we hesitate again to repeat
our action in a similar case. (Rounds of applause from the

French benches.) Very pointedly he deplored the spirit of domination that had been the curse of Europe, and after thanking Briand again for his candid account, finished up by wishing him and his country "every prosperity in that path of unaggressive prosperity which I hope and believe they are now entering." A promise or a warning?

Schanzer followed for Italy, rejoicing over the intention expressed by Briand of a further reduction of the French Army and showing how Italy's Army was down to 200,000 men, whereupon Admiral Kato expressed his sympathies for France and for the losses of Japan's allies. He said that Japan approved of the limitation of land armaments to those necessary for national security and the maintenance of order, forces which could be determined only by special conditions rendering all comparisons difficult. Baron de Cartier followed for Belgium, backing France and praying for the return of conditions permitting a further reduction of land armaments.

Secretary Hughes closed the discussion. After compliments he said that "no words ever spoken by France have fallen upon deaf ears in the United States." What was essential, he said, was the will to peace. Then he went on to say, "in response to a word that has challenged us all, there is no moral isolation for the defenders of liberty and justice." That was the pith, greatly cheered, and the whole matter was then referred back to the Armament Committee. The French were made very happy by the morning's work, but there was not one word said to encourage them to any dubious adventure.

In the late afternoon Geddes received the press and made some very useful statements. Dined in the evening with those dear kind people, the Elliot Goodwins, and found the Simondses, Admiral Grayson and his wife — he was President Wilson's famous doctor — Butler Wright, and a few more. A very pleasant, friendly evening.

Tuesday, November 22, 1921. I was disgusted this morning to read two reports by Stéphane Lauzanne and Mr. James to the effect that the French claimed equality with the Japanese in capital ships, equality with us in submarines, and refused to be bound by the naval holiday. The report had evidently originated in some French official sources, and I promptly sent off a stiff cable to London relating the report and making some severe comment upon it, describing it as most untimely. Told every Frenchman I met what I thought about it.

Mr. Ellery Sedgwick arrived from Boston and came to see me. A good talk. A capable and well-informed man whose *Atlantic Monthly* is the greatest of the great American reviews, and is thoroughly impartial and statesmanlike. Called on Mrs. West and found her charming house in the Georgetown part of the country, notable in its dignity and simple taste and altogether very attractive. She took me on to a tea-fight where we met many people, including the French Chief of Staff, General Buat, whom I set upon at once. I told him that as England had agreed to scrap half her fleet and France had the ambition to double hers, I thought that the best way out was for us to sell him half our navy. Then we should ease our finances and France would more than double her navy all at once. He thought this a splendid idea and was all for it. I reproached him for this morning's announcement, which he tried to minimise.

In the evening to a reception at the Embassy. Some two thousand people. Their Excellencies and Mr. Balfour stood for some four hours receiving the guests as they filed in. A great crowd. Met an immense number of people. Have arrived at the stage of knowing half Washington by sight without being able to put a name to more than a very few of them. Most of the delegates, Ambassadors, and Ministers, including Van Karnebeek, the Dutch Foreign Minister, whom I was glad to meet again after all these years. It was very refreshing to see all the British uniforms again. Back late.

Wednesday, November 23, 1921. The Far East Committee is now at work on China's tariffs, and Riddell gave the press a very useful lecture on the subject this morning calculated to silence some malevolent criticisms which pretended to-day to fasten upon us a double dose of original sin in Chinese affairs. Lunched with Mrs. Minot and a pleasant party at her house. In the afternoon to the Italian Embassy where I had a talk with the Ambassador Ricci and with Senator Bergomini, who is a delegate, and who had just handed over his famous *Corriere della Sera* to his brother. The Italians insist as much as we do on the establishment of a ratio for the Italian and French navies. They are exceedingly critical of France, and they justly point out that before the war they were allied to Austria and now stand alone. They are bent upon a fleet equivalent to France's, but do not care how low the scale is graded down.

To-day there came out alleged interviews with Briand on the naval news of yesterday. It made things no better, as it left the capital ships vague, said nothing of the naval holiday, and went all out for the submarines. The new French plan has put everyone against France, even the Senate. I heard to-day that the plan which I attacked yesterday emanated from Viviani. Briand leaves to-morrow, when Viviani will be in charge. However, if the French are so foolish as not to toe the line with other Powers, we can simply make a reservation and place them in the category with Russia as a State whose actions must determine our future naval policy.

Thursday, November 24, 1921. Briand left to-day for New York and France. As a send-off for him there is published the report of a speech by Curzon which will not be agreeable to the French. This French mission has been muddled. We shall learn some day how it all came about. The French have been entirely out of the picture, and instead of helping matters have rather hampered them. It is a great pity, but the Anglo-French animosities in the Supreme Council have dogged our footsteps here. Briand at his best is a good friend and the sanest of men. I cannot imagine how he arrived here with such serious misconceptions and with such slight knowledge of the atmosphere.

Thanksgiving Day, very wet. Dined with Mrs. Robert Hinckley and a party of about a dozen including Lady Annesley; Mr. and Mrs. R. L. Craigie, of our Embassy; M. and Mme. Gruitch, the Serbian Minister and his wife; M. Corbin, head of the press to the French delegation; and several others whose names escape me. A good talk with Corbin about the navy affair. He puts it all down to Stéphane Lauzanne and some French official. When I named Viviani, he did not plainly deny the imputation, but he says that the ratio will be fixed in due course and that France will not object to equality with Italy. Mme. Gruitch and Miss Gladys Hinckley good neighbours at dinner.

Friday, November 25, 1921. A good lot of particularly poisonous propaganda garbage in the press here to-day from some of our enemies. I wrote a little cable to explain Italy's attitude here, highly commending it. Had hardly finished when Signor Schanzer, who is living at my hotel, asked me to come down, and was very indignant about some "false and malicious" report, as he described it, which had been published in London concerning a supposed violent altercation between him and Briand on the Armaments Committee. I knew nothing of the affair. He asked me to cable to London to deny it on his behalf, which I did. Albertini came in and we had a little talk. Schanzer said that in the Committee, Balfour had spoken to suggest that land armaments should be left open for the later action of the Conference, or at least not be closed. Schanzer had supported him in a very moderate speech, whereupon Briand, instead of answering Balfour, had "vivaciously" answered Schanzer, who had, also "with vivacity," replied. But there were not any high words or insults exchanged, and Briand had even postponed his departure for New York so that the two delegations might dine together. The Italians rightly consider that the tendencious revelation of things taking place, or supposed to be taking place, *en petit comité* is insupportable, and so I think. But one can apparently never stop it when the French are present.

Went to see Mrs. Bliss in the afternoon and found a lot of people there, including Mrs. Brinton, who is here on a visit and returns home soon; Mme. Jusserand, the pleasant wife of the French Ambassador; Princess Cantacuzène, who has worked so hard at relief work in Russia; the Polish Minister, and a number of leading Americans. The Ambassadress hoped that correspondents would not dip their pens in acid. I said that the British here would not, unless their navy, which was the heart of England, were attacked. Lord Riddell gave a good dinner in the evening to one hundred and forty of the correspondents of all nations. A well-managed affair. Balfour, Geddes, and our host spoke. Three capital speeches, Balfour at his very best.

Difficult to keep fit here. The hot rooms suitable for orchids, not Englishmen. Spender says he feels like a kettle, boiling inside and the steam coming out of his mouth.

Length of life said to be seven years less here than at home. Don't wonder. Some people have wood fires, but not many. As a rule coldish wind outside and one's constitution resents the rapid alternations of heat and cold.

Saturday, November 26, 1921. Went to have a talk with Mr. Elihu Root, as wise a head as America contains. I told him of the confidence we had in him and could not avoid praise of his attitude on the affair of the Panama tolls. He said that the opposition to his views on this subject made him almost doubt his own sanity, so clear seemed the text of our treaty. He thinks on the whole that things are going well, but that we had reached the stage when a thousand difficulties of detail presented themselves and these required time to work through. We discussed Curzon's speech. The best opinion here regrets it. It cuts across Balfour's skilful handling of the French case here. It is thought that if the French were in a panic, Curzon's manner was not the best for talking to people in this state. Marianne is a woman, said I; people who take her for a man are not fit to be trusted with courting her. Root thinks that his four points on the China question form a background to which all concrete questions can be referred. He had studied all the treaties of all the Powers for twenty-five years back, and said that Japan was obliged to accept the points or she would have been referred back to her own treaties. He thought that Japan would be stiffest on the naval ratio, and would probably settle the Shantung question out of court. Root thought Japan in the wrong about Shantung, but the Powers who had signed the Versailles Treaty would have a difficulty in opposing her. He considered that Japan intended to become a very great nation, but might not consider the present moment favourable for any fresh expansion. He felt that America was not well versed in economic and financial questions affecting Europe. He had studied them as much as anybody and confessed his own inability to comprehend them all. America was more averse to the League of Nations Convention than ever. The Shantung case was typical of the kind of agreement which the Convention would have compelled America to support. He thought that the political situation dominated the economic in Europe. No confidence could exist while the Bolshevist menace hung over Europe. I thought that it had much diminished, and said that, placing Russia aside, I ventured with diffidence to believe that economics led politics.

We had a talk of my favourite panacea — compulsory arbitration. I found Root entirely shared my opinion. He had helped in creating a list upon which those States agreeing to compulsory arbitration could inscribe their names at The Hague. About a dozen minor States had done so. I told him that if the United States put forward a resolution in favour of it at the end of the Conference, it would be a dramatic curtain for the last act of the play here and would sweep the world, so great was the moral authority of America now. He approved that I should speak to Hughes about it. We walked over to the Conference building after talking. Root is a wise, experienced statesman, invaluable here, but I think he feels that a younger man should take up the fiery cross for the crusade which I alluded to.

Attended Mr. Wile's luncheon party — *Philadelphia Ledger* — to the foreign journalists at the Racquet Club. Mr. Hughes came and made a good speech. He said that the Conference itself was quite a tame affair, but when he read his cuttings at night he was astonished at all that was being read into it and could scarcely sleep. But he thought that we were treating him very fairly and described the Conference as a great education to America. Hughes seems to me to be blossoming out under the rays of the sun of success and to be growing more human and conciliatory. I am more and more impressed with his sincerity and honesty. But one must admit that he has met such good-will on all sides that a high test of his diplomatic ability has not yet presented itself. Mr. Curtis, the proprietor of the *Ledger*, was present.

Our chief news this morning is that President Harding announced last night that he hopes to see "an Association of Nations" arise from the present Conference, and outlined a policy of a conference once a year to consider whatever may menace good understanding, a policy which had been informally suggested to some of the foreign delegates, whose approval has been obtained. In land armaments he said that it was hoped to translate the sentiment of the Conference into a joint declaration of general policy. He added that the Americans held to the 5–5–3 ratio and did not admit a warrant for any change in spite of Japan's objections. China's plea for amelioration of the extraterritorial rights of foreigners had been approved in principle, and modifications with a view to final abolition will be worked out by an international commission of jurists.

All good work and very encouraging. Also quite in accord with the President's speech of July 22, 1920. A statement from the Chinese delegation that the likin duty will be abolished if tariff autonomy be granted creates a very good impression. Attended the Chinese reception and remained for seven minutes. It was not exciting.

Sunday, November 27, 1921. Signor Schanzer spoke to me last night again about the unfortunate telegram published in London about the quite untrue row between him and Briand. He said that the report had created terrible excitement in Italy, that the country was ringing with it, that French consulates were being attacked, that there were interpellations in the Parliament, and in fact that Hades had broken loose and European complications might result. His Excellency was in a great state of mind about it all. I had cabled for information to London, but had had no reply. So I cabled again.

Got through the terrifying Sunday papers. After consulting Mark Sullivan, I have made a list of ten American papers [1] which one should read daily in order to gauge American feeling from the Atlantic to the Pacific. The mere idea of taking on such a job impels one to fly from America. Went off to lunch with Mrs. West at her pretty house, where I found Sir Arthur Willert, Mr. Tennant from the Embassy, Mr. and Mrs. Wilson, and two other ladies. Some amusing talk. The hostess took me on to introduce me to Mr. and Mrs. Adolph Miller. He is on the Federal Reserve Board, and I wished to ascertain his views on the plan for reforming exchanges and currencies which my New York banking friend, Otto Kahn, and I had discussed. Miller thinks that the object is the right one and he does not oppose the use of American gold for the purpose. He prefers to "sanify," as I call it, the currency of one State at a time, withdrawing the debased issue and replacing it by a new on a gold basis. He would like a pretty large committee to begin with, and it would later resolve itself into a "Big Four" who would conduct the business. He admits the need for Government authority and backing, and would bring in the chief national banks of issue in the great countries. But he would make it a banking

1 The *New York Times; New York World; Washington Post; Portland Oregonian; Chicago Tribune; Louisville Courier-Journal* for Southern views; *Indianapolis News; Boston Transcript;* and the *Springfield* (Massachusetts) *Republican* which is the *Manchester Guardian* of America. And one should add a Hearst paper. A mass of folk see and read nothing else.

transaction and not a governmental affair, and he would insist on a certain control and the balancing of the expenditure of all States with their revenue. My only wonder now is why on earth people do not get ahead with the scheme. It sounds a preposterous thing to say that we are waiting on America who is financially uneducated, but after Root's admission I must give the only explanation that I can think of.

The Millers are very nice people and have an attractive house. Mme. Rose came in with Wickham Steed and I made her acquaintance for the first time. Went on to the Simondses and found him inclined to belittle the President's announcement, suggesting that it was a sort of afterthought introduced at the fag-end of his talk, and that Hughes was at the same moment telling the French correspondents that it was better not to announce plans for the future prematurely.

In the evening received a cable from London, explaining the origin of the dangerously false news from Washington. It came from one of our French friends here and he is very contrite and upset about it. I showed Signor Schanzer and Senator Albertini the cable during dinner. I had asked for a reply which I could show to him. We can only surmise the name of the Frenchman's informant, but it was a dirty piece of work on the part of this informant, whoever he was. Discussed with the Italian delegates the position of the League of Nations in relation to Harding's association. Albertini thought that no Power could refuse an invitation to join Harding's next conference, and Schanzer, who is on the League Council, thought that the two bodies might tend to coalesce. If America will not join the League, the League may join America. It is Mahomet and the mountain. In any case I see no reason why the two bodies cannot usefully co-operate.

It seems that Viviani called journalists from their little beds last night to announce to them his acceptance of Harding's association. Doubt whether he was not a trifle premature for an official. We do not really know very much about the new association yet. However, it is all to the good.

Monday, November 28, 1921. Vexed this morning to see that the Italian papers are attributing that d——d message to me, so, as I had an appointment with the real culprit at my hotel, I asked Bullen to go down to the press conference and make a denial at my request, which he did. The culprit arrived, very sad and penitent, admitting that he had written with some *légèreté* and that he had made an error of judgement. He said that X, of the French delegation, had more than once said the things that were in the cable published in London, and so when another Frenchman, who had been present on the now famous occasion, told my friend the story again, he sent it off. It has certainly played the very deuce in Italy. I asked him if he cared to give me the name of his informant. He said that he could not do this and I did not press it. But I asked whether M. Corbin was the guilty party, and my friend obliquely denied it by saying that Corbin had not been present at the Committee.

Mrs. West and another lady, with Mr. Yencken, lunched with me at the Shoreham. Went on to the Embassy for a talk with our commercial attachés and the Ambassador. Explained to the latter the facts about the cable from the Frenchman to London. The subject was brought up to-day in Committee and a very complete denial was given of the whole story. But I doubt that it will ever quite catch up the lie, which has had three days' start.

Wish that I could jot down the abominable mischief that has been practised against us here on two occasions this year, and once quite recently, by a supposed ally. It would make England red-hot with anger. But this Conference is too beneficent an undertaking to permit one to create trouble, even when the most perfidious treachery is practised against us. Our false friend will find that these things have to be paid for. That is all I shall say about it. Hughes seems to have been very firm about the proposals and has not allowed himself to be caught in the net.

Things are going exceedingly well. It is considered quite probable, one of our delegates tells me, that we may settle the battleship ratio by midnight. The French have come to ask that they may rank as 2 in our 5–5–3 scale, but we have been stiff about it. We can be nothing less now that we have the secret of their plans. China gets on well, and we shall keep foreign control of maritime customs, railroads, posts, and banks for the time or the whole system will collapse. The Anglo-Japanese Treaty will drop to the ground when we get the Far Eastern arrangement settled, and this, I am told, may be during the current week too. Am not sure about Shantung yet, but on the whole, unless our delegation are unduly sanguine, we should really make the main settlements within a fortnight, much of them this week, though our officials leap ahead of outside opinion and may make their wish the father of their thought.

In the evening to the Dutch reception and had a good talk with Van Karnebeek. I told him that I thought Hughes might like to hold the next Conference at The Hague. Would it be agreeable and would it be costly in The Netherlands? He said that the Dutch Government would like it very much, but that it should take place in the summer when the Scheveningen hotels were open, as otherwise the delegations would not easily be lodged. It would not cost Holland much and besides the country was well-off. There was the Peace Palace and the Binnenhof, besides our old House in the Wood, and there was ample space. He was quite of my opinion that exchanges and currencies and then armaments were the two great pressing questions.

I told him of my researches here about the gold basis business. He heartily concurred in the ideas which Kahn, Miller, and I shared, and said that the Dutch were thinking furiously on this subject and would fall into line with the plans which I outlined. He was all for the great banks of issue coming in and for Miller's other suggestions. He agreed with me against Root that economics led politics and thought economics by far the most pressing matter. France would not like a control, however. Then she can stand out, I said. K., like Otto Kahn, was for sanifying all the distressed countries at once, and was also for strictly limiting the next Conference to the question of economics and armaments. He was in hopes that co-operation with Geneva could be arranged. It would not do to overburden the agenda of the next Conference. This had been the great fault at Geneva. Van K. told me that the banker Ter Meulen was not wedded to his own scheme so much as some of our enthusiasts are. It was just an idea, not a real cure. He is sending me a paper by Vissering, President of the Netherlands Bank, in the morning. I feel sure that we are on the right track.

Tuesday, November 29, 1921. Attended Riddell's conference in the morning, when I rose and said that Bullen had explained the case of the cable yesterday, but that I was quite ready to answer any question about it that anyone wished to ask. No one spoke except one American, who said that no one supposed that I had had anything to do with it. So the subject dropped. The name of the poor culprit has been given in a New York Italian paper. Went to lunch with Lord Cavan, and Bartholomew and Higgins of his staff, at 1525 Sixteenth Street, a nice little place. There was not much to be said about land armaments, as practically nothing will be done here on this occasion about it except to pass some resolution at the end to keep the affair to the front. So we talked the war, especially in Italy, and our own army affairs and similar subjects; also tennis and football.

Bullen at the same hour attended the President's levée and reported that Harding had somewhat minimised the importance of his statement about an Association of Nations, and had particularly said that it would not be a rival to the League of Nations. But that was quite clear before. I expect that Simonds was right about the previous talk, and also that Hughes had talked to the President after it, and had suggested a certain grading down of the idea till things were more nearly ready for action to be taken.

Wednesday, November 30, 1921. The Japanese are awaiting instructions from Tokio about the battleship ratio. A fuss made about it in some papers. But as it takes four days to get a reply to a cable, the Japs have to hasten slowly. There is no substantial change. At least not yet.

I saw Mr. Balfour in the afternoon at his little flat and had a good talk with him over current events here and the future outlook. He hopes to get away by the end of the month.

December 1, 1921. On the whole a bad day's news. The Japs are adamant about the battleship ratio and the Americans as firm in support of their plan. The Chinese wished to bring Shantung before the full Conference where we, Italy, Belgium, and France, being signatories of the Versailles Treaty, should have been bound to support Japan. But the two parties were persuaded to accept the good offices of England and America and we may be able to patch up some settlement. Sir John Jordan and Mr. Lampson are to act for us. The Japs will not withdraw their troops from the South Manchurian railway, and will withdraw them from other places only when an efficient Chinese police is organised. The Japanese resistance to the ratio blocks all the other naval discussions, since all hangs on the battleship question.

Friday, December 2, 1921. No change. The Japs silent. Lunched with Maurice Low at the Shoreham, who had invited Mrs. Rea of Pittsburgh; Mrs. Frank West; Mrs. Keep, a charming lady, and another, besides H. G. Wells, Ian Hay, and myself. Waited for Wells. Then 'phoned and found that he was still in his black velvet smoking-jacket and that his watch had stopped. What else could one expect of a genius? I was only surprised that the watch had not galloped on twenty centuries to keep pace with its post-historic master. However, he came at last, and we had a most agreeable party.

In the afternoon the foreign press was received by the

President at the White House at 5 P.M. We were ushered into a large room, or at least found our way there, as there was no "aide" to guide us, and waited a quarter of an hour while nothing happened. X very cross because not the sl'ghtest notice had been taken by the President or Hughes of some eight or nine Brit'sh journalists here who think themselves capable of moving British opinion one way or the other. Even now we were all herded together with all the little reporters from the back-veldt of China and Japan. I said that it only made me laugh. I was enormously amused that the State chiefs could not distinguish, and I had taken no steps to secure preferential treatment. It was much more fun to see how the democratic machine worked of its own accord. It afforded me entertainment to discover that the American Court was the most exclusive in the world and was so entirely inaccessible in reality, though so democratic in seeming. The only trouble was that none of us would come again, said X.

Then at last we were ushered into the Presence. Just what Buckingham Palace must be like at a tea-fight for indigent mothers. Inside the door we found some sort of Court dignitary who announced our names, and next to him came the President, a dignified representative American with an attractive presence and a face that pleased. He had time only to say that he "had read a powerful amount of my writings and was glad to meet me face to face," when I found myself presented to his wife, a very agreeable lady, and passed on to a tea-room and out again without further delay.

Went to see the Ambassador and had a good talk. This evening there is a talk going on between Hughes, Balfour, and Kato, and I have an idea that some interesting communication may go to Tokio. I had cabled this week to the *D. T.* suggesting that the best help that the Cabinet could render us here was to concert with Tokio and inform the State Department that, if we agreed here about the Far East, we and Japan would be ready to substitute this agreement for the Anglo-Japan Treaty. It looks as though some such course were being followed, and H.E. spoke of a four-Power agreement to include the United States and France. That would do well, but I thought that the other States represented here should join in too.

Dined at the Frank Simondses and met a number of very pleasant people including the Churchills. Told Simonds that he now had his revenge for the inaccessibility of our leading men of which he had complained so bitterly to me in London during the war. Here our people were saying the same thing. It was worse than Lhassa. It seemed to me that nothing in continental Europe compared with the exclusiveness of a sealed-pattern democracy of the eighteenth-century type. Kings, Presidents, Chancellors, and Foreign Ministers elsewhere I had found to be paragons of accessibility. It amused me hugely. The result was, as in his case in London, that only third-rate men would take the trouble to come on the next occasion were it not for the charms of the "cave-dwellers," as the old families of Washington are called.

Saturday, December 3, 1921. Tremendous excitement about the late talk of the trio yesterday which began at 5.30 P.M. and lasted two hours. Official optimism at the zenith. So everybody thinks that all is over but the shouting and everything arranged. A very little thought should show that we still have a heavy amount of work to do before we get through the agenda. Lunched with Mr. Yokota, who addressed his guests in a long speech in Japanese which was subsequently translated. Full of charming sentiments about America, but he did not mention us. In the evening to Rauscher's, where the Italian Ambassador, supported by his staff and by Schanzer with his delegation, entertained the press. About one hundred and fifty people, I suppose. Wells and most of our people there, I think, but I missed those cool heads, Spender and Nevinson. I was next to the Ambassador and had a good talk with him on many interesting subjects. He is on the committee dealing with the extra-territorial rights, etc., of foreigners in China and told me most of the difficulties which they met with.

He also told me much of interest about the Roman Catholics. There are five million Italians here, but the Irish make a corner in the priesthood, which is all in their hands. He made a good and witty speech in Italian, at the end of which he was much applauded. Except about the submarines, I have not been able to discover a shadow of difference between our policy and that of America or Italy since we have been here. The Italians have got a good team. Bergomini a very capable man and a good second for Schanzer, who has been very open and straightforward.

Sunday, December 4, 1921. A heavy fall of snow. By noon all the town was white. My time has come for returning, so now I must pay some farewell visits, be off to New York, address the Contemporary Club on Thursday, at the Clarks' house after dining with the Morrises, lunch with Mr. Paul D. Cravath and some kindred spirits Friday, dine with Otto Kahn, and hear Chaliapine at the opera, bid adieu to Ferris Greenslet, and embark on the *Olympic* Saturday.

Too early to summarise my impressions, for I have been amassing them in stacks and they are not yet sorted out in my mind. Sorry to leave before the final act is over, but may not learn much more by staying on. I have great hope that the Conference will close with agreement and be a big success, which will give the President and Hughes the requisite authority for going ahead. I hope that in 1922 they will deal with economics first and then with land armaments. That will be quite enough, in all conscience. Then I would like them in 1923 to deal with Russia, all the States combining to restore her to order, and directing their energies by some unified political control of about seven men, or fewer if possible, with Hughes for Chairman. If a good start can be made, then give up 1924 to the cause of obligatory arbitration. At the end of that year we shall be in the throes of another Presidential election and no one can see beyond it. But it may mean the reconstruction of Europe within a single Presidential term. And it is always better to throw for the golden coat even if one gets only the golden sleeve.

The real hope of future success lies in the combination of the characters of the two ruling men here, with the portentous wealth and power of the United States whose word no Power can resist, assuming it continues to ring as true as it does here now. We Europeans are all too much involved and tied up in our treaties, interests, and bickerings in Europe for any European statesman to take the lead in this affair. America stands apart, unseeking, unselfish, righteous, well-intentioned, Olympian in her detachment, yet with means of constraint at need, both moral and material. I see no power but America's to redeem Europe and Asia from all the terrible troubles which my inquiries this year have made too poignantly manifest to me. Responsibility goes with power and has ever so gone since the dawn of history.

This Conference has been a great education to us all and not least to the Americans. The newspapers and magazines teem with wonderfully good accounts of all phases of the programme, written by the first experts in all branches and of all nations. From indifference the public have passed to interest and then to absorption. The knowledge gained by the American press men of their foreign colleagues has been useful to them, and *vice versa*. There has been a very good feeling. The criticisms of the foreigner have been courteous.

The Americans are very national in their sentiments and seem to have no taste at all for internationalism as a form of government. In fact they resent it strongly. They work for themselves first and for America next and all the rest of the time. I think that religion plays a much larger part in public sentiment here than in any other Christian State. I notice also that Labour is sending out seven thousand speakers to advance the cause of general disarmament. Propaganda here is a fine art in politics as in trade.

The way Americans criticise and abuse their political system is disconcerting. They describe it as the lowest and meanest thing on earth, have scarcely a good word to say for any politician, and even rate the Senate low since the election for that body passed from the State Legislatures to the general body of voters. For not more than a small minority of Senators has anybody a good word to say, but one must remember that many good men called Senators are no longer in the Senate. Governors are in the same position, and since Hughes was Governor of New York he has been called Governor Hughes by most people. It is like the French Présidents — Prime Ministers — who are always called M. le Président for the rest of their lives.

I have not been able to get an answer to my question — when is a treaty not a treaty? The treaty-making power is shared by the President and the Senate as everybody knows, and each is jealous of the other's share. But as to precisely where an understanding or a note merges into an agreement and the latter into a Treaty with a big T requiring Senatorial approval, no one has been able to give me a clear explanation. I do not believe that they know themselves, but in the circumstances, and in view of what happened to the League Convention, the Versailles Treaty, and the Anglo-American guarantee to France, I would not give much for an agreement not countersigned by the Senate. He who lets us down once, shame on him. He who lets us down a second time, shame on us. The American Constitution is America's affair. Our affair is merely to make sure that an agreement is valid when it is made, and is so held by the American Legislature. We should be in a nice mess if we scrapped our ships and then found that the Senate did not ratify the arrangement. It would be like the Army and their queues!

I prefer Washington to any European capital for a Conference like the present. The atmosphere is much more serene. There are not all the thousands of distractions and vexations of Paris or London. Everyone can think and work, and meetings are easy owing to short distances. It is a pity that the hotels are so bad and so wickedly expensive, but otherwise life is pleasant. The arrangements for the Conference have all been well made. The hostesses of Washington have overwhelmed us with their kindness and hospitality. Nothing could exceed the natural grace of the womenfolk and the sterling qualities of their men. Scarcely any ostentation or parade. Simple homely houses and many very pleasant ones. One has to refuse abundant invitations, especially in the evenings, or scrap one's work, for a Conference like this occupies nearly all one's time. May Heaven and the hostesses forgive us for all the cards we ought to have left and have not left!

I dare say that we have not done ourselves justice by the publication in the American press of our cables addressed to London. It is not the same thing to write for American readers and English readers. To the latter one tries to convey the American view, which the American does not want to hear. Also the American press cannot make good English out of abbreviated cable messages, and the misprints in the press here are terrible. We are occasionally made to say awful things and sometimes the reverse of what we have said. Another time we must organise this matter and place it on a better footing. The American magazines and American books by the good publishers are as carefully printed and on as good paper and in as good type as the newspapers are the reverse. It is a real *corvée* to read an American paper. The type is so small and vile as to be almost unreadable, and one is constantly arrested by being referred on to some other page and some other column. One rarely sees an English paper here. I have not read one nor even seen one since I came. We get very poor surveys of English opinion here, except from two or three men, and Americans make the same complaint of American news published in London. There is a large field of usefulness open here if the proprietors would set to work upon it.

I hope and believe that one of the chief results of the month's work has been to establish the Anglo-American accord on a firm basis. It has been well and truly laid by Mr. Balfour's wholly admirable and natural gifts, which have never been displayed to greater advantage, while he gives all the credit to Geddes, Lee, Borden, Pearce, and all the younger men who have worked for him. Geddes has also been a tower of strength. If it be true, as an American has told me, that the United States wished at this Conference to discover where they stood and who were their friends, they should know now. Similarly we have found the Americans to be absolutely sincere and entirely devoid of any intention of stealing a march upon us. We hope that they trust us. We are sure that we trust them. A whole mountain of prejudice seems to have been removed from between us during these eventful days, and on our side we must allow the honours to Balfour and Ambassador Geddes. Almost I believe that Americans will some day realise our secret pride in them. And that blessed English language! How can any people who use it be less than brothers?

Only one doubt oppresses, and that is the volatile and unstable character of public opinion here. It has not been precipitated into the British form of solidity by centuries of trials and great events. It is more accustomed to lead its leaders than to be led by them. It knows infinitely less of the world than ours does. The Anglo-Saxon is mixed here with some elements which represent incalculable forces of uncertain properties. So we feel, for all our faith and hope, that explosions are not impossible in the chemical constituents of public opinion. Men may then become anything and the man nothing. Statesmen may be swept away in some convulsion when it comes, and all the bases of their policy may be shattered. There is an unknown quantity. That is the danger.

THE END

INDEX